Algorithms
Sequential & Parallel

A UNIFIED APPROACH

Russ Miller

Laurence Boxer

Prentice Hall, Upper Saddle River, New Jersey 07458

An Alan R. Apt Book

LIBRARY OF CONGRESS INFORMATION AVAILABLE
Miller, Russ.
   A unified approach to sequential and parallel algorithms/
      Russ Miller, Laurence Boxer.
      p. cm.
   Includes bibliographical references and index.
   ISBN 0-13-086373-4
   1. Computer algorithms.   2. Computer programming.
I. Boxer, Laurence. II. Title.
QA76.9.A43   2000
005.1—dc21

99-047207
                                                                                    CIP

Editor-in-chief: *Marcia Horton*
Publisher: *Alan A. Apt*
Project manager: *Ana Arias Terry*
Editorial assistant: *Toni Holm*
Marketing manager: *Jennie Burger*
Production supervision/composition: *D&G Limited, LLC.*
Executive managing editor: *Vince O'Brien*
Managing editor: *David George*
Art director: *Heather Scott*
Cover design: *John Christiana*
Manufacturing buyer: *Beth Sturla*
Assistant vice president of production and manufacturing: *David W. Riccardi*

 ©2000 by Prentice Hall, Inc.
Upper Saddle River, New Jersey 07458

The authors and publisher of this book have used their best efforts in preparing this book.
These efforts include the development, research, and testing of the theories to determine their
effectiveness.

Printed in the United States of America

10 9 8 7 6 5 4 3 2

ISBN 0-13-086373-4

Prentice-Hall International (UK) Limited, *London*
Prentice-Hall of Australia Pty. Limited, *Sydney*
Prentice-Hall Canada Inc., *Toronto*
Prentice-Hall Hispanoamericana, S. A., *Mexico*
Prentice-Hall of India Private Limited, *New Delhi*
Prentice-Hall of Japan, Inc., *Tokyo*
Pearson Education Asia Pte. Ltd., *Singapore*
Editora Prentice-Hall do Brasil, Ltda., *Rio de Janeiro*

To my wife, Celeste, and my children, Melissa, Amanda, and Brian.

— Russ Miller

To my wife, Linda, and my children, Robin and Matthew.

— Laurence Boxer

Preface

A major thrust of computer science is the design, analysis, implementation, and scientific evaluation of algorithms to solve critical problems. In addition, new challenges are being offered to computer scientists in the field of *computational science and engineering*, which includes challenging problems in computational biology, computational fluid dynamics, and computational chemistry, to name a few. As parallel computing continues to merge into the mainstream of computing, it becomes more and more important for students and scientists to understand the application and analysis of algorithmic paradigms to both the (traditional) sequential model of computing and to a variety of parallel models.

Many computer science departments offer courses in "Analysis of Algorithms," "Algorithms," "An Introduction to Algorithms," or "Data Structures and their Algorithms" at the junior or senior level. In addition, a course in "Analysis of Algorithms" is required of most graduate students pursuing a degree in computer science. Throughout the 1980s, the vast majority of these course offerings focused on algorithms for sequential (von Neumann) computers. In fact, not until the late-1980's did courses covering an introduction to parallel algorithms begin to appear in research-oriented departments. Furthermore, these courses in parallel algorithms were typically presented to advanced graduate students. However, by the early 1990s, courses in parallel computing began to emerge at the undergraduate level, especially at progressive 4-year colleges.

It is interesting to note that throughout much of the 1990's, traditional algorithms-based courses changed very little. Gradually, such courses began to incorporate a component of parallel algorithms, typically one to three weeks near the end of the semester. During the later part of the 1990s, however, it was not uncommon to find algorithms courses that contained as much as 1/3 of the material devoted to parallel algorithms.

In this book, we take a very different approach to a traditional algorithms-based course. Parallel computing has become more mainstream, with small multiprocessor machines (which can be ordered by mail from your favorite catalog vendor) flooding the marketplace and with distributed computing systems being efficiently exploited. Therefore, we believe the time is right to teach a fundamental course in algorithms that covers paradigms for both the sequential and parallel models. In fact, the approach we take is to *integrate* the coverage of parallel and sequential algorithms throughout the course.

The philosophy taken in this book is to cover a paradigm, such as divide-and-conquer, and then cover implementation issues for both the sequential and parallel models. Due to the fact that we present design and analysis of paradigms for sequential and parallel models, the reader might notice that the number of paradigms we can treat within a semester is limited.

Several offerings of a course based on a preliminary version of this book have been taught successfully at both the undergraduate and graduate levels at the State University of New York at Buffalo.

Prerequisites: We assume that the reader has a basic knowledge of data structures. That is, the reader should be comfortable with the notion of a stack, queue, list, and binary tree, at a level that is typically taught in a CS2 course. The reader should also be familiar with fundamentals of discrete mathematics and Calculus. Specifically, the reader should be comfortable with limits, summations, and integrals.

OVERVIEW OF CHAPTERS

Background material for the course is presented in Chapters 1, 2, & 3. Chapter 1 introduces the concept of asymptotic analysis. While the reader might have seen some of this material in a course on data structures, we present this material in a fair amount of detail. The reader who is uncomfortable with some of the fundamental material from a Freshman-level Calculus sequence might want to brush up on notions such as limits, summations and integrals, and derivatives, as they naturally arise in the presentation and application of asymptotic analysis. Chapter 2 focuses on fundamentals of induction and recursion. While many students have seen this material in previous courses in computer science and/or mathematics, we have found it important to review this material briefly and to provide the students with a reference for performing the necessary review. In Chapter 3, we present the Master Method, a very useful cookbook-type of system for evaluating recurrence equations that are common in an algorithms-based setting.

Chapter 4 presents an overview of combinational circuits and sorting networks. This work is used to motivate the natural use of parallel models and to demonstrate the blending of architectural and algorithmic approaches. In Chapter 5, we introduce fundamental models of computation, including the RAM (a formal sequential architecture) and a variety of parallel models of computation. The parallel models introduced include the PRAM, mesh, and hypercube, to name a few. In addition, Chapter 5 introduces terminology such as shared-memory and distributed-memory.

The focus of Chapter 6 is the important problem of matrix multiplication, which is considered for a variety of models of computation. In Chapter 7, we introduce the parallel prefix operation. This is a very powerful operation with a wide variety of applications. We discuss implementations and analysis for a number of the models presented in Chapter 5 and give sample applications. In Chapter 8, we introduce *pointer jumping* techniques and show how some list-based algorithms can be efficiently implemented in parallel.

In Chapter 9, we introduce the powerful divide-and-conquer paradigm. We discuss applications of divide-and-conquer to problems involving data movement, including sorting, concurrent reads/writes, and so forth. Algorithms and their analysis are presented for a variety of models.

Chapters 10 & 11 focus on two important application areas, namely, computational geometry and image processing. In these chapters, we focus on interesting problems chosen from these important domains as a way of solidifying the approach of this book in terms of developing machine independent solution strategies, which can then be tailored for specific models, as required.

Chapter 12 focuses on fundamental graph theoretic problems. Initially, we present standard traversal techniques, including breadth-first search, depth-first search, and pointer jumping. We then discuss fundamental problems, including tree contraction and transitive closure. Finally, we couple these techniques with greedy algorithms to solve problems, such as labeling the connected components of a graph, determining a minimal spanning forest of a graph, and problems involving shortest or minimal-weight paths in a graph.

Chapter 13 is an optional chapter concerned with some fundamental numerical problems. The focus of the chapter is on sequential algorithms for polynomial evaluation and approximations of definite integrals.

RECOMMENDED USE

This book has been used in both a junior/senior-level elective and a required first year graduate-level course in the Department of Computer Science and Engineering at the State University of New York at Buffalo (SUNY-Buffalo). The course was presented in 14 weeks, consisting of twenty-four (24) 75-minute lectures, two review classes, and two exams. Recitations were conducted by an advanced graduate student and were used to help the students with homework sets and an understanding of the material. The recitations were especially important early in the semester when mathematically-based background material was being presented. This course is tailored towards students who are not advanced in a mathematical sense, but have a basic, fundamental, background.

CORRESPONDENCE

Please feel free to contact the authors directly with any comments or criticisms (constructive or otherwise) of this book. Russ Miller may be reached at *miller@cse.buffalo.edu* and Laurence Boxer may be reached at *boxer@niagara.edu*. In addition, a Web site for the book is available at *http://www.prenhall.com/millerboxer*. This Web site contains information related to the book, including pointers to education-based pages, relevant parallel computing links, and errata.

ACKNOWLEDGMENTS

The authors would like to thank several anonymous reviewers for providing insightful comments, which have been used to improve the presentation of this book. We would like to thank the students at SUNY-Buffalo who used early drafts of this book in their classes and provided valuable feedback. We would like to thank Ken Smith, a member of the technical support staff at SUNY-Buffalo, for providing assistance with Wintel support. We would also like to thank our families for providing us the support necessary to complete this time-consuming project.

Russ Miller & Laurence Boxer, 1999
www.cs.buffalo.edu/pub/WWW/faculty/miller/research.htm

Contents

1

Asymptotic Analysis

Asymptotic Analysis

A comprehensive study of algorithms includes the design, analysis, implementation, and scientific evaluation through experimentation of algorithms that solve important problems. In this chapter, we introduce some basic tools and techniques that are required in order to tackle effectively both a theoretical and an experimental analysis of algorithms. It is important to realize that without analysis, it is often difficult to justify the choice of one algorithm over another or to justify the need for developing a new algorithm. Therefore, a critical aspect of most advanced data structures or algorithms courses is the development of techniques for estimating the resources (running time, disk space, memory, and so forth) required for a given algorithm. As an aside, we should point out that a course covering proofs of correctness for algorithms is also critical, as having very fast algorithms that produce incorrect results is not desirable. However, for pragmatic reasons, nontrivial proofs of correctness are not typically covered in this text.

Throughout this book, we will focus on resources associated with a given algorithm. Specifically, we will be concerned with quantities that include the number of processors, the size of the memory, and the running time required of an algorithm. This will allow a reasonable comparison to be made between algorithms so that one can make informed choices as to an appropriate algorithm. For example, such analyses will allow us to make a more informed decision on which sorting algorithm to use on a sequential machine, given data with certain properties that are maintained in certain data structures. We should point out that when computing solutions to numerical problems, one must often consider the quality of the solution. Unfortunately, this topic is outside of the scope of this book. In fact, most of the algorithms we consider in this book can be viewed as "nonnumerical" in nature.

In practice, it often turns out that we are more concerned with time than with memory. This may surprise students in the habit of thinking of relatively small class-type projects that, once debugged (or, at least, freed of infinite loops), begin printing their results in tiny fractions of a second. However, many important applications require massive processing of large data sets, requiring hours or even days of CPU time. Examples of such applications are found in areas such as molecular modeling, weather forecasting, image analysis, neural network training, and simulation. Aside from the dollar cost of computer time, human impatience or serious deadlines may limit the use of such applications. For example, it only helps to have a weather forecast if it is made available in advance of the forecast period. By contrast, it is not uncommon to be able to devise algorithms and their associated data structures such that the memory requirements are quite reasonable, often no more than a small multiple of the size of the data set being processed.

In this chapter, we develop mathematical tools for the analysis of resources required by a computer algorithm. Because time is more often the subject of our analysis than memory, we will use time-related terminology; however, the same tools may naturally be applied to the analysis of memory requirements or error tolerance.

NOTATION AND TERMINOLOGY

In this section, we introduce some notation and terminology that will be used throughout the text. We make every effort to adhere to traditional notation and standard terminology. In general, we use the positive integer n to denote the size of the data set processed by an algorithm. We may process an array of n entries, for example, or a linked list, tree, or graph of n nodes. We will use $T(n)$ to represent the running time of an algorithm operating on a data set of size n. (Occasionally, an algorithm is analyzed in terms of more than one parameter; correspondingly, we may use notations such as $T(m,n)$, $T(k,n,p)$ and so forth.)

An algorithm can be implemented on a variety of hardware/software platforms. We expect that the same algorithm operating on the same data values will execute faster if implemented in the assembly language of a supercomputer than if implemented in an interpreted language on a personal computer (PC) from, say, the 1980s. Thus, it rarely makes sense to analyze an algorithm in terms of actual CPU time. Rather, we want our analysis to reflect the intrinsic efficiency of the algorithm without regard to such factors as the speed of the hardware/software environment in which the algorithm is to be implemented; we seek to measure the efficiency of our programming methods, not their actual implementations.

Thus, the analysis of algorithms generally adheres to the following principles:

1. **Ignore machine-dependent constants.** We will not be concerned with how fast an individual processor executes a machine instruction.
2. **Look at *growth* of $T(n)$ as $n \to \infty$.** Even an inefficient algorithm will often finish its work in acceptable time when operating on a small data set. Thus, we are usually interested in $T(n)$, the running time of an algorithm, for large n (recall n is typically the size of the data input to the algorithm).
3. **Growth rate:** Since asymptotic analysis implies that we are interested in the general behavior of the function as the input parameter gets large (*i.e.*, we are interested in the

behavior of $T(n)$ as $n \to \infty$), this implies that low-order terms can (and should) be dropped from the expression. In fact, since we are interested in the *growth rate* of the function as n gets large, we should also ignore constant factors when expressing asymptotic analysis. This is not to say that these terms are irrelevant in practice, just that they are irrelevant in terms of considering the growth rate of a function. So, for example, we say that the function $3n^3 + 10n^2 + n + 17$ grows as n^3. Consider another example. As n gets large, would you prefer to use an algorithm with running time $95n^2 + 405n + 1997$ or one with a running time of $2n^3 + 12$? We hope you chose the former, which has a growth rate of n^2, as opposed to the latter, which has a much slower growth rate of n^3. Naturally, though, if n were small, one *would* prefer the latter ($2n^3 + 12$) to the former ($95n^2 \times 405n + 1997$). In fact, you should be able to determine the value of n that is the break-even point. Figure 1-1 presents an illustration of this situation.

ASYMPTOTIC NOTATION

In this section, we introduce some standard notation that is useful in expressing the asymptotic behavior of a function. Since we often have a function that we wish to express (more simply) in terms of another function, it is easiest to introduce this terminology in terms of two functions. Suppose f and g are positive functions of n. Then

1. $f(n) = \Theta(g(n))$ (read "f of n is **theta** of g of n") *if and only if* there exist positive constants c_1, c_2, and n_0 such that $c_1 g(n) \leq f(n) \leq c_2 g(n)$ whenever $n \geq n_0$. See Figure 1-2.

2. $f(n) = O(g(n))$ (read "f of n is **oh** of g of n") *if and only if* there exist positive constants c and n_0 such that $f(n) \leq cg(n)$ whenever $n \geq n_0$. See Figure 1-3.

3. $f(n) = \Omega(g(n))$ (read "f of n is **omega** of g of n") *if and only if* there exist positive constants c and n_0 such that $cg(n) \leq f(n)$ whenever $n \geq n_0$. See Figure 1-4.

4. $f(n) = o(g(n))$ (read "f of n is **little oh** of g of n") *if and only if* for every positive constant C, there is a positive integer n_0 such that $f(n) < Cg(n)$ whenever $n \geq n_0$. See Figure 1-5.

5. $f(n) = \omega(g(n))$ (read "f of n is **little omega** of g of n") *if and only if* for every positive constant C, there is a positive integer n_0 such that $f(n) > Cg(n)$ whenever $n \geq n_0$. See Figure 1-6.

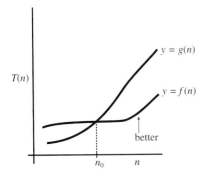

Figure 1-1 An illustration of the growth rate of two functions, $f(n)$ and $g(n)$. Notice that for large values of n, an algorithm with an asymptotic running time of $f(n)$ is typically more desirable than an algorithm with an asymptotic running time of $g(n)$. In this illustration, "large" is defined as $n \geq n_0$.

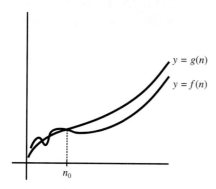

Figure 1-2   An illustration of Θ-notation. $f(n) = \Theta(g(n))$ since functions $f(n)$ and $g(n)$ grow at the same *rate* for all $n \geq n_0$.

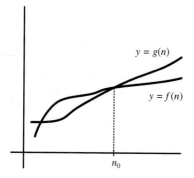

Figure 1-3   An illustration of O-notation. $f(n) = O(g(n))$ since function $f(n)$ is bounded from above by $g(n)$ for all $n \geq n_0$.

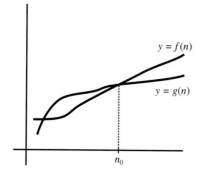

Figure 1-4   An illustration of Ω-notation. $f(n) = \Omega(g(n))$ since function $f(n)$ is bounded from below by $g(n)$ for all $n \geq n_0$.

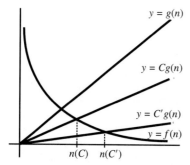

Figure 1-5   An illustration of o-notation: $f(n) = o(g(n))$.

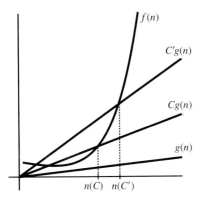

Figure 1-6 An illustration of ω-notation: $f(n) = \omega(g(n))$.

Strictly speaking, Θ, O, Ω, o, and ω are set-valued functions. Therefore, it would be appropriate to write $(3n^2 + 2) \in \Theta(n^2)$. In fact, some authors have tried to use this membership notation "correctly," but it has not caught on. In the literature, it is more common to see this idea expressed as $3n^2 + 2 = \Theta(n^2)$. This is certainly not correct in the mathematical sense; however, it is the standard. The expression $3n^2 + 2 = \Theta(n^2)$ is read as "3 n squared plus 2 *is* **theta** of n squared." Note that one *does not write* $\Theta(n^2) = 3n^2 + 2$.

The set-valued functions Θ, O, Ω, o, and ω are referred to as *asymptotic notation*. Recall that we use asymptotic notation to simplify analysis and capture *growth rate*. Therefore, we want the *simplest* and *best* function as a representative of each Θ, O, Ω, o, and ω expression. Some examples follow.

EXAMPLE

Given $f(t) = 5 + \sin(t)$ and $g(t) = 1$, then $5 + \sin(t) = \Theta(1)$ since $4 \times 1 \leq 5 + \sin(t) \leq 6 \times 1$. (See Figure 1-7.) Note also that $f(t) = O(1)$ and $f(t) = \Omega(1)$, but the best choice for notation is to write $f(t) = \Theta(1)$ since Θ conveys more information than either O or Ω.

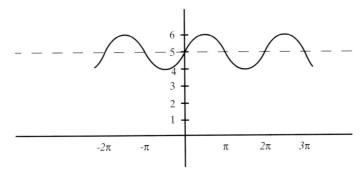

Figure 1-7 An illustration of $f(t) = 5 + \sin(t)$.

EXAMPLE

Show that

$$\sum_{k=1}^{n} k^p = \Theta(n^{p+1})$$

for $p > 1$ a fixed constant. First, we consider an upper bound on the summation. We know that

$$\sum_{k=1}^{n} k^p \leq n \times n^p = n^{p+1}$$

since the summation contains n terms, the largest of which is n^p. Therefore, we know that

$$\sum_{k=1}^{n} k^p = O(n^{p+1}).$$

Next, we consider a lower bound on the inequality. Notice that it is easy to derive a trivial lower bound of $\Omega(n)$, since there are n terms in the summation, the least of which is equal to 1. However, this lower bound is not terribly useful. Let's consider deriving a more useful, larger, lower bound. Notice that

$$\sum_{k=1}^{n} k^p = \sum_{k=1}^{\lfloor n/2 \rfloor} k^p + \sum_{k=\lfloor n/2 \rfloor+1}^{n} k^p \ .$$

Using this result, we know that

$$\sum_{k=1}^{n} k^p \geq \sum_{k=\lfloor n/2 \rfloor+1}^{n} k^p \ .$$

Notice that in

$$\sum_{k=\lfloor n/2 \rfloor+1}^{n} k^p$$

there are $n - \lfloor n/2 \rfloor$ terms, where $(\lfloor n/2 \rfloor + 1)^p$ is the smallest term. Therefore, we know that

$$\sum_{k=1}^{n} k^p \geq (n/2)(n/2)^p = n^{p+1}/2^{p+1} \ .$$

Since 2^{p+1} is a constant, we have

$$\sum_{k=1}^{n} k^p = \Omega(n^{p+1}) \ .$$

Therefore, we know that

$$\sum_{k=1}^{n} k^p = \Theta(n^{p+1}).$$

ASYMPTOTIC RELATIONSHIPS

Useful relationships exist among Θ, O, Ω, o, and ω, some of which are given in the proposition below. The reader might wish to try and prove some of these. (An instructor might wish to assign some of these as homework problems.)

Proposition: *Let f and g be positive functions of n. Then*

1. $f(n) = O(g(n)) \Leftrightarrow g(n) = \Omega(f(n))$.
2. $f(n) = \Theta(g(n)) \Leftrightarrow g(n) = \Theta(f(n))$.
3. $f(n) = \Theta(g(n)) \Leftrightarrow [f(n) = O(g(n)) \text{ and } f(n) = \Omega(g(n))]$.
4. $f(n) = o(g(n)) \Leftrightarrow g(n) = \omega(f(n))$.
5. $f(n) = o(g(n)) \Leftrightarrow \lim_{n \to \infty} \dfrac{f(n)}{g(n)} = 0$.

6. $f(n) = \omega(g(n)) \Leftrightarrow \lim_{n \to \infty} \dfrac{f(n)}{g(n)} = \infty$.

7. $f(n) = o(g(n)) \Rightarrow f(n) = O(g(n))$, but the converse is false.
8. $f(n) = \omega(g(n)) \Rightarrow f(n) = \Omega(g(n))$, but the converse is false.
9. $f(n)$ is bounded above and below by positive constants *if and only if* $f(n) = \Theta(1)$.

ASYMPTOTIC ANALYSIS AND LIMITS

In order to determine the relationship between functions f and g, it is often useful to examine

$$\lim_{n \to \infty} \frac{f(n)}{g(n)} = L.$$

The possible outcomes of this relationship, and their implications, are given below.

1. $L = 0$. This means that $g(n)$ grows at a faster rate than $f(n)$, and hence that $f = O(g)$ (indeed, $f = o(g)$ and $f \neq \Theta(g)$).
2. $L = \infty$. This means that $f(n)$ grows at a faster rate than $g(n)$, and hence that $f = \Omega(g)$ (indeed, $f = \omega(g)$ and $f \neq \Theta(g)$).

3. $L \neq 0$ is finite. This means that $f(n)$ and $g(n)$ grow at the same rate, and hence
    that $f = \Theta(g)$, or equivalently that $g = \Theta(f)$. Notice that this also means that $f = O(g)$,
    $g = O(f), f = \Omega(g)$, and $g = \Omega(f)$.
4. There is no limit. In the case where

$$\lim_{n \to \infty} \frac{f(n)}{g(n)}$$

does not exist, this technique cannot be used to determine the asymptotic relationship between $f(n)$ and $g(n)$.

We now give some examples of how to determine asymptotic relationships based on taking limits of a quotient.

EXAMPLE

Let

$$f(n) = \frac{n(n + 1)}{2} \text{ and } g(n) = n^2.$$

Then we can show that $f(n) = \Theta(g(n))$ since

$$\lim_{n \to \infty} \frac{f(n)}{g(n)} = \lim_{n \to \infty} \frac{n^2 + n}{2n^2} =$$

(dividing both numerator and denominator by n^2)

$$\lim_{n \to \infty} \frac{1 + \dfrac{1}{n}}{2} = \frac{1}{2}.$$

EXAMPLE

If $P(n)$ is a polynomial of degree d, then $P(n) = \Theta(n^d)$.

EXAMPLE

Compare n^{100} and 2^n. We remind the reader of a useful result:

$$\frac{d}{dx} e^{f(x)} = e^{f(x)} f'(x).$$

We have

$$\lim_{n\to\infty} \frac{2^n}{n^{100}} = \lim_{n\to\infty} \frac{e^{\ln 2^n}}{n^{100}}.$$

We can apply L'Hopital's rule to the numerator and denominator of this limit 100 times. After this, we have the following equation:

$$\lim_{n\to\infty} \frac{2^n}{n^{100}} = \lim_{n\to\infty} \frac{e^{\ln 2^n}}{n^{100}} = \lim_{n\to\infty} \frac{(\ln 2)^{100} 2^n}{100!} = \infty.$$

Therefore, we know that $n^{100} = O(2^n)$ and $2^n = \Omega(n^{100})$. In addition, using some of the properties previously presented, we know that $n^{100} = o(2^n)$ and $2^n = \omega(n^{100})$. Further, we know that $n^{100} \neq \Theta(2^n)$.

At this point, it is reasonable to discuss logarithmic notation and to note that logarithms play an important role in asymptotic analysis and will be used frequently throughout this text. As appropriate, we will use fairly standard terminology in referring to logarithms. We write

- $\log_e x$ as $\ln x$,
- $\log_2 x$ as $\lg x$, and
- $\log_{10} x$ as $\log x$.

We now continue with an example that uses logarithms.

EXAMPLE

Let $f(n) = \ln n$ and $g(n) = n$. Then, by applying L'Hopital's Rule, we have

$$\lim_{n\to\infty} \frac{n}{\ln n} = \lim_{n\to\infty} \frac{1}{1/n}$$

which evaluates as

$$\lim_{n\to\infty} \frac{1}{1/n} = \lim_{n\to\infty} n = \infty.$$

Therefore, $\ln n = O(n)$.

We remind the reader that $\log_b x = (\log_b a)(\log_a x)$, for positive a, b, and x with $a \neq 1 \neq b$. Therefore, since $\log_b a$ is a constant, $\log_b x = \Theta(\log_a x)$. That is, the base of a logarithm is irrelevant inside asymptotic notation, except that we assume $a, b > 1$ (so that the logarithms are positive, since we generally have $x \geq 1$ in such contexts).

SUMMATIONS AND INTEGRALS

Since many algorithms involve looping and/or recursion, it is not uncommon for the analysis of an algorithm to include a dependence on some function $f(n)$ that is best expressed as the sum of simpler functions. For example, it may be that the dominant term in an analysis of an algorithm can be expressed as $f(n) = h(1) + h(2) + \ldots + h(n)$. When we consider the worst-case number of comparisons in the insertion sort routine later in this chapter, we will find that the total number of comparisons can be computed as $f(n) = 1 + 2 + 3 + \ldots + n = n(n + 1)/2 = \Theta(n^2)$.

We first consider the case where the function $h(i)$ is nondecreasing. (Notice that the worst-case number of comparisons used in insertion sort, as mentioned above, uses the nondecreasing function $h(i) = i$.) Specifically, let

$$f(n) = \sum_{i=1}^{n} h(i)$$

where h is nondecreasing. (An illustration of this situation is presented in Figure 1-8.)

In order to evaluate $f(n)$, we can consider summing n unit-width rectangles, where the i-th rectangle has height $h(i)$. In Figure 1-8, we present these rectangles in two ways in order to obtain tight bounds on the asymptotic behavior of the total area of the rectangles (in other words,

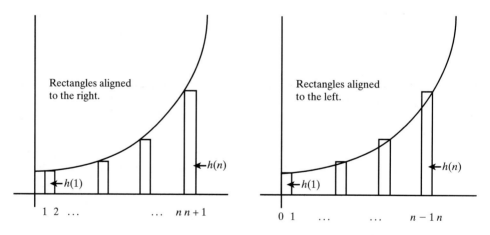

Figure 1-8   An illustration of bounding the summation of a nondecreasing function $\sum_{i=1}^{n} h(i)$ by the integral of the function $h(t)$. On the left, we demonstrate how to use the integral $\int_{1}^{n+1} h(t)dt$ to derive an upper bound on the summation by aligning the rectangles to the right. Notice that $\sum_{i=1}^{n} h(i) \leq \int_{1}^{n+1} h(t)dt$. On the right, we show how to use the integral $\int_{0}^{n} h(t)dt$ to derive a lower bound on the summation by aligning the rectangles to the left. Notice that $\int_{0}^{n} h(t)dt \leq \sum_{i=1}^{n} h(i)$. Therefore, we have $\int_{0}^{n} h(t)dt \leq \sum_{i=1}^{n} h(i) \leq \int_{1}^{n+1} h(t)dt$.

the value of $f(n)$). On the left, we draw the rectangles so that the i-th rectangle is anchored on the left. That is, the left edge of $h(i)$ is at value i on the x-axis. In this way, you will notice that each rectangle is below the curve of $h(t)$, where t takes on values between 1 and $n + 1$ (assuming 1 is the value of the lower bound and n is the value of the upper bound in the sum).

Conversely, on the right of Figure 1-8, we draw the rectangles so that the i-th rectangle is anchored on the right. That is, the right edge of $h(i)$ is at value i on the x-axis. This allows us to use the rectangles to bound the area of the curve, between 0 and n (assuming that 1 is the value of the lower bound and n is the value of the upper bound), from above. Notice that in Figure 1-8, we give the relationships of the area under the curve bounding the rectangles (left figure) and the rectangles bounding the area under the curve (right figure). In addition, we show how to combine these relationships to obtain a bound on the summation by related integrals.

The method of determining asymptotic analysis of a summation by integration is quite powerful. Next, we give several examples, and in doing so, illustrate a variety of techniques and review some basic principles of integration.

EXAMPLE

Find the asymptotic complexity of

$$f(n) = \sum_{i=1}^{n} i.$$

First, we consider the integral bounding principles that were given above. Since the function $h(i) = i$ is nondecreasing, we can apply the conclusion directly and arrive at the bound

$$\int_{0}^{n} t\,dt \le \sum_{i=1}^{n} i \le \int_{1}^{n+1} t\,dt.$$

Evaluating both the left-hand side and right-hand side simultaneously yields

$$\left.\frac{t^2}{2}\right|_{0}^{n} \le \sum_{i=1}^{n} i \le \left.\frac{t^2}{2}\right|_{1}^{n+1}$$

which can be evaluated in a fairly routine fashion, resulting in

$$\frac{n^2}{2} \le \sum_{i=1}^{n} i \le \frac{(n + 1)^2}{2} - \frac{1}{2}.$$

Working with the right-hand side of this inequality, we obtain

$$\frac{(n + 1)^2}{2} - \frac{1}{2} = \frac{1}{2}n^2 + n.$$

Further simplification of the right-hand side can be used to give

$$\frac{1}{2}n^2 + n \le \frac{1}{2}n^2 + n^2$$

for $n \ge 1$. Therefore,

$$\frac{1}{2}n^2 \le \sum_{i=1}^{n} i \le \frac{3}{2}n^2.$$

Since the function

$$f(n) = \sum_{i=1}^{n} i$$

is bounded by a multiple of n^2 on both the left- and right-hand sides, we can conclude that

$$f(n) = \sum_{i=1}^{n} i = \Theta(n^2).$$

EXAMPLE

Find the asymptotic complexity of

$$f(n) = \sum_{k=1}^{n} \frac{1}{k}.$$

First, it is important to realize that the function $1/k$ is a *nonincreasing* function. This requires an update in the analysis presented for nondecreasing functions. In Figure 1-9, we present a figure that illustrates the behavior of a nonincreasing function over the interval $[a, b]$. Notice that with the proper analysis, you should be able to show that

$$\sum_{k=a+1}^{b} f(k) \le \int_{a}^{b} f(x)dx \le \sum_{k=a}^{b-1} f(k).$$

Based on this analysis, we can now attempt to produce an asymptotically tight bound on the function $f(n)$. First, we consider a lower bound on $f(n)$. Our analysis shows that

$$\int_{1}^{n+1} \frac{1}{x} dx \le \sum_{k=1}^{n} \frac{1}{k}.$$

Since

$$\int_1^{n+1} \frac{1}{x}\, dx = \ln x \big|_1^{n+1} = \ln(n+1) - \ln 1 = \ln(n+1) \le \sum_{k=1}^n \frac{1}{k}$$

we know that $f(n)$ is bounded below by $\ln(n+1)$.

Next, we consider an upper bound on $f(n)$. Notice that if we blindly apply the result of our analysis for a nonincreasing function, we obtain

$$\sum_{k=1}^n \frac{1}{k} \le \int_0^n \frac{1}{x}\, dx = \ln x \big|_0^n = \infty .$$

Unfortunately, this result, while providing some information, clearly does not yield a tight enough upper bound. However, notice that the cause of the upper bound resulting in ∞ is evaluation of the integral at the specific point of 0. This problem can be alleviated by carefully rewriting the equation to avoid the problematic point. Let's consider the more restricted inequality

$$\sum_{k=2}^n \frac{1}{k} \le \int_1^n \frac{1}{x}\, dx .$$

Notice that the integral evaluates to $\ln n$. Therefore, if we now add back in the problematic term, we arrive at

$$\sum_{k=1}^n \frac{1}{k} = 1 + \sum_{k=2}^n \frac{1}{k} \le 1 + \ln n .$$

Combining the results of both the upper and lower bounds on $f(n)$, we arrive at

$$\ln n \le \ln(n+1) \le \sum_{k=1}^n f(k) \le 1 + \ln n \le 2 \ln n$$

for n large enough (verify). Therefore,

$$\sum_{k=1}^n \frac{1}{k} = \Theta(\ln n) .$$

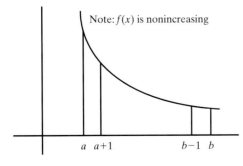

Note: $f(x)$ is nonincreasing

$a \quad a+1 \qquad\qquad b-1 \quad b$

Figure 1-9 An illustration of bounding the summation of a nonincreasing function $\sum_{i=1}^n f(i)$. Notice that for f nonincreasing, we can derive the relationship $\sum_{i=a+1}^b f(i) \le \int_a^b f(x)\, dx \le \sum_{i=a}^{b-1} f(i) .$

EXAMPLE

As our final example of evaluating the asymptotic behavior of a summation by integrals, we consider the function

$$f(n) = \sum_{k=1}^{n} k^p$$

for $p > 0$. We showed earlier that

$$f(n) = \sum_{k=1}^{n} k^p = \Theta(n^{p+1}).$$

However, we now show how to obtain this result by another method. In order to determine whether or not $h(k) = k^p$ is a nondecreasing function, consider the derivative of k^p. For $k > 0$, notice that

$$\frac{d}{dk} k^p = pk^{p-1} > 0.$$

Therefore, the function k^p is term-wise increasing. A quick sketch of an increasing function, in a more general setting than was illustrated earlier, is given in Figure 1-10.

First, let's consider an upper bound on

$$f(n) = \sum_{k=1}^{n} k^p.$$

Using the analysis associated with Figure 1-10, we know that

$$\sum_{k=1}^{n} k^p \leq \int_{1}^{n+1} x^p dx$$

Recall that

$$\int_{1}^{n+1} x^p dx = \frac{x^{p+1}}{p+1}\bigg|_{1}^{n+1} = \frac{(n+1)^{p+1} - 1}{p+1}.$$

Notice that

$$\frac{(n+1)^{p+1} - 1}{p+1} < \frac{(n+1)^{p+1}}{p+1}$$

and since $n + 1 \leq 2n$ for $n \geq 1$, that

$$\frac{(n+1)^{p+1}}{p+1} \leq \frac{(2n)^{p+1}}{p+1}.$$

Therefore, we have

$$f(n) = \sum_{k=1}^{n} k^p \leq \frac{2^{p+1} n^{p+1}}{p+1}.$$

Next, we consider a lower bound on

$$f(n) = \sum_{k=1}^{n} k^p.$$

From our previous analysis, we have

$$\int_{0}^{n} x^p dx \leq \sum_{k=1}^{n} k^p.$$

A straightforward evaluation of the integral results in

$$\frac{1}{p+1} n^{p+1} \leq \sum_{k=1}^{n} k^p.$$

Therefore, we have

$$\frac{1}{p+1} n^{p+1} \leq \sum_{k=1}^{n} k^p \leq \frac{2^{p+1}}{p+1} n^{p+1}$$

which, based on asymptotic properties given earlier in this chapter, yields the expected solution of

$$\sum_{k=1}^{n} k^p = \Theta(n^{p+1}).$$

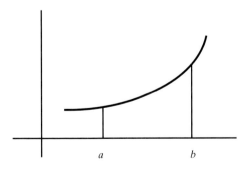

Figure 1-10   An increasing function in the range of a to b. Notice that

$$\sum_{k=a}^{b-1} f(k) \leq \int_{a}^{b} f(x)dx \leq \sum_{k=a+1}^{b} f(k).$$

RULES FOR ANALYSIS OF ALGORITHMS

The application of asymptotic analysis is critical in order to provide an effective means of evaluating both the running time and space of an algorithm as a function of the size of the input. In this section, we present fundamental information about the analysis of algorithms and give several algorithms to illustrate the major points of emphasis.

Fundamental operations execute in $\Theta(1)$ time: Traditionally, it is assumed that "fundamental" operations require a constant amount of time (*i.e.*, a fixed number of computer "clock cycles") to execute. That is, we assume that the running time of a fundamental operation is bounded by a constant, irrespective of the data being processed. Such operations include the following:

- Arithmetic operations ($+, -, \times, /$) as applied to a constant number (typically, 2) of fixed-size operands.
- Comparison operators ($<, \leq, >, \geq, =, \neq$) as applied to two fixed-size operands.
- Logical operators (AND, OR, NOT, XOR) as applied to a constant number of fixed-size operands.
- Bitwise operations, as applied to a constant number of fixed-size operands. (Many of you have seen such operations in C-type languages.)
- I/O operations that are used to read or write a constant number of fixed-size data items. Note this does not include input from a keyboard, mouse, or other human-operated device, as the user's response time is unpredictable.
- Conditional/branch operations.
- The evaluation of certain elementary functions. Notice that such functions need to be considered carefully. For example, when the function $\sin\theta$ is to be evaluated for "moderate-sized" values of θ, it is reasonable to assume that $\Theta(1)$ time is required for each application of the function. However, for very large values of $|\theta|$, a loop dominating the calculation of $\sin\theta$ may require a significant number of operations before stabilizing at an accurate approximation. In this case, it may not be reasonable to assume $\Theta(1)$ time for this operation.

We mention additional fundamental properties.

- Suppose the running times of operations A and B are, respectively, $O(f(n))$ and $O(g(n))$. Then the performance of A followed by B takes $O(f(n) + g(n))$ time. Note that this analysis holds for $\Theta, \Omega, o,$ and ω as well.
- Next, suppose that each application of the body of a loop requires $O(f(n))$ time, and the loop executes its body $O(g(n))$ times. Then the time required to execute the loop (*i.e.*, all performances of its body) is $O(f(n)g(n))$. A similar property holds for $\Theta, \Omega, o,$ and ω.

EXAMPLE

Insertion sort: As an example, we consider the analysis of *insertion sort*, a simple sorting technique that is introduced in most CS1-type courses (Introduction to Computer Science). Suppose we are given a set of data arbitrarily distributed in an array and we wish to rearrange the data so it appears in increasing order. We give pseudocode for the algorithm and then present an analysis of both time and space. Note that later in this book, we compare more advanced algorithms to insertion sort, and also show how insertion sort can be used in critical instances where data is roughly sorted.

Subprogram InsertionSort(*X*)
Input: An array *X* of *n* entries.
Output: The array *X* with its entries in ascending order.
Local Variables: indices *current*, *insertPlace*
Action:
    For *current* = 2 to *n* do
    {The first (*current* − 1) entries of *X* are ordered.
    This is why *current* is initially set to 2.}
        Search *X*[1 . . . *current* − 1] to determine the index, denoted as
            insertPlace ∈ {1, . . . , *current*}, where *X*[*current*] should be inserted.
        Make a copy of *X*[*current*], so as to avoid any loss of data.
        Shift the elements *X*[*insertPlace*, . . . , *current* − 1] down by one
            position into elements *X*[*insertPlace* + 1, . . . , *current*].
        Finally, place the copy of *X*[*current*] into its proper position at
            X[*insertPlace*].
    End For

The description above presents a top-level view of InsertionSort. An example is given in Figure 1-11. We observe that the search called for in the first step of the loop can be performed by a straightforward sequential search that requires $O(k)$ time, where k is the value of *current*. The reader should verify that this requires $\Theta(k)$ time on average. Alternately, a $\Theta(\log k)$-time binary search can be performed, as will be discussed in the chapter on Induction and Recursion. Thus, the total *search* time is

$$O\left(\sum_{k=2}^{n} k\right) = O(n^2)$$

time if sequential searches are used, and

$$O\left(\sum_{k=2}^{n} \log k\right) = O(n \log n)$$

time if binary searches are used. Notice that *O*-notation is used, as both results represent upper bounds on the search time.

Regardless of which search is used to locate the position that *X*[*current*] should be moved to, notice that on average, it will require *current*/2 movements of data items to make room for *X*[*current*]. However, in the worst case, the insert step always requires *X*[*current*] to be moved to position number 1, requiring *current* data items to be moved, while in the best case, *X*[*current*] is always in the proper position (*i.e.*, the initial data is sorted). Therefore, the number of data movement operations is given by

$$T(n) = \sum_{k=2}^{n} movement_k$$

where $movement_k$ is 0 in the best case, k in the worst case, and $k/2$ in the average case. Hence, the running time of InsertionSort is $\Theta(n)$ in the best case (when data is already sorted and a sequential search from $(current - 1)$ downto 1 is used), $\Theta(n^2)$ in the average (or expected) case, and $\Theta(n^2)$ in the worst case. The reader should verify these results by substituting the appropriate values into the summation and simplifying the equation. Notice that the average- and worst-case running times are dominated by the data movement operations.

Finally, notice that $\Theta(n)$ space is required for the algorithm to store the n data items. More importantly, the amount of extra space required for this algorithm is constant ($\Theta(1)$). An insertion routine is presented below.

Subprogram Insert(*X*, *current*, *insertPlace*)
Insert $X[current]$ into the ordered subarray $X[1 \ldots current - 1]$
    in the position *insertPlace*.
We assume $1 \le insertPlace \le current \le n$.
Local variables: index j, entry-type *hold*
Action:
    If $current \ne insertPlace$, then {There's work to do.}
        $hold = X[current]$;
        For $j = current - 1$ downto *insertPlace* do
            $X[j + 1] = X[j]$;
        End For
        $X[insertPlace] = hold$
    End If
End Insert

For completeness, we present an efficient implementation of InsertionSort based on the analysis we have presented.

Subprogram InsertionSort(*x*, *n*)
{This is a simple version of InsertionSort with sequential search.}
    For $i = 2$ to n, do
        $hold = x[i]$
        $position = 1$
        While $(hold > x[position])$, do
            $position = position + 1$
        End While
        If $position < i$, then
            For $j = i$ downto *position*, do
                $x[j] = x[j - 1]$
            End For
            $x[position] = hold$
        End If
    End For
End InsertionSort

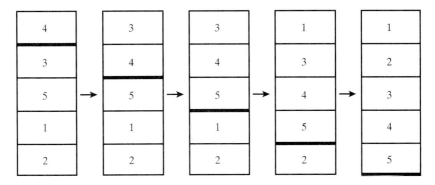

Figure 1-11   An example of InsertionSort. It is initially assumed that the first item (4) is in the correct position. Then the second item (3) is placed into position with respect to all the items in front of it, resulting in (3,4) being properly ordered. The algorithm continues until the last item (2) is placed in its proper position with respect to the items (1,3,4,5) that are in front of it.

It is often possible to modify an algorithm designed for one data structure to accommodate a different data structure. The reader should consider how InsertionSort could be adapted to linked lists (see Exercises).

BINSORT

Sorting is a fundamental problem in computer science since a major use of computers is to maintain order within large collections of data. Perhaps for this reason, researchers have developed many algorithms for sorting. Some of these are considerably faster than others. Yet sometimes the asymptotically slower algorithms are useful because, for example, they may be very fast on relatively small data sets or they may be very fast on sets of data that exhibit certain characteristics. We will present several sorting algorithms in this book in order to examine such issues.

In the previous section, we presented an analysis of InsertionSort. In one of the exercises at the end of this chapter, we present SelectionSort, a fairly straightforward and useful sorting routine that runs in the same worst-case $\Theta(n^2)$ time as InsertionSort, but is typically faster in practice. Later in the book, we present alternative comparison-based sorting algorithms that exhibit an optimal $\Theta(n \log n)$ worst-case running time. In fact, many of you may already be familiar with the result that states that comparison-based sorting requires $\Omega(n \log n)$ time.

While $\Omega(n \log n)$ is a lower bound on general comparison-based sorting, one might ask whether or not it is possible to sort a set of data in $o(n \log n)$ time. In fact, while this is not possible in general, it is possible given a set of data that is not "arbitrary." An important theme that runs through this book is that one should attempt to design a $o(n \log n)$ time sorting algorithm if one knows something about the data *a priori*.

For example, suppose you know that you are required to sort data that is chosen from a restricted set. Maybe you know that the keys can take on only $O(n)$ distinct values. In this case, one can employ a "BinSort" algorithm. BinSort is modeled on the process of placing each member of a collection of numbered items (such as machine parts) into a correspondingly numbered bin. Alternatively, one might think about sorting a deck of cards by going through the deck once, tossing all the Aces in one pile, all the 2s in another, and so on. Once you have gone through all the cards and created your 13 bins (which have four items apiece), then you simply need to concatenate the bins in order to create the final sorted set. An example of BinSort is presented in Figure 1-12.

Below we give a description of BinSort under the assumption that the range of data is the integer values from 1 to n. It is important to note (in terms of the proof that $\Omega(n \log n)$ comparisons are required to sort an arbitrary set of data by a comparison-based sort) that BinSort is not a "comparison-based" sorting algorithm. That is, BinSort does not rely on comparing data items. In fact, the algorithm never compares two data items.

Subprogram BinSort(X)
Sort the array X via the *BinSort* algorithm.
We assume entries of X have integer key values 1 . . . n.
Local variables: indices j, s;
                temp, an array of pointers, each representing a stack
Action:
     1. For $j = 1$ to n, do
          {Make *temp*[j] an empty stack.}
             temp[j] = *null*
     2. For $j = 1$ to n, do
            push(X[j], *temp*[X[j].*key*])
     3. $s = 1$
     4. For $j = 1$ to n, do
            While *emptyStack*(*temp*[s])
                $s \leftarrow s + 1$
            End While
            pop(*temp*[s], X[j])
    End For
End BinSort

An analysis of the algorithm follows. It is easy to see that Steps 1 and 2 each require $\Theta(n)$ time, after which each element is in one of the n bins. Step 3 requires $\Theta(1)$ time. Step 4 requires that every item be examined once. Therefore, Step 4 requires $\Theta(n)$ time. Hence, the entire algorithm requires $\Theta(n)$ time. Further, notice that the algorithm requires $\Theta(n)$ space to store the items and only $\Theta(n)$ additional space (for indices and stack pointers). We observe that the linear amount of additional space requires only a small constant of proportionality, since the items themselves are placed on the stacks (no copies of the items are ever made). Therefore, the algorithm is *optimal* in terms of running time—that is, executing faster (asymptotically) means not examining all of the items, in which case you might miss an item that is out of order—and is efficient in terms of space.

LIMITATIONS OF ASYMPTOTIC ANALYSIS

Suppose a given problem has two equally acceptable solutions. Further, suppose both of these algorithms have the same asymptotic running times and the same asymptotic space requirements. This might make it difficult to choose between the two algorithms; the as-

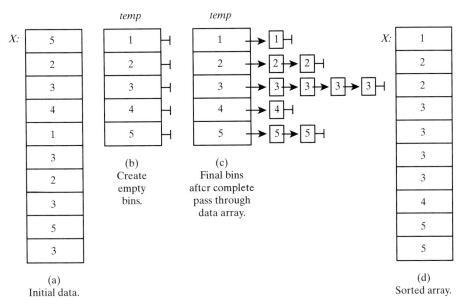

Figure 1-12 BinSort applied to an array of 10 items chosen from 1 . . . 5. In (a), the initial array of data is given. In (b), the set of empty bins is created. In (c), the bins are shown after a complete pass through the array. In (d), the array is recreated by "concatenating" the bins.

ymptotic analysis provides some guidelines for behavior, but we do know that it also hides high-order constants and low-order terms. In fact, suppose that Algorithm A is 5 times faster than Algorithm B for problems of a given size. Since 5 is just a constant, this will be hidden in the O-notation. Similarly, since low-order terms are masked with O-notation, it may be that one algorithm is superior for small data sets (where the low-order terms are important), but not for large data sets (where these low-order terms are, appropriately, masked).

Consider the problem of sorting a set of data, and assume that, based on knowledge of the input, you decide that a general, comparison-based sorting algorithm is required. Among your choices are algorithms that copy data and algorithms that do not copy data (for example, sorting can be done via pointer manipulation, rather than copying data). Suppose, for example, we consider three algorithms whose running times are dominated by the following steps:

a) Algorithm A: $\Theta(n^2)$ comparisons, $\Theta(n^2)$ copying operations;
b) Algorithm B: $\Theta(n^2)$ comparisons, $\Theta(n)$ copying operations;
c) Algorithm C: $\Theta(n^2)$ comparisons, $\Theta(n)$ pointer manipulation operations.

All three algorithms run in $\Theta(n^2)$ time, yet we should expect A to be slower than B, and B to be slower than C. For example, suppose the data being sorted consists of 100 byte data records. Then at the machine level, every copying operation (an assignment statement of the form $x \leftarrow y$) can be thought of as a loop of the following form

For *byteNumber* = 1 to 100, do
    $x[byteNumber] \leftarrow y[byteNumber]$

Therefore, a data-copying operation takes time proportional to the size of the data entity being copied. Thus, given data entries of significant size (where *significant* is machine-dependent—on some machines this may mean data items larger than 100 bytes, while on other machines this may mean data items larger than 1,000 bytes), we expect Algorithm A to be slower than Algorithm B, even though the two algorithms have the same asymptotic running time.

Pointers of four bytes (32 bits) can theoretically be used to address 2^{32} locations of memory. A sorting algorithm that uses $\Theta(n)$ pointer manipulations might involve three to four pointer assignments per data movement. Therefore, such an algorithm would typically be more efficient than an algorithm that copies data, so long as the data items are sufficiently long. Of course, on real machines, some of these conjectures must be tested experimentally, as instruction sets and compilers can play a major role in choosing the most efficient algorithm.

COMMON TERMINOLOGY

We conclude this chapter by giving some common terminology that will be used throughout the text. These terms are fairly standard, appearing in many texts and the scientific literature.

An algorithm with running time	is said to run in
$\Theta(1)$	*constant time*
$\Theta(\log n)$	*logarithmic time*
$\Theta(\log^k n)$, k a positive integer	*polylogarithmic time*
$o(\log n)$	*sublogarithmic time*
$\Theta(n)$	*linear time*
$o(n)$	*sublinear time*
$\Theta(n^2)$	*quadratic time*
$O(f(n))$, where $f(n)$ is a polynomial	*polynomial time*

An algorithm is said to run in *optimal time* if its running time $T(n) = O(f(n))$ is such that any algorithm that solves the same problem requires $\Omega(f(n))$ time. It is important to note that in terms of notions such as *optimality* or *efficiency*, one compares the running time of a given *algorithm* with the lower bound on the running time to solve the *problem* being considered. For example, any algorithm to compute the minimum entry of an unsorted array of n entries must examine every item in the array (because any item skipped could be the minimal item). Therefore, any sequential algorithm to solve this problem requires $\Omega(n)$ time. So, an algorithm that runs in $\Theta(n)$ time is optimal.

Notice that we use the term *optimal* to mean *asymptotically optimal*. An optimal algorithm need not be the fastest possible algorithm to give a correct solution to its problem, but it must be within a constant factor of being the fastest possible algorithm to solve the problem. Proving optimality is often difficult, and there are many problems for which optimal running times are not known. There are, however, problems for which proof of optimality is fairly easy, some of which will appear in this book.

CHAPTER NOTES

The notion of applying asymptotic analysis to algorithms is often credited to Donald E. Knuth (www-cs-faculty.Stanford.EDU/~knuth/). Although it served as the foundation for part of his seminal series *The Art of Computer Programming*, Knuth, in fact, traces *O*-notation back to a number theory textbook by Bachmann in 1892. The *o*-notation was apparently first introduced by Landau in 1909, but the modern use of this notation in algorithms is attributed to a paper by D.E. Knuth that appeared in 1976 ("Big omicron and big omega and big theta," *ACM SIGACT News*, 8(2), 18–23.) Historical developments of the asymptotic notation in computer science can be found in reviews by D.E. Knuth and in *Algorithmics: Theory and Practice* by Brassard and Bratley (Prentice Hall, 1988). One of the early books that earned "classic" status was *The Design and Analysis of Computer Algorithms*, by A.V. Aho, J.E. Hopcroft, and J.D. Ullman, which was released by Addison Wesley in 1974. More recent books that focus on algorithms and their analysis include *Introduction to Algorithms*, by T.H. Cormen, C.E. Leiserson, and R.L. Rivest (McGraw-Hill, New York, 1989), and *Computer Algorithms/C++* by E. Horowitz, S. Sahni, and S. Rajasekaran (Computer Science Press, New York, 1996).

EXERCISES

1. Rank the following by growth rate: n, $n^{1/2}$, $\log n$, $\log(\log n)$, $\log^2 n$, $(1/3)^n$, 4, $(3/2)^n$, $n!$

2. Prove or disprove each of the following.

   a) $f(n) = O(g(n)) \Rightarrow g(n) = O(f(n))$

   b) $f(n) + g(n) = \Theta(\max(f(n), g(n)))$

   c) $f(n) = O((f(n))^2)$

   d) $f(n) = O(g(n)) \Rightarrow g(n) = \Omega(f(n))$

   e) $f(n) + o(f(n)) = \Theta(f(n))$

3. Use O, o, Ω, ω, and Θ to describe the relationship between the following pairs of functions:

   a) $\log^k n$, n^ϵ, where k and ϵ are positive constants

   b) n^k, c^n, where k and c are constants, $k > 0$, $c > 1$

   c) 2^n, $2^{n/2}$

4. Prove that $17n^{1/6} = O(n^{1/5})$.

5. Prove that $\displaystyle\sum_{k=1}^{n} k^{1/6} = \Theta(n^{7/6})$

6. Given a set of n **integer** values in the range of $[1, \ldots, 100]$, give an efficient sequential algorithm to sort these items. Discuss the time, space, and optimality of your solution.

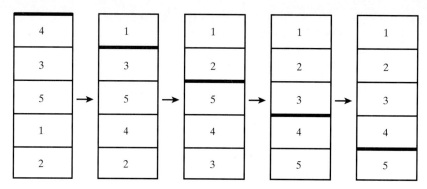

Figure 1-13   An example of SelectionSort. A complete pass is made through the initial set of data in order to determine the item that belongs in the front of the list (1). A swap is performed between this minimum element and the element currently in the front of the list. Next, a pass is made through the remaining four items to determine the minimum (2) of these elements. This minimum element is swapped with the current second item (3). The procedure continues until $n - 1$ items have been properly ordered since this forces all n items to be properly ordered.

7. **(Total function):** Determine the asymptotic running time of the following algorithm to sum a set of values. Show that it is optimal.

> **Function Total(*list*)**
> **Input:** An array *list* of numeric entries indexed from 1 to *n*.
> **Output:** The total of the entries in the array.
> Local variables: integer *index*, numeric *subtotal*
> Action:
> > *Subtotal* = 0
> > For *index* = 1 to *n*, do
> > > *subtotal* = *subtotal* + *list*[*index*]
> > Return *subtotal*

8. **(Selection sort):** Determine the asymptotic running time of the following algorithm, which is used to sort a set of data. See Figure 1-13. Determine the total asymptotic space and the additional asymptotic space required.

> **Subprogram SelectionSort(*List*)**
> **Input:** Array *List*[1 . . . n], to be sorted in ascending order according to the *key* field of the records.
> **Output:** The ordered *List*.
> **Algorithm:** SelectionSort, as follows
> > For each position in the *List*, we
> > Determine the index corresponding to the entry from the unsorted portion of the *List* that is a minimum.
> > Swap the item at the position just determined with the current item.
> Local variables: indices *ListPosition, SwapPlace*
> Action:

{ListPosition is only considered for values up to $n - 1$, because once the first $n - 1$ entries have been swapped into their correct positions, the last item must be in the correct position.}

For *ListPosition* = 1 to $n - 1$,

{Determine the index of correct entry for ListPosition and swap the entries.}

    SwapPlace = *MinimumIndex(List, ListPosition)*;

    Swap(List[SwapPlace], List[ListPosition])

End For

End *Sort*

Subprogram Swap(*A, B*)

Input: Data entities *A, B*.

Output: The input variables with their values interchanged, *e.g.*, if on entry we have $A = 3$ and $B = 5$, then at exit we have $A = 5$ and $B = 3$.

Local variable: *temp*, of the same type as *A* and *B*

Action:

    temp = *A*; {Backup the entry value of *A*.}

    A = *B*;   {*A* gets entry value of *B*.}

    B = *temp*   {*B* gets entry value of *A*.}

End *Swap*

Function MinimumIndex(*List, startIndex*)

Input: *List*[1 . . . *n*], an array of records to be ordered by a *key* field; *startIndex*, which is the first index considered.

Output: Index of the smallest *key* entry among those indexed *startIndex* . . . *n* (the range of indices of the portion of the *List* presumed unordered).

Local variables: indices *bestIndexSoFar, at*

Action:

    bestIndexSoFar = *startIndex*;

    {"at" is used to traverse the rest of the index subrange.}

    For *at* = *startIndex* + 1 to *n*, do

        If *List[at].key* < *List[bestIndexSoFar].key*

        then *bestIndexSoFar* = *at*

    End For

    Return *bestIndexSoFar*

End *MinimumIndex*

9. Earlier in this chapter, we gave an array-based implementation of InsertionSort. In this problem, we consider a linked list-based version of the algorithm.

Subprogram InsertionSort(*X*)

For every *current* entry of the list after the first entry:

    Search the sublist of all entries from the first entry to the *current* entry for the proper placement (indexed *insertPlace*) of the *current* entry in the sublist;

    Insert the *current* entry into the same sublist at the position *insertPlace*.

End For

Suppose we implement the InsertionSort algorithm as just described for a linked list data structure.

a) What is the worst-case running time for a generic iteration of the Search step?

b) What is the worst-case running time for a generic instance of the Insert step?

c) Show that the algorithm has a worst-case running time of $\Theta(n^2)$.

d) Although both the array-based and linked list-based implementations of Insertion-Sort have worst-case running times of $\Theta(n^2)$, in practice, we usually find that the linked list-based implementation (assuming the same data, in the same input order) is faster. Why should this be? (Think in terms of entries consisting of large data records.)

10. Array implementations of both InsertionSort and SelectionSort have $\Theta(n^2)$ worst-case running times. Which is likely to be faster if we time both in the same hardware/software environment for the same input data? Why?

2

Induction and Recursion

Induction and Recursion

In this chapter, we present some fundamental mathematical techniques that are used throughout the book. Many of these techniques, including recursion and mathematical induction, are typically taught in other courses, including calculus and discrete mathematics. For some readers, much of this chapter will serve as a review and require very little time, while for others, a more careful reading may be in order.

Mathematical induction and the related notion of recursion are useful tools in the analysis of algorithms. *Mathematical induction*, which we will often refer to simply as *induction*, is a technique for proving statements about consecutive integers, roughly, by *inducing* our knowledge of the next case from that of its predecessor. *Recursion* is a technique of designing algorithms in which we *i*) **divide** a large problem into smaller subproblems, *ii*) **solve** the subproblems *recursively*, and then *iii*) **combine** (or **stitch** together) the solutions to our subproblems in order to obtain a solution to the original problem. One of the critical steps in this process is that of (recursively) dividing a problem into subproblems. For example, in order to solve a given problem $P(1)$ by recursion, we might first divide $P(1)$ into two subproblems, $P(2)$ and $P(3)$, recursively solve these subproblems, and then stitch their results together to obtain the required result for $P(1)$. In order to solve $P(2)$ and $P(3)$, we might divide problem $P(2)$ into subproblems $P(4)$ and $P(5)$, and similarly divide problem $P(3)$ into subproblems $P(6)$ and $P(7)$. Before stitching together $P(4)$ and $P(5)$, and similarly $P(6)$ and $P(7)$, these problems must first be solved. Therefore, we might recursively divide problems $P(4)$, $P(5)$, $P(6)$, and $P(7)$ into subproblems, recursively solve them, and so on. This recursive subdivision of problems typically continues until subproblems have simple/trivial solutions. Thus, recursion resembles induction in that a recursive algorithm solves a problem by making use of its capability to solve simpler problems, inducing a solution from previous knowledge.

MATHEMATICAL INDUCTION

Suppose we have a statement about positive integers, and we wish to show that the statement is always true. Formally, let $P(n)$ be a *predicate,* a statement that is true or false, depending on its argument n, which we assume to be a positive integer. Suppose we wish to show $P(n)$ is always true.

Principle of Mathematical Induction: Let $P(n)$ be a predicate, where n is an arbitrary positive integer. Suppose we can accomplish the following two steps.

1. Show that $P(1)$ is *true.*
2. Show that whenever $P(k)$ is *true*, we can derive that $P(k + 1)$ is also *true.*

If we can achieve these two goals, then it follows that $P(n)$ is *true* for all positive integers n.

Why does this work? Suppose we have accomplished the two steps given above. Roughly speaking (we'll give a mathematically stronger argument below), we know from Step 1 that $P(1)$ is true, and thus by Step 2 that $P(1 + 1) = P(2)$ is true, and thus by Step 2 that $P(2 + 1) = P(3)$ is true, and thus by Step 2 that $P(3 + 1) = P(4)$ is true, and so forth. That is, Step 2 allows us to induce the truth of $P(n)$ for every positive integer n from the truth of $P(1)$.

The assumption in Step 2 that $P(k)$ = true is called the *inductive hypothesis,* because it is typically used to *induce* the conclusion that the successor statement $P(k + 1)$ is true.

The principle of mathematical induction is stated above as an assertion. Further, we have also given an informal argument as to its validity. For the sake of mathematical completeness, we will prove the assertion below. The proof we give of mathematical induction depends on the following axiom:

Greatest Lower Bound Axiom: Let X be a nonempty subset of the integers such that the members of X have a lower bound (in other words, there is a constant C such that for every $x \in X$, $x \geq C$). Then a greatest lower bound for X exists, *i.e.,* a constant C_0 such that C_0 is a lower bound for the members of X and such that C_0 is greater than any other lower bound for X.

Proof of the Principle of Mathematical Induction: We argue by contradiction. Suppose the Principle of Mathematical Induction is false. Then there is a predicate $P(n)$ on positive integers that yields a counterexample, *i.e.,* for which Steps 1 and 2 are true and yet, for some positive integer k, $P(k)$ is false. Let

$$S = \{n \mid n \text{ is a positive integer and } P(n) = false\}.$$

Then, $k \in S$, so $S \neq \varnothing$. It follows from the greatest lower bound axiom that S has a greatest lower bound $k_0 \in S$, a positive integer. That is, k_0 is the first value of n such that $P(n)$ is false. By Step 1, $P(1) = true$, so $k_0 > 1$. Therefore, $k_0 - 1$ is a positive integer. Notice that by choice of k_0, we must have $P(k_0 - 1) = true$. Finally, it follows from Step 2 of the Principle of Mathematical Induction that $P(k_0) = P((k_0 - 1) + 1) = true$, contrary to the fact that $k_0 \in S$. Since the contradiction results from the assumption that the principle is false, the proof is established.

INDUCTION EXAMPLES

EXAMPLE

Prove that for all positive integers n, $\displaystyle\sum_{i=1}^{n} i = \frac{n(n+1)}{2}$

Proof: We can interpret the equation as claiming that the sum of the first n positive integers is the formula on the right side of the equal sign. For $n = 1$, the left side of the asserted equation is

$$\sum_{i=1}^{1} i = 1$$

and the right side of the asserted equation is is

$$\frac{1(1+1)}{2} = 1 .$$

Thus, for $n = 1$, the asserted equation is true.

Suppose the asserted equation is valid for some positive integer k (notice such an assumption is justified by the previous step). Thus, our inductive hypothesis is the equation

$$\sum_{i=1}^{k} i = \frac{k(k+1)}{2} .$$

Now we want to prove the asserted equation is true for the next term, $n = k + 1$. That is, we want to prove that

$$\sum_{i=1}^{k+1} i = \frac{(k+1)(k+2)}{2} .$$

Consider the left side of this equation. We can rewrite the left side as

$$\sum_{i=1}^{k+1} i = \left(\sum_{i=1}^{k} i \right) + (k+1) .$$

Notice that by the inductive hypothesis, the left side is equal to

$$\left(\sum_{i=1}^{k} i \right) + (k+1) = \frac{k(k+1)}{2} + (k+1) = \frac{(k+1)(k+2)}{2} ,$$

which is the right side of the original equation. Thus, our proof is complete.

EXAMPLE

Prove that $n! > 2^n$ for all integers $n \geq 4$. Notice that you may view this as a statement about all positive integers, not just those greater than or equal to 4, by observing that the assertion is equivalent to the statement that for all positive integers j, $(j + 3)! > 2^{j+3}$. This observation easily generalizes so that mathematical induction can be viewed as a technique for proving the truth of predicates defined for all integers greater than or equal to some fixed integer m. In this generalized view of induction, the first step of an inductive proof requires showing that $P(m) = \textit{true}$. The induction proof follows.

1. We must show the assertion to be true for the base case, which is $n = 4$. Notice that since $4! = 24 > 16 = 2^4$, the assertion is true for our base case of $n = 4$.
2. Suppose $k! > 2^k$ for some integer $k \geq 4$. Based on this, we want to show that $(k + 1)! > 2^{k+1}$. Now, $(k + 1)! = (k + 1)(k!)$, which (by the inductive hypothesis and the assumption that $k \geq 4$) is an expression at least as large as $5(2^k) > 2(2^k) = 2^{k+1}$, as desired. This completes the proof.

EXAMPLE

(Calculus example.) Prove that $\dfrac{d}{dx} x^n = nx^{n-1}$, for all integers n.

Proof: Even though this is a statement about *all* integers, we can use mathematical induction to give the proof for n, an arbitrary positive integer, and then use fundamental rules of calculus to handle other values of n.

First, assume that n is a positive integer. For $n = 1$, the assertion simplifies to

$$\frac{d}{dx} x = 1$$

which is true. Next, consider the inductive step. Suppose the assertion is true for some positive integer k. That is, the inductive hypothesis states that

$$\frac{d}{dx} x^k = kx^{k-1}.$$

Now, consider the case of $k + 1$. By exploiting the product rule of calculus and the inductive hypothesis, we have

$$\frac{d}{dx} x^{k+1} = \frac{d}{dx} x(x^k) = 1x^k + x \frac{d}{dx} x^k = x^k + xkx^{k-1} = (k + 1)x^k,$$

as desired. Thus, the proof is complete for positive integers n.

For $n = 0$, the assertion simplifies to

$$\frac{d}{dx} x^0 = 0,$$

which is true.

Finally, if $n < 0$, we can apply the quotient rule to the result of applying our assertion to the positive integer $-n$. That is,

$$\frac{d}{dx} x^n = \frac{d}{dx} \frac{1}{x^{-n}} = \frac{0x^{-n} - 1(-n)x^{-n-1}}{(x^{-n})^2} = nx^{n-1},$$

as desired. Therefore, we have shown that for all integers n,

$$\frac{d}{dx} x^n = nx^{n-1}.$$

RECURSION

A subprogram that calls upon itself (either directly or indirectly) is called *recursive*. To the beginner unfamiliar with this notion, it may sound like a recipe for an infinite loop, as indeed it may be if not used with care. In fact, recursion is often used as a form of looping. However, recursion should be used so that a recursive subprogram's self-reference is made only with "simpler" data. That is, each time that a program calls itself, it does so with a smaller/simpler instance of the problem. In order to avoid infinite recursion, it is crucial that when the program is invoked with a relatively small (*i.e.*, relatively simple) set of data, the subprogram will compute the required answer and return without issuing another call to itself. This action of returning without issuing another recursive call is critical in allowing the outstanding calls to resolve their problems and return to the routine that called them. In fact, it is critical to proving that recursive calls eventually resolve, which is often shown by proving that successive calls are always to smaller instances of the problem and that there exists a base case for all suitably small instances of the problem that may occur.

Notice, then, the similarity of mathematical induction and recursion. Just as mathematical induction is a technique for inducing conclusions for "large n" from our knowledge of "small n," recursion allows us to process large or complex data sets based on our ability to process smaller or less complex data sets.

A classical example of recursion is computing the *factorial function*, which has a recursive definition. Although it can be proven that for $n > 0$, $n!$ ("*n factorial*") is the product of the integers from 1 to n (and thus a common way of computing $n!$ is to use a simple loop), the definition of $n!$ is recursive and lends itself to a recursive calculation.

DEFINITION

Let n be a nonnegative integer. Then $n!$ is defined by

$$n! = \begin{cases} 1 & \text{if } n=0; \\ n[(n-1)!] & \text{otherwise.} \end{cases}$$

For example, we use the definition to compute $3!$ as follows. From the recursive definition, we know that $3! = 3 \times (2!)$. Thus, we need the value of $2!$. Again (and again, as necessary), we use the second line of the recursive definition. Therefore, we know that $3! = 3 \times (2!) = 3 \times (2 \times (1!)) = 3 \times (2 \times (1 \times (0!)))$. At this point, however, we proceed differently, because the first line of the definition tells us that $0! = 1$. This is the simplest case of n considered by the definition of $n!$, a case that does not require further use of recursion. Such a case is referred to as a *base case* (a recursive definition or algorithm may have more than one base case). It is the existence of one or more base cases, and logic that drives the computation toward base cases, that prevents recursion from producing an infinite loop. In our example, we substitute 1 for $0!$ in order to obtain $0! = 1$, which gives us $1! = 1 \times (0!) = 1 \times 1 = 1$, which yields $2! = 2 \times (1!) = 2 \times 1 = 2$, which finally yields $3! = 3 \times (2!) = 3 \times 2 = 6$.

Below, we give a recursive algorithm for computing the factorial function. It is important to note that this algorithm is given for illustrative purposes only. If one really wants to write an efficient program to compute factorial, a simple tight loop would be much more efficient (depending on compilers).

Integer function factorial (integer n)
Input: n is assumed to be a nonnegative integer.
Algorithm: Produce the value of $n!$ via recursion.
Action:
      If $n = 0$, then return 1
      Else return $n \times$ *factorial* $(n - 1)$

How do we analyze the running time of such an algorithm? Notice that while the size of the data set does not decrease with each invocation of the procedure, the value of n decreases monotonically with each successive call. Therefore, let $T(n)$ denote the running time of the procedure with input value n. We see from the base case of the recursion that $T(0) = \Theta(1)$, since the time to compute $0!$ is constant. From the recurrence given above, we can define the time to compute $n!$, for $n > 0$, as $T(n) = T(n - 1) + \Theta(1)$. The conditions

$$\begin{cases} T(0) = \Theta(1), \\ T(n) = T(n-1) + \Theta(1) \end{cases} \tag{1}$$

form a *recursive (recursion) relation*. We wish to evaluate $T(n)$ in such a way as to express $T(n)$ without recursion. A naive approach uses repeated substitution of the recursive relation. This results in

$$T(n) = T(n-1) + \Theta(1) =$$
$$T(n-2) + \Theta(1) + \Theta(1) = T(n-2) + 2 \times \Theta(1) =$$
$$T(n-3) + \Theta(1) + 2 \times \Theta(1) = T(n-3) + 3 \times \Theta(1).$$

It is important to note the pattern that is emerging: $T(n) = T(n-k) + k \times \Theta(1)$. Such a pattern will lead us to conclude that $T(n) = T(0) + n \times \Theta(1)$, which by the base case of the recursive definition, yields $T(n) = \Theta(1) + n \times \Theta(1) = (n+1) \times \Theta(1) = \Theta(n)$.

Indeed, the conclusion that we have arrived at is correct. However, the "proof" given above is *not* correct. Although naive arguments are often useful for recognizing patterns, they do not serve as proofs. In fact, whenever one detects a pattern and uses such a conclusion in a proof, you can rest assured that there is a logical hole in the proof. Such an approach reminds us of the well-known cartoon in which a scientist explains a difficult step in the derivation of a formula with the phrase "and then a miracle happens." Thus, once we think that we have recognized a solution to a recursion relation, it is still necessary to give a solid mathematical proof.

In the case of the current example, the following proof can be given. We observe that the Θ-notation in condition (1) is a generalization of proportionality. Suppose we consider the simplified recursion relation:

$$\begin{cases} T(0) = 1, \\ T(n) = T(n-1) + 1 \end{cases} \tag{2}$$

Our previous observations lead us to suspect that this turns out to be $T(n) = n + 1$, which we can prove by mathematical induction, as follows.

- For $n = 0$, the assertion is $T(0) = 1$, which is true.
- Suppose the assertion $T(n) = n + 1$ is true for some positive integer k (thus, our inductive hypothesis is the equation $T(k) = k + 1$). We need to show $T(k+1) = k + 2$. Now, using the recursion relation, we have $T(k+1) = T(k) + 1 = (k+1) + 1 = k + 2$, as desired.

Thus, we have completed an inductive proof that our recursion relation (2) simplifies as $T(n) = n + 1 = \Theta(n)$. Since condition (1) is a generalization of (2), in which the Θ-interpretation is not affected by the differences between (1) and (2), it follows that condition (1) satisfies $T(n) = \Theta(n)$. Thus, our recursive algorithm for computing $n!$ requires $\Theta(n)$ time.

BINARY SEARCH

Recursion is perhaps more commonly used when the recursive call involves a large reduction in the *size* of the problem. An example of such a recursive algorithm is *binary search*. Finding data is a fundamental computer operation, in which efficiency is crucial. For example, although we might not mind spending 30 seconds searching a phone book or dictionary for an entry, we probably would mind spending 30 minutes to perform such a task.

Phone books and dictionaries are examples of sorted databases, in which we can take advantage of the fact that the data is ordered when we attempt to find an element. For example, when searching a phone book for "Miller", we would not start at the very beginning and search entry by entry, page by page, in hopes of finding "Miller". Instead, we would open the phone book to the middle and decide whether "Miller" appears on the page(s) before, after, or on the current page being examined.

We now consider the impact of performing a search on a sorted versus an unsorted set of data. First, consider the problem of searching a set of data in which there is no guarantee of order. In this case, we consider a traditional *sequential search* in which each item is examined in sequence. Notice that in the worst case, every item must be examined, since the item we are looking for might not exist or might happen to be the last item listed. So, without loss of generality, let's assume that our sequential search starts at the beginning of the unordered database and examines the items in sequence until either

- the item that is sought is found (the search succeeds), or
- every item has been examined without finding the item sought (the search fails).

Since the data is not known to be ordered, the sequential examination of data items is necessary, because were we to skip over any item, the skipped item could be the one that we wanted (see Figure 2-1).

Thus, we give the following algorithm for a sequential search.

Subprogram SequentialSearch(*X*, *searchValue*, *success*, *foundAt*)
Algorithm: Perform a sequential search on the array $X[1 \ldots n]$ for *searchValue*.
If an element with a key value of *searchValue* is found, then return *success = true*
     and *foundAt*, where *searchValue = X[foundAt]*;
Otherwise, return *success = false*.
Local variable: index *position*
Action:
     position = 1;
     Do
         success = (*searchValue = X[position].key*)
         If *success*, then *foundAt = position*
         Else *position = position* + 1
     While (Not *success*) and (*position* ≤ *n*)
     Return *success*, *foundAt*
End *SequentialSearch*

Analysis: It is easily seen that the set of instructions inside the loop requires $\Theta(1)$ time, that is, constant time per instruction. In the worst case, where either the search is unsuccessful (requiring that we examine every item in order to verify this) or that the item we are searching for is the last item in your search, then the loop body will be executed n times. Thus, one can say that the worst-case sequential search requires $\Theta(n)$ time. Assuming that the data is ordered in a truly random fashion, then a successful search will, on average, succeed after examining half ($n/2$) of the entries. That is, a successful search of an unordered database in which the items are randomly distributed requires $\Theta(n)$ time on average. Of course, we might get lucky and find the item we are searching for immediately, which tells us that the time required for the "best-case search" is $\Theta(1)$.

Now consider the case of searching an ordered database, such as a phone book. Consider trying to design an algorithm that mimics what you would do with a real phone book; that is, a search that would entail grabbing a bunch of pages and flipping back and forth, each time grabbing fewer and fewer pages, until the desired item is located. Notice that this method considers relatively few data values compared to the sequential search. The question we need to consider is whether or not this algorithm is asymptotically faster than the sequential algorithm, since it may be faster by just a high-order constant or low-order term. Before we consider a proper analysis of binary searching, we present a detailed description of the algorithm.

**Subprogram BinarySearch(X, *searchValue, success, foundAt, minIndex,*
maxIndex)**
Algorithm: Binary search algorithm to search subarray
         $X[minIndex \ldots maxIndex]$ for a *key* field equal to *searchValue.*
The algorithm is recursive. In order to search the entire array, the initial call is
         Search(X, searchValue, success, foundAt, 1, n).
If *searchValue* is found in array X in the range of *minIndex* to *maxIndex*, then
         return *success = true* and *foundAt* as the index at which *searchValue* is found;
Otherwise, return *success = false.*
Local variable: index *midIndex*
Action:
     If *minIndex > maxIndex,* then {The subarray is empty.}
         success = false, foundAt = 0
     Else {The subarray is nonempty.}

$$midindex = \left\lfloor \frac{minIndex + maxIndex}{2} \right\rfloor$$

         If *searchValue = X[midIndex].key* then
             success = true, foundAt = midIndex
         Else {*searchValue $\neq$ X[midIndex].key*}
             If *searchValue $<$ X[midIndex].key* then
                 BinarySearch(X, searchValue, success, foundAt, minIndex,
                     midIndex $-$ 1)
             Else {*searchValue $>$ X[midIndex].key*}
                 BinarySearch(X, searchValue, success, foundAt,
                     midIndex $+$ 1, *maxIndex*);
         End {*searchValue $\neq$ X[midIndex].*key}
     End {The subarray is nonempty.}
     Return *success, foundAt*
End *Search*

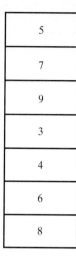

Figure 2-1   An example of sequential search. Given the array of data, a search for the value 4 requires five key comparisons. A search for the value 9 requires three key comparisons. A search for the value 1 requires seven key comparisons in order to determine that the requested value is not present.

Figure 2-2.   An example of binary search. Given the array of data, a search for the value 4 requires two key comparisons (6,4). A search for the value 9 requires three key comparisons (6,8,9). A search for the value 1 requires three key comparisons (6,4,3) in order to determine that the value is not present.

See Figure 2-2. Notice that the running time, $T(n)$, of our binary search algorithm satisfies the recursion relation:

$$T(1) = \Theta(1),$$
$$T(n) \leq T(n/2) + \Theta(1)$$

To analyze the worst-case running time implied by this recursion relation, we can again use the naive approach of repeated substitution into this recursive relation. This results in an expansion that looks like

$T(n) = T(n/2) + \Theta(1) =$
$T(n/4) + \Theta(1) + \Theta(1) = T(n/4) + 2 \times \Theta(1) =$
$T(n/8) + \Theta(1) + 2 \times \Theta(1) = T(n/8) + 3 \times \Theta(1).$

Notice that the pattern beginning to emerge is that $T(n) = T(n/2^k) + k \times \Theta(1)$, where the argument of T reaches the base value $1 = n/2^k$ when $k = \log_2 n$. Such a pattern would lead us to the conclusion that

$$T(n) = T(1) + \log_2 n \times \Theta(1) = \Theta(1) + \log_2 n \times \Theta(1) = \Theta(\log n).$$

Based on this "analysis," we conjecture that a binary search exhibits a worst-case running time of $\Theta(\log n)$. Therefore, we can state that, in general, binary search has a running time of $O(\log n)$.

Notice that in our "analysis" above, we made the simplifying assumption that n is a (positive integer) power of 2. It turns out that this assumption only simplifies the analysis of the running time (see the Exercises).

As before, it is important to realize that once we have recognized what *appears* to be the pattern of the expanded recursion relation, we must prove our conjecture. To do this, we can use mathematical induction. We leave the proof of the running time of binary search as an exercise for the reader.

The term "binary," when applied to this search procedure, is used to suggest that during each iteration of the algorithm, the search is being performed on roughly one half the number of items that were used during the preceding iteration. Although such an assumption makes the analysis more straightforward, it is important for the reader to note that the asymptotic running time holds so long as at the conclusion of each iteration, some fixed fraction of the data is removed from consideration.

MERGING AND MERGESORT

Many efficient sorting algorithms are based on a recursive paradigm in which the list of data to be sorted is split into sublists of approximately equal size, each of the resulting sublists is sorted (recursively), and finally the sorted sublists are combined into a completely sorted list (see Figure 2-3).

The recursion relation that describes the running time of such an algorithm takes the form:

$T(1) = \Theta(1)$
$T(n) = S(n) + 2T(n/2) + C(n)$

where $S(n)$ is the time required by the algorithm to split a list of n entries into two sublists of (approximately) $n/2$ entries apiece, and $C(n)$ is the time required by the algorithm to combine two sorted lists of (approximately) $n/2$ entries apiece into a single sorted list. An example of such an algorithm is *Mergesort*, discussed below.

To *merge* a pair of *ordered* lists X and Y is to form one ordered list from the members of $X \cup Y$. This operation is most natural to describe when the lists are maintained as

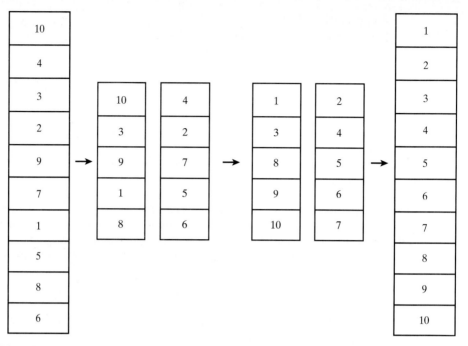

Figure 2-3. Recursively sorting a set of data. Take the initial list and divide it into two lists, each roughly half the size of the original. Recursively sort each of the sublists and then merge these sorted sublists to create the final sorted list.

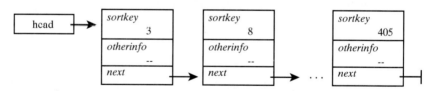

Figure 2-4. An illustration of a linked list in a language that supports dynamic allocation. Notice that the *head* of the list is simply a pointer and not a complete record, and that the last item in the list has its *next* pointer set to *NULL*.

linked (i.e., pointer-based*) lists*. In the following discussion, we consider our data to be arranged as a singly linked list in which each data record has

1. a field called *sortkey*, used as the basis for sorting,
2. a field called *otherinfo*, used to store information pertinent to the record that is not used by the sort routine, and
3. a field called *next*, which is a pointer to the next element of the list.

Remember that a programming language typically has a special pointer constant ("NULL" in C and C++; "nil" in Pascal and LISP) used as the value of a pointer that does not point to anything. Figure 2-4 presents a representation of such a data structure. Notice that in Figure 2-4, we assume the *sortkey* data is of type *integer.*

In the diagram, "head" represents a pointer variable that is necessary to give access to the data structure. An algorithm to merge two ordered linked lists containing a total of n elements in $O(n)$ time is given below (see Figure 2-5).

Subprogram Merge(*head1, head2, headMerge*)
Input: *head1* and *head2* point to two ordered lists that are to be merged. These lists are ordered with respect to field *sortkey*.
Output: This routine produces a merged list addressed by *headMerge*.
Local variable: *atMerge*, a pointer to a link of the merged list
Action:
    If *head1* = *null*, then return *headMerge* = *head2*
    Else {The first input list is nonempty.}
        If *head2* = *null*, then return *headMerge* = *head1*
        Else {Both input lists are nonempty.}
            If *head1.sortkey* $\leq$ *head2.sortkey* then
            {Start merged list with 1st element of 1st list.}
            headMerge = *head1*; *head1* = *head1.next*
        Else
            {Start merged list with 1st element of 2nd list.}
            headMerge = *head2*; *head2* = *head2.next*
        End {Decide first merge element.}
        atMerge = *headMerge*;
        While (*head1* $\neq$ *null* and *head2* $\neq$ *null*), do
            If *head1.sortkey* $\leq$ *head2.sortkey* then
                {Merge element of 1st list.}
                atMerge.next = *head1*;
                atMerge = *head1*;
                head1 = *head1.next*
            Else {Merge element of 2nd list.}
                atMerge.next = *head2*;
                atMerge = *head2*;
                head2 = *head2.next*
            End If
        End While
        {Now, one of the lists is exhausted, but the other isn't. So concatenate the unmerged portion of the unexhausted list to the merged list.}
        If *head1* = *null*, then *atMerge.next* = *head2*
        Else *atMerge.next* = *head1*
        End Else {Both input lists are nonempty.}
    End Else {First input list is nonempty.}
    Return *headMerge*
End *Merge*

It is useful to examine the merge algorithm above for both the *best-case* (minimal) running time and the *worst-case* (maximal) running time. In the best case, one of the input

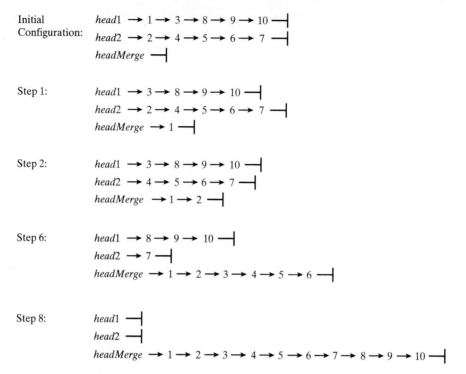

Figure 2-5. An example of merging two ordered lists, *head1* and *head2*, to create an ordered list *headMerge*. Snapshots are presented at various stages of the algorithm.

lists is empty, and the algorithm finishes its work in $\Theta(1)$ time. Now consider the worst-case scenario, in which when one of the input lists is exhausted, only one item remains in the other list. In this case, since each iteration of the While-loop requires a constant amount of work to merge one element into the merged list that is being constructed, the running time for the entire procedure is $\Theta(n)$.

We note also that the algorithm processes every element of one of its input lists. Therefore, the running time of this simple merge algorithm is $\Omega(k)$, where k is the length of the first input list to be exhausted. So if both input lists have length $\Theta(n)$ (if you are merging two lists of length $n/2$, for example), then the running time of this merge algorithm is $\Theta(n)$.

In addition to being able to merge two ordered lists, the Mergesort algorithm requires a routine that will split a list into two sublists of roughly equal size. Suppose you were given a deck of cards and didn't know how many cards were in the deck. A reasonable way to divide the deck into two piles so that each pile had roughly the same number of cards in it would be to deal the cards alternately between the two piles. We give such an algorithm for splitting a list on the following page.

Subprogram Split(*headIn, headOut*)

Algorithm: Split an input list indexed by *headIn* (a pointer to the first element) into two output lists by alternating the output list to which an input element is assigned. The output lists are indexed by *headOut*[0 . . . 1].

Local variables: *current_list*, a switch used to alternate between output lists
temp, a temporary pointer to current link of input list

Action:
{Initialize output lists as empty.}
headOut[0] = *null*;
headOut[1] = *null*;
current_list = 0;
While *headIn* ≠ *null*, do
    temp = *headIn*;
    headIn = *headIn.next*;
    temp.next = *headOut*[*current_list*];
    headOut[*current_list*] = *temp*;
    current_list = 1 − *current_list*
End While
Return *headOut*
End *Split*

In the Split algorithm above, each iteration of the loop takes one element from the input list and places it at the head of one of the output lists. This requires $\Theta(1)$ time. Thus, if the list has *n* elements, the algorithm uses $\Theta(n)$ time.

Since we have introduced and analyzed the tools necessary for Mergesort, we now present algorithm Mergesort.

Subprogram MergeSort(*head*)

Algorithm: Sort a linked list via the Mergesort algorithm.

Input: A linked list indexed by *head*, a pointer to the first element.

Output: An ordered list.

Local variables: *temp*[0 . . . 1], an array of two pointers

Action:
If *head* ≠ *null*, then {Input list is nonempty.}
    If *head.next* ≠ *null*, then
        {There's work to do, as the list has at least two elements.}
        Split(head, temp);
        MergeSort(temp[0]);
        MergeSort(temp[1]);
        Merge(temp[0], *temp*[1], *head*)
    End If
End If
Return *head*
End *Sort*

Before we analyze the Mergesort algorithm above, we make the following observations. The algorithm is recursive, so a question that should be raised is, "What condition represents the base case?" Actually, two base cases are present, but they are both so simple that they are easily missed.

1. Consider the statement "If *head* ≠ *null,* then" in Subprogram MergeSort. The consequent action does not seem like the simple case we expect in a base case of recursion. It does, however, suggest that we consider the opposite case, *head* = *null*. The latter case is not mentioned at all in the algorithm, yet clearly it can happen. This, in fact, is a base case of recursion. Notice that if *head* = *null*, then there is no work to be done, as the list is empty. It is tempting to say that when this happens, no time is used, but we should attribute to this case the $\Theta(1)$ time necessary to recognize that *head* = *null*.

2. Consider the inner "if" clause, "If *head.next* ≠ *null*." Notice that this condition is only tested when the outer if-condition is true and therefore represents the condition of having a list with more than one element. Thus, negation of the inner if-condition represents the condition of having a list with exactly one link (since the outer if's condition being true means there is at least one link). As above, the condition *head.next* = *null* results in no listed action, corresponding to the fact that a list of one element must be ordered. As above, we analyze the case *head.next* = *null* as using $\Theta(1)$ time.

It is important to observe that a piece of code of the form

    If *A,* then
        actionsForA
    End If *A*

is equivalent to

    If *not A,* then   {There is no action.}
    Else   {*A* is true.}
        actionsForA
    End Else *A*

Analysis: Let $T(n)$ be the running time of the MergeSort algorithm, which sorts a linked list of n items. Based on the analysis above, we know that $S(n) = \Theta(n)$, and that $C(n) = \Theta(n)$. Given the time for splitting and combining, we can construct a recurrence equation for the running time of the entire algorithm, as follows.

$T(1) = \Theta(1);$

$T(n) = S(n) + 2T(n/2) + C(n) = 2T(n/2) + \Theta(n)$

Before we proceed further, the reader might notice that the latter equation could be written as

$T(n) = 2T(n/2) + 2 \times \Theta(n)$

However, we leave the demonstration that these equations are equivalent as an exercise to the reader. In order to proceed with the analysis, we again consider using repeated substitution as a means of obtaining a conjecture about the running time. Therefore, we have

$$T(n) = 2T(n/2) + \Theta(n) =$$
$$2[2T(n/4) + \Theta(n/2)] + \Theta(n) = 4T(n/4) + 2 \times \Theta(n) =$$
$$4[2T(n/8) + \Theta(n/4)] + 2 \times \Theta(n) = 8T(n/8) + 3 \times \Theta(n)$$

The emerging pattern appears to be $2^k T(n/2^k) + k \times \Theta(n)$, reaching the base case $1 = n/2^k$ for $k = \log_2 n$. This pattern would result in a conjecture that $T(n) = \Theta(n \log n)$.

Our conjecture can be proved using mathematical induction on k for $n = 2^k$ (see Exercises). Therefore, the running time of our Mergesort algorithm is $\Theta(n \log n)$.

CHAPTER NOTES

A classic reference for the material presented in this chapter is *Fundamental Algorithms*, Volume 1 of *The Art of Computer Programming*, by Donald Knuth. The book, published by Addison-Wesley, originally appeared in 1968, and, along with the companion volumes, is a classic that should be on every computer scientist's desk. An excellent book on discrete mathematics is the book *Discrete Algorithmic Mathematics* by S.B. Maurer & A. Ralston (Addison-Wesley Publishing Company, Reading, Massachusetts, 1991). An interesting book, combining discrete and continuous mathematics, is *Concrete Mathematics* by R.L. Graham, D.E. Knuth, & O. Patashnik, (Addison-Wesley Publishing Company, Reading, Massachusetts, 1989). Finally, we should mention an excellent book, *Introduction to Algorithms*, by T.H. Cormen, C.E. Leiserson, & R.L. Rivest (McGraw-Hill Book Company, New York, 1989). This book covers fundamental mathematics for algorithmic analysis in a thorough fashion.

EXERCISES

1. Devise a $\Theta(n)$ time algorithm that takes as input an array X and produces as output a singly-linked list Y such that the i-th element of Y has the same data as the i-th entry of X. Prove that the algorithm runs in $\Theta(n)$ time.

2. Devise a $\Theta(n)$ time algorithm that takes as input a singly-linked list X and produces as output an array Y such that the i-th entry of Y has the same data as the i-th element of X. Prove that the algorithm runs in $\Theta(n)$ time.

3. (Arithmetic progression.) Show that a recursive algorithm with running time satisfying

$$T(1) = 1$$

$$T(n) = T(n - 1) + \Theta(n)$$

satisfies $T(n) = \Theta(n^2)$.

4. (Geometric progression.) Show that a recursive algorithm with running time satisfying

$$T(1) = 1$$

$$T(n) = T(n/r) + \Theta(n)$$

where $r > 1$ is a constant, satisfies $T(n) = \Theta(n)$.

5. (Binary search.)

a) Show that the recursion relation associated with the binary search algorithm,

$$T(1) = \Theta(1)$$

$$T(n) \le T(n/2) + \Theta(1)$$

satisfies $T(n) = O(\log n)$ when $n = 2^k$ for some nonnegative integer k. **Hint:** Your proof should use mathematical induction on k to show that

$$T(1) = 1$$

$$T(n) \le T(n/2) + 1$$

satisfies $T(n) \le 1 + \log_2 n$.

b) Even if n is not an integer power of 2, the recursion relation above satisfies $T(n) = O(\log n)$. Prove this assertion, using the result for the case of n being a power of 2. **Hint:** Start with the assumption that $2^k < n < 2^{k+1}$ for some positive integer k. One approach is to show that only one more item need be examined, in the worst case, than in the worst case for $n = 2^k$. Another approach is to prove that we could work instead with the recursion relation

$$T(1) = 1$$

$$T(n) \le T\left(\left\lceil \frac{n-1}{2} \right\rceil\right) + 1$$

then show how this, in turn, yields the desired conclusion.

6. Prove that subprogram Mergesort has a running time of $\Theta(n \log n)$ by showing that the recursion relation used in its partial analysis above,

$$T(1) = \Theta(1)$$

$$T(n) = S(n) + 2T(n/2) + C(n) = 2T(n/2) + \Theta(n)$$

satisfies $T(n) = \Theta(n \log n)$. As above, this can be done by an argument based on the assumption that $n = 2^k$, for some nonnegative integer k, using mathematical induction on k.

7. Show that an array of n entries can be sorted in $\Theta(n \log n)$ time by an algorithm that makes use of the Mergesort algorithm given above. **Hint:** See Exercises 1 and 2.

8. The sequence of *Fibonacci numbers*, $f_1, f_2, f_3, \ldots$, is defined recursively as follows:

$$f_1 = f_2 = 1$$
$$f_{n+2} = f_n + f_{n+1}$$

a) Develop a nonrecursive $\Theta(n)$ time algorithm to return the n-th Fibonacci number.

b) Show that the running time of the following recursive algorithm (based on the definition above) to produce the n-th Fibonacci number is $\omega(n)$ (the moral is that the use of recursion isn't always a good idea).

Integer Function Fibonacci(n)
Output: The n-th Fibonacci number.
Input: n, a nonnegative integer.
Action:
    If n $\leq$ 2, then return 1
    Else return *fibonacci*($n - 2$) + *fibonacci*($n - 1$)
End *Fibonacci*

Hint: The analysis can be achieved by the following steps.

■ Show that the running time $T(n)$ can be analyzed via a recursion relation $T(n) = T(n - 1) + T(n - 2) + \Theta(1)$.

■ Show the recursion relation obtained above implies $T(n) > 2T(n - 2)$.

■ Use the above to show that $f_n = \omega(n)$. Note it is not necessary to find an explicit formula for either f_n or $T(n)$ to achieve this step.

3

The Master Method

The Master Method

Computer scientists don't like to reinvent the wheel. It's much more efficient to exploit tools and techniques that have previously been developed than to start from scratch. Of course, students must often develop solutions from scratch in order to master fundamental methodologies. However, students must also make the gradual transition from novice to expert. In the analysis of algorithms, it is desirable to develop general-purpose methods of analysis, as we have seen in previous examples. The Master Method is an extremely important tool that can be used to provide a solution to a large class of recursion relations.

Consider a recurrence of the form

$$T(n) = aT\left(\frac{n}{b}\right) + f(n)$$

where $a \geq 1$ and $b > 1$ are constants, and $f(n)$ is a positive function. If $T(n)$ is the running time of a problem of size $\Theta(n)$, we can interpret this recurrence as defining $T(n)$ to be the time to solve a subproblems of size n/b plus $f(n)$, which is the sum of

- the time to divide the original problem into the a subproblems, and
- the time to combine the subproblems' solutions in order to obtain the solution to the original problem.

Consider the problem of sorting a linked list of data using the MergeSort algorithm (see Figure 3-1). Assume that we split a list of length n into two lists, each of length $n/2$, recursively sort these new lists, and then merge them together. In terms of our general recurrence equation, this gives $a = 2$ subproblems to solve, each of size $n/2$ (*i.e.*, $b = 2$).

Further, the interpretation is that $f(n)$ is the time to split the list of length n into two lists of length $n/2$ each, plus the time to merge two ordered lists of length $n/2$ each into an ordered list of length n. See Figure 3-2.

The *Master Method* is summarized in the following "**Master Theorem**."

No. of Problems   Each Problem size   Time

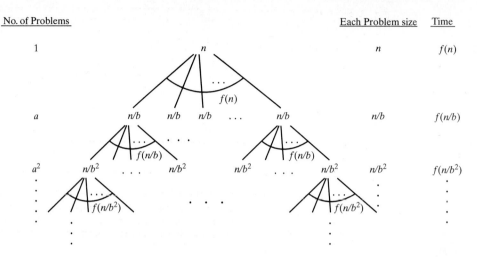

Figure 3-1 A recursion tree representing the recurrence equation $T(n) = aT(n/b) + f(n)$. The number of problems to be solved at each (horizontal) level of recursion is listed along with the size of each problem at that level. Time is used to represent the time per problem, not counting recursion, at each level.

No. of Problems   Each Problem size   Time

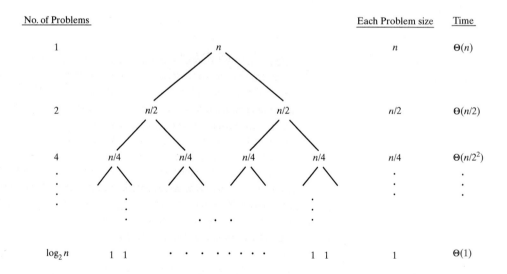

Figure 3-2 A recursion tree for MergeSort, as represented by $T(n) = 2T(n/2) + \Theta(n)$. Notice that level i of the recursion tree (i.e., $\{1, 2, \ldots, \log_2 n\}$) requires a total of $2^i \times \Theta(n/2^i) = \Theta(n)$ time.

    The reader should observe that the **Master Theorem** does not cover all instances of the equation (3.1).

    On the following pages, we sketch a proof for the **Master Theorem**, which should probably be skipped by many readers. We provide the proof as a convenience to those readers with solid mathematical skills, coupled with the desire and background to appreciate it.

MASTER THEOREM

Let $a \geq 1$ and $b > 1$ be constants. Let $f(n)$ be a positive function defined on the positive integers. Let $T(n)$ be defined on the positive integers by

$$T(n) = aT\left(\frac{n}{b}\right) + f(n) \qquad (3.1)$$

where we can interpret n/b as meaning either $\lfloor n/b \rfloor$ or $\lceil n/b \rceil$. Then the following hold:

1. Suppose $f(n) = O(n^{\log_b a - \varepsilon})$ for some constant $\varepsilon > 0$. Then $T(n) = \Theta(n^{\log_b a})$.
2. Suppose $f(n) = \Theta(n^{\log_b a})$. Then $T(n) = \Theta(n^{\log_b a} \log n)$.
3. Suppose $f(n) = \Omega(n^{\log_b a + \varepsilon})$ for some constant $\varepsilon > 0$, and there are constants $c < 1$ and $N > 0$ such that $(n/b) > N \Rightarrow af(n/b) \leq cf(n)$. Then $T(n) = \Theta(f(n))$.

PROOF OF THE MASTER THEOREM (OPTIONAL)

We start under the simplifying assumption that the values of n considered are nonnegative integral powers of b. The advantage of this assumption lies in the fact that at every level of recursion, n/b is an integer. Later, we show how to handle the general case.

Lemma 1: Let $a \geq 1$ and $b > 1$ be constants, and let $f(n)$ be a nonnegative function defined on integral powers of b. Let $T(n)$ be defined on integral powers of b by the recurrence:

$$T(n) = \begin{cases} \Theta(1) \text{ if } n = 1; \\ aT\left(\dfrac{n}{b}\right) + f(n) \text{ if } n = b^i \text{ for some positive integer } i. \end{cases}$$

Then

$$T(n) = \Theta(n^{\log_b a}) + \sum_{k=0}^{\log_b n - 1} a^k f\left(\frac{n}{b^k}\right).$$

Remarks: The asserted pattern can be guessed at by simplifying an iterated expansion of the recurrence

$$T(n) = f(n) + aT\left(\frac{n}{b}\right) = f(n) + af\left(\frac{n}{b}\right) + a^2 T\left(\frac{n}{b^2}\right) = \ldots =$$

$$f(n) + af\left(\frac{n}{b}\right) + a^2 f\left(\frac{n}{b^2}\right) + \ldots + a^{\log_b n - 1} f\left(\frac{n}{b^{\log_b n - 1}}\right) + a^{\log_b n} T(1).$$

Since $a^{\log_b n} = n^{\log_b a}$ and $T(1) = \Theta(1)$, the last term in the expanded recurrence is $\Theta(n^{\log_b a})$, and the other terms yield

$$\sum_{k=0}^{\log_b n - 1} a^k f(n/b^k)$$

as asserted above. Once we have guessed the pattern, we prove it by mathematical induction.

Proof of Lemma 1: We establish our claim by showing that

$$T(n) = n^{\log_b a}T(1) + \sum_{k=0}^{\log_b n - 1} a^k f\left(\frac{n}{b^k}\right)$$

where we consider $n = b^i$ for nonnegative integers i. Therefore, the base case is $i = 0$ (*i.e.*, $n = 1$). In this case, the

$$\sum_{k=0}^{\log_b n - 1} a^k f(n/b^k)$$

term of the assertion is an empty sum, which by convention has value 0. Therefore, the assertion is true since the right side of the asserted equation is

$$1^{\log_b a}T(1) + \sum_{k=0}^{\log_b n - 1} a^k f(n/b^k) = T(1) + 0 = T(1).$$

Thus, the base case of the induction is established.

Suppose the assertion is true for integer powers i of b, where $0 \le i \le p$. In particular, the assertion is true for $n = b^p$. Then, we have

$$T(b^p) = b^{p \log_b a}T(1) + \sum_{k=0}^{p-1} a^k f\left(\frac{n}{b^k}\right) = a^p T(1) + \sum_{k=0}^{p-1} a^k f\left(b^{p-k}\right).$$

Now, consider $n = b^{p+1}$. By the hypothesized recurrence, we have

$$T(b^{p+1}) = aT(b^p) + f(b^{p+1}) =$$

{using the inductive hypothesis}

$$a\left[a^p T(1) + \sum_{k=0}^{p-1} a^k f(b^{p-k})\right] + f(b^{p+1}) =$$

$$a^{p+1}T(1) + \left[a\sum_{k=0}^{p-1} a^k f(b^{p-k})\right] + f(b^{p+1}) =$$

{since $b^{\log_b a} = a$}

$$b^{(p+1)\log_b a}T(1) + \sum_{k=0}^{p} a^k f(b^{p+1-k}) = n^{\log_b a}T(1) + \sum_{k=0}^{p} a^k f\left(\frac{n}{b^k}\right)$$

which, since $p = \log_b n - 1$, is the desired result. This completes the induction proof.

Next, we give asymptotic bounds for the summation term that appears in the conclusion of the statement of Lemma 1.

Lemma 2:   Let $a \ge 1$ and $b > 1$ be constants, and let $f(n)$ be a nonnegative function defined on nonnegative integral powers of b. Let $g(n)$ be a function defined on integral powers of b by

$$g(n) = \sum_{k=0}^{\log_b n - 1} a^k f\left(\frac{n}{b^k}\right) \tag{3.2}$$

1. If $f(n) = O(n^{\log_b a - \varepsilon})$ for some constant $\varepsilon > 0$, then $g(n) = O(n^{\log_b a})$.
2. If $f(n) = \Theta(n^{\log_b a})$, then $g(n) = \Theta(n^{\log_b a} \log n)$.
3. If there is a positive constant $c < 1$ such that $n \geq b \Rightarrow af(n/b) \leq cf(n)$, then $g(n) = \Theta(f(n))$.

Proof: For case 1, substituting the hypothesis of the case into the definition of the function $g(n)$ yields

$$g(n) = O\left(\sum_{k=0}^{\log_b n - 1} a^k \left(\frac{n}{b^k}\right)^{\log_b a - \varepsilon} \right) = O\left[n^{\log_b a - \varepsilon} \sum_{k=0}^{\log_b n - 1} \left(\frac{ab^\varepsilon}{b^{\log_b a}} \right)^k \right] =$$

$$O\left[n^{\log_b a - \varepsilon} \sum_{k=0}^{\log_b n - 1} (b^\varepsilon)^k \right] =$$

{using the formula for the sum of a geometric series}

$$O\left[n^{\log_b a - \varepsilon} \left(\frac{b^{\varepsilon \log_b n} - 1}{b^\varepsilon - 1} \right) \right] = O\left[n^{\log_b a - \varepsilon} \left(\frac{n^\varepsilon - 1}{b^\varepsilon - 1} \right) \right] =$$

{since b and ε are constants}

$$O(n^{\log_b a}), \text{ as claimed.}$$

For case 2, it follows from the hypothesis of the case that $f(n/b^k) = \Theta((n/b^k)^{\log_b a})$. When we substitute the latter into (3.2), we have

$$g(n) = \Theta\left[\sum_{k=0}^{\log_b n - 1} a^k \left(\frac{n}{b^k}\right)^{\log_b a} \right] = \Theta\left[n^{\log_b a} \sum_{k=0}^{\log_b n - 1} \left(\frac{a}{b^{\log_b a}} \right)^k \right] =$$

$$\Theta\left(n^{\log_b a} \sum_{k=0}^{\log_b n - 1} 1 \right) = \Theta(n^{\log_b a} \log n)$$

as claimed.

For case 3, observe that all terms of the sum in (3.2) are nonnegative, and the term corresponding to $k = 0$ is $f(n)$. Therefore, $g(n) = \Omega(f(n))$. The hypothesis of the case, that there is a constant $c < 1$ such that $af(n/b) \leq cf(n)$, implies (by an easy induction argument that is left to the reader) that $n \geq b^k \Rightarrow a^k f(n/b^k) \leq c^k f(n)$. When we substitute the latter into (3.2), we get

$$g(n) = \sum_{k=0}^{\log_b n - 1} a^k f\left(\frac{n}{b^k}\right) \leq \sum_{k=0}^{\log_b n - 1} c^k f(n) = f(n) \sum_{k=0}^{\log_b n - 1} c^k.$$

Since the latter summation is a geometric series with decreasing terms, it follows that

$$g(n) \leq f(n)\left(\frac{1}{1-c}\right) \Rightarrow g(n) = O(f(n)).$$

Since we previously showed that $g(n) = \Omega(f(n))$, it follows that $g(n) = \Theta(f(n))$, as claimed.

Now we prove a version of the *Master Method* for the case in which n is a nonnegative integral power of b.

Lemma 3: Let $a \geq 1$ and $b > 1$ be constants, and let $f(n)$ be a nonnegative function defined on integral powers of b. Let $T(n)$ be defined on integral powers of b by the recurrence

$$T(n) = \begin{cases} \Theta(1) \text{ if } n = 1; \\ aT\left(\dfrac{n}{b}\right) + f(n) \text{ if } n = b^k \text{ for some positive integer } k. \end{cases}$$

Then we have the following:

1. If $f(n) = O(n^{\log_b a - \varepsilon})$ for some constant $\varepsilon > 0$, then $T(n) = \Theta(n^{\log_b a})$.
2. If $f(n) = \Theta(n^{\log_a b})$, then $T(n) = \Theta(n^{\log_b a} \log n)$.
3. If $f(n) = \Omega(n^{\log_b a + \varepsilon})$ for some constant $\varepsilon > 0$, and if $n \geq b \Rightarrow af(n/b) \leq cf(n)$ for some positive constants $c < 1$ and N, then $T(n) = \Theta(f(n))$.

Proof: First, we observe by Lemma 1 that $T(n) = \Theta(n^{\log_b a}) + g(n)$, where

$$g(n) = \sum_{k=0}^{\log_b n - 1} a^k f\left(\frac{n}{b^k}\right).$$

In case 1, it follows from case 1 of Lemma 2 that

$$T(n) = \Theta(n^{\log_b a}) + g(n) = \Theta(n^{\log_b a} + n^{\log_b a}) = \Theta(n^{\log_b a}).$$

In case 2, it follows from case 2 of Lemma 2 that

$$T(n) = f(n) + g(n) = \Theta(n^{\log_b a} + n^{\log_b a} \log n) = \Theta(n^{\log_b a} \log n).$$

In case 3, it follows from case 3 of Lemma 2 that $g(n) = \Theta(f(n))$ and (by Lemma 1)

$$T(n) = \Theta(n^{\log_b a}) + g(n) = \Theta(n^{\log_b a} + f(n)).$$

Since $f(n) = \Omega(n^{\log_b a + \varepsilon})$, it follows that $T(n) = \Theta(f(n))$.

The general case: Lemma 3 states the *Master Method* for the case that n is a nonnegative integral power of b. Recall that the importance of this case is to guarantee that at every level of recursion the expression n/b is an integer. For general n, however, the expression n/b need not be an integer. We can therefore substitute $\lceil n/b \rceil$ or $\lfloor n/b \rfloor$ for n/b in the recurrence (3.1) and attempt to obtain similar results. Since

$$\frac{n}{b} - 1 < \left\lfloor \frac{n}{b} \right\rfloor \leq \left\lceil \frac{n}{b} \right\rceil < \frac{n}{b} + 1$$

this will enable us to demonstrate that a small discrepancy in the value of the independent variable often makes no difference in asymptotic evaluation. In the following, we develop a version of the *Master Method* using the expression $\lceil n/b \rceil$ for n/b in the recurrence (3.1); a similar argument can be given if, instead, we use $\lfloor n/b \rfloor$ for n/b in (3.1).

Consider the sequences defined by the recursive formulas

$$m_i = \begin{cases} n & \text{if } i = 0 \\ \left\lfloor \dfrac{m_{i-1}}{b} \right\rfloor & \text{if } i > 0 \end{cases}$$

and

$$n_i = \begin{cases} n & \text{if } i = 0 \\ \left\lceil \dfrac{n_{i-1}}{b} \right\rceil & \text{if } i > 0. \end{cases}$$

Since $b > 1$, these are nonincreasing sequences of integers. We have

$$m_0 = n_0 = n,$$

$$\frac{n}{b} - 1 < m_1 \le n_1 < \frac{n}{b} + 1,$$

$$\frac{n}{b^2} - \frac{1}{b} - 1 < m_2 \le n_2 < \frac{n_1}{b} + 1 < \frac{n}{b^2} + \frac{1}{b} + 1,$$

and more generally (the reader should be able to prove the following lower bound for m_i and the following upper bound for n_i, via simple induction arguments),

$$\frac{n}{b^i} - \frac{b}{b-1} =$$

$$\frac{n}{b^i} - \sum_{k=0}^{\infty} \frac{1}{b^k} < \frac{n}{b^i} - \sum_{k=0}^{i-1} \frac{1}{b^k} < m_i \le n_i < \frac{n}{b^i} + \sum_{k=0}^{i-1} \frac{1}{b^k} < \frac{n}{b^i} + \sum_{k=0}^{\infty} \frac{1}{b^k} =$$

$$\frac{n}{b^i} + \frac{b}{b-1}.$$

Thus,

$$i \ge \lceil \log_b n \rceil \Rightarrow b^i \ge n \Rightarrow n_i < 1 + \frac{b}{b-1}.$$

Since n_i is integer-valued, we have

$$i \ge \lceil \log_b n \rceil \Rightarrow m_i \le n_i \le \left\lfloor 1 + \frac{b}{b-1} \right\rfloor = \Theta(1).$$

Suppose, then, that we use the recurrence

$$T(n) = aT\left(\left\lceil \frac{n}{b} \right\rceil\right) + f(n) \tag{3.3}$$

and expand this recurrence iteratively in order to obtain

$$T(n) = f(n_0) + aT(n_1) = f(n_0) + af(n_1) + a^2 T(n_2) = \dots$$

The reader should be able to prove by induction that for $0 \le i \le \lceil \log_b n \rceil - 1$,

$$T(n) = \left[\sum_{k=0}^{i} a^k f(n_k) \right] + a^{i+1} T(n_{i+1}).$$

In particular, for $i = \lceil \log_b n \rceil - 1$,

$$T(n) = a^{\lceil \log_b n \rceil} T(n_{\lceil \log_b n \rceil}) + \sum_{k=0}^{\lceil \log_b n \rceil - 1} a^k f(n_k).$$

Now,

$$a^{\log_b n} \le a^{\lceil \log_b n \rceil} < a a^{\log_b n} \Rightarrow a^{\lceil \log_b n \rceil} = \Theta(a^{\log_b n}) = \Theta(n^{\log_b a}).$$

Since $n_{\lceil \log_b n \rceil} = \Theta(1)$, we have $T(n_{\lceil \log_b n \rceil}) = \Theta(1)$. Substituting these last two results into the last equation for $T(n)$, we have

$$T(n) = \Theta(n^{\log_b a}) + \sum_{k=0}^{\lceil \log_b n \rceil - 1} a^k f(n_k).$$

This is an equation much like that of the conclusion of Lemma 1.

Similarly, if we modify (3.3) to obtain the recurrence

$$T'(n) = a T'\left(\left\lfloor \frac{n}{b} \right\rfloor \right) + f(n) \tag{3.4}$$

then we similarly obtain

$$T'(n) = \Theta(n^{\log_b a}) + \sum_{k=0}^{\lceil \log_b n \rceil - 1} a^k f(m_k).$$

Let

$$g(n) = \sum_{k=0}^{\lceil \log_b n \rceil - 1} a^k f(n_k)$$

and

$$g'(n) = \sum_{k=0}^{\lceil \log_b n \rceil - 1} a^k f(m_k).$$

We wish to evaluate $g(n)$ and $g'(n)$ asymptotically.

In case 1, we have the hypothesis that $f(n) = O(n^{\log_b a - \varepsilon})$ for some constant $\varepsilon > 0$. Without loss of generality, we have $\log_b a - \varepsilon \ge 0$. There is a constant $c > 0$ such that for sufficiently large n_k, say, $n_k > N$,

$$f(n_k) \le c(n_k^{\log_b a - \varepsilon}) \le c\left(\frac{n}{b^k} + \frac{b}{b-1} \right)^{\log_b a - \varepsilon} = c\left[\left(\frac{n}{b^k} \right) \left(1 + \frac{b^k}{n} \times \frac{b}{b-1} \right) \right]^{\log_b a - \varepsilon}$$

$$= c\left(\frac{n^{\log_b a - \varepsilon}}{a^k b^{-k\varepsilon}} \right) \left[1 + \left(\frac{b^k}{n} \times \frac{b}{b-1} \right) \right]^{\log_b a - \varepsilon} \le c\left(\frac{n^{\log_b a - \varepsilon}}{a^k} b^{k\varepsilon} \right) \left(1 + \frac{b}{b-1} \right)^{\log_b a - \varepsilon}$$

$$= \frac{d n^{\log_b a - \varepsilon} b^{k\varepsilon}}{a^k}$$

where

$$d = c\left(1 + \frac{b}{b-1}\right)^{\log_b a - \varepsilon}$$

is a constant.

For such k, $a^k f(n_k) \leq dn^{\log_b a - \varepsilon} b^{k\varepsilon}$. It follows that

$$g(n) = \sum_{k \in \{0, \dots \lceil \log_b n \rceil - 1\}, n_k \leq N} a^k f(n_k) + \sum_{k \in \{0, \dots \lceil \log_b n \rceil - 1\}, n_k > N} a^k f(n_k)$$

$$\leq \Theta(1) \sum_{k \in \{0, \dots \lceil \log_b n \rceil - 1\}, n_k \leq N} a^k + dn^{\log_b a - \varepsilon} \sum_{k \in \{0, \dots \lceil \log_b n \rceil - 1\}, n_k > N} b^{ek}.$$

The former summation, a geometric series, evaluates as $O(a^{\log_b n}) = O(n^{\log_b a})$. In the latter summation, there are $\Theta(1)$ terms, as $n_k > N$ corresponds to small values of k. It follows that

$$g(n) \leq O(n^{\log_b a}) + dn^{\log_b a - \varepsilon}\Theta(1) = O(n^{\log_b a}).$$

Hence, $T(n) = \Theta(n^{\log_b a}) + g(n) = \Theta(n^{\log_b a})$, as desired. A similar argument shows $T'(n) = \Theta(n^{\log_b a})$.

In case 2, the hypothesis that $f(n) = \Theta(n^{\log_b a})$ implies there are positive constants c and C such that for sufficiently large m_k and n_k, say, $m_k, n_k > N$,

$$f(n_k) \leq c(n_k^{\log_b a}) \leq c\left(\frac{n}{b^k} + \frac{b}{b-1}\right)^{\log_b a} = c\left(\frac{n^{\log_b a}}{a^k}\right)\left[1 + \left(\frac{b^k}{n} \times \frac{b}{b-1}\right)\right]^{\log_b a}$$

$$\leq c\left(\frac{n^{\log_b a}}{a^k}\right)\left(1 + \frac{b}{b-1}\right)^{\log_b a} = \frac{dn^{\log_b a}}{a^k}$$

where $d = c\left(1 + \frac{b}{b-1}\right)^{\log_b a}$ is a constant, and similarly, there is a constant $D > 0$ such that

$$f(m_k) \geq \frac{Dn^{\log_b a}}{a^k}.$$

Therefore, for such k, $a^k f(n_k) \leq dn^{\log_b a}$ and $a^k f(m_k) > Dn^{\log_b a}$. So,

$$g(n) = \sum_{k \in \{0, \dots, \lceil \log_b n \rceil - 1\}, n_k \leq N} a^k f(n_k) + \sum_{k \in \{0, \dots, \lceil \log_b n \rceil - 1\}, n_k > N} a^k f(n_k).$$

In the first summation, the values of $f(n_k)$ are bounded, since $n_k \leq N$. Thus, the summation is bounded asymptotically by the geometric series

$$\sum_{k=0}^{\lceil \log_b n \rceil - 1} a^k = O(a^{\log_b n}) = O(n^{\log_b a}).$$

The second summation evaluates as follows:

$$\sum_{k\in\{0,\dots,\lceil\log_b n\rceil-1\},\, n_k>N} a^k f(n_k) \le \sum_{k=0}^{\lceil\log_b n\rceil-1} dn^{\log_b a} = O(n^{\log_b a}\log n).$$

Substituting these into the previous equation for $g(n)$, we obtain

$$g(n) = O(n^{\log_b a}) + O(n^{\log_b a}\log n) = O(n^{\log_b a}\log n).$$

Hence, $T(n) = O(n^{\log_b a}\log n)$. Similarly,

$$g'(n) = \sum_{k\in\{0,\dots,\lceil\log_b n\rceil-1\},\, m_k\le N} a^k f(m_k) + \sum_{k\in\{0,\dots,\lceil\log_b n\rceil-1\},\, m_k>N} a^k f(m_k)$$

$$= \Omega(1) + \Omega(n^{\log_b a}\log n) = \Omega(n^{\log_b a}\log n).$$

Notice that

$$\{(m_k \le n_k)\text{ and }[f(n) = \Theta(n^{\log_b a})]\} \Rightarrow$$

$$\sum_{k\in\{0,1,\dots,\lceil\log_b n\rceil-1\},\, m_k>N} a^k f(m_k) = O\left(\sum_{k\in\{0,1,\dots,\lceil\log_b n\rceil-1\},\, n_k>N} a^k f(n_k)\right).$$

Therefore,

$$g'(n) = \sum_{k\in\{0,\dots\lceil\log_b n\rceil-1\},\, m_k\le N} a^k f(m_k) + \sum_{k\in\{0,\dots\lceil\log_b n\rceil-1\},\, m_k>N} a^k f(m_k)$$

$$= O\left(\sum_{k=0}^{\lceil\log_b n\rceil-1} a^k\right) + O\left(\sum_{k\in\{0,1,\dots,\lceil\log_b n\rceil-1\},\, n_k>N} a^k f(n_k)\right) = O(g(n)).$$

It follows that $g(n) = \Theta(n^{\log_b a}\log n)$ and $g'(n) = \Theta(n^{\log_b a}\log n)$. Therefore,

$$T(n) = \Theta(n^{\log_b a}\log n)\ \text{ and }\ T'(n) = \Theta(n^{\log_b a}\log n).$$

In case 3, an analysis similar to that given for case 3 of Lemma 2 shows $g(n) = \Theta(f(n))$, as follows. Recall the hypotheses of this case: $f(n) = \Omega(n^{\log_b a+\varepsilon})$ for some constant $\varepsilon > 0$, and there are constants $c < 1$ and $N > 0$ such that $(n/b) > N \Rightarrow af(n/b) \le cf(n)$. As above, it follows by a simple induction argument that for

$$\frac{n}{b^k} > N \text{ or, equivalently, } k \le \left\lfloor \log_b\left(\frac{n}{N}\right)\right\rfloor,$$

we have

$$a^k f\left(\frac{n}{b^k}\right) \leq c^k f(n).$$

Therefore,

$$g(n) = \sum_{k=0}^{\lfloor \log_b(n/N)\rfloor} a^k f\left(\frac{n}{b^k}\right) + \sum_{k=\lfloor \log_b(n/N)\rfloor+1}^{\lceil \log_b n\rceil-1} a^k f\left(\frac{n}{b^k}\right) \leq$$

$$f(n) \sum_{k=0}^{\lfloor \log_b(n/N)\rfloor} c^k + a^{\lceil \log_b n\rceil-1}(\log_b N) \max_{k \geq \lfloor \log_b(n/N)\rfloor+1} f\left(\frac{n}{b^k}\right) <$$

$$f(n)\frac{1}{1-c} + \Theta(a^{\log_b n}) = O(f(n) + a^{\log_b n}).$$

Since $f(n) = \Omega(n^{\log_b a + \varepsilon})$ and $a^{\log_b n} = n^{\log_b a}$, we have $g(n) = O(f(n))$, and therefore $T(n) = \Theta(n^{\log_b a} + g(n)) = O(f(n))$.

Since equation (3.3) implies $T(n) = \Omega(f(n))$, it follows that $T(n) = \Theta(f(n))$, as desired. A similar argument shows $T'(n) = \Theta(f(n))$.

Thus, in all cases, whether we use $\lceil n/b\rceil$ or $\lfloor n/b\rfloor$ as our interpretation of n/b in (3.1), we have obtained the results asserted in the statement of the **Master Theorem**. Therefore, the proof of the **Master Theorem** is complete.

EXAMPLE

Consider the recurrence

$$T(n) = T\left(\frac{n}{2}\right) + 1$$

that occurs in the analysis of Binary Search. Then $f(n) = 1 = n^{\log_2 1}$, so by case 2 of the **Master Theorem**, $T(n) = \Theta(\log n)$.

EXAMPLE

Consider the recurrence

$$T(n) = 2T\left(\frac{n}{2}\right) + n$$

that occurs in the analysis of MergeSort. We have $a = 2$, $b = 2$, $f(n) = n = n^{\log_b a}$. So, by case 2 of the **Master Theorem**, $T(n) = \Theta(n \log n)$.

EXAMPLE

Consider the recurrence

$$T(n) = T\left(\frac{n}{4}\right) + n^{1/2}$$

that occurs in the analysis of many mesh computer algorithms that will be presented later in the text. We have

$$a = 1, b = 4, f(n) = n^{1/2} = \Omega(n^{\log_b a + 0.5}),$$

$$af(n/b) = (n/4)^{1/2} = n^{1/2}/2 = 0.5f(n).$$

So, by case 3 of the **Master Theorem**, $T(n) = \Theta(n^{1/2})$.

CHAPTER NOTES

In this chapter, we focus on the Master Method, a cookbook approach to solving recurrences of the form $T(n) = aT(n/b) + f(n)$. This approach has been well utilized in texts by E. Horowitz and S. Sahni, including *Computer Algorithms/C++*, by E. Horowitz, S. Sahni, and S. Rajasekaran (Computer Science Press, New York, 1996). Our proof is based on the one given in *Introduction to Algorithms* by T.H. Cormen, C.E. Leiserson, and R.L. Rivest (McGraw-Hill Book Company, New York, 1990). The paper, "A general method for solving divide-and-conquer recurrences," by J.L. Bentley, D. Haken, and J.B. Saxe, *SIGACT News*, 12(3), 1980, 36–44, appears to serve as one of the earliest references to this technique.

EXERCISES

For each of the following recurrences, either solve via the **Master Theorem**, or show it is not applicable, as appropriate. If the **Master Theorem** is not applicable, try to solve the recurrence by another means.

1. $T(n) = 2T\left(\frac{n}{2}\right) + 1$

2. $T(n) = T(n - 2) + 1$

3. $T(n) = 4T\left(\frac{n}{2}\right) + n^2$

4. $T(n) = 4T\left(\frac{n}{2}\right) + n^{3/2}$

5. $T(n) = 3T\left(\dfrac{n}{2}\right) + n^2$

6. $T(n) = 8T\left(\dfrac{n}{2}\right) + \dfrac{n^2}{\log_2 n}$

7. $T(n) = 16T\left(\dfrac{n}{4}\right) + \dfrac{n^3}{\log_2 n}$

4

Combinational Circuits

Combinational Circuits and Sorting Networks

A significant portion of the computing cycles on early sequential machines was spent on sorting data. As a result, a substantial effort has been put into developing efficient sorting techniques for both software and hardware. In this section, we consider an early hardware-based implementation of sorting, proposed by Ken Batcher in 1968. In his seminal 1968 paper, Batcher proposed two sorting algorithms, namely, *BitonicSort* and *Odd-Even MergeSort*. Both of these algorithms are based on a MergeSort framework, both were presented for hardware, and in the case of the former, Batcher made the insightful observation that such an algorithm would very efficient on a parallel computer with certain interconnection properties. The focus of this chapter is on Batcher's Bitonic Sort.

We begin this chapter with a presentation of combinational circuits, a simple hardware model involving a unidirectional (one-way) flow of data from input to output through a series of basic functional units. When we present diagrams of combinational circuits, the flow of information is represented by lines and the functional units are represented by boxes. It is understood that information flows along the lines from left to right. After this introduction, we discuss Batcher's Bitonic Merge Unit, as applied to combinational circuits. We then present an indepth analysis of the running time on this model. Finally, we conclude with a combinational circuit implementation and analysis of Bitonic MergeSort, which exploits this very interesting Bitonic Merge unit.

Combinational circuits were among the earliest models developed in terms of providing a systematic study of parallel algorithms. They have the advantage of being simple, and many algorithms that are developed for this model serve as the basis for algorithms presented later in this book for more advanced models of parallel computing. A combinational circuit can be thought of as taking input from the left, allowing data to flow through a series of functional units in a systematic fashion, and producing output to the right. The functional units in the circuit are quite simple. Each such unit performs a single operation in constant time. These operations include logical operations such as **and**, **or**, and **not**, comparisons such as <, >, and =, and fundamental arithmetic operations such as addition, subtraction, minimum, and maximum. These functional units are connected to each other by *unidirectional* links, which serve to transport the data. Further, these functional units are assumed to have constant *fan-in* (in other words, the number of links entering a processor is bounded by a constant) and constant *fan-out* (the number of links exiting a unit is bounded by a constant).

In this chapter, we restrict our attention to comparison-based networks in which each functional unit simply takes two values as input and presents these values ordered on its output lines. Finally, it should be noted that there is no feedback (*i.e.*, no cycles) in these circuits.

Sorting Networks: We consider a comparison-based combinational circuit that can be used as a general-purpose sorting network. Such *sorting networks* are said to be *oblivious* to their inputs since this model fixes the sequence of comparisons in advance. That is, the sequence of comparisons is not a function of the input values. Notice that some traditional sorting routines, such as Quicksort or Heapsort, are not oblivious in that they perform comparisons that are dependent on their input.

Bitonic Sort was originally defined in terms of sorting networks. It was intended to be used not only as a sorting network, but as a simple switching network for routing multiple inputs to multiple outputs. The basic element of a sorting network is the *comparison element*, which receives two inputs, say, A and B, and produces both the minimum of A and B and the maximum of A and B as output, as shown in Figure 4-1.

DEFINITION

A sequence $a = \langle a_1, a_2, \ldots, a_p \rangle$ of p numbers is said to be *bitonic* if and only if

1. $a_1 \le a_2 \le \ldots \le a_k \ge \ldots \ge a_p$, for some k, or
2. $a_1 \ge a_2 \ge \ldots \ge a_k \le \ldots \le a_p$, for some k, or
3. a can be split into two parts that can be interchanged to give either of the first two cases.

The reader should notice that by including the third case in the **Definition**, the first two cases become equivalent, and thus redundant. The third case can be interpreted as stating that a circular rotation of the members of the sequence yields an example of one of the first two cases. For example, the sequence $\langle 3,2,1,6,8,24,15,10 \rangle$ is bitonic, since there is a circular rotation of the sequence that yields $\langle 6,8,24,15,10,3,2,1 \rangle$, which satisfies case 1.

A bitonic sequence can therefore be thought of as a circular list that obeys the following condition. Start a traversal at the entry in the list of minimal value, which we will refer to as x. Then as you traverse the list in either direction, you will encounter elements in nondecreasing order until you reach the maximum element in the list, after which you

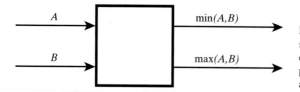

Figure 4-1   An illustration of a comparison element. This is the fundamental element of a sorting network. The comparison element receives inputs A and B and produces min(A,B) and max(A,B).

will encounter elements in nonincreasing order until you return to x. Notice that if we have duplicate elements in the sequence (list), then there are plateaus in the list, where multiple items of the same value appear contiguously, as we perform this traversal.

Before introducing a critical theorem about bitonic sequences, we make an important observation about two *monotonic* sequences. Given one ascending sequence and one descending sequence, they can be concatenated to form a bitonic sequence. Therefore, a network that sorts a bitonic sequence into monotonic order can be used as a *merging* network to merge (sort) a pair of monotonic sequences (which are preprocessed by such a concatenation step).

Theorem: Given a **bitonic** sequence $a = \langle a_1, a_2, \ldots, a_{2n} \rangle$, the following hold.

a) $d = \langle \min\{a_i, a_{n+i}\} \rangle_{i=1}^{n} = \langle \min\{a_1, a_{n+1}\}, \min\{a_2, a_{n+2}\}, \ldots, \min\{a_n, a_{2n}\} \rangle$ is bitonic.

b) $e = \langle \max\{a_i, a_{n+i}\} \rangle_{i=1}^{n} = \langle \max\{a_1, a_{n+1}\}, \max\{a_2, a_{n+2}\}, \ldots, \max\{a_n, a_{2n}\} \rangle$ is bitonic.

c) $\max(d) \leq \min(e)$.

Proof: Let $d_i = \min\{a_i, a_{n+i}\}$ and $e_i = \max\{a_i, a_{n+i}\}$, $1 \leq i \leq n$. We must prove that *i*) d is bitonic, *ii*) e is bitonic, and *iii*) $\max(d) \leq \min(e)$. Without loss of generality, we can assume that $a_1 \leq a_2 \leq \ldots a_{j-1} \leq a_j \geq a_{j+1} \geq \ldots \geq a_{2n}$, for some j such that $n \leq j \leq 2n$.

■ Suppose $a_n \leq a_{2n}$. For $1 \leq i \leq n$, if $n + i < j$, then the choice of j implies $a_i \leq a_{n+i}$, while if $n + i \geq j$, then $a_i \leq a_n \leq a_{2n} \leq a_{n+i}$. (See Figure 4-2.) Therefore, if $a_n \leq a_{2n}$, we have $d_i = a_i$ and $e_i = a_{n+i}$. Further, since $\max(d) = a_n$ and $\min(e) = \min(a_{n+1}, a_{2n})$, we also have $\max(d) \leq \min(e)$. This completes the proof for the case where $a_n \leq a_{2n}$.

■ Now consider the case where $a_n > a_{2n}$. Since a is nondecreasing for $i \leq j$ and nonincreasing for $i \geq j$, and since $a_{j-n} \leq a_j$, then there is an index k, $j \leq k < 2n$, for which $a_{k-n} \leq a_k$ and $a_{k-n+1} > a_{k+1}$. This is illustrated in Figure 4-3.

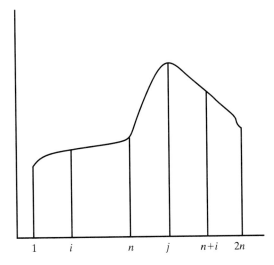

Figure 4-2 An illustration of a bitonic sequence $\langle a \rangle$ in which $a_n \leq a_{2n}$, and a_j is a maximal element of $\langle a \rangle$, where $n \leq j \leq 2n$.

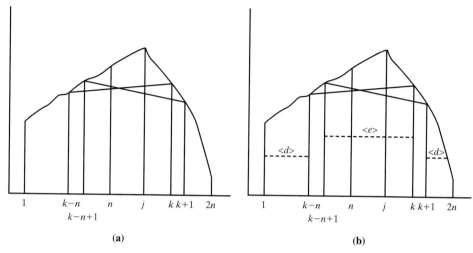

Figure 4-3 An illustration of a bitonic sequence $<a>$ in which $a_n > a_{2n}$, a_j is a maximal element of $<a>$, where $n \leq j \leq 2n$, and there exists a pivot element k such that $a_{k-n} \leq a_k$ and $a_{k-n+1} > a_{k+1}$.

First, consider the sequence d. For $1 \leq i \leq k - n$, we have either

- $i + n \leq j$, which implies $a_i \leq a_{i+n}$, or

- $i + n > j$, in which case

$$a_i \leq a_{k-n} \leq a_k \leq a_{i+n},$$

the last inequality in the chain following from

$$(i \leq k - n) \Rightarrow (j < i + n \leq k).$$

Thus, for $1 \leq i \leq k - n$, we have $d_i = a_i$. Further, this subsequence of d is nondecreasing. Next, notice that $d_i = a_{n+i}$ for $k - n < i \leq n$, since for such i,

$$a_i \geq a_{k-n+1} \quad \{\text{Since } k - n + 1 \leq i \leq n \leq j.\}$$

$$\geq a_{k+1} \quad \{\text{By choice of } k.\}$$

$$\geq a_{i+n} \quad \{\text{Since } j < k + 1 \leq i + n.\}$$

Further, this subsequence of d is nonincreasing. Therefore, d is comprised of a nondecreasing subsequence followed by a nonincreasing subsequence. By the first part of the bitonic sequence definition, we know that d is bitonic.

Now consider the sequence e. Notice that $e_i = a_{n+i}$ for $1 \leq i \leq j - n$. Further, this subsequence of e is nondecreasing. Next, notice that $e_i = a_{n+i}$ for $j - n \leq i \leq k - n$. Further, this subsequence is easily seen to be nonincreasing. Finally, notice that $e_i = a_i$ for $k - n < i \leq n$. This final subsequence of e is nondecreasing. Therefore, e is bitonic by case three from the definition since we also have that $e_n = a_n \leq a_{n+1} = e_1$. See Figure 4-3b.

Now, consider the relationship between bitonic sequences d and e. Notice that $\max(d) = \max\{a_{k-n}, a_{k+1}\}$ and $\min(e) = \min\{a_k, a_{k-n+1}\}$. It follows easily that $\max(d) \leq \min(e)$, completing the proof for the case of $a_n > a_{2n}$.

Bitonic Merge: The previous theorem gives the iterative rule for constructing a bitonic *merge* unit. That is, a unit that will take a bitonic sequence as input (recall that a bitonic sequence is easily created from two monotonic sequences), and produce a monotonic sequence as output. (See Figure 4-4.) Please be careful. It is very important to note that this is only the merge step, and that this merge step works on bitonic sequences. After we finish our discussion and analysis of the *merge* unit, we will show how to utilize this merge unit to sort data via BitonicSort.

We now present the bitonic merge algorithm. The input to the routine is the bitonic sequence A and the direction that A is to be sorted into (ascending or descending). The routine will produce a monotonic sequence Z, ordered as requested.

Subprogram BitonicMerge(A, Z, *direction*)
Procedure: Merge bitonic list A, assumed at top level of recursion to be of size
$\qquad\qquad$ $2n$, to produce list Z, where Z is ordered according to the *function*
$\qquad\qquad$ *direction*, which can be viewed as a function with values < or >.
Local variables: i: list index
$\qquad\qquad\qquad$ Z_d, Z'_d, Z_e, Z'_e: lists, initially empty
Action:
$\qquad$ If $|A| < 2$, then return $Z = A$ {This is a base case of recursion.}
$\qquad$ Else
$\qquad\qquad$ For $i=1$ to n, do
$\qquad\qquad\qquad$ If **direction** (A_i, A_{n+i}), then
$\qquad\qquad\qquad\qquad$ append A_i to Z_d and append A_{n+i} to Z_e
$\qquad\qquad\qquad$ Else append A_{n+i} to Z_d and append A_i to Z_e
$\qquad\qquad$ End For
$\qquad\qquad$ *BitonicMerge*(Z_d, Z'_d, *direction*)
$\qquad\qquad$ *BitonicMerge*(Z_e, Z'_e, *direction*)
$\qquad\qquad$ Concatenate(Z'_d, Z'_e, Z)
$\qquad$ End Else
$\qquad$ End *BitonicMerge*

Bitonic Merge Unit

Input: a **bitonic** sequence

Output: a **monotonic** (ordered) sequence

Figure 4-4 Input and output for a bitonic merge unit.

Notice the strong resemblance between BitonicMerge and both MergeSort and Quicksort.

- BitonicMerge is similar to MergeSort in that it requires a list of elements to be split into two even sublists, recursively sorted, and then concatenated (the concatenation serves as a merge step, by part c) of the theorem). Be aware, though, that MergeSort takes as input an *unordered* list, which is sorted to produce an ordered list, while BitonicMerge takes as input a bitonically ordered list in order to produce an ordered list.

- BitonicMerge is similar to Quicksort in that it splits a list into sublists, recursively solves the problem on the sublists, and then concatenates the sublists into the final list. In fact, notice that in the case of BitonicMerge and QuickSort, the two intermediate sublists that are produced both have the property that every element in one of the lists is greater than or equal to every element in the other list.

As described, a bitonic merge unit for $2n$ numbers is constructed from n comparitors and two n-item bitonic merge units. Two items can be merged with a single comparison unit. In fact, n pairs of items can be simultaneously merged using one level of merge units. That is, if $L(x)$ is the number of levels of comparitors required to merge simultaneously $x/2$ pairs of items, we know that the base case is $L(2) = 1$. In general, to merge two bitonic sequences, each of size n, requires $L(2n) = L(n) + 1 = \log_2 2n$ levels.

In terms of our analysis of running time, we assume that it takes $\Theta(1)$ time for a comparison unit to perform its operation. So, each level of a sorting network contributes $\Theta(1)$ to the running time. Therefore, a bitonic merge unit for $2n$ numbers performs a bitonic merge in $\Theta(\log n)$ time.

Now consider implementing BitonicMerge on a sequential machine. The algorithm requires $\Theta(\log n)$ iterations of a procedure that makes n comparisons. Therefore, the total running time for this *merge* routine on a sequential machine is $\Theta(n \log n)$. As a means of comparison, recall that *i*) the time for MergeSort to merge two lists with a total of n items is $\Theta(n)$, and *ii*) the time for Quicksort to partition a set of n items is $\Theta(n)$.

In Figure 4-5, we present a $2n$-item bitonic merge unit. It is important to note that the input sequence, $<a>$, is bitonic and that the output sequence, $<c>$, is sorted. The boxes represent the comparitors that accept two inputs and produce two outputs: L, which represents the lower (minimum) of the two input values, and H, which represents the higher (maximum) of the two input values.

Figures 4-6 and 4-7 present examples of a four-element bitonic merge unit and an eight-element bitonic merge unit, respectively. The input sequence $<a>$ in both figures is assumed to be bitonic. Further, as in Figure 4-5, we let L denote the low (minimum) result of the comparison, and H represents the high (maximum) result.

Bitonic Sort: BitonicSort is a sorting routine based on MergeSort. Given a list of n elements, MergeSort can be viewed in a bottom-up fashion as first merging n single elements into $n/2$ pairs of ordered elements. The next step consists of pair-wise merging these $n/2$ ordered pairs of elements into $n/4$ ordered groups of quadruples. This process continues until the last stage, which consists of merging two ordered groups of elements, each of size $n/2$, into a single ordered list of size n. BitonicSort works in much the same way.

Given an initial input list of random elements, notice that every pair of elements is bitonic. Therefore, in the first stage of BitonicSort, bitonic sequences of size 2 are merged to cre-

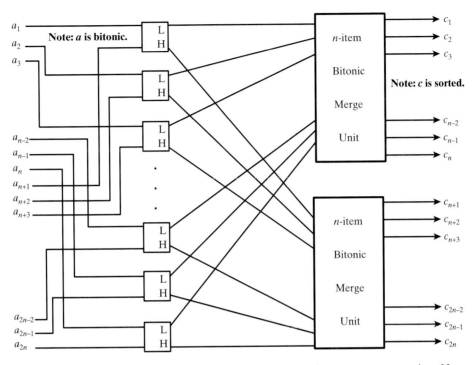

Figure 4-5 The iterative rule for constructing a bitonic merge unit. The input sequence <*a*> consists of 2*n* items and is *bitonic*. The 2*n* item output sequence <*c*> is sorted.

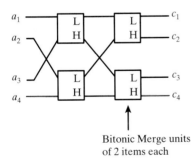

Bitonic Merge units
of 2 items each

$$
\begin{aligned}
\text{Levels} = L(2n) = L(2 \times 2) &= 1 + L(n) \\
&= 1 + L(2) \\
&= 2 \\
&= \log_2(2 \times 2)
\end{aligned}
$$

Figure 4-6 A four-item *bitonic merge unit*. Note that <a_1, a_2, a_3, a_4> is the bitonic input sequence and <c_1, c_2, c_3, c_4> is the sorted output sequence. The number of levels $L(2n)$ can be determined as $L(2n) = L(2 \times 2) = 1 + L(n) = 1 + L(2) = 2 = \log_2 2n$.

ate ordered lists of size 2. Notice that if these lists alternate between being ordered into increasing and decreasing order, then at the end of this first stage of merging, we actually have $n/4$ bitonic sequences of size 4. In the next stage, bitonic sequences of size 4 are merged into sorted sequences of size 4, alternately into increasing and decreasing order, so as to form $n/8$ bitonic sequences of size 8. Given an unordered sequence of size $2n$, notice that exactly $\log_2 2n$

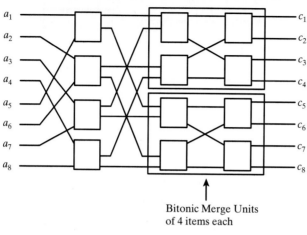

Bitonic Merge Units
of 4 items each

Levels = $L(2n) = L(2 \times 4) = 1 + L(4) = 1 + 2 = 3$
$= \log_2(2 \times 4)$

Figure 4-7 An 8-item *bitonic merge unit.* Note that the input sequence $<a_1, \ldots, a_8>$ is bitonic and the output sequence $<c_1, \ldots, c_8>$ is sorted. The number of levels $L(2n)$ can be determined as $L(2n) = L(2 \times 4) = 1 + L(4) = 1 + 2 = 3 = \log_2(2 \times 4) = \log_2 8$.

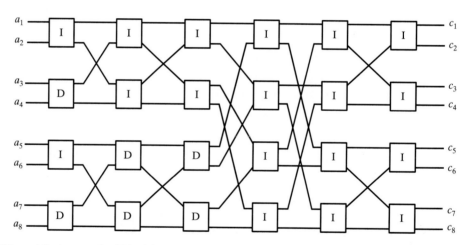

Figure 4-8 An example of BitonicSort on eight data items. Note that the input sequence $<a>$ is initially unordered, and the output sequence $<c>$ is sorted into nondecreasing order. The symbol "I" means that the comparison is done so that the top output item is less than or equal to the bottom output item (increasing order if the items are unique). The symbol "D" represents that the comparison is done with respect to nonincreasing order (decreasing order if unique items).

stages of merging are required to produce a completely ordered list. (We have assumed, for the sake of simplicity, that $2n = 2^k$, for some positive integer k.) See Figure 4-8.

Now consider the merging stages. Each of the $\log_2 2n$ stages of BitonicSort utilizes a different number of comparitors. In fact, notice that in Stage 1, each bitonic list of size 2 is merged with one comparitor. In Stage 2, each bitonic sequence of size 4 is merged with two *levels* of comparitors, as per our previous example. In fact, at stage i, the BitonicMerge requires i levels of comparitors.

We now consider the total number of levels of comparitors required to sort an *arbitrary* set of $2n$ input items with BitonicSort. Again, there are $\log_2 2n$ stages of merging, and each stage i requires i levels of comparisons. Therefore, the number of levels of comparitors is given by

$$\sum_{i=1}^{\log_2 2n} i = \frac{(\log_2 2n)(\log_2 2n + 1)}{2} = \frac{(\log_2 2n)^2}{2} + \frac{\log_2 2n}{2}$$

So, $\Theta(\log^2 n)$ levels of comparitors are required to sort completely an unordered list of size $2n$. That is, an input list of $2n$ values can be sorted in this (combinational circuit) model with $\Theta(\log^2 n)$ delay.

Now consider how this algorithm compares to traditional sorting algorithms operating on the sequential model. Notice that for $2n$ input values, each of the $\Theta(\log^2 n)$ levels of comparitors actually uses n comparitors. That is, a total of $\Theta(n \log^2 n)$ comparitors is required to sort $2n$ input items with BitonicSort. Therefore, if properly implemented in software, this algorithm requires $\Theta(n \log^2 n)$ time on a sequential machine.

Subprogram BitonicSort(X)
Procedure: Sort the list $X[1, \ldots, 2n]$, using the bitonic sort algorithm.
Local variables: integers *segmentLength, i*
Action:
      segmentLength = 1;
      Do
            For $i = 1$ to *n/segmentLength,* do in parallel
                BitonicMerge(
                    $X[(2i - 2) \times segmentLength + 1 \ldots (2i - 1) \times segmentLength]$,
                    $X[(2i - 1) \times segmentLength + 1 \ldots 2i \times segmentLength]$,
                    $X[(2i - 2) \times segmentLength + 1 \ldots 2i \times segmentLength]$,
                    ascending = odd(i))
            End For;
            segmentLength = 2 $\times$ segmentLength;
          While *segmentLength* $<$ $2n$ {End Do.}
      End *BitonicSort*

There is an alternative view of sorting networks that some find easier to grasp. We present such a view in Figure 4-9 for BitonicSort, as applied to an eight-element unordered sequence. The input elements are given on the left of the diagram. Each line is labeled with a unique three-bit binary number. Please do not confuse these labels with the values that are contained on the lines (not shown in this figure). Horizontal lines are used to represent the flow of data from left to right. A vertical line is used to illustrate a comparitor between the elements on the endpoints of its line. The letters next to the vertical lines indicate whether the comparison being performed is $\leq$ (represented as I, giving the intuition of *increasing*) or $\geq$ (represented as D, giving the intuition of *decreasing*). Note that dashed vertical lines are used to separate the $3 = \log_2 8$ merge stages of the algorithm. The reader might want to draw a diagram of an eight-element bitonic sorting network using the lines and comparitors that have been used previously in this chapter and verify that such a diagram is consistent with this one.

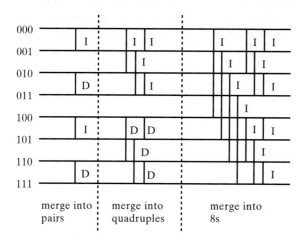

Figure 4-9 A different view of Bitonic-Sort for eight elements. The horizontal lines represent wires and the solid vertical lines represent comparison-exchange elements. That is, the vertical lines represent points in time at which two items are compared and ordered according to the label I (increasing order) or D (decreasing order). Notice that the $\log_2 8 = 3$ bitonic merge stages are separated by dotted vertical lines.

Finally, Batcher made a very interesting observation in his seminal 1968 paper that included Bitonic Sort and Odd-Even MergeSort. Consider the alternative view of Bitonic Sort just presented. Batcher noticed that at each stage of the algorithm, the only elements ever compared are those on lines that differ in exactly one bit of their line labels. Suppose that we are given a parallel machine consisting of a set of $2n$ processors and we have one item per processor that we wish to sort. Batcher noted that if every processor were connected to all other processors that differ in exactly one bit position, the sorting would be performed in $\Theta(\log^2 n)$ time. In fact, such a model corresponds to the interconnection of a hypercube, which will be discussed later in this book.

Processor	Entry	Neighbor processors
000	a_0	001, 010, and 100
001	a_1	000, 011, and 101
010	a_2	011, 000, and 110
011	a_3	010, 001, and 111
100	a_4	101, 110, and 000
101	a_5	100, 111, and 001
110	a_6	111, 100, and 010
111	a_7	110, 101, and 011

Summary   In conclusion, we note that Bitonic Sort will sort n items

- in $\Theta(\log^2 n)$ time using a sorting network,
- in $\Theta(\log^2 n)$ time on a machine in which processors that differ in a single bit in their unique, consecutively labeled indices, are directly connected (a hypercube),
- in $\Theta(\log^2 n)$ time on a parallel machine that allows any two 2 processors to communicate in constant time (such as a PRAM, which is also presented later in this book), and
- in $\Theta(n \log^2 n)$ time on a sequential machine (RAM).

CHAPTER NOTES

In 1968, Ken Batcher presented a short paper that introduced Bitonic Sort and Odd-Even MergeSort, and made the insightful observation that both sorting networks would operate efficiently on a hypercube network of processors. The work from this paper, "Sorting networks and their applications," (K.E. Batcher, *Proceedings of the AFIPS Spring Joint Computer Conference* 32, 1968, pp. 307–314) has been covered in traditional courses on data structures and algorithms by many instructors over the past 20 years. The material has become more integral to such a curriculum as parallel computing has reached the mainstream. This material has recently been incorporated into textbooks. A nice presentation of this material can be found in *Introduction to Algorithms*, by T.H. Cormen, C.E. Leiserson, and R.L. Rivest (McGraw-Hill Book Company, New York, 1992).

EXERCISES

1. Define a **transposition network** to be a comparison network in which comparisons are only made between elements on adjacent lines. Prove that sorting n input elements on a transposition network requires $\Omega(n^2)$ comparison units.

2. What is the smallest number of elements for which you can construct a sequence that is not bitonic? Prove your result.

3. Consider a comparison network C that takes a sequence of elements $X = \{x_1, x_2, \ldots, x_n\}$ as input. Further, suppose that the output of C is the same set of n elements, but in some predetermined order. Let the output sequence be denoted as $\{y_1, y_2, \ldots, y_n\}$.

   a) Given a monotonically increasing function F, prove that if C is given the sequence $\{F(x_1), F(x_2), \ldots, F(x_n)\}$ as input, it will produce $\{F(y_1), F(y_2), \ldots, F(y_n)\}$ as output.

   b) Suppose that input set X consists only of 0s and 1s. That is, the input is a set of n bits. Further, suppose that the output produced by C consists of all the 0s followed by all the 1s. That is, C can be used to sort any permutation of 0s and 1s. Prove that such a circuit (one that can sort an arbitrary sequence of n bits) can correctly sort any sequence of arbitrary numbers (not necessarily 0s and 1s). This result is known as the 0-1 *sorting principle*.

4. Use the 0-1 *sorting principle* to prove that the following *odd-even merging network* correctly merges sorted sequences $\{x_1, x_2, \ldots, x_n\}$ and $\{y_1, y_2, \ldots, y_n\}$.

   a) The odd-indexed elements of the two sequences, that is $\{x_1, x_3, \ldots, x_{n-1}\}$ and $\{y_1, y_3, \ldots, y_{n-1}\}$, are merged to produce a *sorted* sequence $\{u_1, u_2, \ldots, u_n\}$.

   b) Simultaneously, the even-indexed elements of the two sequences, $\{x_2, x_4, \ldots, x_n\}$ and $\{y_2, y_4, \ldots, y_n\}$, are merged to produce a *sorted* sequence $\{v_1, v_2, \ldots, v_n\}$.

   c) Finally, the output sequence $\{z_1, z_2, \ldots, z_{2n}\}$ is obtained from $z_1 = u_1$, $z_{2n} = v_n$, $z_{2i} = \min(u_{i+1}, v_i)$, $z_{2i+1} = \max(u_{i+1}, v_i)$, for all $1 \le i \le n - 1$.

5

Models of Computation

Models of Computation

In this chapter, we introduce a variety of models of computation that will be used throughout the book. Initially, we introduce the random access machine (RAM), which is the traditional sequential model of computation (also called the von Neumann model). The RAM has been an extremely successful model in terms of the design and analysis of sequential algorithms targeted at serial computers. Next, we introduce the parallel random access machine (PRAM), which is the most popular parallel model of computation. The PRAM was designed so that the user could design and analyze parallel algorithms without concern for communication (either between processors and memory or within sets of processors). Following our introduction to the PRAM, and a variety of fundamental examples, we introduce parallel models of computation that rely on specific interconnection networks, either between processors and memory or between processors that contain on-board memory. Such models include the mesh, tree, pyramid, mesh-of-trees, and hypercube. Finally, we conclude the chapter with a presentation of some standard terminology.

RAM (Random Access Machine): The RAM is the traditional sequential model of computation, as shown in Figure 5-1. It has proved to be quite successful since algorithms designed for the RAM tend to perform as predicted on the majority of sequential (uniprocessor) machines.

The RAM has the following characteristics:

Memory: Assume that the RAM has M memory locations, where M is a (large) finite number. Each memory location has a unique address and is capable of storing a single piece of data. The memory locations can be accessed in a random (direct) fashion. That is, there is a constant $C > 0$ such that given any memory address A, the data stored at address A can be accessed in at most C time. Thus, memory access on a RAM is assumed to take $\Theta(1)$ time, regardless of the number of memory locations or the particular location of the memory access.

Processor: The RAM contains a single processor, which operates under the control of a sequential algorithm. One instruction at a time is issued. Each instruction is performed to completion before continuing with the next instruction. We assume that the processor can perform a variety of fundamental operations. These operations include loading and storing data from and to memory, respectively, as well as performing basic arithmetic and logical operations.

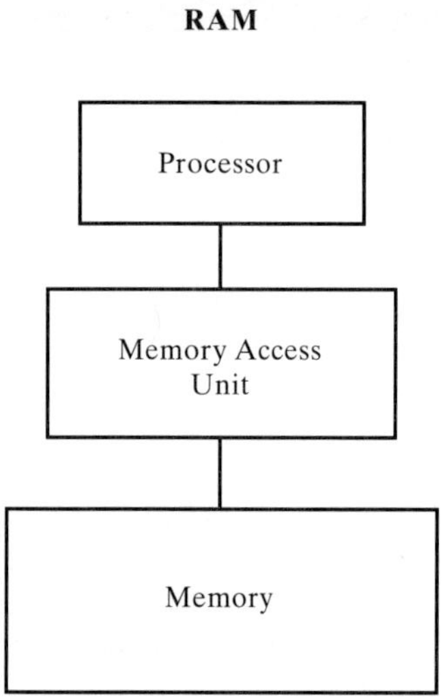

RAM

Figure 5-1 The RAM (random access machine) is a traditional sequential model of computation. It consists of a single processor and memory. The processor is able to access any location of memory in $\Theta(1)$ time through the memory access unit.

Memory Access Unit: The memory access unit is used to create a path (a direct connection) between the processor and a memory location.

Execution: Each step of an algorithm consists of three phases: a *read phase*, a *compute phase*, and a *write phase*. In the read phase, the processor has the opportunity to read data from memory into one of its registers. In the compute phase, the processor has the opportunity to perform basic operations on the contents of its registers. Finally, during the write phase, the processor has the opportunity to send the contents of one of its registers to a specific memory location. This is a high-level interpretation of a step of an algorithm, corresponding typically to several machine (or assembly language) instructions. There is no distortion of analysis in such an interpretation, as several machine instructions can certainly be executed in $\Theta(1)$ time, as discussed below.

Running Time: We need to consider the time that each of these three phases requires. First, it is important to note that each register in the processor must be of size greater than or equal to $\log_2 M$ bits in order to accommodate M distinct memory locations (the reader should verify this). Due to the fan-out of "wires" between the processor and memory, any access to memory will require $O(\log M)$ time. Notice, however, that it is often possible for k consecutive memory accesses to be pipelined to run in $O(k + \log M)$ time on a slightly enhanced model of a RAM. Based on this analysis, and the fact that many computations are amenable to pipelining for memory access, we assume that both the read and the write phase of an execution cycle requires $\Theta(1)$ time.

Now consider the compute phase of the execution cycle. Given a set of k-bit registers, many of the fundamental operations can be performed in $\Theta(\log k)$ time. The reader unfamiliar with these results might wish to consult a basic book on computer architecture and read about carry-lookahead adders, which provide an excellent example. Therefore, since each register has $k = \Theta(\log M)$ bits, the compute phase of each execution cycle can be performed in $O(\log M)$ time.

Typically, one assumes that every cycle of a RAM algorithm requires $\Theta(1)$ time. This is due to the fact that neither the $O(k + \log M)$ time required for memory access nor the $O(\log \log M)$ time required to perform fundamental operations on registers typically affects the comparison of running time between algorithms. Further, these two terms are relatively small in practice, so much so that the running time of an algorithm is almost always dominated by other considerations such as

- the amount of data being processed,
- the instructions executed, and
- (in an approximate algorithm) the error tolerance.

It is important to note that this $\Theta(1)$ time model is the standard, and that most authors do not go into the analysis or justification of it. However, this model is properly referred to as the *uniform analysis* variant of the RAM. This is the model that we will assume throughout the book when we refer to the RAM and, as mentioned, it is the model that is used in all standard algorithms and data structures books.

PRAM (Parallel Random Access Machine):   The PRAM is the most widely utilized parallel model of computation. When it was developed, the hope was that it would do for parallel computing what the RAM model did for sequential computing. That is, the PRAM was developed in order to provide a platform upon which people could design theoretical algorithms that would behave as predicted by the asymptotic analysis on real parallel computers. The advantage of the PRAM is that it ignores communication issues and allows the user to focus on the potential parallelism available in the design of an efficient solution to the given problem. The PRAM has the following characteristics (see Figure 5-2).

Processors: The PRAM maintains n processors, $P_1, P_2, \ldots, P_n$, each of which is identical to a RAM processor. These processors are often referred to as *processing elements, PEs*, or simply *processors.*

Memory: As with the RAM, there is a common (sometimes referred to as a "global") memory. It is typically assumed that there are $m \geq n$ memory locations.

Memory Access unit: The memory access unit of the PRAM is similar to that of the RAM in that it assumes that every processor has equal $\Theta(1)$ time access to every memory location.

It is important to note that *the processors are not directly connected to each other.* So if two processors wish to communicate in their effort to solve a problem, they must do so through the common memory. That is, PRAM algorithms often treat the common memory as a blackboard (to borrow a term from *Artificial Intelligence*). For example, suppose processor P_1 maintains the sum of elements in array X in one of its registers. Then in order for another processor to view or use this value, P_1 must write the value to a location in the global memory. Once it is there, other processors can then read and use the value.

PRAM

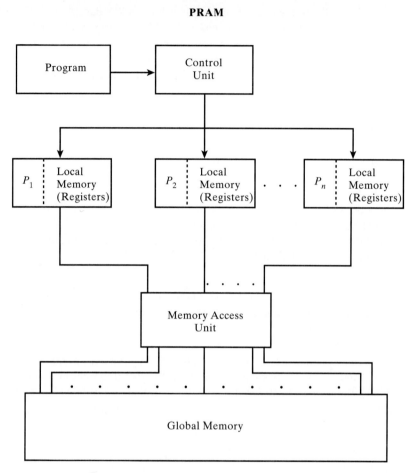

Figure 5-2   Characteristics of a PRAM (parallel random access machine). The PRAM consists of a set of processing elements connected to a global memory through a memory access unit. All memory accesses are assumed to take $\Theta(1)$ time.

Execution: As with the RAM, each step of an algorithm consists of three phases, a *read phase*, a *compute phase*, and a *write phase*. During the read phase, all n processors have the opportunity to read simultaneously a piece of data from a, not necessarily unique, memory location. Each processor places the data item into one of its registers. In the compute phase, every processor has the opportunity to perform a fundamental operation on the contents of its registers. This phase is identical to that of the RAM, but remember that n independent operations can be performed simultaneously (one in each processor). During the write phase, every processor can (simultaneously) write an item from one of its registers to the global memory. Again, the write stage is very similar to the write stage of the RAM, with the exception that simultaneous writes can occur. It is important to note that conflicts can occur during both the read and write phases. We will consider resolutions to such conflicts shortly.

Running Time: The analysis of running time per cycle is virtually identical to that of the RAM. Again, we need to consider the time that each of these three phases takes. An analysis of the read and write phases will again show that the time required for each processor to access any of the m memory locations, due to constraints in fan-in, is $O(\log m)$. As discussed previously, this can be improved by pipelining to allow k consecutive requests from all n processors to be handled in $O(k + \log m)$ time. Similarly, every processor can perform fundamental operations on its own k-bit registers in $O(\log k)$ time. Finally, by assuming a uniform access model, we can assume that every cycle can be performed in $\Theta(1)$ time. Although this uniform-access model is not perfect, it suits most of our needs.

Memory Access (Resolving Data Access Conflicts):   Conflicts in memory access can arise during both the read phase and the write phase of a cycle. How should one handle this? For example, if two processors are trying to read from the same memory location, should only one succeed? If so, which? If two processors are trying to write to the same memory location (the classical "race condition"), which one succeeds? Is a processor notified if it doesn't succeed? We discuss the traditional variants of the PRAM model in terms of memory access. Once the read and write access options have been defined, they can be coupled in a variety of ways to yield the common PRAM models.

Read Conflicts: Handling read conflicts is fairly straightforward. Two basic models exist:

1. *Exclusive Read (ER):* Only one processor is allowed to read from a given memory location during a cycle. That is, it is considered an illegal instruction (*i.e.*, a compile-time or run-time programming error, if you will) if at any point during the execution of a procedure, two or more processors attempt to read from the same memory location.
2. *Concurrent Read (CR):* Multiple processors are allowed to read from the same memory location during a clock cycle.

Write Conflicts: Handling write conflicts is much more complex, and a variety of options exist.

1. *Exclusive Write (EW):* The exclusive write model allows only one processor to write to a given memory location during a clock cycle. That is, it is considered to be a compile-time or run-time error if a piece of code requires two or more processors to write to the same memory location during the same clock cycle.
2. *Concurrent Write (CW):* The concurrent write model allows multiple processors to write to the same memory location simultaneously (*i.e.*, during the same clock cycle). This brings up a very interesting point. How should one resolve write conflicts? A variety of arbitration schemes have been used in the literature. We list some of the popular ones.
   (a) *Priority CW:* The *priority CW* model assumes that if two or more processors attempt to write to the same memory location during the same clock cycle, the processor with the highest priority succeeds. In this case, it is assumed that processors have been assigned priorities in advance of such an operation, and that the

priorities are unique. Notice that there is no feedback to the processors as to which one succeeds and which ones fail.

(b) *Common CW:* The *common CW* model assumes that all processors attempting a simultaneous write to a given memory location will write the same value.

(c) *Arbitrary CW:* The *arbitrary CW* model is quite interesting. This model assumes that if multiple processors try to write simultaneously to a given memory location, then one of them, arbitrarily, will succeed.

(d) *Combining CW:* The *combining CW* model assumes that when multiple processors attempt to write simultaneously to the same memory location, the values written by these multiple processors are (magically) combined, and this combined value will be written to the memory location in question. Popular operations for the combining CW model include arithmetic functions such as SUM and PRODUCT, logical functions such as AND, OR, and XOR, and higher-level fundamental operations such as MIN or MAX.

Popular PRAM Models: Now that we have defined some of the common ways in which reads and writes are arbitrated with the PRAM, we can discuss the four popular PRAM models.

1. *CREW:* The *CREW PRAM* is one of the most popular models because it represents an intuitively appealing machine. Namely, it assumes that concurrent reads may occur, but it forbids concurrent writes.

2. *EREW:* The *EREW PRAM* is the most restrictive form of a PRAM in that it forbids both concurrent reads and concurrent writes. Since only exclusive reads and writes are permitted, it is much more of a challenge to design efficient algorithms for this model. Further, due to the severe restrictions placed on the EREW PRAM model, notice that any algorithm designed for the EREW PRAM will run on any of the other models. Note, however, that an optimal EREW algorithm may not be optimal on other PRAM models.

3. *CRCW:* The *CRCW PRAM* allows for both concurrent reads and concurrent writes. When we use such a model, the details of the concurrent write must be specified. Several choices of CW were discussed above.

4. *ERCW:* The *ERCW PRAM* rounds out the four obvious combinations of reads and writes. However, this model has very little to offer and is rarely considered. Notice that intuitively, if one can assume that hardware can perform concurrent writes, it is not very satisfying to assume that concurrent reads could not be managed.

Discussion: The PRAM is one of the earliest and most widely studied parallel models of computation. However, it is important to realize that the PRAM is not a physically realizable machine. That is, while a machine with PRAM-type characteristics could be built with relatively few processors, such a machine could not be built with an extremely large number of processors. In part, this is due to current technological limitations in connecting processors and memory. Regardless of the practical implications, the PRAM is a powerful model for studying the logical structure of parallel computation under conditions that permit theoretically optimal communication. Therefore, the PRAM offers a model for exploring the limits of parallel computation, in the sense that the asymptotic running time of an optimal PRAM algorithm should be at least as fast as that of an optimal algorithm on any other architecture with the same number of processors. (There are some exceptions to this last statement, but they are outside the scope of this book.)

The great speed we claim for the PRAM is due to its fast communications, an issue that will be discussed in greater detail later. The idea is that data may be communicated between a source and a destination processor in $\Theta(1)$ time via

1. the source processor writing the data value to memory, followed by
2. the destination processor reading this data value from memory.

By contrast, parallel computers with other architectures may require a nonconstant amount of time for communication between distant processors, as the data must be passed step-by-step between neighboring processors in an interconnection network until the data reaches the desired destination.

EXAMPLES: SIMPLE ALGORITHMS

Now that we have introduced many of the critical aspects of the PRAM, it is appropriate for us to present several simple algorithms, along with some basic analysis of time and space. The first operation we consider is that of *broadcasting* a piece of information. For example, suppose a particular processor contains a piece of information in one of its registers that is required by all other processors. We can use a broadcast operation to distribute this information from the given processor to all others. Broadcasting will serve as a nice, simple example to get us started. The first broadcasting algorithm we present is targeted at the CR PRAM. Notice that the algorithm we present exploits the fundamental CR capabilities. Therefore, it will not work on the ER models.

CR PRAM Algorithm for Broadcasting a Unit of Data
Initial Condition: One processor, P_i, stores a value d in its register $r_{i,j}$ that is to be broadcast.

Exit Condition: All processors store the value d.

Action:
1. Processor P_i writes the value d from register $r_{i,j}$ to shared memory location X
2. In parallel, all processors read d from shared memory location X

End Broadcast

Step 1 only requires a $\Theta(1)$ time exclusive write, assuming that all processors know whether or not they are the one to be broadcasting the data (a reasonable assumption). Step 2 requires $\Theta(1)$ time because the model has the concurrent read property. The reader should note that this algorithm runs in $\Theta(1)$ time regardless of the number of processors.

Now consider the broadcast problem for an ER PRAM. A simple modification to the previous algorithm could be made to allow each processor, in sequence, to read the data item from shared memory location X. However, this would result in an algorithm that runs in time linear in the number of processors, which is less than desirable. That is, given an ER PRAM with n processors, such an algorithm would run in $\Theta(n)$ time. Alternately, we could make multiple copies of the data, one for each processor, and then allow each processor to simultaneously read "its" copy. We will take this approach. The algorithm follows.

ER PRAM Algorithm for Broadcasting a Unit of Data

Assumption: The ER PRAM has n processors.

Initial Condition: One processor, P_i, has the data value d stored in its register $r_{i,j}$.

Exit Condition: All processors have the value d.

Action:

    Processor P_i writes the value d from register $r_{i,j}$ to shared memory location d_1.

    For $i = 1$ to $\lceil \log_2 n \rceil$, do

        In parallel, processors $P_j, j \in \{1, \dots, 2^{i-1}\}$, do

            read d from d_j

            If $j + 2^{i-1} \leq n$, then write d to $d_{j+2^{i-1}}$

        End parallel

    End For

End Broadcast

This is an example of a *recursive doubling procedure*, in which during each generic step of the algorithm, the number of copies of the initial data item has doubled (exactly or approximately). As is the case with many parallel algorithms, it also implies that the number of processors that maintain a copy of the data doubles during each successive step. Notice that this has the flavor of a tree-like algorithm. Initially, there is one copy of the data (at the root). After the first step, there are now two copies of the data (at the children). After the second step, there are four copies of the data (at the grandchildren), and so on. Since each step of reading and writing only requires $\Theta(1)$ time, regardless of the number of processors participating in the operation, we know that an ER PRAM with n processors can perform a broadcast operation in logarithmic time, *i.e.*, in $\Theta(\log n)$ time.

Next, we consider PRAM solutions to several fundamental operations involving arrays of data. Let's assume that the input to these problems consists of an array $X = [x_1, x_2, \dots, x_n]$ where each entry, x_i, might be a record containing multiple fields and where the array X may itself be ordered, as appropriate. When there is no confusion, we will make references to the key fields simply by referring to an entry x_i.

A *semigroup operation* is a *binary associative operation*. That is, a semigroup operation has the property that $(x \otimes y) \otimes z = x \otimes (y \otimes z)$, where $\otimes$ is a well-defined operation on two operands. Popular semigroup operators include **maximum, minimum, sum, product, OR,** and so forth. Sometimes we find it easier to present a concrete example. Therefore, we will choose **minimum** as our operator for several of the semigroup operations that follow. We first consider an efficient algorithm on a RAM to compute the minimum of a set X.

RAM Minimum Algorithm
Input: Array X.
Output: Minimum entry of X.
Local variables: i, *min_so_far*
Action:
  min_so_far $= x_1$
  For $i = 2$ to n, do
      If $x_i <$ *min_so_far* then *min_so_far* $= x_i$
  End For
  return min_so_far
End Minimum

The analysis of this algorithm's running time is fairly straightforward. Given an array of size n, each entry is examined exactly once in $\Theta(1)$ time. Therefore, the running time is $\Theta(n)$. Further, given an unordered set of data, this is optimal since if we avoid any of the n elements, we may produce the wrong answer. Next, we consider the space requirements of this algorithm. Notice that $\Theta(n)$ space is used to store the array of data, and that the algorithm uses $\Theta(1)$ additional space.

Now consider a semigroup operation for the PRAM. The first algorithm we present is fairly intuitive for the reader who has studied tree-like data structures. The algorithm uses a bottom-up, tree-like computation, as shown in Figure 5-3, computing the minimum of disjoint pairs of items, then the minimum of disjoint pairs of these results, and so on until the global minimum has been determined. In Figure 5-4, we show how the processors cooperate in order to compute the minimum. The reader should note that the processing presented in Figure 5-4 performs the computations that are presented in Figure 5-3. To simplify our presentation, we assume the size of the problem, n, is a power of 2.

PRAM Minimum Algorithm (initial attempt)
Assumption: The PRAM (CR or ER) has $n/2$ processors.
Input: An array $X = [x_1, x_2, \ldots, x_n]$, in which the entries are drawn from a linearly
      ordered set.
Output: The smallest entry of X.
Action:
  1. Copy X to a temporary array T
  2. For $i = 1$ to $\log_2 n$, do
        In parallel, processors P_j, $j \in \{1, \ldots, 2^{(\log_2 n) - i}\}$, do
            a) Read t_{2j-1} and t_{2j};
            b) Write $\min\{t_{2j-1}, t_{2j}\}$ to t_j;
          End parallel
      End For
  3. If desired, broadcast $t_1 = \min\{x_1, x_2, \ldots, x_n\}$
End Minimum

Step 1 of the algorithm requires constant time since all processors can simultaneously copy a unique element in $\Theta(1)$ time. Notice that if we do not care about preserving the input

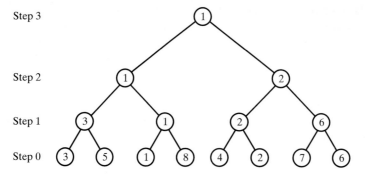

Figure 5-3 A bottom-up, tree-like computation to compute the minimum of eight values. The global minimum can be computed in three parallel steps. Each step reduces the total number of candidates by half.

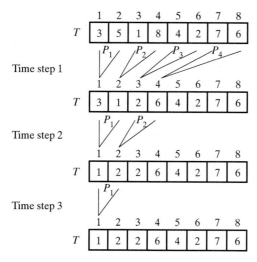

Figure 5-4 Another view of the minimum operation presented in Figure 5-3. This shows the action of a set of four processors. The data is presented as residing in a horizontal array. The processors that operate on data are shown between each of the three time steps.

data, then we could omit Step 1. Step 2 requires $\Theta(\log n)$ time to perform the bottom-up, tree-type operation. The broadcast operation can be performed in $O(\log n)$ time ($\Theta(1)$ time on a CR PRAM and $\Theta(\log n)$ time on an ER PRAM). Thus, the algorithm requires $\Theta(\log n)$ total time. Unfortunately, time is not the only measure of the quality of an algorithm. Sometimes we care about the efficient utilization of additional resources. We define a measure that considers both running time and productivity of the processors, as follows.

DEFINITION

Let $T_{par}(n)$ be the time required for an algorithm on a parallel machine with n processors. The *cost* of such an algorithm is defined as $cost = n \times T_{par}(n)$, which represents the total number of cycles available during the execution of the given algorithm.

Since we assume that $n/2$ processors are available in the preceding PRAM algorithm to determine the minimum value of an array, the cost of the algorithm is $n/2 \times \Theta(\log n) = \Theta(n \log n)$. That is, during the time that the algorithm is executing, the machine has the capability to perform $\Theta(n \log n)$ operations, regardless of how many operations it actually performs. Since the machine has the opportunity to perform $\Theta(n \log n)$ operations, and the *problem* can be solved with $\Theta(n)$ operations, we know that this PRAM algorithm is *not cost-optimal*. However, it may or may not be the best we can do for this particular architecture.

Let's consider how we might improve this algorithm. In order to improve the cost of the algorithm, we must either reduce the number of processors, reduce the running time, or both. We might argue that with the model we have defined, we cannot combine more than a fixed number of data values in one clock cycle. Therefore, it must take a logarithmic number of clock cycles to combine the input data. Since our argument suggests that $\Theta(\log n)$ time is required, we might consider reducing the number of processors. So let's consider the question: how many processors are required in order to obtain a cost-optimal algorithm? That is, what is the value of P, representing the number of processors, that will yield $P \times \Theta(\log n) = \Theta(n)$, assuming that the $\Theta(\log n)$ running time does not change? Clearly, the solution to this equation shows that if we can keep the running time at $\Theta(\log n)$, then we want the number of processors to be $P = \Theta(n / \log n)$. The algorithm that follows shows how to exploit $P = \Theta(n / \log n)$ processors in order to determine the global minimum of n values in $\Theta(\log n)$ time on a PRAM. The reader is referred to Figures 5-5 and 5-6.

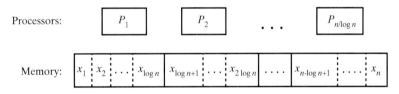

Figure 5-5   Improving the performance of a PRAM algorithm by requiring each of $n/\log n$ processors to be responsible for $\log n$ data items.

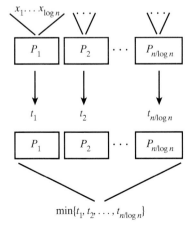

Figure 5-6   An algorithm for computing the minimum of n items with $n/\log_2 n$ processors on a PRAM. Initially, every processor sequentially determines the minimum of the $\log_2 n$ items that it is responsible for. Once these $n/\log n$ results are known, then the minimum of these values can be determined in $\log (n/\log n) = \log n - \log \log n = \Theta(\log n)$ time on a PRAM with $n/\log n$ processors.

PRAM Minimum Algorithm (*Optimal*)

Assumption: The PRAM (ER or CR) has $n/\log n$ processors.

Input: An array $X = [x_1, x_2, \ldots, x_n]$, drawn from a linearly ordered set.

Output: The smallest entry of X.

Action:

1. Conceptually partition the data into $n/\log n$ disjoint sets of $\log n$ items each. In parallel, every processor P_j computes $t_j = \min\{x_{(j-1)\log n+1}, x_{(j-1)\log n+2}, \ldots, x_{j\log n}\}$ using an optimal RAM algorithm, given previously. Since the data set operated on by P_j has size $\Theta(\log n)$, this takes $\Theta(\log n)$ time.

2. Use the previous PRAM algorithm to compute $\min\{t_1, t_2, \ldots, t_{n/\log n}\}$ with $n/\log n$ processors in $\Theta(\log (n/\log n)) = \Theta(\log n)$ time.

End *Minimum*

The algorithm just described takes an interesting approach. We use asymptotically fewer processors than there are data items of concern. We divide the data items over the number of processors. For example, suppose there are P processors and D data items. Then we assume every processor has approximately D/P items. Each processor first works on its set of D/P items in a sequential manner. After the sequential phase of the algorithm completes, then each processor has reduced its information to only one item of concern, which in this case is the minimum of the items for which the processor is responsible. Finally, one item per processor is used as input into the simple, nonoptimal parallel algorithm to complete the task. Notice that this final parallel operation uses P items with P processors. Therefore, this PRAM algorithm runs in $\Theta(\log n)$ time on $n/\log n$ processors. This results in a cost of $(n/\log n) \times \Theta(\log n) = \Theta(n)$, which is optimal. Therefore, we have a cost-optimal PRAM algorithm for computing the minimum entry of an array of size n that also runs in time-optimal $\Theta(\log n)$ time.

Now let's consider the problem of searching an *ordered* array on a PRAM. That is, given an array $X = [x_1, \ldots, x_n]$, in which the elements are in some predetermined order, construct an efficient algorithm to determine if a given query element q is present. Without loss of generality, let's assume that our array X is given in nondecreasing order. If q is present in X, we will return an index i such that $x_i = q$. Notice that i is not necessarily unique.

First, let's consider a traditional binary search on a RAM. Given an ordered set of data, we have discussed in Chapter 2 how to perform a binary search in $\Theta(\log n)$ time. Using this result as the base case for the parallel models, we know that we are aiming for algorithms with a total cost of $\Theta(\log n)$, which is an extremely tight bound. The first model we consider is the CRCW PRAM.

CRCW PRAM Algorithm to Search an Ordered Array (Initial Attempt)

Assumption: The *combining* CRCW PRAM has n processors and uses the combining operator *minimum*.

Input: An ordered array, $X = [x_1, x_2, \ldots, x_n]$, and the *search_value*.

Output: *succeeds*, a flag indicating whether or not the search succeeds, and *location*, an index at which the search succeeds (if it does).

Action:

Processor P_1 initializes *succeeds = false*;

In parallel, every processor P_i does the following:
    read *search_value* and x_i {Note that CR is used to read *search_value*.}
    If $x_i = search\_value$ then
        succeeds = *true*;
        location = i;
    End If
    End Parallel
End *Search*

When this CRCW algorithm terminates, the value of the Boolean variable *succeeds* will be set to *true* if and only if *search_value* is found in the array. In the event that the item is found, the variable *location* is set to a (not necessarily unique) position in the array where *search_value* exists. Now let's consider the running time of the algorithm. Notice that the initial concurrent read takes $\Theta(1)$ time. The time required for every processor (simultaneously) to compare its element to the query element takes $\Theta(1)$ time. Finally, the two concurrent write operations take $\Theta(1)$ time. Notice that the second concurrent write exploits the combining property of the CRCW PRAM (using the operation of minimum). Therefore, the total running time of the algorithm is $\Theta(1)$. Now we should consider the cost of the algorithm on this architecture. Since $\Theta(1)$ time is required on a machine with n processors, the total cost is a less-than-wonderful $\Theta(n)$. (Recall that a binary search requires $\Theta(\log n)$ time on a RAM.) Next, we present an alternative algorithm that is somewhat slower but more cost-efficient than the previous algorithm.

CRCW PRAM Algorithm to Search an Ordered Array (Optimal)
Assumption: The *combining* CRCW PRAM has $f(n) = O(n)$ processors and uses
              combining operator *minimum*. (For simplicity, assume that $f(n)$ is a
              factor of n.)
Input: An ordered array, $X = [x_1, x_2, \ldots, x_n]$, and *search_value*, the item to
        search for.
Action:
    Processor P_1 initializes *success* = *false*;
    In parallel, every processor P_i conducts a binary search on

$$\left[x_{\frac{(i-1)n}{f(n)}+1}, x_{\frac{(i-1)n}{f(n)}+2}, \ldots, x_{\frac{in}{f(n)}} \right]$$

End *Minimum*

The algorithm above is interesting in that it presents the user with a continuum of options in terms of the number of processors utilized and the effect that this number will have on the running time and total cost. So if your primary concern is minimizing cost, notice that by using one processor, the running time will be $\Theta(\log n)$ and the cost will be $\Theta(\log n)$, which is optimal. In fact, with the number of processors set to one, notice that this is the RAM binary search algorithm.

Now suppose you care about minimizing the running time. If running time is your main concern, then the more processors you use, the better off you are in this case, at least up to n processors. Using more than n processors has no positive effect on the running time. In the case of an n processor system, we have already seen that the running time is $\Theta(1)$. In general, the running time of this algorithm is $\Theta(\log(n/f(n)))$, and the cost is $\Theta(f(n)\log(n/f(n)))$. In particular, notice that if you use $f(n) = \Theta(\log n)$ processors, the running time will be $\Theta(\log n)$, as in the case of the RAM, but presumably with a smaller constant of proportionality. In other words, this PRAM implementation should run significantly faster if other factors such as chip speed, optimized code, and so on, are the same. The cost of $\Theta(\log^2 n)$ will also be very good, though not quite optimal.

FUNDAMENTAL TERMINOLOGY

In this section, we introduce some common terminology concerned with interconnection networks. The terminology we present is standard in the field and will be used throughout the book. It should be noted that, in general, we do our best to avoid technical terminology. We try to use such terms only when they provide for a more precise presentation of material. In fact, we wait until the end of this chapter to provide a more comprehensive set of terms.

Distributed Memory Versus Shared Memory: Multiprocessor machines are constructed with some combination of shared and distributed memory. When we discuss such memory, it is important to note that we are discussing traditional, off-chip, secondary memory. Such memory explicitly excludes cache-type memory. A *shared-memory machine* provides physically shared memory for the processors, as shown on the left side of Figure 5-7. For small shared-memory machines, networks can be constructed so that every processor can access every memory location in the same amount of time. Unfortunately, such machines cannot currently scale to large numbers of processors while preserving uniformly fast access time to memory. This has been discussed previously in connection with the PRAM.

In a *distributed-memory machine*, each processor only has access to its own private (local) memory, as shown on the right side of Figure 5-7. On such machines, processors

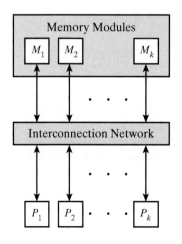
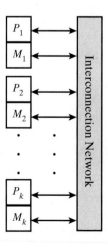

Figure 5-7   A traditional *shared-memory machine* is presented on the left, in which all processors operate through an interconnection network and have equal unit-time access to all memory locations. A traditional *distributed-memory machine* is presented on the right, in which every processing element (processor and memory pair) communicates with every other processing element through an interconnection network.

communicate by sending messages to each other through the interconnection network. So, for example, if processor A needs information stored in the memory of processor B, then this information must be transported from processor B to processor A. This is typically done by having A initiate a request for information, which is sent to processor B, followed by B sending the requested information back to processor A. However, it is often the case that the overhead and delay can be reduced if the computation is synchronized so that B simply sends the information to A without receiving such a request.

Distributed Address Space Versus Shared Address Space: Recently, there has been an interest in creating a programming model that provides a global (shared) *address space*. Such a model enables the user to program the machine under the assumption that all processors have equal access to memory, regardless of how the machine is physically constructed. Clearly, this presents a lot of advantages to the programmer. However, it mainly serves to postpone the consideration of a variety of real issues, including differences between *NUMA* (*non-uniform memory access*) machines and *UMA* (*uniform memory access*) machines. That is, shared-memory systems containing a large number of processors are typically constructed as processor/memory modules. So while the memory may be logically shared, in terms of algorithmic performance, the machine behaves as a distributed-memory machine. In such a case, memory that is close to a processor can be accessed more quickly than memory that is far from a processor.

In this book, we will focus on the physical models to arrive at an appropriate analysis of the algorithms under consideration. Therefore, it is time to consider options for connecting processors to each other (*i.e.,* options for the distributed-memory model).

INTERCONNECTION NETWORKS

In this section, we consider distributed-memory machines, which are constructed as processor-memory pairs connected to each other in a well-defined pattern. These processor-memory pairs are often referred to as *processing elements,* or *PEs*, or sometimes just as *processors*, when this term will not cause confusion. The efficient use of an interconnection network of a parallel machine is often critical in the development of an algorithm. The quality of an interconnection network can be evaluated in a variety of ways, including the following.

1. **Degree of the network**: The term *degree* comes from graph theory. The *degree of a processor* is defined to be the number of (bidirectional) communication links attached to the processor. That is, the degree of processor A corresponds to the number of other processors to which processor A is *directly* connected. So if you think of the processors as corresponding to vertices and the communication links as corresponding to edges in an undirected graph, the degree of a processor is the degree of the corresponding vertex. Similarly, the *degree of a network* refers to the maximum degree of any processor in the network. Naturally, networks of high degree become very difficult to manufacture. Therefore, it is desirable to use networks of low degree whenever possible, especially if we are concerned with scaling the network to extremely large numbers of processors.

2. **Communication Diameter**: The *communication diameter* of a network is defined to be the maximum of the minimum distance between any pair of processors. That is, it represents the longest path between any two processors, assuming that a best (shortest) path between processors is always chosen. Therefore, a machine (network) with a low communication diameter is highly desirable, in that it allows for efficient communication between arbitrary pairs of processors.

3. **Bisection Width**: The *bisection width* of a network is defined to be the minimum number of wires that have to be removed (severed) in order to disconnect the network into two approximately equal size subnetworks. In general, machines with a high bisection width are difficult (more costly) to build, but they provide users with the possibility of moving large amounts of data efficiently.

4. **I/O Bandwidth**: The input/output bandwidth is not a primary concern in this book, as it is often reasonable to assume that the data is already in the machine before our algorithms are initiated. However, when considering the construction of a real machine, I/O bandwidth is certainly important.

5. **Running Time**: When comparing models of computation, it is often enlightening to consider the time required to perform fundamental operations. Such operations include semigroup computations (min, max, global sum, and so forth), prefix computations (to be defined later), and fundamental data movement operations such as sorting. In fact, as we introduce some of the network models below, we will consider the efficiency of such routines.

To summarize, we want to design the interconnection network of a distributed-memory machine with the following characteristics. In order to reduce the cost of building a processor, we would like to minimize the degree of the network. In order to minimize the time necessary for individual messages to be sent long distances, we want to minimize the communication diameter. Finally, in order to reduce the probability of contention between multiple messages in the system, we want to maximize the bisection width. Unfortunately, it is often difficult to balance these design criteria. In fact, we also would prefer to use a simple design, in that simplicity reduces the hardware and software design costs. Further, we would like the machine (*i.e.*, network) to be scalable, so that machines of various sizes can be built (and sold).

PROCESSOR ORGANIZATIONS

In this section, we introduce a variety of processor organizations (*i.e.*, sets of processing elements and their interconnection networks). These network models are characterized by *i*) the interconnection scheme between the processors, and *ii*) the fact that the memory is distributed among the processors (there is no shared memory). In particular, it is the interconnection pattern that distinguishes these *distributed-memory* architectures. As we introduce several such models, we will consider some of the measures discussed above. Notice, for example, that the communication diameter often serves as a limiting factor in the running time of an algorithm. This measure serves as an upper bound on the time required for any (arbitrary) pair of processors to exchange information, and therefore as a lower bound on the running time of any algorithm that requires global exchanges of information.

Terminology: We say that two processors in a network are *neighbors* if and only if they are directly connected by a communication link. We assume these communication links are *bidirectional*. That is, if processor A and processor B are connected by a communication link, we assume that A can send data to B and that B can send data to A. Since sorting is a critical operation in network-based parallel machines, we need to define what it means to sort on such architectures. Suppose we have a list, $X = \{x_1, \ldots, x_n\}$, with entries stored in the processors of a distributed-memory machine. In order for the members of X to be considered ordered, there must be a meaningful ordering not only of those entries that are stored in the same processor, but also of entries in different processors. We assume that there is an ordering of the processors. The notation $R(i)$ is used to denote the ranking function for the processor labeled i. We say the list X is in ascending order if the following conditions are satisfied:

1. $i < j \Rightarrow x_i \le x_j$ and
2. $i < j$, x_i is stored in P_m, x_j is stored in P_n, and $m \ne n$ implies $R(m) < R(n)$.

Similar statements can be made for data stored in descending order.

Linear Array: A *linear array of size n* consists of a string of n processors, $P_1, \ldots, P_n$, where every generic processor is connected to its two neighbors (see Figure 5-8). Specifically, processor P_i is connected to its two neighbors, P_{i+1} and P_{i-1}, for all $2 \le i \le n - 1$. However, the two end processors, P_1 and P_n, are each only connected to one neighbor. Given a linear array of size n, let's consider some of the basic measures. Since $n - 2$ processors have degree 2 and two processors have degree 1, the degree of the network is 2. Now consider the communication diameter, the maximum over the minimum distances between any two processors. Consider the minimum number of communication links that need to be traversed in order for processors P_1 and P_n to exchange information. The only way that a piece of data originating in P_1 can reach processor P_n is by traversing through all of the other $n - 2$ processors. Therefore, the communication diameter is $\Theta(n)$. This is important in that it tells us that time linear in the number of processors is required to compute any function for which all processors may need to know the final answer. Now consider the minimum time required for a computation to be performed on two arbitrary pieces of data. Notice that information from processors P_1 and P_n could meet in processor $P_{\lceil n/2 \rceil}$. However, this still requires $\lceil n/2 \rceil - 1$ communication steps. Therefore, time linear in the number of processors is required, even in the best case, to solve a problem that requires arbitrary pairs of data to be combined.

Next we consider the bisection width of a linear array of size n. The bisection width of a linear array of size n is 1, as the communication link between processors $P_{n/2}$ and $P_{(n/2)+1}$ can be severed, and the result would be two linear arrays, each of size $n/2$. Now let's move on and consider some basic operations.

Assume that a set of data, $X = [x_1, \ldots, x_n]$, is distributed so that processor P_i stores data element x_i. First, we consider the problem of determining the minimum element of

Figure 5-8   A *linear array* of size n.

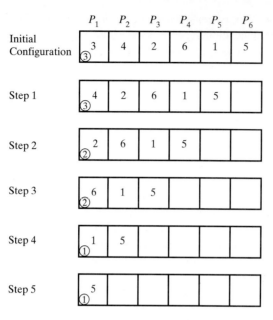

Figure 5-9 Computing the minimum of n items initially distributed one per processor on a linear array of size n. Notice that the data is passed in lockstep fashion to the left during every time step. The leftmost processor (P_1) keeps the running minimum (lower-left corner of P_1).

array X. This can be done in several ways. Our first approach is one in which all the data will march left in lockstep fashion, and as the data reaches processor P_1, this leftmost processor will compute the running minimum, as shown in Figure 5-9. That is, initially, processor P_1 sets a register *running_min* to x_1. During the first step of the algorithm, in lockstep fashion, processors $P_2, \ldots, P_n$ each send their data elements to the left. Now processor P_1 sets *running_min* = min(*running_min*, x_2). The procedure continues so that after i steps, processor P_1 has the value of min($x_1, \ldots, x_{i+1}$). Therefore, after $n - 1$ steps, the minimum of X is stored in processor P_1.

Suppose every processor needs to know this minimum value, which is currently stored in processor P_1. Initially, processor P_1 (viewed as the leftmost processor in the linear array), can send this value to the right (to processor P_2). If this value continues to move to the right during each step, then after a total of $n - 1$ such steps, all n processors will know the minimum of X. Therefore, the minimum (or any other semigroup operation) can be determined and distributed to all processors in $\Theta(n)$ time on a linear array of size n. Notice that such a $\Theta(n)$ time algorithm on a set of n processors yields a cost of $n \times \Theta(n) = \Theta(n^2)$. This is not very appealing, considering that such problems can be easily solved in $\Theta(n)$ time on a RAM. Therefore, we should consider whether or not it is possible to do better on a linear array of size n. Notice that we simply cannot do better, due to the $\Theta(n)$ communication diameter.

Next, consider whether or not we can reduce the number of processors and arrive at a cost-optimal algorithm. Clearly, if we use only one processor, we will be able to determine the minimum in $\Theta(n)$ time, which would yield an optimal cost of $\Theta(n)$. However, this is not very desirable, since the running time has not been reduced over that of the RAM. So while we have considered the two extremes in terms of numbers of processors (both 1 and n), let's now consider some intermediate value. What value should we consider? We would like to balance the amount of work performed by each processor with the work performed by the network. That is, we would like to balance the number of data elements per processor, since the local minimum algorithm runs in time linear in the number of elements, with the number of processors, since the communication diameter is linear in the number of processors. Therefore, we should consider a linear array of size $n^{1/2}$, where each processor is responsible for $n^{1/2}$ items, as shown in Figures 5-10 and 5-11. An algorithm to compute the minimum of n data items, evenly distributed on a linear array of size $n^{1/2}$, can be constructed with two major steps. First, each processor runs the linear time sequential algorithm on its own set of data. Next, the linear array algorithm is run on these $n^{1/2}$ partial results in order to obtain the final global result (minimum). Therefore, the running time of the algorithm is dominated by the $\Theta(n^{1/2})$ time to perform the RAM algorithm simultaneously on all processors, followed by the $\Theta(n^{1/2})$ time to determine the minimum of these $n^{1/2}$ local minima, distributed one per processor on a linear array of size $n^{1/2}$. Hence, the running time of the algorithm is $\Theta(n^{1/2})$, which results in an optimal cost of $\Theta(n)$. Finally, this yields a cost-optimal algorithm with optimal running time for a linear array.

Suppose we have a linear array of size n, but that the data does not initially reside in the processors. That is, suppose we have to input the data as part of the problem. For lack of a better term, we will call this model an *input-based linear array*. Assume that the data is input to the leftmost processor (processor P_1) and only one piece of data can be input per unit time. Assume that the data is input in reverse order and that at the end of the operation, every processor P_i must know x_i and the minimum of X. This can be accomplished by the following algorithm. In the first step, processor P_1 takes as input x_n and initializes *running_min* to x_n. In the next step, processor P_1 sends x_n to processor P_2, inputs x_{n-1}, and assigns *running_min* = *min(running_min, x_{n-1})*. In general, during each step of the

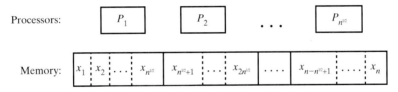

Processors:

Memory:

Figure 5-10 Partitioning the data in preparation for computing the minimum of n items initially distributed on a linear array of size $n^{1/2}$ in such a fashion that each of the $n^{1/2}$ processors stores $n^{1/2}$ items.

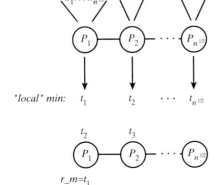

"*local*" min:

Figure 5-11 Computing the minimum of n items initially distributed on a linear array of size $n^{1/2}$ in such a fashion that each of the $n^{1/2}$ processors stores $n^{1/2}$ items. In the first step, every processor sequentially computes the minimum of the $n^{1/2}$ items that it is responsible for. In the second step, the minimum of these $n^{1/2}$ minima are computed on the linear array of size $n^{1/2}$ by the typical lockstep algorithm.

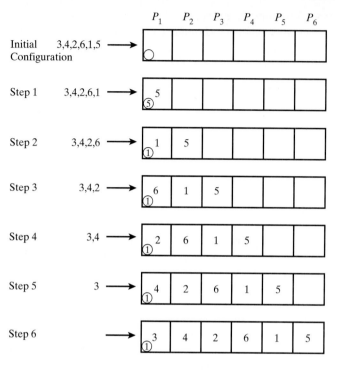

Figure 5-12   Computing the minimum on an *input-based linear array* of size 6. During step 1, processor P_1 takes as input $x_6 = 5$ and initializes *running_min* to 5. During step 2, processor P_1 sends x_6 to processor P_2, inputs $x_{n-1} = 1$, and assigns *running_min* = min(*running_min*, x_{n-1}) = 1, which is the minimum of 5 and 1, respectively. The algorithm continues in this fashion as shown, sending data to the right in lockstep fashion, while the first processor keeps track of the minimum value of the input data.

algorithm, the data continues to march in lockstep fashion to the right, and the leftmost processor continues to store the running minimum, as shown in Figure 5-12. After n steps, all processors have their data element, and the leftmost processor stores the minimum of all n elements of X. As before, processor P_1 can broadcast the minimum to all other processors in $n - 1$ additional steps. Therefore, we have an optimal $\Theta(n)$ time algorithm for the input-based linear array.

We introduced this input-based variant of the linear array so that we could extrapolate an algorithmic strategy. Suppose we wanted to emulate this input-based linear array algorithm on a traditional linear array of size n, in which the data is initially stored in the array. This could be done with a *tractor-tread* algorithm, where the data moves as one might observe on the tractor-tread of many large construction vehicles or tanks. In the initial phase, view the data as marching to the right, so that when a data element hits the right wall, it turns around and marches to the left (see Figure 5-13). That is, every processor initially starts by sending its data to the right (with the exception of the rightmost processor). When the rightmost processor receives data, it reverses its direction.

In general, every processor will continue to pass all the data it receives in the direction it is going, with the exception of the first and last processors, which emulate the walls and serve to reverse the direction of data. So after the initial $n - 1$ steps, notice that processor P_1 will store a copy of x_n, processor P_2 will store a copy of x_{n-1}, and so forth. That is, the data is now positioned so that processor P_1 is prepared to accept as "input" x_n, as in the input-based linear array algorithm. In fact, the input-based linear array algorithm can now

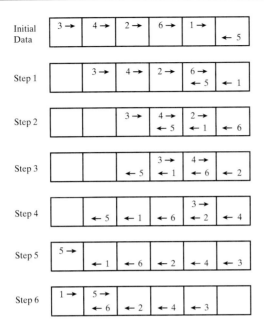

Figure 5-13 A *tractor-tread* algorithm. Data in the linear array moves to the right until it hits the right wall, where it reverses itself and starts to march to the left. Once the data hits the left wall, it again reverses itself. A revolution of the tractor-tread algorithm is complete once the initial data resides in its original set of processors. Given a linear array of size n, this algorithm allows every processor to view all n data items in $\Theta(n)$ time.

be emulated with a loss in running time of these initial $n - 1$ steps. Therefore, the asymptotic running time of the algorithm remains as $\Theta(n)$.

Notice that this tractor-tread algorithm is quite powerful. It can be used, for example, to rotate all of the data through all of the processors of the linear array. This gives every processor the opportunity to view all of the data. Therefore, such an approach can be used to allow every processor to compute the result of a semigroup operation in parallel. Notice that we have traded off an initial setup phase for the postprocessing broadcast phase. However, as we shall soon see, this approach is even more powerful than it might initially appear.

Consider the problem of sorting. The communication diameter tells us that $\Omega(n)$ time is required to sort n pieces of data distributed in an arbitrary fashion one item per processor on a linear array of size n. Similarly, by considering the bisection width, we know that in the worst case, if the $n/2$ items on the left side of the linear array belong on the right side of the array, and vice versa, then in order for n items to cross the single middle wire, $\Theta(n/1) = \Theta(n)$ time is required.

We now show how to construct such a time-optimal sorting algorithm for this model. First, consider the input-based linear array model. Notice that the first processor will view all n data items as they come in. If that processor retains the smallest data item and never passes it to the right, then at the end of the algorithm, processor P_1 will store the minimum data item. Now, if processor P_2 performs the same minimum-keeping algorithm as processor P_1 does, then at the end of the algorithm, processor P_2 will store the minimum data item of all $n - 1$ items that it viewed (see Figure 5-14). That is, processor P_2 would store the minimum of all items with the exception of the smallest item, which processor P_1 never passed along. Therefore, at the end of the algorithm, processor P_2 would store the second

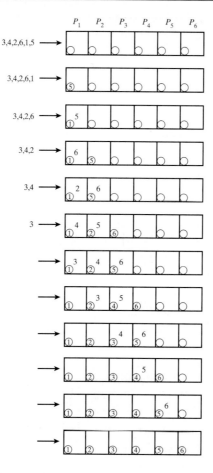

Figure 5-14 Sorting data on an input-based linear array. Every processor simply retains the item that represents the minimum value it has seen to date. All other data continues to pass in lockstep fashion to the right. Notice that this is a minor generalization of the minimum algorithm illustrated in Figure 5-12.

smallest data item. (This algorithm can be illustrated quite nicely in the classroom. Each row of students can simulate this algorithm running on such a machine, where the input comes from the instructor standing in the aisle.)

We now have an optimal $\Theta(n)$ time algorithm for this model. By using the tractor-tread method, we can emulate this algorithm to produce a time-optimal $\Theta(n)$ time algorithm for a linear array of size n. As an aside, we should mention that this sorting algorithm can be viewed as a parallel version of Selection Sort. That is, the first processor views all of the data and selects the minimum. The next processor views all of the remaining data and selects the minimum, and so forth.

The final algorithm we consider for the linear array is that of computing the parallel prefix of $X = [x_1, \ldots, x_n]$. When the algorithm terminates, processor P_i must store the i-th prefix, $x_1 \otimes \ldots \otimes x_i$, where $\otimes$ is a binary associative operator. The algorithm follows. First, we note that processor P_1 initially stores what is its final value. During the first step, processor P_1 sends a copy of x_1 to processor P_2, which computes and stores the second prefix, $x_1 \otimes x_2$. During the second step, processor P_2 sends a copy of its prefix value to processor P_3, which computes and stores the third prefix value, $x_1 \otimes x_2 \otimes x_3$. The algorithm continues in this fashion for $n - 1$ steps, after which every processor P_i stores the i-th prefix, as required. It is important to note that during step i, the i-th prefix is passed from processor P_i to processor P_{i+1}. That is, processor P_i passes a single value, which is the result of $x_1 \otimes \ldots \otimes x_i$, to processor P_{i+1}. If processor P_i passed all of the components of this result, $x_1, \ldots, x_i$, to processor P_{i+1}, the running time for the i-th step would be $\Theta(i)$, and the total running time for the algorithm would therefore be

$$\Theta\left(\sum_{i=1}^{n-1} i\right) = \Theta(n^2).$$

By requiring only one data item to be passed between neighboring processors during each iteration of the algorithm, the running time of this algorithm is $\Theta(n)$. Notice that this is optimal for a linear array of size n since the data entries stored at maximum distance must be combined (argument based on communication diameter). In this case, no argument can be made with respect to the bisection width, since this problem does not require large data movement.

Ring: A ring is simply a linear array of processors in which the two end processors are connected to each other, as shown in Figure 5-15. That is, a *ring of size n* consists of string of n processors, $P_1, \ldots, P_n$, where every processor is connected to its two neighbors. That is, processor P_i is connected to its two neighbors, P_{i+1} and P_{i-1}, for $2 \le i \le n - 1$, and processors P_1 and P_n are connected to each other.

Let's examine some of our measures to see what advantages the ring has over the linear array. The degree of both networks is 2. The communication diameter of a ring of size n is approximately $n/2$, which compares favorably with the $n - 1$ of the linear array. However, notice that this factor of approximately 1/2 is only a multiplicative constant. Thus, both architectures have the same asymptotic communication diameter of $\Theta(n)$. Although the bisection width does not really make sense in this model, if one assumes that the ring could be broken and then each subring sealed back up, this would require severing/patching $\Theta(1)$ communication links, which is the same as the linear array. In fact, when we consider the ring compared to the linear array, the best we could hope for is a factor of 2 improvement in the running time of algorithms. Since this book is concerned primarily with

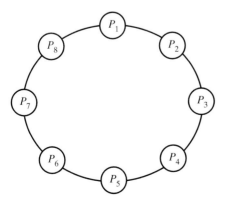

Figure 5-15   A *ring* of size 8. All processors in a ring are connected to two neighbors.

the design and *asymptotic* analysis of algorithms, the ring presents an uninteresting variant of the linear array and will not be discussed further.

Mesh: We will use the term *mesh* in this book to refer to a 2-dimensional, checkerboard-
type, mesh-based computer. A variety of 2-dimensional meshes have been proposed in the
literature. In the most traditional of meshes, each generic processor has four neighbors and
the mesh itself is constructed either as a rectangular or square array of processors, as shown
in Figure 5-16. A simple variant of the four-connected mesh is an eight-connected mesh in
which each generic processor is connected to its traditional north, south, east, and west neighbors, as well as to its northeast, northwest, southwest, and southeast neighbors. Meshes have
also been proposed in which each processor has six (hexagonal) neighbors.

In this text, we restrict our attention to a traditional 2-dimensional square mesh, which
will be referred to as a *mesh of size n*, where $n = 4^k$ for k a positive integer. Throughout the
text, we will show how to exploit a divide-and-conquer solution strategy on the mesh. This
will be done by showing how to divide a problem into two (or four) independent subproblems, map each of these to a submesh, recursively solve the smaller problems on each submesh, and then stitch the results together.

Now let's consider several of the measures that we have discussed. Notice that all the interior processors have degree 4, the four corner processors each have degree 2, and the remaining
edge processors all have degree 3. Therefore, the degree of a mesh of size n is 4. That is, the
mesh is a fixed degree network. The communication diameter represents the maximum distance
of shortest paths over every pair of processors in the network. Notice that on a mesh of size n,

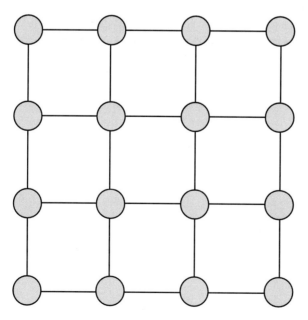

Figure 5-16   A *mesh* of size 16. Each
generic processor in a traditional mesh
is connected to its four nearest neighbors. Notice that there are no wrap-
around connections and that the
processors located along the edges of
the mesh have less than four neighbors.

there are $n^{1/2}$ rows and $n^{1/2}$ columns. So, transporting a piece of data from the northwest processor to the southeast processor requires traversing $n^{1/2} - 1$ rows and $n^{1/2} - 1$ columns. That is, a message originating in one corner of the mesh and traveling to the opposite corner of the mesh requires traversing a minimum of $2n^{1/2} - 2$ communication links. Therefore, the communication diameter of a mesh of size n is $\Theta(n^{1/2})$. Notice that if we are interested in *combining*, as opposed to exchanging, information from two processors at opposite corners, such information could be sent to one of the middle processors in less than $2n^{1/2} - 2$ steps. While the time to combine distant data may be an improvement over the time to transmit such data, notice that the improvement is only by a constant factor.

Determining the bisection width of a mesh of size n is fairly straightforward. If one cuts the links between the middle two columns, then we are left with two (rectangular) meshes of size $n/2$. If this is not intellectually satisfying, then we could sever the links between the middle two rows and the middle two columns and be left with four square meshes, each of size $n/4$. In any event, it is clear that the bisection width of a mesh of size n is $\Theta(n^{1/2})$. Before considering some fundamental operations, we should note that the bisection width can be used to provide a lower bound on the worst-case time to sort a set of data distributed one piece per processor. For example, suppose all the data elements initially stored in the first $n/2$ columns need to move to the last $n/2$ columns and vice versa. Moving n pieces of data between the middle two columns, which are joined by $n^{1/2}$ communication links, requires $\Theta(n/n^{1/2}) = \Theta(n^{1/2})$ time.

We will now turn our attention to some fundamental mesh operations. Since the mesh can be viewed as a collection of linear arrays stacked one on top of the other and interconnected in a natural fashion, we start by recalling that the mesh can implement linear array algorithms independently in every row and/or column of the mesh. Of immediate interest is the fact that the mesh can perform a row (column) rotation simultaneously in every row (column), so that each processor will have the opportunity to view all information stored in its row (column). As discussed above, a row rotation consists of sending data from every processor in lockstep fashion to the right. When data reaches the rightmost processor, it reverses itself and marches to the left until it reaches the leftmost processor, at which point it reverses itself again and continues moving to the right until it reaches the processor where it originated. Notice that at any point during the algorithm, a processor is responsible for at most two pieces of data that are involved in the rotation, one that is moving from left to right (viewed as the top of the tractor tread) and the other that is moving from right to left (viewed as the bottom of the tractor tread). A careful analysis will show that exactly $2n^{1/2} - 2$ steps are required to perform a complete rotation. Recall that this operation is asymptotically optimal for the linear array.

Since a rotation allows every processor in a row (or column) to view all other pieces of information in its row (or column), this operation can be used to solve a variety of problems. For example, if it is required that all processors determine the result of applying some semigroup operation (min, max, sum) to a set of values distributed over all the processors in its row/column, a rotation can be used to provide a time-optimal solution.

We now provide an algorithm for performing a semigroup operation over a set, $X = [x_1, \ldots, x_n]$, initially distributed one item per processor on a mesh of size n. This operation consists of performing a sequence of rotations. First, a row rotation is performed in every row so that every processor knows the result of applying the operation to the data elements in its row. Next, a column rotation is performed so that every processor can determine the final result (which is a combination of every row-restricted result).

Mesh Semigroup Algorithm

Input: An input set X, consisting of n elements, such that every processor $P_{i,j}$ initially stores data value $x_{i,j}$.

Output: Every processor stores the result of applying the semigroup operation $\otimes$ to all of the input values.

Action:

In parallel, every row i performs a row rotation so that every processor in row i knows the product $r_i = \otimes_{j=1}^{n^{1/2}} x_{i,j}$

In parallel, every column j performs a column rotation so that every processor in column j knows the product $p = \otimes_{i=1}^{n^{1/2}} r_i$ (which is equal to the desired product $\otimes_{i=1}^{n^{1/2}} \otimes_{j=1}^{n^{1/2}} x_{i,j}$)

End *Semigroup Algorithm*

This algorithm requires $\Theta(n^{1/2})$ time, which is optimal for a mesh of size n. However, on a RAM, a simple scan through the data will solve the problem in $\Theta(n)$ time. Therefore, this mesh algorithm is not cost-optimal since it allows for $\Theta(n \times n^{1/2}) = \Theta(n^{3/2})$ operations to be performed. Now let's try to construct a cost-optimal algorithm of minimal running time for a mesh. In order to balance the local computation time with communication time based on the communication diameter, consider an $n^{1/3} \times n^{1/3}$ mesh, in which each processor stores $n^{1/3}$ of the data items. Initially, every processor can perform a sequential semigroup operation on its set of $n^{1/3}$ data items. Next, the $n^{2/3}$ partial results, one per processor on the $n^{1/3} \times n^{1/3}$ mesh, can be used as input to the fine-grained mesh algorithm just presented. Notice that the sequential component of the algorithm, which operates on $n^{1/3}$ data items, can be performed in $\Theta(n^{1/3})$ time. The parallel semigroup component also requires $\Theta(n^{1/3})$ time. Therefore, the algorithm is complete in $\Theta(n^{1/3})$ time on a mesh of size $n^{2/3}$, which results in an optimal cost of $\Theta(n^{2/3} \times n^{1/3}) = \Theta(n)$.

In addition to semigroup operations, row and column rotations are important components of data gathering and broadcasting operations for the mesh. Suppose a data value x is stored in an arbitrary processor $P_{i,j}$ of a mesh of size n, and we need to broadcast x to all of the other $n - 1$ processors. Then a single row rotation, followed by $n^{1/2}$ simultaneous column rotations, can be used to solve this problem, as follows (see Figure 5-17).

Mesh Broadcast Algorithm

Procedure: Broadcast the data value x, initially stored in processor $P_{i,j}$, the processor in row i and column j, to all processors of the mesh.

Action:

Use a row rotation in row i to broadcast x to all processors in row i

In parallel, for all columns $j \in \{1, 2, \ldots, n^{1/2}\}$, use a column rotation to broadcast x to every processor in column j

End *Broadcast*

An analysis of the running time of the broadcast operation is straightforward. It consists of two $\Theta(n^{1/2})$ time rotations. Based on the communication diameter of a mesh of size n, we know that the running time for the algorithm is optimal for this architecture. Now consider the cost of this operation. In $\Theta(n^{1/2})$ time, n processors have the opportunity to perform $\Theta(n \times n^{1/2}) = \Theta(n^{3/2})$ operations. Therefore, this algorithm is not cost-optimal.

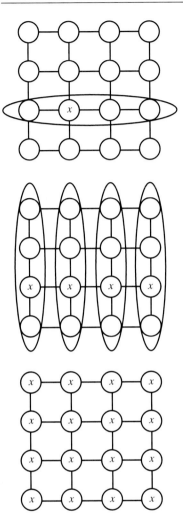

Figure 5-17 Broadcasting a piece of data on a mesh. First, a row rotation is performed in order to broadcast the critical data item to all processors in its row. Next, column rotations are performed simultaneously in every column in order to broadcast the critical data item to all remaining processors.

As we did previously, let's consider reducing the number of processors to the point where we balance the sequential processing time within each processor with the communication time required by the network. Notice that if we construct an $n^{1/3} \times n^{1/3}$ mesh, each of these $n^{2/3}$ processors would store $n^{1/3}$ of the data items. So, using the rotations as described, a single piece of information could be broadcast from one processor to all $n^{2/3}$ processors in $\Theta(n^{1/3})$ time. Once this is complete, each processor can make $n^{1/3}$ copies of this data item. (This might come up, for example, if it is desired to initialize every member of an array of size n with the value that must be broadcast.) Therefore, the algorithm is complete in $\Theta(n^{1/3})$ time on a mesh of size $n^{2/3}$, which results in an optimal cost of $\Theta(n)$.

Tree: A *tree of base size n* is constructed as a full binary tree with n processors at the base level. In graph terms, this is a tree with n leaves. Therefore, a tree of base size n has $2n - 1$ total processors (see Figure 5-18). The root processor is connected to its two children. Each

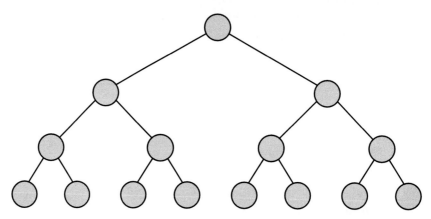

Figure 5-18   A *tree of base size* 8. Notice that base processors have only a single neighbor (parent processor), the root has only two neighbors (children processors), and the remaining processors have three neighbors (one parent and two children processors).

of the n leaf processors is connected only to its parent. All other (interior) processors are connected to three other processors, namely, one parent and two children. Therefore, the degree of a tree network is 3. Notice that a tree with n leaves contains nodes at $1 + \log_2 n$ levels. Thus, any processor in the tree can send a piece of information to any other processor in the tree by traversing $O(\log n)$ communication links. This is done by having the piece of information follow the unique path between the two processors involving their least common ancestor. That is, information flows from one processor up the tree to their least common ancestor and then down the tree to the other processor. Therefore, the communication diameter of a tree of base size n is far superior to the other network models that we have considered. Now let's consider the bisection width. The bisection width of a tree of base size n is $\Theta(1)$ since if the two links are cut between the root and its children, a tree of base size n will be partitioned into two trees, each of base size $n/2$.

A tree presents a nice (low) communication diameter, but a less than desirable (low) bisection width. This leaves us with a good news, bad news scenario. The good news is that fundamental semigroup operations can be performed in $\Theta(\log n)$ time, as follows. Assume that n pieces of data are initially distributed one per base processor. Then in order to compute a semigroup operation (min, max, sum, etc.) over this set of data, the semigroup operator can be applied to disjoint pairs of partial results in parallel as data moves up the tree level by level. Notice that after $\Theta(\log n)$ steps, the final result will be known in the root processor. Naturally, if all processors need to know the final result, it can be broadcast from the root to all processors in a straightforward top-down fashion in $\Theta(\log n)$ time. So semigroup, broadcast, and combine-type operations can be performed in $\Theta(\log n)$ time and with $\Theta(n \log n)$ cost on a tree of base size n. Notice that the running time of $\Theta(\log n)$ is optimal for a tree of base size n, and that the cost of $\Theta(n \log n)$, while not optimal, is only a factor of $\Theta(\log n)$ from optimal since a RAM can perform these operations in $\Theta(n)$ time.

Now for the bad news. Consider the problem of sorting or any routing operation that requires moving data from the leftmost $n/2$ base processors to the rightmost $n/2$ processors and vice versa. Unfortunately, the root serves as a bottleneck, since it can only process a constant amount of traffic during each clock cycle. Therefore, in order to move n pieces of data from one side of the tree to the other requires $\Omega(n)$ time.

In summary, the tree provides a major benefit over the linear array and mesh in terms of combining information, but is not well equipped to deal with situations that require extensive data movement. At this point, it makes sense to consider an architecture that combines the best features of the tree (fast broadcast, report, and semigroup operations) with the best features of the mesh (increased numbers of communication links that provide the capability to move large amounts of data in an efficient fashion). The pyramid computer is such a machine.

Pyramid: A *pyramid of base size* n combines the advantages of both the tree and the mesh architectures (see Figure 5-19). It can be viewed as a set of processors connected as a 4-ary tree (a tree in which every generic node has four children), where at each level the processors are connected as a 2-dimensional mesh. Alternately, the pyramid can be thought of as a tapering array of meshes, in which each mesh level is connected to the preceding and succeeding levels with 4-ary tree-type connections. Thus, the base level of the pyramid of base size n is a mesh of size n, the next level up is a mesh of size $n/4$, and so on until you reach the single processor at the root. A careful count of the number of processors reveals that a pyramid of base size n contains $(4n - 1)/3$ processors. The root of a pyramid only has links to its four children. Each base processor has links to its four base-level mesh neighbors and an additional link to a parent. In general, a generic processor somewhere in the middle of a pyramid is connected to one parent, four children, and has four mesh-connected neighbors. Therefore, the degree of the pyramid network is nine. The communication diameter of a pyramid of base size n is $\Theta(\log n)$, since a message can be sent from the northwest base processor to the southeast base processor by traversing $2 \log_4 n$ links, which represents a worst-case scenario. (This can be done by sending a piece of data upwards from the base to the root and then downwards from the root to the base.)

Now consider the bisection width of a pyramid of base size n. The reader might picture a plane (a flat geometric object) passing through the pyramid, positioned so that it passes just next to the root and winds up severing connections between the middle two columns of the base. We now need to count the number of links that have been broken. There are $n^{1/2}/2$ at the base, $n^{1/2}/4$ at the next level, and so on up the pyramid, for a total of $\Theta(n^{1/2})$ such links. Consider passing two planes through the root, one that passes between the middle two rows of the base and the other that passes through the middle two columns of the base. This will result in four pyramids, each of base size $n/4$, with roots that were originally the children of the root processor. Therefore, as with the mesh of size n, the bisection width of a pyramid of base size n is $\Theta(n^{1/2})$.

Now consider fundamental semigroup and combination-type operations. Such operations can be performed on a pyramid of base size n in $\Theta(\log n)$ time by using tree-type algorithms, as previously described. However, for algorithms that require extensive data movement (such as moving $\Theta(n)$ data between halves of the pyramid), the mesh lower bound of $\Omega(n^{1/2})$ applies. Therefore, the pyramid combines the advantages of both the tree and mesh architectures without a net asymptotic increase in the number of processors. However, one of the reasons that the pyramid has not been more popular in the commercial marketplace is that laying out a scalable pyramid in hardware is a difficult process.

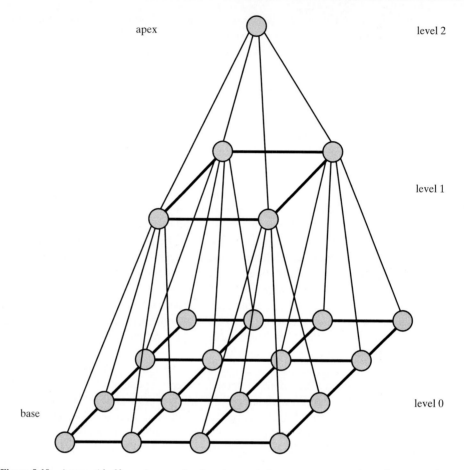

Figure 5-19   A *pyramid of base size n* can be viewed as a set of processors connected as a 4-ary tree, where at each level in the pyramid, the processors at that level are connected as a 2-dimensional mesh. Alternately, it can be thought of as a tapering array of meshes. The root of a pyramid only has links to its four children. Each base processor has links to its four base-level mesh neighbors and an additional link to a parent. In general, a generic processor somewhere in the middle of a pyramid is connected to one parent, four children, and has four mesh-connected neighbors.

Mesh-of-Trees: We now consider another interconnection network that combines the advantages of the tree connections with the mesh connections. However, this architecture does it in a very different way than the pyramid. Essentially, the mesh-of-trees is a standard mesh computer with a tree above every row and a tree above every column, as shown in Figure 5-20. So a *mesh-of-trees of base size n* consists of a mesh of size n at the base with a tree above each of the $n^{1/2}$ columns and a tree above each of the $n^{1/2}$ rows. Notice that these $2n^{1/2}$ trees are completely disjoint except at the base. That is, row tree i and column tree j only

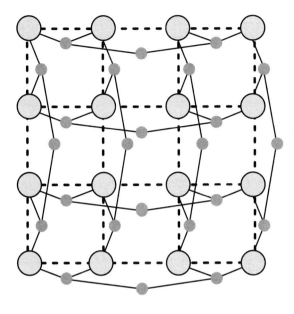

Processing Element in the base

Processing Element in a tree over the base

Figure 5-20   A *mesh-of-trees of base size n* consists of a mesh of size n at the base with a tree above each of the $n^{1/2}$ columns and a tree above each of the $n^{1/2}$ rows. Notice that the trees are completely disjoint except at the base. The mesh-of-trees of base size n has n processors in the base mesh, $2n^{1/2} - 1$ processors in each of the $n^{1/2}$ row trees, and $2n^{1/2} - 1$ processors in each of the $n^{1/2}$ column trees. The communication links corresponding to the mesh connectors are shown by dashed lines, while the communication links between tree processors are shown as solid lines.

have base processor $P_{i,j}$ in common. So the mesh-of-trees of base size n has n processors in the base mesh, $2n^{1/2} - 1$ processors in each of the $n^{1/2}$ row trees, and $2n^{1/2} - 1$ processors in each of the $n^{1/2}$ column trees. Since the n base processors appear both in the row trees and the column trees, the mesh-of-trees has a total of $2n^{1/2}[(2n^{1/2} - 1)] - n = 3n - 2n^{1/2}$ processors. Therefore, as with the pyramid, the number of processors in the entire machine is linear in the number of base processors.

First, as has been our tradition, let's consider the degree of the network. A generic base processor is connected to four mesh neighbors, one parent in a row tree, and one parent in a column tree. Notice that processors along the edge of the mesh have fewer mesh connections, as previously discussed. The root processor of every tree is connected to two children, and interior tree nodes are connected to one parent and two children. Note that leaf processors are mesh processors, so we need not consider them again. Therefore, the degree of the mesh-of-trees of base size n is six.

Next, consider the communication diameter of a mesh-of-trees of base size n. Without loss of generality, assume that base processor $P_{a,b}$ needs to send a piece of information, call it x, to base processor $P_{c,d}$. Notice that processor $P_{a,b}$ can use the tree over row a to send x to base processor $P_{a,d}$ in $O(\log n^{1/2}) = O(\log n)$ time. Now, processor $P_{a,d}$ can use the tree over column d to send x to base processor $P_{c,d}$ in $O(\log n)$ time. Therefore, any two base processors can communicate by exploiting one row tree and one column tree in $O(\log n)$ time.

The bisection width of a mesh-of-trees can be determined by passing a plane through the middle two rows or columns (or both) of the base mesh. The analysis is similar to the pyramid, where the total number of links severed is $\Theta(n^{1/2})$.

Therefore, some of the objective measures of the pyramid and mesh-of-trees are similar. The difference between the two is that in a pyramid, the apex (root of the pyramid) serves as a bottleneck, while for the mesh-of-trees, there is no such bottleneck. In fact, the mesh-of-trees offers more paths between processors. So, one might hope that more efficient algorithms can be designed for the mesh-of-trees than for the pyramid. However, the bisection width tells us that this is not possible for problems that require significant data movement. For example, for problems such as sorting, in which all data on the left half of the base mesh might need to move to the right half, and vice versa, a lower bound of $\Omega(n/n^{1/2}) = \Omega(n^{1/2})$ still holds. One can only hope that problems which require a moderate amount of data movement can be solved faster than on the pyramid.

Let's first consider the problem of computing a semigroup operation on a set $X = [x_1, x_2, \ldots, x_n]$, initially distributed one item per base processor. Within each row (simultaneously), use the row tree to compute the operation over the set of data that resides in the row. Once the result is known in the root of a tree, it can be passed down to all of its leaves (the base processors in the row). In $\Theta(\log n)$ time, every base processor will know the result of applying the semigroup operation to the elements of X that are stored in its row. Next, perform a semigroup operation (simultaneously) on this data within each column by using the tree above each column. Notice that when the root processors of the column trees have the result, they all have the identical final result, which they can again pass back down to the leaf (base) processors. Therefore, after two $\Theta(\log n)$ time tree-based semigroup operations, all processors know the final answer. As with the tree and pyramid, this is a time-optimal algorithm. However, the cost of the algorithm is again $\Theta(n \log n)$, which is $\Theta(\log n)$ from optimal.

Next, we consider a very interesting problem of sorting a reduced amount of data. This problem surfaces quite often in the middle of a wide variety of algorithms. Formally, we are given a unique set of data, $D = [d_1, d_2, \ldots, d_{n^{1/2}}]$, distributed one per processor along the first row of the base mesh in a mesh-of-trees of base size n such that processor $P_{1,i}$ stores d_i. We wish to sort the data so that the i-th largest element in D will be stored in processor $P_{1,i}$. The method we use will be that of counting sort. That is, for each element $d \in D$, we will count the number of elements smaller than d in order to determine the final position of d. In order to use this counting sort, we first create a cross-product of the data so that each pair (d_i, d_j) is stored in some processor, as shown in Figure 5-21. Notice that since the number of elements in D is $n^{1/2}$, we have room in the base mesh to store all $n^{1/2} \times n^{1/2} = n$ such pairs. This cross-product is created as follows (see Figure 5-22). First, use the column trees to broadcast d_j in column j. At the conclusion of this $\Theta(\log n)$ time step, every base proces-

(d_1,d_1) — (d_1,d_2) — (d_1,d_3) — (d_1,d_4)

(d_2,d_1) — (d_2,d_2) — (d_2,d_3) — (d_2,d_4)

(d_3,d_1) — (d_3,d_2) — (d_3,d_3) — (d_3,d_4)

(d_4,d_1) — (d_4,d_2) — (d_4,d_3) — (d_4,d_4)

Figure 5-21 Creating a cross-product of items $<d_1, d_2, d_3, d_4>$. Notice that processor $P_{i,j}$ will store a copy of d_i and d_j. That is, every processor in row i will store a copy of d_i and every processor in column j will store a copy of d_j.

sor $P_{i,j}$ will store a copy of d_j. Now using the row trees in every row i, broadcast item d_i from processor $P_{i,i}$ to all processors in row i. This operation also requires $\Theta(\log n)$ time. Therefore, after a row and column broadcast, every processor $P_{i,j}$ will store a copy of d_j (obtained from the column broadcast) and a copy of d_i (obtained from the row broadcast). At this point, the creation of the cross-product is complete.

Let row i be responsible for determining the rank of element d_i. Simultaneously for every processor $P_{i,j}$, set register *count* to 1 if $d_j < d_i$, and to 0 otherwise. Now use the row trees to sum the count registers in every row. Notice that in every row i, this sum, call it $r(i)$, corresponds to the *rank* of d_i, the number of elements of D that precede d_i. Finally, a column broadcast is used within every column to broadcast d_i from processor $P_{i,r(i)+1}$ to processor $P_{1,r(i)+1}$, completing the procedure.

The time to create the cross-product is $\Theta(\log n)$, as is the time to determine the rank of every entry, and the time to broadcast each entry to its final position. Therefore, the running time of the algorithm is $\Theta(\log n)$, which is worst-case optimal for the mesh-of-trees, due to the $\Theta(\log n)$ communication diameter and the fact that d_1 and $d_{n^{1/2}}$ might need to change places (processors $P_{1,1}$ and $P_{1,n^{1/2}}$ might need to exchange information). The cost of the algorithm is $\Theta(n \log n)$. Notice that the cost is not optimal since $\Theta(n^{1/2})$ items can be sorted in $\Theta(n^{1/2} \log n)$ time on a RAM.

Hypercube: The final network model we consider is the hypercube, as shown in Figure 5-23. The hypercube presents a topology that provides a low communication diameter and a high bisection width. The communication diameter is logarithmic in the number of processors, which allows for fast semigroup and combination-based algorithms. This is the same as for the tree, pyramid, and mesh-of-trees. However, the bisection width of the hypercube is linear in the number of processors, which is a significant improvement over the bisection width for the mesh, pyramid, and mesh-of-trees. Therefore, there is the possibility of moving large amounts of data quite efficiently.

Formally, a *hypercube of size n* consists of n processors indexed by the integers $\{0, 1, \ldots, n - 1\}$, where n is an integral power of 2. Processors A and B are connected *if and only if* their unique $\log_2 n$-bit strings differ in *exactly* one position. So suppose that $n = 8$. Then the processor with binary index 011 is connected to three other processors, namely those with indices 111, 001, and 010.

It is often useful to think of constructing a hypercube in a recursive fashion, as shown in Figure 5-24. A hypercube of size n can be constructed from two hypercubes of size $n/2$,

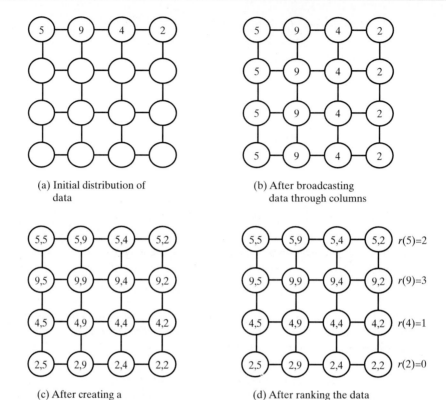

(a) Initial distribution of
data

(b) After broadcasting
data through columns

(c) After creating a
cross-product of data

(d) After ranking the data

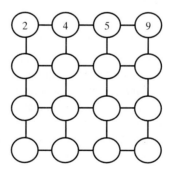

(e) After redistributing data
by rank

Figure 5-22   Sorting a reduced set of data on a mesh-of-trees. (a) The initial distribution of data consists of
a single row of elements. (b) The data after using the column trees to broadcast the data element in every column. (c) The result after using the row trees to broadcast the diagonal elements along every row. At this point,
a cross-product of the initial data exists in the base mesh of the mesh-of-trees. (d) The result of performing
row-rankings of the diagonal element in each row. This step is accomplished by performing a comparison in
the base mesh followed by a semigroup operation of every row tree. (e) The result after performing the final
routing step of the diagonal elements to their proper position according to the rankings.

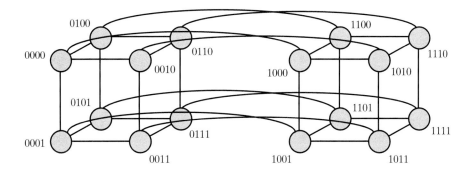

Figure 5-23   A hypercube of size 16 with the processors indexed by the integers {0, 1, . . . , 15}. Pairs of processors are connected *if and only if* their unique $\log_2 16 = 4$ bit strings differ in *exactly* one position.

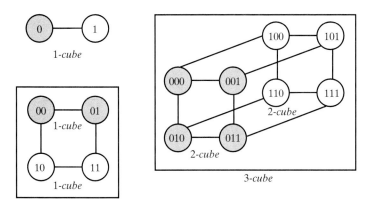

Figure 5-24   Constructing a hypercube of size n from two subcubes each of size $n/2$. First, attach elements of subcube A to elements of subcube B with the same index. Then prepend a 0 to indices of subcube A and prepend a 1 to all indices of subcube B. Subcube A is shaded in all diagrams for ease of presentation.

which we refer to as H_1 and H_2, as follows. Place H_1 and H_2 side by side with every processor labeled according to their $\log_2(n/2)$-bit string. Notice that there are now two copies of every index, one associated with H_1 and one associated with H_2. We need to resolve these conflicts and also to connect H_1 and H_2 in order to form a hypercube of size n. In order to distinguish the labels of H_1 from those of H_2, we will add a leading zero to every index of H_1 and add a leading 1 to every index of H_2. Finally, we need to connect the corresponding nodes of H_1 and H_2. That is, we need to connect those nodes that differ only in their (new) leading bit. This completes our construction of a hypercube of size n.

Based on this construction scheme, the reader should note that the number of communication links affiliated with every processor must increase as the size of the network increases. That is, unlike the mesh, tree, pyramid, and mesh-of-trees, the hypercube is not a fixed degree network. Specifically, notice that a processor in a hypercube of size n is labeled with a unique index of $\log_2 n$ bits and is therefore connected to exactly $\log_2 n$ other processors. So the degree of a hypercube of size n is $\log_2 n$, and unlike the mesh, pyramid, tree, and mesh-of-trees, all nodes of a hypercube are identical with respect to the number of attached communication links.

Next, we consider the communication diameter of a hypercube of size n. Notice that if processor 011 needs to send a piece of information to processor 100, then one option is for the piece of information to traverse systematically the path from $011 \rightarrow 111 \rightarrow 101 \rightarrow 100$. This traversal scheme works from the leftmost bit to the rightmost bit, correcting each bit that differs between the current processor and the destination. Of course, one could "correct" the logarithmic number of bits in any order. The important point is that one can send a message from any processor to any other by visiting a sequence of nodes that *must be connected* (by definition of a hypercube) since they differ in exactly one bit position. Therefore, the communication diameter of a hypercube of size n is $\log_2 n$. However, unlike the tree and pyramid, multiple minimal-length paths traverse $O(\log n)$ communication links between many pairs of processors. This is an appealing property in that the hypercube shows promise of avoiding some of the bottlenecks that occurred in the previously defined network architectures.

Now consider the bisection width. From the construction procedure described near the beginning of this section, it is clear that any two disjoint subcubes of size $n/2$ are connected by exactly $n/2$ communication links. That is, the bisection width of a hypercube of size n is $\Theta(n)$. Therefore, we now have the *possibility* of being able to sort n pieces of data in $\Theta(\log n)$ time, which would be cost-optimal. In fact, in Chapter 4, a bitonic sort algorithm was presented that demonstrated that n pieces of data, initially distributed one piece per processor on a hypercube of size n, can be sorted in $\Theta(\log^2 n)$ time. This result represents a significant improvement over the mesh, tree, pyramid, and mesh-of-trees. Of course, the drawback is that the hypercube is not a fixed interconnection network, which makes it very hard to produce a generic hypercube processor and to lay out the machine so that it is expandable (scalable).

We should note that the hypercube is both node- and edge-symmetric in that nodes can be relabeled so that we can map one index scheme to a new index scheme and preserve connectivity. This is a very nice property and also means that unlike some of the other architectures, there are no special nodes. That is, there are no special root nodes, edge nodes, or leaf nodes, and so forth. And yet, we can often use algorithms designed for other architectures such as meshes or trees, since if we merely ignore the existence of some of a hypercube's interprocessor connections, we may find the remaining connections form a mesh, tree, or other parallel architecture (or in some cases, an "approximation" of another interesting architecture).

In terms of fundamental algorithms on the hypercube, let's consider a semigroup operation. A description of an algorithm to perform such an operation will illustrate a variety of algorithmic techniques for the hypercube. In this description, we will use the term *k-dimensional edges* to refer to a set of communication links in the hypercube that connect processors that differ in the k-th bit position of their indices. Without loss of generality, suppose we want to compute the minimum of $X = [x_0, x_1, \ldots, x_{n-1}]$, where x_i is initially stored in processor P_i (the processor with its binary label equivalent to i base 10). The algorithm we describe makes use of the observation that by ignoring some interprocessor connections, the remainder of the hypercube is a tree.

Consider the simple case of a hypercube of size 16, as shown in Figure 5-25. In the first step, we send entries from all processors with a 1 in the most significant bit to their neighbors that have a 0 in the most significant bit. That is, we use the 1-dimensional edges to pass information. The processors that receive information, compute the minimum of the received value and their element and store this result as a running minimum. In the next step, we send running minima from all processors with a 1 in their next most significant bit and that received data during the previous step, to their neighbors with a 0 in that bit position, using the 2-dimensional edges. The receiving processors again compute the minimum of the value received and the value stored. The third step consists of sending data along the 3-dimensional edges and determining the minima (for processors 0001 and 0000). The final step consists of sending the running minimum along the 4-dimensional edge from processor 0001 to processor 0000, which computes the final result. Therefore, after $\log_2 n = \log_2 16 = 4$ steps, the final result is known in processor P_0 (see Figure 5-26).

If we now wish to distribute the final result to all processors, we can simply reverse the process and in the i-th step, send the final result along $(\log_2 n - i + 1)$-dimensional edges from processors with a 0 in the $(\log_2 n - i + 1)$-th bit to those with a 1 in the $(\log_2 n - i + 1)$-th bit. Again, this takes $\log_2 n = \log_2 16 = 4$ steps. Clearly, a generalization of this algorithm simply requires combining data by cycling through the bits of the indices and sending data appropriately in order to determine the final result. If desired, this result can be distributed to all processors by reversing the communication mechanism just described. Therefore, semigroup, reporting, broadcasting, and general combination-based algorithms can be performed on a hypercube of size n in $\Theta(\log n)$ time.

ADDITIONAL TERMINOLOGY

In this chapter, we have presented an introduction to the models of computation that will be used throughout the book. We have also presented fundamental algorithms for these models so that the reader can appreciate some of the fundamental similarities and differences among these models. We have intentionally avoided using too much terminology. At this point, however, we feel it is reasonable to introduce some terminology that will be found in the scientific literature and used as appropriate throughout the rest of this book.

Flynn's Taxonomy: In 1966, Flynn defined a taxonomy of computer architectures based on the concepts of both instruction stream and data stream. Briefly, an *instruction stream* is defined to be a sequence of instructions performed by the computer, while a *data stream* is defined to be the sequence of data items that are operated on by the instruction stream. Flynn defines the instruction stream as being either single or multiple, and also defines the data stream as being either single or multiple. This leads to four basic categories:

A *single instruction stream, single data stream* (*SISD*) machine consists of a single processor and a single set of data that is operated on by the processor as it carries out the sequential set of instructions. The RAM model is a SISD model, and most serial computers fall into this category, including PCs and workstations. This is the von Neumann model of computing.

A *single instruction stream, multiple data stream* (*SIMD*) machine consists of a set of processors (with local memory), a control unit, and an interconnection network. The control unit stores the program and broadcasts the instructions, one per clock cycle, to all processors simultaneously. All processors execute the same instruction at the same time,

Initial Configuration

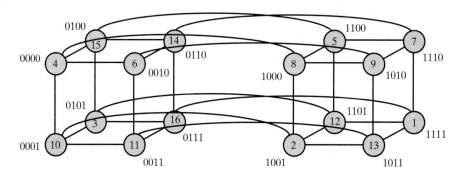

Figure 5-25a Initial distribution of data. Data values are presented inside of the circles that represent the processors. The labels of the processors are presented as binary numbers and are positioned beside the processors in the figure.

Step 1

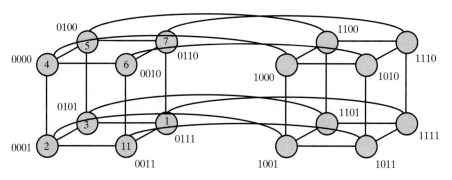

Figure 5-25b Step 1: Transmit-and-compare along 1-dimensional edges (*i.e.*, the processors that differ in the most significant bit).

Step 2

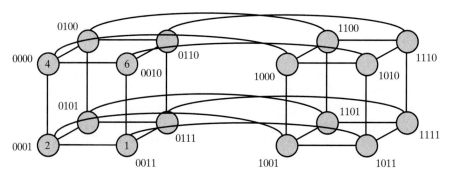

Figure 5-25c Step 2: Transmit-and-compare along 2-dimensional edges.

Step 3

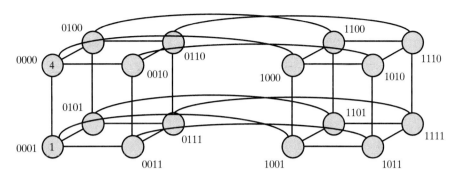

Figure 5-25d Step 3: Transmit-and-compare along 3-dimensional edges.

Step 4

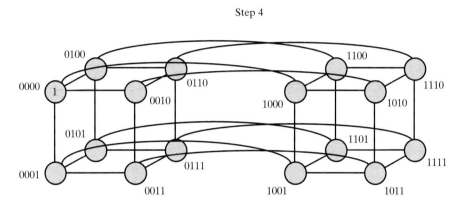

Figure 5-25e Step 4: Transmit-and-compare along 4-dimensional edges. The result is the global minimum being stored in processor 0000.

Figure 5–25 An example of computing a semigroup operation on a hypercube of size 16. For this example, we use minimum as the semigroup operation. In the first step, we send entries from all processors with a 1 in the most significant bit to their neighbors that have a 0 in the most significant bit. That is, elements from the right subcube of size 8 are sent to their neighboring nodes in the left subcube of size 8. The receiving processors compare the two values and keep the minimum. The algorithm continues within the left subcube of size 8. After $\log_2 16 = 4$ transmission-and-compare operations, the minimum value (1) is known in processor 0000.

but on the contents of their own local memory. However, through the use of a mask, processors can be in either an active or inactive state at any time during the execution of a program. Further, these masks can be determined dynamically. Networks of processors, such as the mesh, pyramid, and hypercube, can be built as SIMD machines. In fact, the algorithms that we have described so far for these network models have been described in a SIMD fashion.

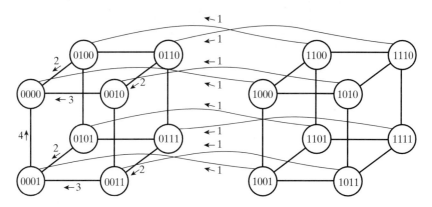

Figure 5-26 Data movement in a semigroup operation on a hypercube. The links of the hypercube of size 16 are labeled based on the step in which they are used to move data in the semigroup operation shown in Figure 5-25.

A *multiple instruction stream, single data stream* (*MISD*) machine is a model that doesn't make much sense. One might argue that systolic arrays fall into that category, but such a discussion is not productive within the context of this book.

A *multiple instruction stream, multiple data stream* (*MIMD*) machine typically consists of a set of processors (with local memory) and an interconnection network. In contrast to the SIMD model, the MIMD model allows each processor to store and execute its own program. However, in reality, in order for multiple processors to cooperate to solve a given problem, these programs must at least occasionally synchronize and cooperate. In fact, it is quite common for an algorithm to be implemented in such a fashion that all processors execute the same program. This is referred to as the *single-program multiple-data* (*SPMD*) programming style. Notice that this style is popular since it is typically infeasible to write a large number of different programs that will be executed simultaneously on different processors. Most commercially available multiprocessor machines fall into the MIMD category, including departmental computers that contain multiple processors and either a physically or virtually "shared memory." Further, most large codes fall into the SPMD category.

Granularity: Machines can also be classified according to their *granularity*. That is, machines can be classified according to the number and/or complexity of their processors. For example, a commercial machine with a dozen or so very fast (and complex) processors would be classified as a *coarse-grained machine*, while a machine with tens of thousands of very simple processors would be classified as a *fine-grained machine*. Most commercially available multiprocessor machines fall into the coarse-grained MIMD category. Of course, such terminology is quite subjective.

We now define some general performance measures. These are common terms that the user is likely to come across while reading the scientific literature.

Throughput: The term *throughput* refers to the number of results produced per unit time. This is a critical measure of the effectiveness of your problem-solving environment, which includes not only your algorithm and computer, but also the quality of any queue-ing system and other operating system features.

Cost/Work: Let $T_{par}(n)$ represent the length of time that an algorithm with n processors takes to complete a problem. Then the *cost* of such a parallel algorithm, as previously discussed, can be defined as $C(n) = n \times T_{par}(n)$. That is, the cost of an algorithm is defined as the number of potential instructions that could be executed during the running time of the algorithm, which is clearly the product of the running time and the number of processors. A related term is *work*, which is typically defined to be the actual number of instructions performed.

Speedup: We define *speedup* as the ratio between the time taken for the *most effi-cient* sequential algorithm to perform a task and the time taken for the *most efficient* par-allel algorithm to perform the same task on a machine with n processors, which we denote as $S_n = T_{seq}/T_{par}(n)$. The term *linear speedup* refers to a speedup of $S_n = n$. In general, lin-ear speedup cannot be achieved since the coordination and cooperation of processors to solve a given problem must take some time. An interesting debate concerns the concept of su-perlinear speedup, or the situation where $S_n > n$.

The question of how superlinear speedup can occur is an interesting one. For example, if you consider asymptotic analysis, then it would seem that a sequential algorithm could al-ways be written to emulate the parallel algorithm with $O(n)$ slowdown, which implies that su-perlinear speedup is not possible. However, assume that the algorithms are chosen in advance. Then several situations could occur. First, in a nondeterministic search-type algorithm, a mul-tiprocessor search might simply get lucky and discover the solution before such an emulation of the algorithm might. That is, the parallel algorithm has an increased probability of getting lucky in certain situations. Second, effects of memory hierarchy might come into play. For ex-ample, a set of very lucky or unlucky cache hits could have a drastic effect on running time.

Efficiency: The *efficiency* of an algorithm is a measure of how well utilized the processors are. That is, efficiency is the ratio of sequential running time and the cost on an n-processor machine, which is equivalent to the ratio between the n-processor speedup and n. So efficiency is given as $E_n = T_{seq}/C(n) = S_n/n$.

Amdahl's Law: When we discuss speedup, we should mention an interesting concept called *Amdahl's Law*. Basically, Amdahl's Law states that the maximum speedup achievable by an n-processor machine is given by $S_n \leq 1/[f + (1 - f)/n]$, where f is the fraction of op-erations in the computation that must be performed sequentially. So, for example, if five per-cent of the operations in a given computation must be performed sequentially, then the speedup can never be greater than 20, *regardless of how many processors are used*. That is, a small number of sequential operations can significantly limit the speedup of an algorithm on a par-allel machine. Fortunately, what Amdahl's Law overlooks is the fact that for many algorithms, the percentage of required sequential operations decreases as the size of the *problem* increases. Further, it is often the case that as one scales up a parallel machine, scientists often want to solve larger and larger problems, and not just the same problems more efficiently. That is, it is common enough to find that for a given machine, a scientist will want to solve the largest problem that fits on that machine (and complain that the machine isn't just a bit bigger so that they could solve the problem they really want to consider).

Scalability: We say that an algorithm is *scalable* if the level of parallelism increases at least linearly with the problem size. We say that an architecture is scalable if the machine continues to yield the same performance per processor as the number of processors increases. In general, scalability is important in that it allows users to solve larger problems in the same amount of time by purchasing a machine with more processors.

CHAPTER NOTES

The emphasis of this chapter is on introducing the reader to a variety of parallel models of computation. A nice, relatively concise presentation is given in "Algorithmic Techniques for Networks of Processors," by R. Miller and Q.F. Stout in the *CRC Handbook of Algorithms and Theory of Computation*, M.J. Atallah, ed. A general text targeted at undergraduates that covers algorithms, models, real machines, and some applications, is *Parallel Computing Theory and Practice* by M.J. Quinn (McGraw-Hill, Inc., New York, 1994). For a book that covers PRAM algorithms at a graduate level, the reader is referred to *An Introduction to Parallel Algorithms*, by J. Já Já (Addison-Wesley, Reading, MA., 1992), while advanced undergraduate students or graduate students interested primarily in mesh and pyramid algorithms might refer to *Parallel Algorithms for Regular Architectures: Meshes and Pyramids* by R. Miller and Q.F. Stout (The MIT Press, Cambridge, MA., 1996). For the reader interested in a text devoted to hypercube algorithms, see *Hypercube Algorithms for Image Processing and Pattern Recognition* by S. Ranka and S. Sahni, (Springer-Verlag, 1990). A comprehensive parallel algorithms book that focuses on models related to those presented in this chapter is *Introduction to Parallel Algorithms and Architectures: Arrays, Trees, Hypercubes* by F.T. Leighton (Morgan Kaufmann Publishers, San Mateo, CA., 1992). While Amdahl's law is discussed or mentioned in most texts on parallel algorithms, we feel it is worth mentioning the original paper, "Validity of the single processor approach to achieving large scale computing capabilities" by G. Amdahl, *AFIPS Conference Proceedings*, Vol. 30, Thompson Books, 1967, pp. 483–485. Similarly, Flynn's taxonomy is a standard in texts devoted to parallel computing. The original articles by Flynn are "Very high-speed computing systems" by M.J. Flynn, *Proceedings of the IEEE*, 54 (12), 1966, pp. 1901–1909, and "Some computer organizations and their effectiveness" by M.J. Flynn, *IEEE Transactions on Computers*, C-21, 1972, pp. 948–960.

EXERCISES

1. Consider the "star-shaped" architecture shown in Figure 5-27, which consists of n processors, labeled from 0 to $n - 1$, where processor P_0 is directly connected to all other processors, but for $i, j > 0$, $i \neq j$, processors P_i and P_j are not directly connected. Explain why this architecture has a "serial bottleneck" at processor P_0. To do this, consider the time required by a fundamental operation such as computing a semigroup operation $\bigotimes_{i=0}^{n-1} x_i$, where x_i is stored in processor P_i. Does the star-shaped configuration seem to be a useful arrangement of processors for parallel computation?

2. Consider an architecture of n processors partitioned into two disjoint subsets, A and B, each with $n/2$ processors. Further, assume that each processor in A is joined to each processor in B, but no pair of processors having both members in A or in B are joined. See Figure 5-28 for an example.

   a) Can fundamental operations be executed on this architecture faster than on the star-shaped architecture described above? For example, devise an efficient parallel algorithm for computing a semigroup operation $\bigotimes_{i=0}^{n-1} x_i$, where x_i is stored in processor P_i, on this architecture, and analyze its running time.

   b) What is the bisection width of this architecture? What does this imply about the practicality of this architecture?

3. Define an X-tree to be a tree machine in which neighboring nodes on a level are connected. That is, each interior node has two additional links, one to each of its left and right neighbors. Nodes on the outer edge of the tree (with the exception of the root) have one additional link, to its neighboring node in its level.

   a) What is the communication diameter of an X-tree? Explain.

   b) What is the bisection width of an X-tree? Explain.

   c) Give a lower bound on sorting for the X-tree. Explain.

4. Suppose that you have constructed a CRCW PRAM algorithm to solve problem A in $O(t(n))$ time. Now when you begin to consider solutions to problem A on a CREW PRAM, what do you already know about an upper bound on the running time to solve this problem on a CREW PRAM? Why?

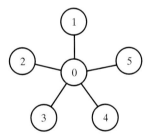

Figure 5-27 A *star-shaped* computer of size 6.

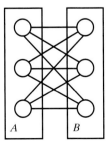

Figure 5-28 An architecture in which n processors are partitioned into two disjoint subsets of $n/2$ processors each.

5. Suppose that you have a CREW PRAM algorithm to solve problem A in $\Theta(t(n))$ time. If you now consider a solution to this problem on an EREW PRAM, how does the CREW PRAM algorithm help you in determining a lower bound on the running time to solve this problem on an EREW PRAM?

6. Give an asymptotically optimal algorithm to sum n values on a 3-dimensional mesh. Discuss the running time and cost of your algorithm. Give a precise definition of your model.

7. Give an efficient algorithm to sum n values on a hypercube.

8. Define a *linear array of size n* with a bus to be a 1-dimensional mesh of size n augmented with a single global bus. Every processor is connected to the bus and in each unit of time one processor can write to the bus and all processors can read from the bus (*i.e.*, the bus is a CREW bus).

   a) Give an efficient algorithm to sum n values, initially distributed one per processor. Discuss the time and cost of your algorithm.

   b) Give an efficient algorithm to compute the parallel prefix of n values, initially distributed one per processor. Discuss the time and cost of your algorithm.

9. Show that a pyramid computer with base size n contains $(4n - 1)/3$ processors. Hint: Let $n = 4^k$ for integer $k \geq 0$, and use mathematical induction on k.

10. Why is it unrealistic to expect to solve an *NP*-complete problem on the PRAM in polylogarithmic time using a polynomial number of processors?

6

Matrix Operations

Matrix Operations

Computational science is an emerging discipline that unites computers and science. It is already being called the third science, complementing *theoretical science* and *laboratory science*. Programs in computational science are widespread at universities and colleges, and are even being introduced into the K–12 curriculum. One of the major focuses of computational science is on the knowledge and techniques required to perform computer simulation. The importance of simulation can be found in "grand challenge" problems in areas such as structural biology, materials science, high-energy physics, economics, fluid dynamics, and global climate change, to name a few. In fact, designers of automobiles and airplanes are beginning to exploit simulation in an effort to reduce the costs of prototypes, to test models, and to provide alternatives to expensive wind tunnels. Computational science is an interdisciplinary subject, uniting computer technology with disciplinary research in biology, chemistry, physics, and other applied and engineering fields. Since operations on matrices are central to computational science, we consider the problems of matrix multiplication and Gaussian elimination on a variety of models of computation.

MATRIX MULTIPLICATION

Suppose a matrix A has p rows and q columns, which we denote as $A_{p,q}$. Given matrices $A_{p,q}$ and $B_{q,r}$, the matrix product of A and B is written informally as $C = A \times B$ and more formally as $C_{p,r} = A_{p,q} \times B_{q,r}$. The element $c_{i,j} \in C_{p,r}$, that is, the element of C in the i-th row and j-th column, for $1 \leq i \leq p$ and $1 \leq j \leq r$, is defined as

$$c_{i,j} = \sum_{k=1}^{q} a_{i,k} b_{k,j}.$$

Notice that the number of columns of A must be the same as the number of rows of B, since each entry of the product corresponds to the dot product of one row of A and one column of B. That is, the (i,j) entry of matrix C is equal to the dot product of the i-th row of A and the j-th column of B, as given in the definition above. In fact, in order to determine the product of A and B, the dot product of every row of A with every column of B is typically computed (see Figure 6-1).

A traditional, sequential dot product of two vectors, each of length q, requires q multiplications and $q - 1$ additions. Therefore, such a sequential operation can be performed in $\Theta(q)$ time. Hence, the $p \times r$ dot products, each of length q, used to perform a traditional matrix multiplication can be computed in a straightforward fashion in $\Theta(prq)$ time on a RAM. Therefore, the total number of operations performed in a brute-force matrix multiplication on a RAM, as described, is $\Theta(prq)$. Such an algorithm follows.

> **Input:** A $p \times q$ matrix A, and a $q \times r$ matrix B.
> **Output:** The matrix product $C_{p,r} = A_{p,q} \times B_{q,r}$.
> For $i = 1$ to p, do   {Loop through rows of A.}
>   For $j = 1$ to r, do   {Loop through columns of B.}
>   {Perform the dot product of a row of A and a column of B.}
> $C(i, j) = 0$
>   For $k = 1$ to q, do
> $C(i, j) = C(i, j) + A(i, k) \times B(k, j)$
>   End For k
>   End For j
> End For i
> End *Matrix Product*

$$\begin{bmatrix} 1 & 2 & 3 & 4 \\ 5 & 6 & 7 & 8 \\ 9 & 10 & 11 & 12 \end{bmatrix} \times \begin{bmatrix} 1 & 0 & 2 & 0 & 4 \\ 0 & 1 & 0 & 2 & 0 \\ 1 & 0 & 2 & 0 & 4 \\ 0 & 1 & 0 & 2 & 0 \end{bmatrix} = \begin{bmatrix} 4 & 6 & 8 & 12 & 16 \\ 12 & 14 & 24 & 28 & 48 \\ 20 & 22 & 40 & 44 & 80 \end{bmatrix}$$
$$A_{3 \times 4} \qquad\qquad\qquad B_{4 \times 5} \qquad\qquad\qquad C_{3 \times 5}$$

Figure 6-1   An example of matrix multiplication. Notice that $c_{2,3}$ is the product of the second row of A (5, 6, 7, 8) and the third column of B (2, 0, 2, 0), which yields $5 \times 2 + 6 \times 0 + 7 \times 2 + 8 \times 0 = 10 + 0 + 14 + 0 = 24$.

We now consider matrix multiplication on a variety of models of computation. For simplicity, we will assume that all matrices are of size $n \times n$.

RAM: A traditional sequential algorithm, as given above, will multiply $A_{n \times n} \times B_{n \times n}$ to produce $C_{n \times n}$ in $\Theta(n^3)$ time. There are better algorithms, however. In fact, due to the importance of matrix multiplication and its relatively large running time, this problem has been the focus of research for many years. In 1968, Strassen presented a divide-and-conquer algorithm to perform matrix multiplication in $O(n^{2.81})$ time. This result was quite surprising, as it had been previously conjectured that $\Omega(n^3)$ operations were required in order to perform matrix multiplication. Due to the importance of this problem, research in this area remains quite active. In fact, recently, algorithms have been presented that run in $o(n^{2.81})$ time. Unfortunately, the details of such algorithms are beyond the scope of this book.

PRAM: Consider the design of an efficient matrix multiplication algorithm for a CR PRAM. Suppose you are given a PRAM with n^3 processors, where each processor has a unique label, (i, j, k), where $1 \leq i, j, k < n$ are integers. (Notice that processors $P_1, \ldots, P_{n^3}$ can be relabeled as $P_{1,1,1}, \ldots, P_{n,n,n}$ in $\Theta(1)$ time.) One can consider this representation as associating processor $P_{i,j,k}$ with $a_{i,k}b_{k,j}$, the k-th product between the i-th row of A and the j-th column of B. Notice that this product is one of the terms that contributes to $c_{i,j}$. So suppose that initially, every processor $P_{i,j,k}$ computes the result of $a_{i,k}b_{k,j}$. After this single step, notice that all $\Theta(n^3)$ multiplications have been performed. All that remains is to compute the summation of each dot product's $\Theta(n)$ terms. This can be done in $\Theta(\log n)$ time by performing $\Theta(n^2)$ independent semigroup operations, where the operator is addition. So in $\Theta(\log n)$ time, processors $P_{i,j,k}, k \in \{1, 2, \ldots, n\}$, can perform a semigroup operation to determine the value of $c_{i,j}$, which can then be written into the appropriate cell in memory in constant time. Therefore, the running time of the algorithm is $\Theta(\log n)$, and the total cost is $\Theta(n^3 \log n)$.

Unfortunately, while efficient, this algorithm is not cost-optimal. Therefore, we can consider trying to reduce the running time by a factor of $\Theta(\log n)$ or the number of processors by a factor of $\Theta(\log n)$. Since reducing the running time is a difficult challenge, let's consider a CR PRAM with $n^3/\log_2 n$ processors. First, let each processor be responsible for a unique set of $\Theta(\log n)$ multiplications. For example, processor P_1 can perform the multiplication operations that processors $P_1, \ldots, P_{\log_2 n}$ performed in the previous algorithm, processor P_2 can perform the multiplication operations that processors $P_{1 + \log_2 n}, \ldots, P_{2 \log_2 n}$ performed in the previous algorithm, and so on. Next, each processor can sum the products it computed above in $\Theta(\log n)$ time. Finally, in $\Theta(\log n)$ time, each of the n^2 values $c_{i,j}$ could be computed by parallel semigroup operations (addition), with each semigroup operation performed by a group of $\Theta(n/\log n)$ of the $\Theta(n^3/\log n)$ processors associated with $c_{i,j}$. The algorithm follows.

PRAM Matrix Product Algorithm using $\Theta(n^3/\log n)$ processors

Input: A $p \times q$ matrix A, and a $q \times r$ matrix B.

Output: The matrix product $C_{p,r} = A_{p,q} \times B_{q,r}$.

To simplify our analysis, we assume $p = q = r = n$.

      For each processor, determine the logarithmic number of products that it is responsible for. That is, logically determine a partition of the triples (i,k,j), $1 \le i \le p$, $1 \le k \le q$, $1 \le j \le r$, so each processor knows the subset of $\Theta(\log n)$ products that it is responsible for.

      In parallel, each processor computes its $\Theta(\log n)$ products $p_{i,j,k} = a_{i,k} b_{k,j}$. This takes $\Theta(\log n)$ time.

      Compute each of the n^2 values $c_{i,j} = \sum_{k=1}^{n} p_{i,k,j}$ by parallel semigroup (addition) operations (as described above). This takes $\Theta(\log n)$ time.

End *Matrix Product*

Therefore, the running time of the algorithm is $\Theta(\log n)$ and the cost of the algorithm is $\Theta(n^3)$, which is optimal when compared to the traditional matrix multiplication algorithm.

Finally, we consider a CR PRAM with n^2 processors. The algorithm is straightforward. Every processor simultaneously computes the result of a distinct entry in matrix C. Notice that every processor implements a traditional sequential algorithm for multiplying a row of A by a column of B (*i.e.*, a dot product). This is done in $\Theta(n)$ time, simultaneously for every row and column. Therefore, the n^2 entries of C are determined in $\Theta(n)$ time with n^2 processors, which results in a cost-optimal, $\Theta(n^3)$ operations algorithm (with respect to the traditional matrix multiplication algorithm).

Mesh: Consider the problem of determining $C = A \times B$ on a mesh computer, where A, B, and C are $n \times n$ matrices. Let's consider the case in which no processor stores more than one initial entry of A. Similarly, we assume that no processor stores more than one initial entry of B. Further, we assume that at the conclusion of the algorithm, no processor stores more than one entry of the product matrix C.

Initially, we will consider a $2n \times 2n$ mesh, where matrix A is stored in the lower-left quadrant, matrix B is stored in the upper-right quadrant, and matrix C will be produced in the lower-right quadrant, as shown in Figure 6-2. Let's consider the operations necessary

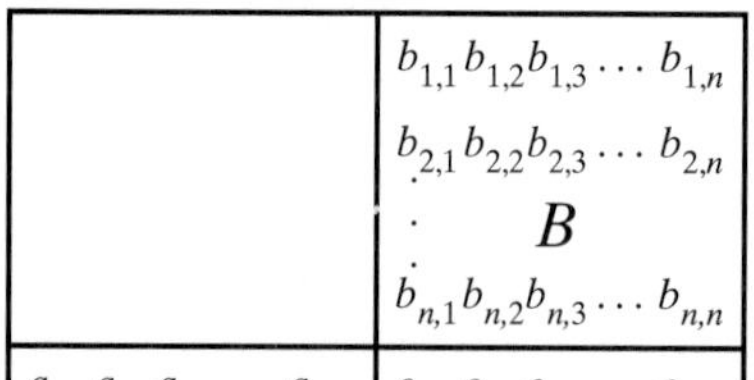

Figure 6-2   Matrix multiplication on a $2n \times 2n$ mesh. Matrix $A_{n \times n}$ initially resides in the lower-left quadrant and matrix $B_{n \times n}$ initially resides in the upper-right quadrant of the mesh. The matrix product $C_{n \times n} = A_{n \times n} \times B_{n \times n}$ is stored in the lower-right quadrant of the mesh.

to compute the entries of C in place. That is, let's design an algorithm so that the entries of A and B flow through the lower-right quadrant of the $2n \times 2n$ mesh and arrive in processors where they can be of use at an appropriate time.

Consider the first step of the algorithm. Notice that if all processors containing an element of the first row of A send their entries to the right and all processors containing an entry of the first column of B simultaneously send their entries down, the processor responsible for $c_{1,1}$ will have entries $a_{1,n}$ and $b_{n,1}$ (see Figures 6-3a and 6-3b). Since $a_{1,n} \times b_{n,1}$ is one of the terms necessary to compute $c_{1,1}$, this partial result can be used to initialize the running sum for $c_{1,1}$ in the northwest processor of the lower-right quadrant. Notice that initially $a_{1,n}$ and $b_{n,1}$ represent the only pair of elements that could meet during the first step and produce a useful result.

Now consider the second step of such an algorithm. Notice that if the elements in row 1 of A move to the right again, and that if the elements of column 1 of B move down again, then $a_{1,n-1}$ and $b_{n-1,1}$ will meet in the processor responsible for $c_{1,1}$ that can add their product to its running sum. In addition, notice that if the second row of A and the second column of B begin to move to the right and down, respectively, during this second time step, the processors responsible for entries $c_{2,1}$ and $c_{1,2}$ could begin to initialize their running sums

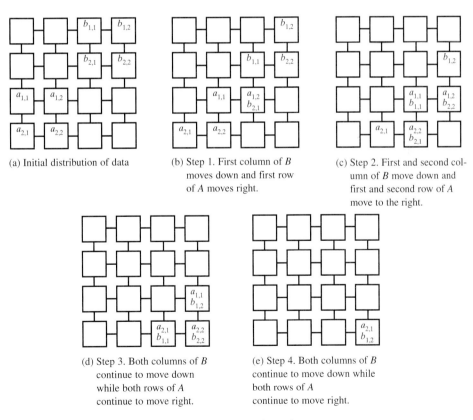

(a) Initial distribution of data

(b) Step 1. First column of B moves down and first row of A moves right.

(c) Step 2. First and second column of B move down and first and second row of A move to the right.

(d) Step 3. Both columns of B continue to move down while both rows of A continue to move right.

(e) Step 4. Both columns of B continue to move down while both rows of A continue to move right.

Figure 6-3 Data flow for matrix multiplication on a $2n \times 2n$ mesh.

with a partial result (see Figure 6-3c). Continuing in this line of thinking, notice that in general this algorithm operates so that at time i, the i-th row of A and the i-th column of B initiate their journeys to the right and down, respectively. Further, at time i, rows $1 \ldots i - 1$ and columns $1 \ldots i - 1$ will continue on their journeys. Eventually, all of the elements of C will be computed.

Now let's consider the running time of the algorithm. Notice that at time n, the last row of A and the last column of B begin their journeys. During every subsequent time step, the last row of A will continue to move one position to the right, and the last column of B will continue to move one position down. At time $3n - 2$, elements $a_{n,1}$ and $b_{1,n}$ will finally meet in the processor responsible for computing $c_{n,n}$, the last element to be computed. Therefore, the running time for this algorithm is $\Theta(n)$. Is this good? Consider the fact that in matrix multiplication, every pair of elements must be combined. Therefore, it is easy to see that this algorithm is asymptotically optimal in terms of running time on a mesh of size $4n^2$. This is due to the $\Theta(n)$ communication diameter of a mesh of size $4n^2$. Now consider the total cost of the algorithm. Since this algorithm runs in $\Theta(n)$ time on a machine with $\Theta(n^2)$ processors, the total cost of the algorithm is $\Theta(n^3)$. Therefore, this algorithm is cost-optimal with respect to the traditional sequential algorithm.

While the previous algorithm is time- and cost-optimal on a $2n \times 2n$ mesh computer, let's consider a matrix multiplication algorithm targeted at an $n \times n$ mesh. Assume that processor $P_{i,j}$ initially stores element $a_{i,j}$ of matrix A and element $b_{i,j}$ of matrix B. When the algorithm terminates, processor $P_{i,j}$ will store element $c_{i,j}$ of the product matrix C. Since we already have an optimal algorithm for a slightly expanded mesh, we consider adapting the algorithm just presented to an $n \times n$ mesh. To do this, we simply use row and column rotations, as we did when we adapted the selection sort algorithm from the input-based linear array to run on the traditional linear array. Specifically, in order to prepare to simulate the previous algorithm, start by performing a row rotation so that processor $P_{i,j}$ contains element $a_{i,(n-j+1)}$ of matrix A, followed by a column rotation so that processor $P_{i,j}$ contains element $b_{(n-i+1),j}$ of matrix B (see Figure 6-4).

At this point, the strategy described in the previous algorithm can be followed while we make the natural adjustments to accommodate the rotations that are necessary to continue moving the data properly, as well as the fact that data is starting in the first row and the first column. The details are left to the reader. Notice that the additional rotations, which can be thought of as serving as a "preprocessing" step, require $\Theta(n)$ time. Therefore, the asymptotic analysis of this algorithm results in the same time- and cost-optimal results as previously discussed.

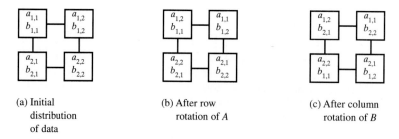

(a) Initial	(b) After row	(c) After column
distribution	rotation of A	rotation of B
of data		

Figure 6-4   Row and column rotations—preprocessing steps for matrix multiplication on an $n \times n$ matrix.

GAUSSIAN ELIMINATION

The technique of *Gaussian elimination* is widely used for such applications as finding the inverse of an $n \times n$ matrix and solving a system of n linear equations in n unknowns. In our presentation, we focus on the problem of finding an inverse matrix.

The $n \times n$ matrix I_n, called the *identity matrix*, is the matrix in which the entry in row i and column j is

$$1 \text{ if } i = j;$$

$$0 \text{ if } i \neq j.$$

It is well known that for $n \times n$ matrix A, we have $A \times I_n = A$ and $I_n \times A = A$. We say an $n \times n$ matrix A is *invertible* (or *nonsingular*) if there is an $n \times n$ matrix B such that $A \times B = B \times A = I_n$. If such a matrix B exists, it is the *inverse* of A, and we write $B = A^{-1}$.

Given an $n \times n$ matrix A, each of the following is said to be an *elementary row operation*.

- Interchange distinct rows of A (see Figure 6-5).
- Multiply (or divide) a row of A by a nonzero constant. That is, for some $c \neq 0$, replace each element $a_{i,j}$ of row i by $ca_{i,j}$ (see Figure 6-6).
- Add (or subtract) a constant multiple of row i to (a different) row j. That is, for some constant c, replace each element $a_{j,k}$ of row j by $a_{j,k} + ca_{i,k}$ (see Figure 6-7).

It is well known that if a sequence σ of elementary row operations applied to an $n \times n$ matrix A transforms A into I_n, then the same sequence σ of elementary row operations applied to I_n transforms I_n into A^{-1}. Thus, we can implement an algorithm to find A^{-1} by finding a sequence σ of elementary row operations that transforms the "augmented matrix" $[A|I_n]$ to $[I_n|A^{-1}]$.

$$
\begin{bmatrix} 5 & 0 & 6 & -2 \\ 0 & -2 & 4 & 5 \\ 1 & 1 & -3 & 7 \\ 2 & -4 & 9 & 15 \end{bmatrix} \rightarrow \begin{bmatrix} 1 & 1 & -3 & 7 \\ 0 & -2 & 4 & 5 \\ 5 & 0 & 6 & -2 \\ 2 & -4 & 9 & 15 \end{bmatrix}
$$

Figure 6-5   Interchange of row_1 and row_3.

$$
\begin{bmatrix} 5 & 0 & 6 & -2 \\ 0 & -2 & 4 & 5 \\ 1 & 1 & -3 & 7 \\ 2 & -4 & 9 & 15 \end{bmatrix} \rightarrow \begin{bmatrix} 1 & 0 & 1.2 & -0.4 \\ 0 & -2 & 4 & 5 \\ 1 & 1 & -3 & 7 \\ 2 & -4 & 9 & 15 \end{bmatrix}
$$

Figure 6-6   Replace row_1 by $0.2 \times row_1$.

$$
\begin{bmatrix} 1 & 6 & -8 \\ -5 & 20 & 10 \\ 3 & 8 & 15 \end{bmatrix} \rightarrow \begin{bmatrix} 1 & 6 & -8 \\ 0 & 50 & -30 \\ 3 & 8 & 15 \end{bmatrix}
$$

Figure 6-7   Replace row_2 by $row_2 + 5 \times row_1$.

Consider an example. Let

$$A = \begin{bmatrix} 5 & -3 & 2 \\ -3 & 2 & -1 \\ -3 & 2 & -2 \end{bmatrix}.$$

We can find A^{-1} as follows. Start with the augmented matrix

$$[A|I_3] = \left[\begin{array}{ccc|ccc} 5 & -3 & 2 & 1 & 0 & 0 \\ -3 & 2 & -1 & 0 & 1 & 0 \\ -3 & 2 & -2 & 0 & 0 & 1 \end{array}\right].$$

The first phase of our procedure is the "Gaussian elimination" phase, in which, one column at a time from left to right, we perform elementary row operations to create entries of 1 along the *diagonal* of A and 0s below the diagonal. That is, after Gaussian elimination on $A_{n \times n}$, all $a_{i,i} = 1$, $1 \le i \le n$, and all $a_{i,j} = 0$, $1 \le j < i \le n$. Follow these steps:

1. Divide row 1 by 5 to obtain

$$\left[\begin{array}{ccc|ccc} 1 & -0.6 & 0.4 & 0.2 & 0 & 0 \\ -3 & 2 & -1 & 0 & 1 & 0 \\ -3 & 2 & -2 & 0 & 0 & 1 \end{array}\right].$$

2. Add 3 times row 1 to row 2, and 3 times row 1 to row 3, to obtain

$$\left[\begin{array}{ccc|ccc} 1 & -0.6 & 0.4 & 0.2 & 0 & 0 \\ 0 & 0.2 & 0.2 & 0.6 & 1 & 0 \\ 0 & 0.2 & -0.8 & 0.6 & 0 & 1 \end{array}\right].$$

Notice column 1 now has the desired form. We proceed with Gaussian elimination steps on column 2.

3. Divide row 2 by 0.2 to obtain

$$\left[\begin{array}{ccc|ccc} 1 & -0.6 & 0.4 & 0.2 & 0 & 0 \\ 0 & 1 & 1 & 3 & 5 & 0 \\ 0 & 0.2 & -0.8 & 0.6 & 0 & 1 \end{array}\right].$$

4. Subtract 0.2 times row 2 from row 3 to obtain

$$\left[\begin{array}{ccc|ccc} 1 & -0.6 & 0.4 & 0.2 & 0 & 0 \\ 0 & 1 & 1 & 3 & 5 & 0 \\ 0 & 0 & -1 & 0 & -1 & 1 \end{array}\right].$$

Note column 2 now has the desired form.

5. Divide row 3 by -1 to obtain

$$\left[\begin{array}{ccc|ccc} 1 & -0.6 & 0.4 & 0.2 & 0 & 0 \\ 0 & 1 & 1 & 3 & 5 & 0 \\ 0 & 0 & 1 & 0 & 1 & -1 \end{array}\right].$$

This completes the Gaussian elimination phase of the procedure.

Now we proceed with the "back substitution" phase, in which, for one column at a time from right to left, we use elementary row operations to eliminate nonzero entries above the diagonal. In a sense, this is more Gaussian elimination, as we use similar techniques for a similar purpose. We proceed as follows:

1. Subtract 0.4 times row 3 from row 1, and 1 times row 3 from row 2, to obtain

$$\begin{bmatrix} 1 & -0.6 & 0 & | & 0.2 & -0.4 & 0.4 \\ 0 & 1 & 0 & | & 3 & 4 & 1 \\ 0 & 0 & 1 & | & 0 & 1 & -1 \end{bmatrix}.$$

2. Add 0.6 times row 2 to row 1, to obtain

$$\begin{bmatrix} 1 & 0 & 0 & | & 2 & 2 & 1 \\ 0 & 1 & 0 & | & 3 & 4 & 1 \\ 0 & 0 & 1 & | & 0 & 1 & -1 \end{bmatrix}.$$

Since the left side of the augmented matrix is now I_3, the right side is the desired inverse:

$$A^{-1} = \begin{bmatrix} 2 & 2 & 1 \\ 3 & 4 & 1 \\ 0 & 1 & -1 \end{bmatrix}.$$

This can be verified easily by showing that the products $A \times A^{-1}$ and $A^{-1} \times A$ both coincide with I_3.

The example given above illustrates our general algorithm for finding the inverse of an $n \times n$ matrix A. In the algorithm presented below, we assume that array $A[1 \ldots n, 1 \ldots n]$ is used to represent the matrix we wish to invert, and the matrix $I[1 \ldots n, 1 \ldots n]$ is initialized to represent the $n \times n$ identity matrix. Here we demonstrate a procedure for either finding the inverse of A or determining that such an inverse does not exist:

1. {Gaussian elimination phase: use elementary operations to transform *A* into an upper triangular matrix, *i.e.*, a matrix in which every diagonal entry has value 1 and every entry below the diagonal has value 0.}

   For $i = 1$ to n, do

   ■ If $A[i,i] = 0$ and $A[m,i] = 0$ for all $m > i$, conclude that A^{-1} does not exist and halt the algorithm.

   ■ If $A[i,i] = 0$ and $A[m,i] \neq 0$ for some smallest $m > i$, interchange rows i and m in the array A and in the array I.

   ■ Now we assume $A[i,i] \neq 0$. Divide row i of A and row I of I by $A[i,i]$. That is, let $scale = A[i,i]$ and then for $j = 1$ to n, set $A[i,j] \leftarrow A[i,j] \,/\, scale$ (actually, it suffices to do this for $j = i$ to n, since the Gaussian elimination has caused $A[i,j] = 0$ for $j < i$). Similarly, for $j = 1$ to n, set $I[i,j] \leftarrow I[i,j] / scale$. Note we now have $A[k,k] = 1$ for $k \leq i$, and $A[m,j] = 0$ if $j < i$ and $j < m$.

- Now we have $A[i,i] = 1$. If $i < n$, then for $r > i$, subtract $A[r,i]$ times row i from row j in both the arrays A and I (this zeroes out the entries in A of column i below the diagonal without destroying the 0s below the diagonal in columns further to the left). That is,

If $i < n$, then
    For $row = i + 1$ to n
        $factor \leftarrow A[row,i]$
        For $col = 1$ to n
            $A[row,col] \leftarrow A[row,col] - factor \times A[i,col]$
            $I[row,col] \leftarrow I[row,col] - factor \times I[i,col]$
        End for col
    End for row
End If
    {Note we now have $A[k,k] = 1$ for $k \leq i$, and $A[m,j] = 0$ if $j \leq i$ and $j < m$.}
End for i

2. {Back substitution phase: eliminate the nonzero entries above the diagonal of A.}

For $elim = n$ downto 2
    For $row = elim - 1$ downto 1
        $factor \leftarrow A[row,elim]$
        For $col = 1$ to n
            $A[row,col] \leftarrow A[row,col] - factor \times A[elim,col]$
            $I[row,col] \leftarrow I[row,col] - factor \times I[elim,col]$
        End for col
    End for row
End for $elim$

We now discuss the analysis of Gaussian elimination on sequential and parallel models of computation.

RAM: A straightforward implementation of the algorithm given above on a RAM requires $\Theta(n^3)$ time in the worst case, when the matrix inverse exists and is determined. The best case running time is $\Theta(n)$, when it is determined by examining the first column that an inverse does not exist.

Parallel models: We must be careful. For example, it is easy to see how some of our inner loops may be parallelized, but some of our outer loops seem inherently sequential. Thus, on a PRAM it is easy to see how to obtain significant speedup over the RAM, but perhaps not how to obtain optimal performance. Further, on distributed memory models such as the mesh, some of the advantages of parallelism may seem negated by delays needed to broadcast key data values throughout rows or columns of the mesh. Below, we discuss how the basic algorithm presented above can be implemented efficiently on various parallel models.

PRAM of n^2 processors: Let's assume we are using a PRAM with the EW property. Then each decision on whether or not to halt as described in the algorithm can be performed by a semigroup operation in $\Theta(\log n)$ time. Assuming the decision is not to halt, a row interchange can be done in $\Theta(1)$ time. Scalar multiplication or division of a row can be done on a CR PRAM in $\Theta(1)$ time; an ER PRAM requires $\Theta(\log n)$ time, since a broadcast of the scalar to all processors associated with a row is required. Notice that the row subtraction of the last step of the Gaussian elimination phase can be done in parallel; that is, the outer For j loop may be parallelized as there is no sequential dependence between the rows in its operations and the inner For k loop parallelizes. As in the scalar multiplication step, the outer For j loop executes its operations in $\Theta(1)$ time on a CR PRAM and in $\Theta(\log n)$ time on an ER PRAM. Thus, a straightforward implementation of the Gaussian elimination phase requires $\Theta(n \log n)$ time on a PRAM (CR or ER).

For the back substitution phase, we can similarly parallelize the inner and the intermediate-nested loop to conclude this phase, which requires $\Theta(n)$ time on a CR PRAM and $\Theta(n \log n)$ time on an ER PRAM. Thus, a straightforward implementation of this algorithm requires $\Theta(n \log n)$ time on an EW PRAM. The total cost is $\Theta(n^3 \log n)$. Note that relative to the cost of our RAM implementation, the PRAM implementation of Gaussian elimination to invert a matrix is not optimal. We leave as an exercise the question of obtaining an optimal implementation of the algorithm on a PRAM.

Mesh with n^2 processors: As usual, we assume entries of the arrays A and I are distributed among the processors of the mesh so that the processor $P_{i,j}$ in row i and column j of the mesh contains both $A[i,j]$ and $I[i,j]$.

Several of the steps of our general algorithm require communication of data across a row or column of the mesh. For example, scalar multiplication of a row requires communication of the scalar across the row. If every processor in the row waits for this communication to finish, the scalar multiplication step would take $\Theta(n)$ time. It's easy to see how this would yield a running time of $\Theta(n^2)$, which is not optimal, since the total cost is then $\Theta(n^2 \times n^2) = \Theta(n^4)$.

We obtain better mesh performance by *pipelining* and *pivoting*. Notice the following is true of each of the steps of the inner loops of our algorithm. Once a processor has the data it needs to operate upon, its participation in the current step requires $\Theta(1)$ additional time, after which the processor can proceed to its participation in the next step of the algorithm regardless of whether other processors have finished their work for the current step (thus, the instructions are pipelined). Therefore, if we could be sure that no processor experiences a total of more than $O(n)$ time waiting for data to reach it, it would follow that the algorithm requires $\Theta(n)$ time ($O(n)$ time for waits and $\Theta(n)$ time for the "active" execution of instructions in each processor).

However, there is one place where the algorithm as described above could have processors that experience $\omega(1)$ delays of $O(n)$ time apiece to receive data. That is, the step that calls conditionally for exchanging a row of A having a 0 diagonal entry with a row below it having a nonzero entry in the same column. In order to ensure this situation does not cost us too much time via frequent occurrence, we modify our algorithm via the technique of *pivoting*, which we describe now. If processor $P_{i,i}$ detects that $A[i,i] = 0$, then $P_{i,i}$ sends a message down column i to search for the first nonzero $A[j,i]$ with $j > i$. If such a j is found, row j is called the *pivot row* and plays the role similar to that otherwise played by row i: Row j is used for Gaussian elimination in the rows below it (creating 0 entries in the i-th column of each such row); rows between row i and row j (if any) have entries of 0 in column i, hence require no row combination at this stage; and row j "bubbles up" to row i in a wave-like fashion (using both vertical and horizontal pipelining), while row i bubbles down to row j, executing the row interchange.

On the other hand, if no such j is found, processor $P_{i,n}$ broadcasts a message to halt throughout the mesh.

In this fashion, we pipeline the row interchange step with the following steps of the algorithm in order to ensure that each processor spends $O(n)$ time awaiting data. It follows, as described above, that we can compute the inverse of an $n \times n$ matrix or decide, when appropriate, that it is not invertible, through Gaussian elimination on an $n \times n$ mesh in $\Theta(n)$ time, which is optimal relative to our RAM implementation.

Roundoff error: It should be noted that the Gaussian elimination algorithm is sensitive to roundoff error. Roundoff error occurs whenever an exact calculation requires more decimal places (or binary bits) than are actually used for storage of the result. Occasionally, roundoff error can cause an incorrect conclusion with respect to whether or not the input matrix has an inverse, or with respect to which row should be the pivot row. Such a situation could be caused by an entry that should be 0, computed as having a small nonzero absolute value. Also, a roundoff error in a small nonzero entry could have a powerfully distorting effect if the entry becomes a pivot element, since the pivot row is divided by the pivot element and combined with other rows.

It is tempting to think such problems could be corrected by selecting a small positive number ϵ and establishing a rule that whenever a step of the algorithm computes an entry with absolute value less than ϵ, the value of the entry is set to 0. However, such an approach can create other problems since a nonzero entry in the matrix with an absolute value less than ϵ may be correct.

Measures used to prevent major errors due to roundoff errors in Gaussian elimination are beyond the scope of this book. However, a crude test of the accuracy of the matrix B computed as the inverse of A is to determine the matrix products $A \times B$ and $B \times A$. If all entries of both products are sufficiently close to the respective entries of the identity matrix I_n to which they correspond, then B is likely a good approximation of A^{-1}.

CHAPTER NOTES

A traditional sequential algorithm to multiply $A_{n \times n} \times B_{n \times n}$ runs in $\Theta(n^3)$ time. However, in 1968, the paper "Gaussian elimination is not optimal," by V. Strassen, *Numerische Mathematik* 14(3), 1969, pp. 354–356, showed that a divide-and-conquer algorithm could be exploited to perform matrix multiplication in $O(n^{2.81})$ time. The mesh matrix algorithm presented in this chapter is derived from the one presented in *Parallel Algorithms for Regular Architectures* by R. Miller and Q.F. Stout (The MIT Press, Cambridge, 1996). Our algorithm for Gaussian elimination is traditional. Its presentation is similar to that found in *Parallel Algorithms for Regular Architectures*.

Two additional books that concentrate on algorithms for problems in computational science are G.S. Almasi and A. Gottlieb's *Highly Parallel Computing* (The Benjamin/Cummings Publishing Company, New York, 1994) and G.W. Stout's *High Performance Computing* (Addison-Wesley Publishing Company, New York, 1995).

EXERCISES

1. The PRAM algorithms presented in this chapter for matrix multiplication are simpler under the assumption of the CR property. Why? In other words, in what step or steps of our algorithms is there a computational advantage in assuming the CR property as opposed to the ER property?

2. Give an algorithm for a CR PRAM with n processors that solves the matrix multiplication problem in $\Theta(n^2)$ time.

3. In this chapter, we present a mesh algorithm for computing the product of two $n \times n$ matrices on an $n \times n$ mesh. A somewhat different algorithm for an $n \times n$ mesh can be given, in which we more closely simulate the algorithm given above for a $2n \times 2n$ mesh. If we compress matrices A and B into $n/2 \times n/2$ submeshes, it becomes easy to simulate the $2n \times 2n$ mesh algorithm given in this chapter.

   a) Give an algorithm that runs in $\Theta(n)$ time to compress the matrix A, where A is initially stored so that $a_{i,j}$ is in processor $P_{i,j}$, $1 \leq i \leq n$, $1 \leq j \leq n$. At the end of the compression, A should be stored so that processor $P_{i,j}$, $1 \leq i \leq n/2$, $1 \leq j \leq n/2$, stores $a_{k,m}$, for $k \in \{2i - 1, 2i\}$, $m \in \{2j - 1, 2j\}$. Show that your algorithm is correct.

   b) Give an algorithm that runs in $\Theta(n)$ time to inflate the matrix C, where the initial storage of the matrix is such that processor $P_{i,j}$, $n/2 < i \leq n$, $n/2 < j \leq n$, contains $c_{k,m}$, for $k \in \{2i - n - 1, 2i - n\}$, $m \in \{2j - n - 1, 2j - n\}$. At the end of the inflation, processor $P_{i,j}$ should store $c_{i,j}$ for $1 \leq i \leq n$, $1 \leq j \leq n$. Show that your algorithm is correct.

4. Show how our algorithm for Gaussian elimination to invert an $n \times n$ matrix can be implemented on a PRAM of $n^2/\log n$ processors in $\Theta(n \log n)$ time.

5. Show how the array changes (as determined by pipelining, pivoting, and replacement computations) via our matrix inversion algorithm as implemented on a 3×3 mesh for the matrix

$$A = \begin{bmatrix} 0 & 2 & 5 \\ 4 & -1 & 1 \\ -8 & 2 & 1 \end{bmatrix}.$$

That is, you should show the appearance of A at each time step, in which a processor performs any of the following operations:

■ Send a unit of data to an adjacent processor (if necessary, after a $\Theta(1)$ time decision).

■ Receive a unit of data from an adjacent processor (if necessary, after a $\Theta(1)$ time decision).

■ Calculate in $\Theta(1)$ time and store a new value of its entry of A (if necessary, after a $\Theta(1)$ time decision).

7

Parallel Prefix

Parallel Prefix

The focus of this chapter is on efficient algorithms for performing the parallel prefix computation. Parallel prefix is a powerful operation that can be used to sum elements, find the minimum or maximum of a set of data, broadcast values, compress (or compact) data, and so forth. We will find many uses for the parallel prefix operation as we go through the more advanced chapters of this book. In fact, parallel prefix is such an important operation that it has been implemented at the lowest levels on many machines and is typically available to the user as a library call.

Parallel Prefix: First, we provide a definition of parallel prefix. Let $X = \{x_1, x_2, \ldots, x_n\}$ be a set of elements contained in a set Y. Let $\otimes$ be a *binary*, *associative* operator that is *closed* with respect to Y. The term *binary* refers to the fact that the operator $\otimes$ takes two operands, say x_1 and x_2, as input. The term *closed* refers to the fact that the result of $x_1 \otimes x_2$ is a member of Y. The term *associative* refers to the fact that the operator $\otimes$ obeys the relation $(x_i \otimes x_j) \otimes x_k = x_i \otimes (x_j \otimes x_k)$. (The reader should note that we *do not* require $\otimes$ to be *commutative*. That is, we do *not* require $x_i \otimes x_j = x_j \otimes x_i$ to be true.)

The result of $x_1 \otimes x_2 \otimes \ldots \otimes x_k$ is referred to as the *k*-th prefix. The computation of all *n* prefixes, $x_1, x_1 \otimes x_2, x_1 \otimes x_2 \otimes x_3, \ldots, x_1 \otimes \ldots \otimes x_n$, is referred to as the *parallel prefix computation*. Another common term for this operation is *scan*. Since parallel prefix can be performed quite simply on a sequential machine by making a single pass through the data, it is also sometimes referred to as a *sweep* operation (an operation that can be performed by *sweeping* through the data).

The operator $\otimes$ is typically a unit-time operator; that is, an operator that requires $\Theta(1)$ time to perform. Sample operators include addition ($+$), multiplication ($\times$), MIN, MAX, AND, OR, and XOR.

Lower Bound: The number of operations required to perform a complete parallel prefix is $\Omega(n)$, since the *n*-th prefix involves operating on *n* values.

RAM Algorithm: Let's consider a straightforward sequential algorithm for computing the *n* prefixes $p_1, p_2, \ldots, p_n$, where $p_1 = x_1$, and $p_{i+1} = p_i \otimes x_{i+1}$, for $i \in \{1, 2, \ldots, n-1\}$. The algorithm follows.

$p_1 = x_1$; {This is the constant time assignment.}
for $i = 1$ to $n-1$, do {This is the linear scan through the elements.}
    $p_{i+1} = p_i \otimes x_{i+1}$ {This is the constant time operation.}

Since the running time of the sequential parallel prefix algorithm is dominated by the work done within the loop, it is easy to see that this algorithm runs in $\Theta(n)$ time. Further, this algorithm is optimal, to within a constant factor, since $\Omega(n)$ time is required to solve this problem (see Figures 7-1 and 7-2).

Parallel Algorithms: When we consider parallel models of computation, we will assume that the data is initially stored in a contiguous fashion. Thus, we assume that data is stored in contiguous memory locations in the shared memory of a PRAM or in contiguous processors (typically one per processor) on a distributed memory machine. Note that this situation is analogous to the one just discussed for the RAM in that we assume the input is an *array* of data.

Parallel Prefix on the PRAM: The first parallel model of computation we consider is the PRAM. In this section, we will use the term *segment* to refer to a nonempty subset of consecutively indexed entries of an array. We denote a segment covering entries i through j, $i \le j$, as $S_{i,j}$. Using this terminology, we can say that the parallel prefix problem requires the computation of prefix values for all n segments, $S_{1,1}, S_{1,2}, \ldots, S_{1,n}$.

The first algorithm we present is fairly naive. Given an input set of data, $X = \{x_1, \ldots, x_n\}$, and a set of n processors, $P_1, \ldots, P_n$, let processor P_i be associated with data item x_i. The

X	P
4	4
3	7
6	13
2	15
1	16
5	21

Figure 7-1   An example of parallel prefix on a set X of six items. The operation $\otimes$ is addition. The resulting prefix sums are given in array P.

X	P
4	4
3	3
6	3
2	2
1	1
5	1

Figure 7-2   An example of parallel prefix on a set X of six items. The operation $\otimes$ is minimum. The resulting prefixes are given in array P.

algorithm operates by recursive-halving, that is, by combining pairs of elements, then pairs of pairs, and so forth. So, for example, $S_{1,9}$ is computed, in sequence, as x_9, then $x_8 \otimes x_9$, then $x_6 \otimes x_7 \otimes x_8 \otimes x_9$, then $x_2 \otimes x_3 \otimes x_4 \otimes x_5 \otimes x_6 \otimes x_7 \otimes x_8 \otimes x_9$, and finally as $x_1 \otimes x_2 \otimes x_3 \otimes x_4 \otimes x_5 \otimes x_6 \otimes x_7 \otimes x_8 \otimes x_9$. That is, initially, it combines the pair x_8 and x_9. In the next step, it combines the $x_8 \otimes x_9$ pair with the $x_6 \otimes x_7$ pair. In the third step, it combines prefixes of four items, and so on. Let's consider another example. First, we will denote $x_i \otimes \ldots \otimes x_j$ as $[x_i - x_j]$. Now consider the order of computation for $S_{1,19}$. The computation sequence consists of x_{19}, then $[x_{18} - x_{19}]$, then $[x_{16} - x_{19}]$, then $[x_{12} - x_{19}]$, then $[x_4 - x_{19}]$, and then finally $[x_1 - x_{19}]$. The algorithm follows (see the example shown in Figure 7-3.)

> For $i = 1$ to n, do in parallel
>> $p_i . prefix = x_i;$
>> $p_i . first\_in\_segment = i;$
> End For

> For $i = 2$ to n, do in parallel
> {Compute the i-th prefix by repeated doubling of the length of the segment over
>   which it is computed.}
>> While $p_i . first\_in\_segment > 1$ do
>>> $j = p_i . first\_in\_segment - 1;$
>>> $p_i . prefix = p_j . prefix \otimes p_i . prefix;$
>>> $p_i . first\_in\_segment = p_j . first\_in\_segment;$
>> End While
> End For

Due to the recursive doubling nature of the algorithm, the running time is $\Theta(\log n)$. The reader is advised to go through the algorithm carefully with an example. Notice that in every iteration of the algorithm, the number of terms in every incomplete prefix will double. In fact, with a little work, one can determine that the i-th prefix will be complete after $\lceil \log_2 i \rceil$ iterations.

We now consider a version of parallel prefix with the same time and processor bounds, but with different algorithmic characteristics. The principal of this algorithm is similar to that of the combine operation in MergeSort. Initially, we "compute" single prefix values

$n = 11; \lceil \log_2 11 \rceil = 4; \otimes$ is addition										
Initial Values	1	2	3	4	5	6	7	8	9	10	11
Step 1	1	3	5	7	9	11	13	15	17	19	21
Step 2	1	3	6	10	14	18	22	26	30	34	38
Step 3	1	3	6	10	15	21	28	36	44	52	60
Step 4	1	3	6	10	15	21	28	36	45	55	66

Figure 7-3 A recursive doubling algorithm to compute the parallel prefix of 11 values on a PRAM in which each processor is responsible for one data item. The algorithm requires $\lceil \log_2 11 \rceil = 4$ parallel steps.

$\langle x_1, x_2, \ldots, x_n \rangle$. In the next step, we combine the single prefix values to determine prefix values of pairs, resulting in the determination of $\langle [x_1 - x_2], [x_3 - x_4], \ldots, [x_{n-1} - x_n] \rangle$. Next, we combine pairs of prefix values in order to determine prefix values of pairs of pairs, which results in the determination of $\langle [x_1 - x_4], [x_5 - x_8], \ldots, [x_{n-3} - x_n] \rangle$, and so forth. The algorithm continues for $\lceil \log_2 n \rceil$ iterations, at which point all prefix values have been determined for certain segments that have lengths that are powers of 2 or that end at x_n. See Figure 7-4 for an example.

In an additional $\Theta(\log n)$ time, in parallel each processor P_i can build up the prefix $[x_1 - x_i]$ by a process that mimics the construction of the value i as a string of binary bits, from prefix values computed in previous steps.

Notice that the cost of either algorithm, which is a product of the running time and number of available processors, is $\Theta(n \log n)$. Unfortunately, this is not optimal since we know from the running time of the RAM algorithm that this problem can be solved with $\Theta(n)$ operations.

Now let's consider options for developing a time- and cost-optimal PRAM algorithm for performing a parallel prefix. With respect to the algorithm just introduced, we can either try to reduce the running time from $\Theta(\log n)$ to $\Theta(1)$, which is unlikely, or reduce the number of processors from n to $\Theta(n / \log n)$ while retaining the $\Theta(\log n)$ running time. The latter approach is the one we will take. This is similar to the approach we took earlier in the book when we introduced a time- and cost-optimal PRAM algorithm for computing a semigroup operation. That is, we let each processor assume responsibility for a logarithmic number of data items. Initially, each processor sequentially computes the parallel prefix over its set of $\Theta(\log n)$ items. A global prefix is then computed over these $\Theta(n / \log n)$ final, local prefix results. Finally, each processor uses the global prefix associated with the previous processor to update each of its $\Theta(\log n)$ prefix values. The algorithm follows (see the example shown in Figure 7-5).

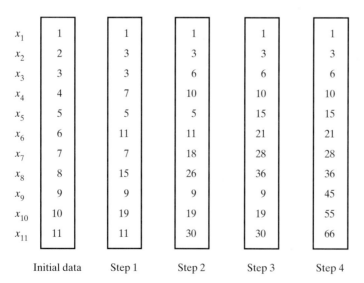

	Initial data	Step 1	Step 2	Step 3	Step 4
x_1	1	1	1	1	1
x_2	2	3	3	3	3
x_3	3	3	6	6	6
x_4	4	7	10	10	10
x_5	5	5	5	15	15
x_6	6	11	11	21	21
x_7	7	7	18	28	28
x_8	8	15	26	36	36
x_9	9	9	9	9	45
x_{10}	10	19	19	19	55
x_{11}	11	11	30	30	66

Figure 7-4 An example of computing parallel prefix by continually combining results of disjoint pairs of items. The operation $\otimes$ used in this example is addition. Notice that the algorithm requires $\lceil \log_2 11 \rceil + 1 = 4$ steps. At the conclusion of Step 1, we have computed $\langle [x_1 - x_2], [x_3 - x_4], [x_5 - x_6], [x_7 - x_8], [x_9 - x_{10}], x_{11} \rangle$. At the end of Step 2, we have computed $\langle [x_1 - x_4], [x_5 - x_8], [x_9 - x_{11}] \rangle$. At the end of Step 3, we have computed $\langle [x_1 - x_8], [x_9 - x_{11}] \rangle$. At the end of Step 4, we have computed $\langle [x_1 - x_{11}] \rangle$.

Values	1	2	3	4	5	6	7	8	9	10	11	12	13	14	15	16
P (step 1)	1	3	6	10	5	11	18	26	9	19	30	42	13	27	42	58
P (step 2)				10				36				78				136
P (step 3)	1	3	6	10	15	21	28	36	45	55	66	78	91	105	120	136

Figure 7-5 An example of computing the parallel prefix on a PRAM with $\Theta(n / \log n)$ processors. In this example, we are given $n = 16$ data items, the operation is addition, there are $\log_2 n = 4$ processors, and each processor is responsible for $n / \log_2 n = 16/4 = 4$ data items.

Step 1:

For $i = 1$ to $\dfrac{n}{\log_2 n}$, do in parallel

$p_{[(i-1)\log_2 n]+1} = x_{[(i-1)\log_2 n]+1}$;

   For $j = 2$ to $\log_2 n$, do

   $p_{[(i-1)\log_2 n]+j} = p_{[(i-1)\log_2 n]+j-1} \otimes x_{[(i-1)\log_2 n]+j}$

End For i;

Comment: After Step 1, processor P_1 has the correct final prefix values stored for the first $\log_2 n$ prefix terms. Similarly, processor P_2 now knows the prefix value of the $\lceil n/\log_2 n \rceil$ entries stored in processor P_2, and so forth. In fact, every processor P_i stores $p_{[(i-1)\log_2 n]+j}$, the prefix computed over the segment of the array X indexed by $[(i-1)\log_2 n]+1 \ldots [(i-1)\log_2 n]+j$, for all $j \in \{1, 2, \ldots, \log_2 n\}$.

Step 2: Compute the global prefixes over the $n/\log_2 n$ final prefix values, currently stored one per processor.

$r_1 = p_{\log_2 n}$

Let

$$r_i = r_{i-1} \otimes p_{i \log_2 n}, i \in \left\{2, 3, \ldots, \dfrac{n}{\log_2 n}\right\}$$

Comments: Note that r_i is a prefix over the segment of the array X indexed by $1 \ldots i \log_2 n$. This prefix of $n / \log_2 n$ terms is computed in $\Theta(\log n)$ time by the previous algorithm since the step uses one piece of data stored in each of the $n/\log_2 n$ processors.

Step 3: The final stage of the algorithm consists of distributing, within each processor, the final prefix value determined by the previous processor.

For $i = 2$ to $\dfrac{n}{\log_2 n}$, do in parallel

   For $j = 1$ to $\log_2 n$, do

   $p_{[(i-1)\log_2 n]+j} = r_{i-1} \otimes p_{[(i-1)\log_2 n]+j}$

End For i

Comment: Note that $p_{[(i-1)\log_2 n]+j}$ has the desired final value, as it is now calculated over the segment of X indexed $1 \ldots [(i-1)\log_2 n] + j$.

Mesh: In this section, we consider the problem of computing the parallel prefix on a mesh computer. As discussed earlier, when considering an operation that involves an ordering imposed on the data, we must first consider an ordering of the processors. In this section, we will consider a simple *row-major ordering* of the processors, as shown below. Formally, the row-major index of processor $P_{i,j}$, $i, j \in \{1, \ldots, n^{1/2}\}$, is $(i-1)n^{1/2} + j$ (see Figure 7-6).

The input to our parallel prefix problem consists of a data set $X = \{x_1, \ldots, x_n\}$, distributed one item per processor on an $n^{1/2} \times n^{1/2}$ mesh. That is, processor P_i (denoted by its row-major index) initially contains x_i, $1 \le i \le n$. When the algorithm terminates, processor P_i should contain the i-th prefix $x_1 \otimes \ldots \otimes x_i$. We describe the algorithm in terms of mesh operations that we developed earlier in the book.

First, perform a row rotation within every row. At the conclusion of this rotation, the rightmost processor in every row knows the final prefix value of the entries in its row. Notice that this step is similar to Step 1 of the PRAM algorithm just described, in which every processor computes the prefix of entries initially stored in its processor. Next, using only the processors in the rightmost column, perform a column rotation to determine the parallel prefix of these partial results. Again, note that this step is similar to Step 2 of the PRAM algorithm, which computes the global parallel prefix of the partial results determined in Step 1.

At this point, notice that the rightmost processors in every row contain their correct final answers. Furthermore, the value stored in the rightmost processor of row i needs to be applied to all of the partial prefix values determined by the processors in row $i+1$ (during Step 1). This can be done by first moving the appropriate prefix values determined at the end of Step 2 down one processor (from the rightmost processor in row i to the rightmost processor in row $i+1$). Once this is done, every row (with the exception of the first row) can perform a row rotation to propagate this value to all processors in its row so that they can apply the value appropriately.

Therefore, the algorithm consists of a row rotation, a column rotation, a communication step between neighboring processors, and a final row rotation. Each of these steps

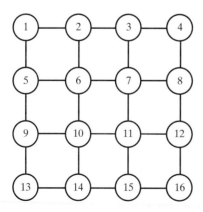

Figure 7-6   The row-major index scheme imposed on a mesh of size 16.

can be performed in $O(n^{1/2})$ on a mesh of size n. In fact, since the rotations take $\Theta(n^{1/2})$ time, the running time of the algorithm is $\Theta(n^{1/2})$. Of course, we are now presented with what is becoming a routine question, namely, "How good is this algorithm?" Since the mesh of size n has a $\Theta(n^{1/2})$ communication diameter, and since every pair of data elements is required for the determination of the n-th prefix, we can conclude that the running time is optimal for this architecture. Now, consider the cost. The algorithm requires $\Theta(n^{1/2})$ operations to be performed on a set of $\Theta(n)$ processors, which results in a cost of $\Theta(n^{3/2})$. Since we know that only $\Theta(n)$ operations are required, we can conclude that this is not cost-optimal.

So this brings us to one of our favorite questions: Can we design an algorithm that is more cost-effective than our current algorithm? The major limitation for the mesh, in this case, is the communication diameter. That is, there is no inherent problem with the bisection width. In order to reduce the communication diameter, we must reduce the size of the mesh. This will have the effect of increasing the number of data elements that each processor is responsible for, including the number of input elements, the number of final results, and the number of intermediate results.

Notice that at the extreme, we could consider a mesh of size 1, or a RAM. The algorithm would run in a very slow $\Theta(n)$ time, but would also have an optimal cost of $\Theta(n)$. However, this is not quite what we envisioned when we thought about reducing the size of a mesh. In fact, consider keeping the cost of the mesh optimal, but improving the running time from that of a fine-grained mesh. In such a case, we want to balance the communication diameter with the amount of work each processor must perform. Given an $n^{1/3} \times n^{1/3}$ mesh, notice that each of these $n^{2/3}$ processors would store $n^{1/3}$ elements of X and would be responsible for storing $n^{1/3}$ final prefix results. This is similar to the PRAM algorithm in which we required every processor to be responsible for $\Theta(\log n)$ input elements and final results.

So let's consider a mesh of size $n^{2/3}$, $i.e.$, a mesh of size $n^{1/3} \times n^{1/3}$, where each processor initially stores $n^{1/3}$ entries of X. The algorithm follows the time- and cost-optimal PRAM algorithm presented in the last section, combined with the global operations and techniques presented in the nonoptimal $n^{1/2} \times n^{1/2}$ mesh algorithm just presented. First, every processor computes the prefix of its $n^{1/3}$ entries in $\Theta(n^{1/3})$ time by the standard sequential (RAM) algorithm. Now, consider the final restricted prefix value in each of the $n^{2/3}$ processors. The previous (nonoptimal) mesh algorithm can be applied to these $n^{2/3}$ entries, stored one per processor on the $n^{1/3} \times n^{1/3}$ mesh. Since this mesh algorithm runs in time proportional to the communication diameter of the mesh, this step will take $\Theta(n^{1/3})$ time. At the conclusion of this step, every processor will now have to obtain the previous prefix value and go through and determine each of its final $n^{1/3}$ results, as we did in the PRAM algorithm. Clearly, this can be done in $\Theta(n^{1/3})$ time. Therefore, the running time of the algorithm is $\Theta(n^{1/3})$. This is due to the fact that we balanced the time required for data movement with the time required for sequential computing. Since the algorithm runs in $\Theta(n^{1/3})$ time on a machine with $\Theta(n^{2/3})$ processors, the cost of the algorithm is $\Theta(n^{1/3}) \times \Theta(n^{2/3}) = \Theta(n^{1/3} \times n^{2/3}) = \Theta(n)$, which is optimal.

Hypercube: In this section, we consider the problem of computing the parallel prefix on a hypercube computer. As with the mesh, when considering an operation that involves an ordering imposed on the data, we must first consider an ordering of the processors. In this section, we assume that the data set $X = \{x_0, \ldots, x_{n-1}\}$ is distributed so that processor P_i initially contains data item x_i. Notice that we have changed the indexing of the set X from $[1, \ldots, n]$, which was used for the RAM, Mesh, and PRAM, to $[0, \ldots, n-1]$. The reason we did this was to accommodate the natural indexing of a hypercube of size n, in which the $\log_2 n$-bit indices are in the range of $[0, \ldots, n-1]$. (Recall that two processors are connected *if and only if* their binary addresses differ in exactly one bit.) So, we assume that every processor P_i initially contains data item x_i, and at the conclusion of the algorithm, every processor P_i will store the i-th prefix, $x_0 \otimes \ldots \otimes x_i$.

The procedure we present is similar to the recursive doubling algorithm we presented earlier in connection with an efficient hypercube broadcasting algorithm. The algorithm operates by cycling through the $\log_2 n$ bits of the processor indices. At iteration i, every processor determines the prefix for the subhypercube that it is in with respect to the $i + 1$ least significant bits of its index. In addition, every processor uses this partial information, as appropriate, to compute its required prefix value. The algorithm follows (see Figure 7-7).

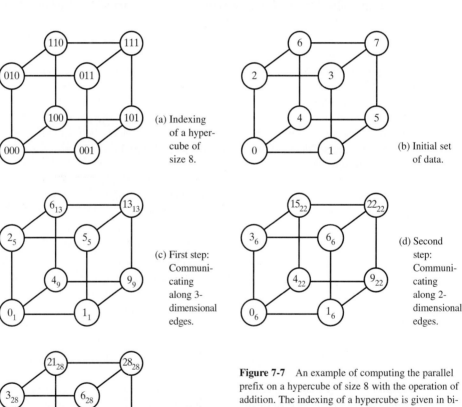

(a) Indexing of a hypercube of size 8.

(b) Initial set of data.

(c) First step: Communicating along 3-dimensional edges.

(d) Second step: Communicating along 2-dimensional edges.

(e) Third step: Communicating along 1-dimensional edges.

Figure 7-7 An example of computing the parallel prefix on a hypercube of size 8 with the operation of addition. The indexing of a hypercube is given in binary representation in (a). In (b), the initial set of data items is presented. In (c), (d), and (e), we show the results after the first, second, and third steps of the algorithm, respectively. Processor prefix values are large in (c), (d), and (e); subcube prefix values are small.

Input: Processor P_i contains data element x_i, $0 \le i \le n-1$.
Output: Processor P_i contains the i-th prefix $x_1 \otimes \ldots \otimes x_i$.
In parallel, every processor P_i does the following:
      subcube_prefix = x_i {This is the prefix for current subcube.}
      processor_prefix = x_i {This is the prefix of desired result.}
      {*lsb* = least significant bit and *msb* = most significant bit.}
      For b = *lsb* to *msb*, do
      {In this loop, we consider the binary processor indices from the rightmost bit
        to the leftmost bit.}
          send *subcube_prefix* to *b-neighbor*
          receive *temp_prefix* from *b-neighbor*
          If the b-th bit of processor P_i is a 1, then
              processor_prefix = *temp_prefix* $\otimes$ *processor_prefix*
              subcube_prefix = *temp_prefix* $\otimes$ *subcube_prefix*
          Else
              subcube_prefix = *subcube_prefix* $\otimes$ *temp_prefix*
          End If
      End For
End *Parallel*

Analysis: The analysis of this algorithm is fairly straightforward. Notice that the n processors are uniquely indexed with $\log_2 n$ bits. The algorithm iterates over these bits, each time performing $\Theta(1)$ operations (sending/receiving data over a link and performing a fixed number of unit-time operations on the contents of local memory). Therefore, given n elements initially distributed one per processor on a hypercube of size n, the running time of the algorithm is $\Theta(\log n)$. Although the running time of the algorithm is optimal on this architecture, due to the $\Theta(\log n)$ communication diameter, the total cost of the algorithm is $\Theta(n \log n)$, which is not optimal. In order to reduce the cost to $\Theta(n)$, we might consider reducing the number of processors from n to $n/\log_2 n$ while still maintaining a running time of $\Theta(\log n)$. We leave this problem as an exercise.

APPLICATION: MAXIMUM SUM SUBSEQUENCE

In this section, we consider an application of the parallel prefix computation. The problem we consider is that of determining a *subsequence* of a data set that sums to the maximum value with respect to any subsequence of the data set. Formally, we are given a sequence, $X = \langle x_0 x_1 \ldots x_{n-1} \rangle$, and we are required to find (not necessarily distinct) indices u and v, $u \le v$, such that the subsequence $\langle x_u x_{u+1} \ldots x_v \rangle$ has the largest possible sum, $x_u + x_{u+1} + \ldots + x_v$, among all possible subsequences of X.

    We should first make an observation. Notice that if all the elements of X are nonnegative, then the problem is trivial, as the entire sequence represents the solution. Similarly, if all elements of X are nonpositive, an empty subsequence is the solution, since by convention the sum of the elements of an empty set of numbers is 0. So this problem is interesting only when positive and negative values are allowed. This is the case we consider for several models.

RAM: The lower bound to solve this problem on a RAM is $\Omega(n)$, since if any one element is not examined, it is possible that an incorrect solution may be obtained. We will now attempt to develop an optimal $\Theta(n)$ time solution to this problem. Consider the situation of scanning the list from the first element to the last while maintaining some basic information about the maximum subsequence observed and the contribution that the current element can make to the current subsequence under investigation. A first draft of the algorithm follows.

1. Solve the problem for $\langle x_0 \, x_1 \ldots x_{i-1} \rangle$. One can think of this as either a recursive or iterative step.

2. Extend the solution to include the next element, x_i. Notice that the maximum sum in $\langle x_0 \, x_1 \ldots x_i \rangle$ is the maximum of

    a) the sum of a maximum sum subsequence in $\langle x_0 x_1 \ldots x_{i-1} \rangle$, referred to as *Global_Max*, and

    b) the sum of a subsequence ending with x_i, referred to as *Current_Max*.

The details of the algorithm are straightforward. (Also see the example presented in Figure 7-8.)

> *Global_Max* $\leftarrow x_0$
> $u \leftarrow 0$ {Start index of global max subsequence.}
> $v \leftarrow 0$ {End index of global max subsequence.}
> *Current_Max* $\leftarrow x_0$
> $q \leftarrow 0$ {Initialize index of current subsequence.}
>
> For $i = 1$ to $n-1$, do {Traverse list.}
>   If *Current_Max* ≥ 0
>   Then *Current_Max* $\leftarrow$ *Current_Max* $+ x_i$
>   Else *Current_Max* $\leftarrow x_i$
> $q \leftarrow i$ {Reset index of current subsequence.}
>   End Else
>
>   If   *Current_Max* $>$ *Global_Max*
>   Then *Global_Max* $\leftarrow$ *Current_Max*
> $u \leftarrow q$
> $v \leftarrow i$
>   End If
> End For

The five initialization steps each take $\Theta(1)$ time. Each pass through the for loop also takes $\Theta(1)$ time. Since the loop is performed $\Theta(n)$ times, it follows that the running time of the algorithm is $\Theta(n)$, which is optimal, as all n entries of the input array X must be examined.

i	x	Global_Max	u	v	Current_Max	q
0	5	5	0	0	5	0
1	3	8	0	1	8	0
2	-2	8	0	1	6	0
3	4	10	0	3	10	0
4	-6	10	0	3	4	0
5	-5	10	0	3	-1	0
6	1	10	0	3	1	6
7	10	11	6	7	11	6
8	-2	11	6	7	9	6

Figure 7-8   An example of the maximum sum subsequence problem.

PRAM: Consider an efficient solution to the maximum sum subsequence problem for the PRAM. Let's attempt to design a PRAM algorithm that is efficient in its running time and optimal in its use of resources (cost-optimal). Based on our previous experience with designing cost-effective PRAM algorithms, it makes sense to target a $\Theta(\log n)$ time algorithm on a machine with $\Theta(n/\log n)$ processors. Such an algorithm would be time- and cost-optimal.

Suppose we first compute the parallel prefix sums $\{s_0, s_1, \ldots, s_{n-1}\}$ of $X = \{x_0, x_1, \ldots, x_{n-1}\}$, where $s_i = x_0 \otimes \ldots \otimes x_i$. This can be done in $\Theta(\log n)$ time by the cost-optimal parallel prefix algorithm presented in the previous section. Next, compute the *parallel postfix maximum* of $S = \{s_0, s_1, \ldots, s_{n-1}\}$ so that for each index i, the maximum $s_j, j \geq i$, is determined, along with the value j. (The *parallel postfix* computation is similar to the parallel prefix computation: Given data values $\{y_0, y_1, \ldots, y_{n-1}\}$, the parallel postfix computation using the operator $\otimes$ computes the values $y_0 \otimes y_1 \otimes y_2 \otimes \ldots \otimes y_{n-1}, y_1 \otimes y_2 \otimes \ldots \otimes y_{n-1}$, $y_2 \otimes \ldots \otimes y_{n-1}, \ldots, y_{n-2} \otimes y_{n-1}, y_{n-1}$.) So, in this case, we compute the parallel postfix maximum of $\{s_0, s_1, \ldots, s_{n-1}\}$, which, since the maximum operator is commutative, is equivalent to computing the parallel prefix maximum of $\{s_{n-1}, s_{n-2}, \ldots, s_0\}$. Let m_i denote the value of the postfix-max at position i, and let a_i be the associated index ($s_{a_i} = \max \{s_i, s_{i+1}, \ldots, s_{n-1}\}$). This parallel postfix is completed in $\Theta(\log n)$ time by the algorithm presented in the previous section.

Next, for each i, compute $b_i = m_i - s_i + x_i$, the maximum prefix value of anything to the right (in other words, with a higher index) minus the prefix sum plus the current value. (Note that x_i must be added back in since it appears in term m_i as well as in term s_i.) This operation can be performed in $\Theta(\log n)$ time by having each processor (sequentially) compute the value of b for each of its $\Theta(\log n)$ entries. Finally, the solution corresponds to the maximum of the b_is, where u is the index of the position where the maximum of the bs is found and $v = a_u$. This final step can be computed by a semigroup operation in $\Theta(\log n)$ time.

Therefore, the algorithm runs in optimal $\Theta(\log n)$ time on a PRAM with $n/\log_2 n$ processors, which yields an optimal cost of $\Theta(n)$.

We now give an example for this problem. Consider the input sequence $X = \langle -3, 5, 2, -1, -4, 8, 10, -2 \rangle$. The parallel prefix sum of X is $S = \langle -3, 2, 4, 3, -1, 7, 17, 15 \rangle$.

$m_0 = 17$	$a_0 = 6$	$b_0 = 17 - (-3) + (-3) = 17$
$m_1 = 17$	$a_1 = 6$	$b_1 = 17 - 2 + 5 = 20$
$m_2 = 17$	$a_2 = 6$	$b_2 = 17 - 4 + 2 = 15$
$m_3 = 17$	$a_3 = 6$	$b_3 = 17 - 3 + (-1) = 13$
$m_4 = 17$	$a_4 = 6$	$b_4 = 17 - (-1) + (-4) = 14$
$m_5 = 17$	$a_5 = 6$	$b_5 = 17 - 7 + 8 = 18$
$m_6 = 17$	$a_6 = 6$	$b_6 = 17 - 17 + 10 = 10$
$m_7 = 15$	$a_7 = 7$	$b_7 = 15 - 15 + (-2) = -2$

As the example shows, we have a maximum subsequence sum of $b_1 = 20$. This corresponds to $u = 1$ and $v = a_1 = 6$, or the subsequence $\langle 5, 2, -1, -4, 8, 10 \rangle$. It is also interesting to observe (for any doubters) that the maximum sum subsequence for this example is a subsequence that contains positive and negative terms.

Mesh: We now consider a mesh. Notice that an optimal PRAM algorithm for solving the maximum sum subsequence problem relies on a parallel prefix, a parallel postfix, a semigroup operation, and some local unit-time computations. Also notice that a semigroup computation can be implemented via a parallel prefix computation. This means that the maximum sum subsequence problem can be solved via three parallel prefix operations (one, the parallel "postfix" computation, that runs in reverse order) and some local computations. This means that, in designing an algorithm for the mesh, we can simply follow the general guidelines of the PRAM algorithm while implementing the appropriate mesh algorithms (in this case, predominantly parallel prefix) in an efficient manner. So, we know that we can solve the maximum sum subsequence problem in $\Theta(n^{1/3})$ time on a mesh of size $n^{2/3}$ (on an $n^{1/3} \times n^{1/3}$ mesh). Since this algorithm requires $\Theta(n^{1/3})$ time on a machine with $n^{2/3}$ processors, we know that the cost is $\Theta(n^{1/3} \times n^{2/3}) = \Theta(n)$, which is optimal. Further, as discussed previously, this is the minimal running time on a mesh for a cost-optimal solution.

ARRAY PACKING

In this section, we consider an interesting problem that results in a global rearrangement of data. The problem consists of taking an input data set, in which a subset of the items are *marked*, and rearranging the data set so that all of the marked items precede all of the unmarked items. Formally, we are given an array X of items. Each item has an associated label field that is initially set to one of two values: *marked* or *unmarked*. The task is to pack the items so that all of the *marked* items appear before all of the *unmarked* items in the array. Notice that this problem is equivalent to sorting a set of 0s and 1s. In fact, if you consider 0 to represent *marked* and 1 to represent *unmarked,* then this problem is equivalent to sorting a set of 0s and 1s into nondecreasing order (all 0s preceding all 1s).

RAM: The first model of computation that we consider is the RAM. Since this problem is equivalent to sorting a set of 0s and 1s, we could solve this problem quite simply in $O(n \log n)$ time by any one of a number of $\Theta(n \log n)$-time worst-case sorting routines. However, since we know something about the data (the restricted nature of the input), we should consider an alternative to a general sorting routine. In this case, we know that the keys of the items to be sorted can only take on one of two values. Using this information, we can consider scan-based sorts such as *counting sort* or *radix sort*.

Consider counting sort. If we are sorting an array of n entries, we could simply make one pass through the array and count the number of 0s and the number of 1s. We could then make another pass through and write out the appropriate number of 0s, followed by the appropriate number of 1s. The situation is slightly more complicated if the keys are associated with larger records. In such a case, we could create two linked lists (dynamic allocation) and then traverse the array element by element. As we encounter each element in the array, we create and initialize a record with the pertinent information and add it onto the head of either the 0s list or the 1s list. This traversal is complete in $\Theta(n)$ time. We can then scan through the 0s list, element by element, and write the pertinent information into the next available place in the array. We then do the same with the 1s list. Again, this step takes $\Theta(n)$ time, and hence the algorithm is complete in asymptotically optimal $\Theta(n)$ time. The reader should observe that this algorithm is closely related to the BinSort algorithm discussed in Chapter 1.

Suppose we are given an array of n complex entries (that is, records) and we are required to perform array packing in place. That is, suppose that the space requirements in the machine are such that we cannot duplicate more than some fixed number of items. In this case, we can use the array-based partition routine from QuickSort (see Chapter 9) to rearrange the items. This partition routine is implemented by considering one index L that moves from the beginning to the end of the array and another index R that moves from the end to the beginning of the array. Index L stops when it encounters an *unmarked* item, while index R stops when it encounters a *marked* item. When both L and R have found an out-of-place item, and L precedes R in the array, then the items are swapped and the search continues. When L does not precede R, the algorithm terminates. The running time of the algorithm is linear in the number of items in the array. That is, the running time is $\Theta(n)$.

PRAM: Now consider the PRAM. As with the maximum sum subsequence problem, we realize that in order to obtain an efficient and cost-effective algorithm, we should try to develop an algorithm that runs in $\Theta(\log n)$ time using only $\Theta(n/\log n)$ processors. This problem is solved easily using a parallel prefix sum to determine the rank of each 0 with respect to all 0s and the rank of each 1 with respect to all 1s. That is, suppose you first determine for each 0 the number of 0s that precede it, and similarly for each 1 the number of 1s that precede it. Further, assume that the total number of 0s is computed as part of the process of ranking the 0s. Then during a write stage, every 0 can be written to its proper location, the index of which is one more than the number of 0s that precede it. Also, during this write state, every 1 can be written to its proper location, the index of which is one plus the number of 1s that precede it plus the number of 0s (that also precede it).

Let's consider the running time of such an algorithm. Given a PRAM with $\Theta(n/\log n)$ processors, the parallel prefix computation can be performed in $\Theta(\log n)$ time, as previously described. Along with this computation, the total number of 0s is determined easily in an additional $\Theta(\log n)$ time. Therefore, the write stage of the algorithm can be performed in $\Theta(\log n)$ time (each processor is responsible for writing out $\Theta(\log n)$ items). Hence, the total running time of the algorithm is $\Theta(\log n)$, and the cost of the algorithm on a machine with $\Theta(n/\log n)$ processors is $\Theta(\log n \times n/\log n) = \Theta(n)$, which is optimal. It is important to note that this algorithm can be adapted easily to sort a set of values chosen from a constant size set. In fact, the algorithm can be adapted easily to sort records, where each key is chosen from a constant size set.

Network Models: Now let's consider the problem of array packing for the general network model. Suppose one simply cares about sorting the data set, which consists of 0s and 1s. Then the algorithm is straightforward. Using either a semigroup operation or a parallel prefix computation, determine the total number of 0s and 1s. These values are then broadcast to all processors. Assume there are k 0s in the set. Then all processors P_i, $i \leq k$, record their final result as 0, while all other processors record their final result as 1. This results in all 0s appearing before all 1s in the final (sorted) list. Notice that this is a simple implementation of the *counting sort* algorithm we have used previously.

Suppose that instead of simply sorting keys, one needs the actual data to be rearranged. That is, assume that we are performing array packing on labeled records where all records that are marked are to appear before all records that are not marked. This is a fundamentally different problem from sorting a set of 0s and 1s. Notice that for this variant of the problem, it may be that all of the records are on the "wrong" half of the machine under consideration. Therefore, the lower bound for solving the problem is a function of the bisection width. For example, on a mesh of size n, if all n records need to move across the links that connect the middle two columns, a lower bound on the running time is $\Omega(n/n^{1/2}) = \Omega(n^{1/2})$. On a hypercube of size n, the bisection width gives us a lower bound of $\Omega(n/(n/2)) = \Omega(1)$. However, the communication diameter yields a better lower bound of $\Omega(\log n)$. The reader should consider bounds on other machines, such as the pyramid and mesh-of-trees.

Since the record-based variant of the array packing problem reduces to sorting, the solution can be obtained by performing an efficient general-purpose sorting algorithm on the architecture of interest. Such algorithms will be discussed later in this book.

INTERVAL (SEGMENT) BROADCASTING

It is shown easily that parallel prefix can be used to broadcast a piece of information (see Exercises). This is particularly useful in the ER PRAM model or on network-based models. In this section, we consider a variant of the parallel prefix problem. Assume that we are given a sequence of data items. Further, we assume that some subset of these items is "marked." We can view these marked data items as separating the complete sequence of data items into logical subsequences, where the first item of every subsequence is a marked data item. The problem we consider is that of broadcasting a marked data item to all of the records in its subsequence. It is important to note that in each subsequence, there is one and only one marked data item, and, in fact, it is the first item of the subsequence. For this reason, the marked data items are often referred to as "leaders." We now give a more concise description of the problem.

Suppose you are given an array X of n data items with a subset of the elements marked as "leaders." Broadcast the value associated with each leader to all elements that follow it in X up to but not including the next leader. An example is given below.

Processor Index:	0	1	2	3	4	5	6	7	8	9
Leader	1	0	0	1	0	1	1	0	0	0
Data	18	22	4	36	-3	72	28	100	54	0

Processor Index:	0	1	2	3	4	5	6	7	8	9
Leader	1	0	0	1	0	1	1	0	0	0
Data	18	22	4	36	-3	72	28	100	54	0
LeaderData	18	18	18	36	36	72	28	28	28	28

Figure 7-9 An example of a segmented broadcast. The top table shows the initial state *(i.e.,* the information before the segmented broadcast). Thus, by examining the Leader field in each processor, we know that the interval leaders are processors 0, 3, 5, and 6. In the bottom table, we show the information after the segmented broadcast. Notice that information from each leader has been propagated (broadcast) to all processors to the right (higher index values) up to, but not including, the next leader.

The top table in Figure 7-9 gives the information before the segmented broadcast. Notice that the leaders correspond to those entries for which the "Leader" component is equal to 1.

In the table at the bottom of Figure 7-9, we show the information after this segmented broadcast. At this point, every entry knows the information broadcast from its leader.

Solution Strategy: The interval broadcasting problem can be solved in a fairly straightforward fashion by exploiting a parallel prefix computation, as follows. For each leader (or marked entry) x_i in X, create the record (i, x_i). For each data item x_i that does not correspond to a leader in X, create the record $(-1, -1)$. Now define our prefix operator $\otimes$ as:

$$(i, a) \otimes (j, b) = \begin{cases} (i, a) \text{ if } i > j; \\ (j, b) \text{ otherwise.} \end{cases}$$

The reader should verify that our operator $\otimes$ is legal, as defined for parallel prefix. That is, the reader should verify that this operator is binary, closed, and associative. Recall that $\otimes$ need not be commutative. Notice that a straightforward application of a parallel prefix will now serve to broadcast the data associated with each leader to the members of its interval.

Analysis: Consider the RAM. A parallel prefix is implemented as a linear time scan operation, making a single pass through the data. So given an array X of n elements, the running time of the algorithm on a RAM is $\Theta(n)$, which is asymptotically optimal. Notice that the solution to the interval broadcasting problem simply consists of a careful definition of the prefix operator $\otimes$, coupled with a straightforward implementation of parallel prefix. Therefore, the analysis of running time, space, and cost on the PRAM and network models is identical to that which has been presented earlier in this chapter.

(SIMPLE) POINT DOMINATION QUERY

In this section, we consider an interesting problem from *computational geometry*, a branch of computer science concerned with designing efficient algorithms to solve geometric problems. Such problems typically involve points, lines, polygons, and other geometric figures. Consider a set of n data items, where each item consists of m fields. Further, suppose that each field is drawn from some linearly ordered set. That is, within each field, one can compare two entries and determine whether or not the first entry is less than the second entry. To cast the problem in two dimensions (that is, $m = 2$), we say that a point $q_1 = (x_1, y_1)$ *dominates* a point $q_2 = (x_2, y_2)$ *if and only if* $x_1 > x_2$ *and* $y_1 > y_2$. This is an important problem in the field of databases. For example, it is often important to determine for a given set of points, $Q = \{q_1, q_2, \ldots, q_n\}$ all the points that are *not* dominated by any point in Q.

Suppose you are interested in performing a study to identify the set of students for which no other student has both a higher grade point average (GPA) *and* owns more compact discs (CDs). An example is given in Figure 7-10, where the x-axis represents the number of CDs and the y-axis represents GPA. Exactly three points from this set of nine students satisfy our query.

Suppose that the input to our problem consists of a set of n points, $Q = \{q_1, q_2, \ldots, q_n\}$, where each point $q_i = (x_i, y_i)$, and where Q is initially ordered with respect to the x-coordinate of the records. Further, assume that no two points have the same x- or y-coordinate. We want to find all members of Q that are not dominated by any other member of Q.

Solution Strategy: Since the records are initially ordered with respect to the x-coordinate, the points can be thought of as lying ordered along the x-axis. The first step of the algorithm is to perform a *parallel postfix* operation, where the operator is *maximum-y-value*. Since the *maximum* operation is commutative, this is equivalent to performing a parallel prefix operation on the sequence of data $\langle q_n, q_{n-1}, \ldots, q_1 \rangle$. Let p_i denote the parallel prefix value associated with record q_i. Notice that at the conclusion of the parallel prefix algorithm, the desired set of points consists of all q_i for which $i < n$ and $p_i > p_{i+1}$. Also, q_n is one of the desired points. We now consider the time- and space-complexity of the algorithm on the RAM, PRAM, and network models.

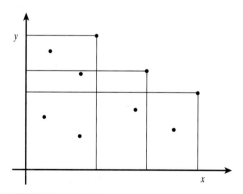

Figure 7-10   An example of the *point domination problem*. In this example, exactly three points have no other point both above and to the right. The remainder of the points are *dominated* by at least one of these three points.

RAM: Given an (ordered) array of data, a prefix operation can be performed on the n entries in $\Theta(n)$ time using a constant amount of additional space. A final pass through the data can be used to identify the desired set of records. (We should note that this second pass could be avoided by incorporating the logic to recognize undominated points into the parallel prefix operation.) As usual, it is easy to argue that the running time is optimal. The only way to complete the algorithm faster would be not to examine all of the entries, which could result in an incorrect result.

PRAM and Network Models: Notice that the solution to the 2-dimensional point domination query, where the input is given ordered by x-axis, is dominated by a parallel prefix operation. Therefore, the running time, space, and cost analysis is consistent with the analysis of parallel prefix given earlier in this chapter.

COMPUTING OVERLAPPING LINE SEGMENTS

In this section, we consider other (simple) problems from computational geometry. These problems involve a set of line segments that lie along the same line. We can think of this as a set of line segments that lie along the x-axis, as shown in Figure 7-11, where the segments are shown raised above the x-axis for clarity. The line segments are allowed to overlap (or not) in any possible combination. The first problem that we consider in this section is whether or not the set of line segments completely covers the x-axis between a given set of y-coordinates. The second problem is to determine a point on the x-axis that is covered by the most line segments.

Formally, we assume that the input consists of a set $S = \{s_1, s_2, \ldots, s_n\}$ of n uniquely labeled line segments, all of which lie along the same horizontal line. Each member of S is represented by two records, one corresponding to each endpoint. Each such record consists of the x-coordinate of the endpoint, the label of the line segment, and a flag indicating whether the point is the left or right endpoint of the line segment. Further, we assume that these $2n$ records are ordered with respect to the x-coordinate of the records, and if there is a tie (two records with the same x-coordinate), the tie is broken by having a record with a left endpoint precede a record with a right endpoint.

Coverage Query: The first problem we consider is determining whether or not the x-axis is completely covered by the set S of n line segments between two given x-coordinates, A and B, where $A < B$.

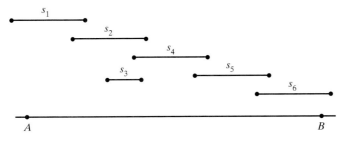

Figure 7-11 An example of problems involving *overlapping line segments*. The line segments are all assumed to lie on the x-axis, though they are drawn superimposed for viewing purposes.

Solution: We give a machine-independent solution strategy and then discuss the analysis for a variety of models.

1. Determine whether or not $left(s_1) \leq A$ and $B \leq \max\{right(s_i)\}_{i=1}^n$. If this is the case, then we can proceed. If not, we can halt with the answer that the coverage query is false.

2. For each of the $2n$ records, create a fourth field that is set to 1 if the record represents a left endpoint and -1 if the record represents a right endpoint. We will refer to this field as the *operand field*.

3. Considering all $2n$ records, perform a parallel prefix sum operation on the values in this operand field. The result of the i-th prefix will be stored in a fifth field of the i-th record, for each of the $2n$ records.

4. Notice that any parallel prefix sum of 0 must correspond to a right endpoint. Suppose that such a right endpoint is at x-coordinate c. Then all line segments with a left endpoint in $(-\infty, c]$ must also have their right endpoint in $(-\infty, c]$. Notice that due to the ordering of the records (in case of a tie in the x-coordinate, the left endpoint precedes the right endpoint), this means that the record that follows must be a left endpoint with x-coordinate strictly greater than c. That is, there is a break in the coverage of the x-axis at point c. So we determine the first record with parallel prefix sum equal to 0. If the x-coordinate of the endpoint is greater than B, then the answer to the coverage query is true, while otherwise it is false (see Figure 7-12).

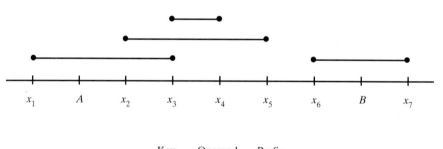

Key	Operand	Prefix
x_1	1	1
x_2	1	2
x_3	1	3
x_3	-1	2
x_4	-1	1
x_5	-1	0
x_6	1	1
x_7	-1	0

Figure 7-12   Transforming the coverage query problem to the parentheses matching problem. For this example, notice that there is a break in coverage between x_5 and x_6, as indicated by the 0 in the prefix value of x_5.

RAM: Consider an implementation of this algorithm on a RAM. The input consists of an array S with $2n$ entries and the values of A and B. Step 1 requires the comparison of the first element of S with the scalar quantity A and, since the records are ordered, a comparison of B with the last point. Therefore, Step 1 can be performed in $\Theta(1)$ time. Step 2 is completed with a simple $\Theta(n)$ time scan through the array. Similarly, the parallel prefix is performed on an array of $2n$ items with a scan that takes $\Theta(n)$ time. One final scan can be used to determine the first break in the coverage of the line segments before determining in $\Theta(1)$ time whether or not this endpoint precedes B. Therefore, the running time of the RAM algorithm is $\Theta(n)$, which is optimal.

PRAM: In order to attempt to derive a cost-optimal algorithm for this problem on the PRAM, we will consider a PRAM with $\Theta(n/\log n)$ processors. In the first step, the values of A and B can be broadcast to all processors in $O(\log n)$ time, even if the PRAM is ER, as shown previously. This is followed by a $\Theta(\log n)$ time (OR) semigroup operation to compute the desired comparison for A and then B, and a $\Theta(1)$ time (CR) or $\Theta(\log n)$ time (ER) broadcast of the decision concerning halting. Step 2 requires $\Theta(\log n)$ time since every processor must examine all $\Theta(\log n)$ of the records for which it is responsible. Step 3 is a straightforward parallel prefix, which can be performed on a PRAM with $\Theta(n/\log n)$ processors in $\Theta(\log n)$ time, as discussed previously. A $\Theta(\log n)$ time semigroup operation can be used to determine the first endpoint that breaks coverage, and a $\Theta(1)$ time comparison can be used to resolve the final query. Therefore, the running time of the algorithm is $\Theta(\log n)$ on a PRAM with $\Theta(n/\log n)$ processors, resulting in an optimal cost of $\Theta(n)$.

Mesh: As we have done previously when attempting to derive an algorithm with $\Theta(n)$ cost on a mesh, we consider an $n^{1/3} \times n^{1/3}$ mesh, in which each of these $n^{2/3}$ processors contains $n^{1/3}$ items from S. If we follow the flow of the PRAM algorithm, as implemented on a mesh of size $n^{2/3}$, we know that the broadcasts and parallel prefix operations can be performed in $\Theta(n^{1/3})$ time. Since these operations dominate the running time of the algorithm, we have a $\Theta(n^{1/3})$ time algorithm on a mesh with $n^{2/3}$ processors, which results in an optimal cost of $\Theta(n)$.

Maximal Overlapping Point: The next variant of the overlapping line segments problem that we consider is the problem of determining a point on the x-axis that is covered by the most line segments. The input to this problem consists of the set S of n line segments along with A and B, which represent the range on the x-axis under consideration.

Solution: The solution we present for the maximal overlapping point problem is very similar to the solution just presented for the coverage query problem.

1. For each of the $2n$ records, create a fourth field that is set to 1 if the record represents a left endpoint and -1 if the record represents a right endpoint. We will refer to this field as the *operand field*.

2. Considering all $2n$ records, perform a parallel prefix sum operation on the values in

this operand field. For each of the $2n$ records, the result of the i-th prefix will be stored in the fifth field of the i-th record.

3. Determine the maximum value of these prefix sums, denoted as M. All points with a prefix sum of M in the fifth field of their record correspond to points that are overlapped by a maximal number of line segments.

Analysis: The analysis of this algorithm follows that of the coverage query problem quite closely. Both problems are dominated by operations that are efficiently performed by parallel prefix computations. Therefore, the RAM algorithm is optimal at $\Theta(n)$ time. A PRAM algorithm can be constructed with $\Theta(n/\log n)$ processors that runs in $\Theta(\log n)$ time, yielding an optimal cost of $\Theta(n)$. Finally, a mesh algorithm can be constructed with $\Theta(n^{2/3})$ processors, running in $\Theta(n^{1/3})$ time, which also yields an algorithm with optimal $\Theta(n)$ cost.

CHAPTER NOTES

In this chapter, we studied the implementation and application of parallel prefix, an extremely powerful operation, especially on parallel computers. Parallel prefix-based algorithms are presented in R. Miller and Q.F. Stout's *Parallel Algorithms for Regular Architectures* (The MIT Press, Cambridge, 1996) to solve fundamental problems as well as to solve application-oriented problems from fields including image processing and computational geometry for mesh and pyramid computers. A similar treatment is presented for the PRAM in J. Já Já's *An Introduction to Parallel Algorithms* (Addison-Wesley Publishing Company, New York, 1992). Parallel prefix is presented in a straightforward fashion in the introductory text by M.J. Quinn's *Parallel Computing Theory and Practice* (McGraw-Hill, Inc., New York, 1994). Finally, the Ph.D. thesis by G.E. Blelloch, *Vector Models for Data-Parallel Computing* (The MIT Press, Cambridge, 1990), considers a model of computation that includes parallel prefix as a fundamental unit-time operation.

EXERCISES

1. Show that a hypercube with $\Theta(n/\log n)$ processors can compute a parallel prefix operation for a set of n data, $\{x_0, x_1, \ldots, x_{n-1}\}$, distributed $\Theta(\log n)$ items per processor, in $\Theta(\log n)$ time.

2. The *interval prefix computation* is defined as performing a parallel prefix within predefined disjoint subsequences of the data set. Give an efficient solution to this problem for the RAM, PRAM, and Mesh. Discuss the running time, space, and cost of your algorithm.

3. Show how a parallel prefix operation can be used to broadcast data to all the processors of a parallel computer in the asymptotic time of a parallel prefix operation. This should be done by providing an algorithm that can be implemented on any parallel model,

with the running time of the algorithm dominated by a parallel prefix operation.

4. Define *InsertionSort* in terms of parallel prefix operations for the RAM and PRAM. Give an analysis of running time, space, and cost of the algorithm.

5. Give an *optimal* EREW PRAM algorithm to compute the parallel prefix of n values $x_1, x_2, \ldots, x_n$.

6. Give an efficient algorithm to perform *Carry-Lookahead Addition* of two n-bit numbers on a PRAM. Hint: Keep track of whether each one-bit subaddition stops (s) a carry, propagates (p) a carry, or generates (g) a carry. See the example below. Notice that if the i-th carry is p, then the i-th carry is a 1 if and only if the leftmost non-p to the right of the i-th position is a g.

$$01001110101100100010$$
$$01100101101010101011100$$
$$sgpspgppgsgppsgppps$$

7. Give an efficient algorithm for computing the parallel prefix of n values, initially distributed one per processor on a q-dimensional mesh of size n. Discuss the time and cost of your algorithm.

8. Suppose that you are given a set of n pairwise disjoint line segments in the first quadrant of the Euclidean plane, each of which has one of its endpoints on the x-axis. Think of these segments as representing the skyline of a city. You may also assume the input is ordered from left to right. Give an efficient algorithm for computing the piece of each line segment that is observable from the origin. You may assume that the viewer does not have x-ray vision. That is, the viewer cannot see through any piece of a line segment. Discuss the time, space, and cost complexity of your algorithms for each of the following models of computation.

   a) PRAM

   b) Mesh

   c) Hypercube

9. Give an efficient algorithm for computing the parallel prefix of n values stored one per processor in

   a) the leaves of a tree machine;

   b) the base of a mesh-of-trees of base size n.

   Discuss the time and cost complexity of your algorithms.

10. Consider the array-packing algorithms presented in this chapter. Which of the routines is stable? That is, given duplicate items in the initial list, which of the routines will preserve the initial ordering with respect to duplicate items?

8

Pointer Jumping

Pointer Jumping

In this chapter, we consider algorithms for manipulating linked lists. We assume that the linked list under consideration is arbitrarily distributed throughout the memory of the model under consideration. Each element of the list consists of a data record and a *next* field. The *next* field contains the address of the next element in the list. In addition, we assume that the *next* field of the last entry in the list is set to *null*.

On a RAM, the list is arbitrarily distributed throughout the memory, and we assume that the location of the first element is known. On a PRAM, we assume that the list is arbitrarily distributed throughout the shared memory. Consider a linked list with n elements distributed throughout the memory of a PRAM with n processors. In this situation, we assume that every processor knows the location of a unique list element and that the location of the first element in the list is known. Given a PRAM with $m \leq n$ processors, each processor will be responsible for $\Theta(n/m)$ such elements.

For the network models, we assume that the list is evenly distributed in an arbitrary fashion throughout the memory of the processing elements. Given a linked list of size n, distributed one item per processor on a network model with n processors, every processor will store one element. Each element consists of a data record and a *next* pointer, which contains the processor ID of the next element in the list. Given a network model with $m \leq n$ processors, every processor will store approximately n/m elements, and each pointer will now include the processor ID and the index of the next element within that processor.

RAM: A linked list and a sequential machine provide a model for traversing the data that is inherently sequential. Therefore, given a list of size n, problems including linked list searches, linked list traversals, semigroup operations, and parallel prefixes, to name a few, can be solved in a straightforward fashion in $\Theta(n)$ time by a linear search.

Network Models: Given that the data is arbitrarily distributed among the processors, the communication diameter of a network model serves as a lower bound on the time required for a single link to be traversed. The time for all links to be traversed simultaneously is bounded by the bisection width. Therefore, it is often advantageous simply to consider a linked list of data as an unordered array of data and operate on it with high-powered data movement operations. Such operations will be discussed later in the book.

PRAM: The most interesting model to discuss in terms of linked list operations is the PRAM. This is due to the fact that the communication diameter is $\Theta(1)$ and the bisection width of a PRAM with n processors is equivalent to $\Theta(n)$. For many years, it was believed that list-based operations were inherently sequential. However, some clever techniques have been used to circumvent this notion. We demonstrate some of these *pointer jumping* techniques in the context of two problems. The problems are *list ranking* and *parallel prefix* (for linked lists). A description of the problems, along with PRAM implementations and analyses, follow.

LIST RANKING

Suppose that we are given a linked list L of size n, and we wish to determine the distance from each element to the end of the list. That is, for list element $L(i)$, we want to compute the distance, call it $d(i)$, to the end of the list. Recall that this is a linked list of elements, so that except for the first element in the list, the position of any element is initially unknown. We define the distance, $d(i)$, as follows.

$$d(i) = \begin{cases} 0 & \text{if } next(i) = null; \\ 1 + d(next(i)) & \text{if } next(i) \neq null. \end{cases}$$

The PRAM algorithm we present operates by a recursive doubling procedure. Initially, every processor finds the next element in the list, that is, the element one place away from it (closer to the end of the list). In the next step, every element locates the element two places away from it. In the next step, every element locates the element four places away from it, and so on. Notice that in the first step, every element has a pointer to the next element. During the course of the algorithm, these pointers are updated (otherwise, every element would need to maintain more than a fixed number of pointers). During every step of the algorithm, each element $L(i)$ knows that $L(next(i))$ is at distance, say, $current\_dist(i)$ from it. In order to determine the element at distance $\max\{2 \times current\_dist(i), d(i)\}$, $L(i)$ simply locates $L(next(next(i)))$, as shown in Figure 8-1. As the process progresses, every element needs to keep track of the number of such links traversed in order to determine its distance to the end of the list. In fact, some care needs to be taken for computing distances at the end of the list. The details follow.

Input: A linked list L consisting of n elements, arbitrarily stored in the shared memory of a PRAM with n processors.

Output: For every element $L(i)$, determine the distance $d(i)$ from that element to the end of the list.

{First, initialize the distance entries.}

For all $L(i)$ do

    $d(i) \leftarrow 0$ if $next(i) = null$

    $d(i) \leftarrow 1$ if $next(i) \neq null$

End For all

{Perform pointer-jumping algorithm. The actual pointer jumping step is

  $next(i) \leftarrow next(next(i))$.}

While there exists an i such that $next(i) \neq null$, do

    For all $L(i)$ do

$$\text{If } next(i) \neq null \text{ then } \begin{cases} d(i) \leftarrow d(i) + d(next(i)) \\ next(i) \leftarrow next(next(i)) \end{cases}$$

End For all
End *While*

Analysis: Given a PRAM of size *n*, the running time of this algorithm is $\Theta(\log n)$. This can be seen by the fact that the first element in the list must traverse $\lceil \log_2 n \rceil + 1$ links in order to reach the end of the list. Since the cost for a PRAM of size *n* to solve the list ranking problem for a list of size *n* is $\Theta(\log n)$, the total cost is $\Theta(n \log n)$, which we know is suboptimal.

In order to reduce this cost, we can consider a PRAM with $n/\log_2 n$ processors. In this case, we can attempt to make modifications to this algorithm as we have done previously. That is, we can attempt to create a hybrid algorithm in which each processor first

(a) Initial list with data values set to 1. Every processor knows the list element one place away.

(b) Pointer jump to determine list element two places away.

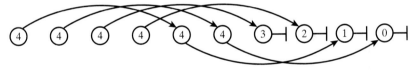

(c) Pointer jump to determine list element four places away.

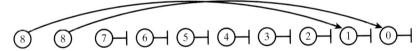

(d) Pointer jump to determine list element eight places away.

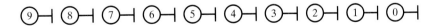

(e) Final data values after recursive doubling.

Figure 8-1   An example of *list ranking*. Given a linked list, determine for each element the number of elements in the list that follow it. The algorithm follows a recursive doubling procedure of traversing links while adding data values, which are initially set to 1 (see top list). Initially, every processor finds the next element in the list. In the next step, every element locates the element two places away from it, and so on. Given a list with 10 elements, five iterations are required ($\lceil \log_2 10 \rceil + 1 = 5$).

solves the problem locally in $\Theta(\log n)$ time, and then the algorithm just described is run on this set of partial results. Finally, in $\Theta(\log n)$ time, we can make a final local pass through the data. However, consider this algorithm carefully. It is important to note that if each processor were responsible for $\Theta(\log n)$ items, there is no guarantee that these items form a contiguous segment of the linked list. Therefore, there is no easy way to consider merging the $\Theta(\log n)$ items that a processor is responsible for into a single partial result that can be used during the remainder of the computation. In this case, such a transformation fails, and we are left with a cost-suboptimal algorithm.

LINKED LIST PARALLEL PREFIX

Now let's consider the parallel prefix problem. Although the problem is the same as we have considered earlier in the book, the input is significantly different. Previously, whenever we considered the parallel prefix problem, we had the advantage of knowing that the data was ordered in a random access structure, that is, an array. Now we have to consider access to the data in the form of a linked list. Notice that if we simply perform a scan on the data, then the running time will be $\Theta(n)$, which is equivalent to the RAM algorithm. Instead, we consider applying techniques of pointer jumping so that we can make progress simultaneously on multiple prefix results. For completeness, recall that we are given a set of data, $x_1, x_2, \ldots, x_n$, and a binary associative operator $\otimes$, from which we are required to compute $x_1, x_1 \otimes x_2, \ldots, x_1 \otimes x_2 \otimes \ldots \otimes x_n$, where the k-th prefix is defined as $p_k = x_1 \otimes x_2 \otimes \ldots \otimes x_k$. We now present an algorithm for computing the parallel prefix of a linked list of size n on a PRAM of size n, based on the concept of pointer jumping.

```
{pi is used to store the i-th prefix.}
For all i, pi ← xi
{Perform a pointer-jumping algorithm.}
While there exists an i such that next(i) ≠ null, do
      For all xi, do
            If next(i) ≠ null, then
                  Pnext(i) ← pi ⊗ Pnext(i)
                  next(i) ← next(next(i))
            End If
      End For all
End While
```

An example of this algorithm is given in Figure 8-2, where we show the application of a parallel prefix on a PRAM to a linked list of size 6. While going through the algorithm, it is important to implement the update steps presented inside of the "For all" statement in lockstep fashion across the processors.

Analysis: This algorithm is similar to that of the list-ranking algorithm just presented. That is, given a PRAM of size n, the running time of this algorithm is $\Theta(\log n)$. This can be seen by the fact that the first element in the list must traverse $\lceil \log_2 n \rceil + 1$ links in order

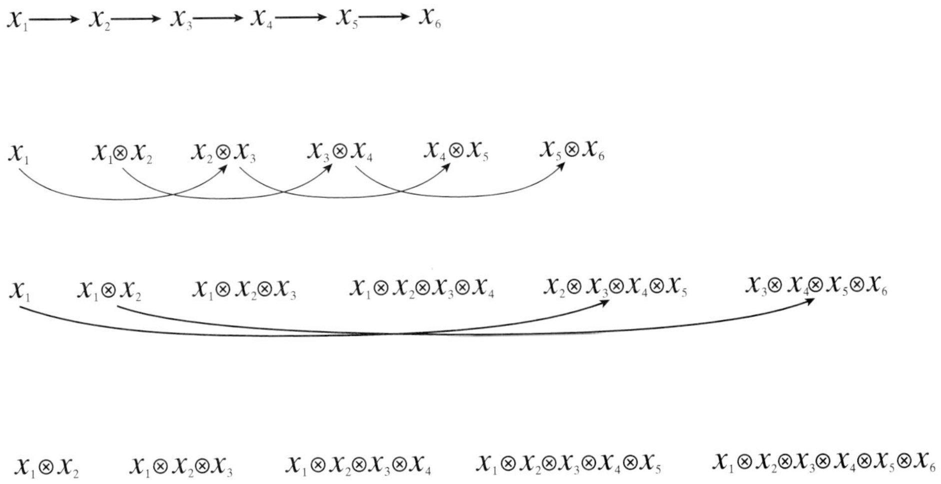

$$X_1 \longrightarrow X_2 \longrightarrow X_3 \longrightarrow X_4 \longrightarrow X_5 \longrightarrow X_6$$

$$X_1 \qquad X_1 \otimes X_2 \qquad X_2 \otimes X_3 \qquad X_3 \otimes X_4 \qquad X_4 \otimes X_5 \qquad X_5 \otimes X_6$$

$$X_1 \qquad X_1 \otimes X_2 \qquad X_1 \otimes X_2 \otimes X_3 \qquad X_1 \otimes X_2 \otimes X_3 \otimes X_4 \qquad X_2 \otimes X_3 \otimes X_4 \otimes X_5 \qquad X_3 \otimes X_4 \otimes X_5 \otimes X_6$$

$$X_1 \otimes X_2 \qquad X_1 \otimes X_2 \otimes X_3 \qquad X_1 \otimes X_2 \otimes X_3 \otimes X_4 \qquad X_1 \otimes X_2 \otimes X_3 \otimes X_4 \otimes X_5 \qquad X_1 \otimes X_2 \otimes X_3 \otimes X_4 \otimes X_5 \otimes X_6$$

Figure 8-2   An example of *parallel prefix* on a PRAM with linked list input. Given a list of size 6, the recursive doubling procedure requires three iterations to complete the prefix computation, plus an additional iteration to determine that the process should terminate ($\lceil \log_2 6 \rceil + 1 = 4$).

to propagate x_1 to all n prefix values. Since the time for a PRAM of size n to compute the parallel prefix on a list of size n is $\Theta(\log n)$, the total cost of the algorithm is $\Theta(n \log n)$. As with the list ranking algorithm, the cost of the parallel prefix computation is suboptimal.

CHAPTER NOTES

The focus of this chapter is on pointer-jumping algorithms providing efficient solutions to problems involving linked lists, an inherently sequential structure. An excellent chapter was written on this subject by R.M. Karp and V. Ramachandran, entitled "A survey of parallel algorithms and shared memory machines," which appeared in the *Handbook of Theoretical Computer Science: Algorithms and Complexity* (A.J. van Leeuwen, ed., Elsevier, New York, 1990, pp. 869–941). It contains numerous techniques and applications to interesting problems. In addition, pointer-jumping algorithms are discussed in *An Introduction to Parallel Algorithms*, by J. JáJá (Addison-Wesley Publishing Company, New York, 1992).

EXERCISES

1. The *component labeling* problem has several variants in graph theory, computational geometry, and image analysis. Suppose we have a set $S = \{p_1, \ldots, p_n\}$, the members of which could be points in a Euclidean space, vertices of a graph, or pixels of a digital image. Further, suppose we have a well-defined notion of neighboring points that

is *symmetric* (p_i and p_j are neighbors if and only if p_j and p_i are neighbors) and *anti-reflexive* (no point is a neighbor of itself). We say p_i and p_j are *connected* if either p_i and p_j are neighbors or there is a sequence $\{p_{i_0}, p_{i_1}, \ldots, p_{i_k}\} \subset S$ such that $p_i = p_{i_0}$, $p_j = p_{i_k}$, and p_{i_j} and $p_{i_{j+1}}$ are neighbors, $0 \leq j < k$. A *component* C is a maximal subset of S such that all members of C are connected. The label of C is the smallest index i (or some equivalent such as a pointer to a unique member of C) such that $p_i \in C$. The component labeling problem is to associate with each member p_i of S the label of the component of S containing p_i.

Given a set of linked lists, solve this version of the component labeling problem. That is, given several linked lists with a total of n elements, regard each list as a component of the totality of links; neighbors are links that are adjacent in the same list. Give RAM and PRAM algorithms that efficiently solve the component labeling problem. The RAM solution should run in $\Theta(n)$ time. The PRAM solution should have a cost of $\Theta(n \log n)$. (Hint: a PRAM solution could use the pointer-jumping techniques illustrated in this chapter.)

2. Give an efficient algorithm to solve the following problem. Given a collection of linked lists with a total of n links, let every link know how many links are in its list and how far the link is from the front of the list (the head link is number 1, the next link is number 2, and so on). Analyze for the RAM and the PRAM.

3. Give an efficient algorithm to solve the following problem. For a linked list with n links, report the number of links with a given data value x. Analyze for the RAM and the PRAM.

4. Give an efficient algorithm to solve the following problem. For a set of ordered linked lists with a total of n links, report to each link the median value of the link's list (in an ordered list of length k for even k, the median value can be taken either as the value in link $(k/2)$ or link $(k/2 + 1)$ from the head). Do not assume that it is known at the start of the algorithm how many links are in any of the lists. Analyze for the RAM and the PRAM.

9

Divide-and-Conquer

Divide-and-Conquer

The phrase "divide-and-conquer" is used in the study of algorithms to refer to a method of solving a problem that typically involves *i*) partitioning the problem into smaller subproblems, *ii*) recursively solving these subproblems, and then *iii*) stitching these partial solutions together in order to obtain a solution to the original problem. Thus, the solution strategy involves doing some work in order to partition the problem into a number of subproblems of the same form. Each of these subproblems is then solved recursively. Finally, the solutions to these subproblems are combined in order to solve the original problem. The divide-and-conquer-strategy is summarized below.

1. *Divide* the problem into subproblems, each of which is of a smaller size than the original;
2. *Conquer* all of the subproblems recursively (general case), unless a subproblem is small enough that recursion is unnecessary (base case of recursion);
3. *Combine/stitch* the solutions to the subproblems together in order to obtain a solution to the original problem.

MERGESORT (REVISITED)

The divide-and-conquer paradigm is exhibited in *MergeSort,* a sorting algorithm that we have previously discussed (see Chapter 2). MergeSort serves as a nice example for a concrete discussion of divide-and-conquer. Recall that the input to the MergeSort routine consists of an unordered list of n elements, and the output consists of an ordered list of the n elements. A high-level description of MergeSort, in divide-and-conquer terminology, follows.

1. **Divide:** Divide the unordered n-element input sequence into two unordered subsequences, each containing $n/2$ items.
2. **Conquer:** Recursively sort each of the two subsequences (general case). If a subsequence has only one item, then the subsequence need not be recursively sorted since a single item is already sorted (base case).
3. **Stitch:** Combine the two sorted sequences by *merging* them into the sorted result.

We should point out that this is a "top-down" divide-and-conquer description of MergeSort. This is in contrast to a "bottom-up" description that many students see in their early courses. A bottom-up description is typically presented as follows: "Merge pairs of (ordered) sequences of length 1 into ordered sequences of length 2. Next, merge pairs of ordered sequences of length 2 into ordered sequences of length 4, and so on." Notice that while these two descriptions differ significantly, the algorithm described, and therefore the work performed, is identical.

We now consider the time and space analysis of MergeSort on a variety of models of computation.

RAM: The analysis for the RAM should be familiar to readers who have taken a traditional year-long introduction to computer science or a course on data structures. Let's first consider a schematic of the operations performed by the MergeSort algorithm on a RAM. The n elements in the list are initially divided into two lists, each of which is recursively sorted. These two sorted lists are then merged into a single ordered list. Notice that a traditional, sequential merge routine on n items requires $\Theta(n)$ time. So, regardless of the details of the data structure, and whether or not the splitting is done in $\Theta(1)$ or $\Theta(n)$ time, the total running time required for the initial split and the final merge is $\Theta(n)$. In fact, we can be a little more precise and say that the running time for the highest-level split and merge is Cn, for some constant C.

Now consider each list of size $n/2$. Again, we argue that the split and merge routines are a function of the size of the input. That is, the running time to perform the split and merge for each input set of size $n/2$ can be expressed as $C_1(n/2)$ for some constant C_1. In general, the running time of the algorithm behaves as is shown in Figure 9-1.

Recursion Tree for MergeSort: The top-down description and analysis of MergeSort can be used to derive the running time of the algorithm in the form of a recurrence $T(n) = 2T(n/2) + \Theta(n)$. From the *Master Method*, we know that this recurrence has a solution of $T(n) = \Theta(n \log n)$. This is not surprising considering the *recursion tree* presented in Figure 9-1.

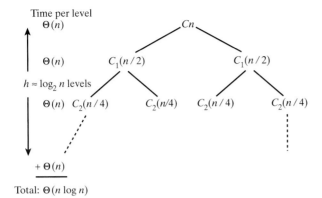

Figure 9-1 A recursion tree giving insight into the time required to perform a traditional MergeSort algorithm on a RAM.

Linear Array: We now consider an implementation of MergeSort on a linear array. Assume that the elements of the list are arbitrarily distributed one per processor on a linear array of size n, where for the sake of presentation, we assume that n is power of 2. Let's consider the stitch step of the algorithm. That is, assume that processors $P_1, \ldots, P_{n/2}$ contain an ordered subset of the data and that processors $P_{(n/2)+1}, \ldots, P_n$ contain the remaining elements in sorted order (see Figure 9-2). By knowing its processor ID, every processor knows the rank of its element in its subsequence of size $n/2$ (see Figure 9-3). That is, processor P_i, $1 \leq i \leq n/2$, knows that the element it currently contains is the i-th element with respect to those elements stored in processors $P_1, \ldots, P_{n/2}$. Similarly, processor P_i, $(n/2) + 1 \leq i \leq n$, knows that the element it currently contains has a rank of $i - (n/2)$ with respect to those elements stored in processors $P_{(n/2)+1}, \ldots, P_n$. Based on this information and knowledge of where an element ranks in the other subsequence, every processor will know the final position of the element it contains. That is, if the element in processor P_i, $1 \leq i \leq n/2$, is such that s elements in processors $P_{(n/2)+1}, \ldots, P_n$ are less than it, then the final position for the element in processor P_i is $i + s$. Similarly, if the element in processor P_i, $(n/2) < i \leq n$, is such that t elements in processors $P_1, \ldots, P_{n/2}$ are less than it, then the final position for the element in processor P_i is $i - (n/2) + t$ (see Figure 9-4).

In order to determine the rank of an element with respect to the other subsequence, simply perform a rotation of the data and allow every processor to count the number of elements from the other subsequence that are less than the one that it is currently maintaining. A final rotation can then be used to send every element to its correct sorted position. The running time of such an algorithm is given by the recurrence $T(n) = T(n/2) + \Theta(n)$, which has a solution of $T(n) = \Theta(n)$. Notice that is optimal for the linear array. We make the following observations:

1. The algorithm, as described, requires that during each recursive step a rotation is *only performed within the pairs of subsequences being merged*. That is, a complete rotation is not performed each time. If a complete $\Theta(n)$ time rotation were performed during each of the $\Theta(\log n)$ iterations, the resulting running time would be $\Theta(n \log n)$.

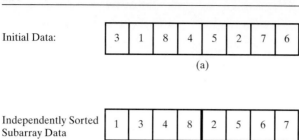

Initial Data:

| 3 | 1 | 8 | 4 | 5 | 2 | 7 | 6 |

(a)

Figure 9-2   A snapshot of Merge-Sort on a linear array of size 8. The initial data is given in (a), and the result of independently sorting both the left and right subarrays is shown in (b).

Independently Sorted
Subarray Data

| 1 | 3 | 4 | 8 | 2 | 5 | 6 | 7 |

(b)

Data

| 1 | 3 | 4 | 8 | 2 | 5 | 6 | 7 |

Local Rank

| 1 | 2 | 3 | 4 | 1 | 2 | 3 | 4 |

Figure 9-3   A snapshot of MergeSort on a linear array of size 8, using the data from Figure 9-2. The snapshot shows the data and local ranks that are determined after the independent sorts on both the left and right subarrays.

Data

| 1 | 3 | 4 | 8 | 2 | 5 | 6 | 7 |

Local Rank

| 1 | 2 | 3 | 4 | 1 | 2 | 3 | 4 |

Rank in Other
Subarray

| 0 | 1 | 1 | 4 | 1 | 3 | 3 | 3 |

Figure 9-4   A snapshot of MergeSort on a linear array of size 8 after the independent sorts on both the left and right subarrays. The data, local ranks, and ranks with respect to the opposite subarray are all given. The data is from Figure 9-2.

2. Although the running time of this algorithm is asymptotically equivalent to the tractor-tread/rotation-based sorting algorithm presented earlier for the linear array, it is clear that the high order constants for this MergeSort routine are significantly higher than that of the tractor-tread algorithm. This is clear from the fact that the last iteration of the MergeSort procedure requires two complete rotations, whereas the rotation-based sort requires only one rotation in total.

   Finally, consider the cost of the MergeSort algorithm. The running time is $\Theta(n)$ on a linear array with n processors, which yields a total cost of $\Theta(n^2)$. Notice that this is significantly larger than the $\Theta(n \log n)$ lower-bound result on the number of operations required for comparison-based sorting. Consider the $\Theta(n)$ communication diameter of the linear array. From this we know that it is not possible to reduce the running time of Merge-Sort on a linear array of n processors. Therefore, our only reasonable option for developing a MergeSort-based algorithm that is cost-optimal on a linear array is to consider reducing the number of processors. Notice that if we reduce the number of processors to one, then the cost-optimal RAM algorithm can be executed. Since this yields no improvement in running time, we would like to consider a linear array with more than a fixed number of processors but less than a linear number of processors in the size of the input, in an asymptotic sense. We leave this problem as an exercise.

SELECTION

In this section, we consider the *selection* problem, which requires the identification of the k-th smallest element from a list of n elements, where the integer k is given as input to the procedure and where we assume that $1 \le k \le n$. Notice that this problem serves as a generalization of several important problems, including the following:

- The *minimum problem* (find a minimal entry), which corresponds to $k = 1$.
- The *maximum problem* (find a maximal entry), which corresponds to $k = n$.
- The *median problem* (find the median value), which corresponds to either $k = \lfloor n/2 \rfloor$ or $k = \lceil n/2 \rceil$.

A naive algorithm for the selection problem consists of

1. sorting the data, and then
2. reporting the entry that now resides in the k-th position of this ordered list.

Assume that on the given model of computation, the running time for the sort step (Step 1) dominates the running time for the report step (Step 2). Given this situation, the asymptotic running time for selection is bounded by the running time for sorting. So, on a RAM, our naive algorithm for arbitrary input data has a running time of $O(n \log n)$.

We know that a lower bound on a solution to the selection problem requires that every element is examined. In fact, for the restricted problem of finding the minimum or maximum element, we know that a more efficient solution can be obtained by a semigroup operation, which may or may not be implemented by a prefix-based algorithm. For example, a simple scan through the data on a RAM provides an asymptotically optimal $\Theta(n)$ time solution for determining either the minimum or the maximum element of the list. These observations suggest the possibility of solving the more general selection problem in $o(n \log n)$ time.

We first consider an efficient $\Theta(n)$ time algorithm for the RAM, which is followed by a discussion of selection on parallel machines.

RAM: The fact that a simple scan of the data will result in a $\Theta(n)$ time solution to the minimum or maximum problem motivates us to consider developing a solution to the general selection problem that does not require sorting. We now present an efficient semigroup-based algorithm to the general selection problem. We assume that the n data items are initially stored in arbitrary order in an array. For ease of explanation, we assume that n, the number of elements in the array, is a multiple of 5.

The algorithm may appear to be more complex than those that have been presented previously in this text. However, it is really quite straightforward. Initially, we take the unordered array as input and sort disjoint strings of five items (see Figure 9-5). That is, given

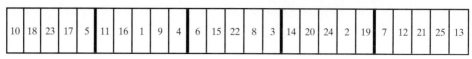

(a) Initial array of size 25

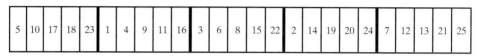

(b) Array after independent sorts

Figure 9-5   Using the partition routine to solve the Selection Problem. An initial input array of size 25 is given in (a). In (b), the array is shown after independently sorting disjoint subarrays of size 5. (Note: contrary to the algorithm presented in the chapter, for ease of presentation we ignore the fact the algorithm should stop when it reaches a subarray of size 50 or smaller.)

smallList → 5 → 10 → 1 → 4 → 9 → 11 → 3 → 6 → 8 → 2 → 7 → 12 ⊣

equalList → 13 ⊣

bigList → 17 → 18 → 23 → 16 → 15 → 22 → 14 → 19 → 20 → 24 → 21 → 25 ⊣

Figure 9-6   Creating three buckets based on $AM = 13$, the median of the five medians (17, 9, 8, 19, 13) given in Figure 9-5b. The data given in Figure 9-5b is traversed from the beginning to the end of the array, with every element less than 13 being placed in *smallList*, every item equal to 13 being placed in *equalList*, and every item greater than 13 being placed in *bigList*. Notice that the items should be placed in these lists in a manner that allows for $\Theta(1)$ time insertion. So given the order shown in this figure, one might assume that tail pointers were maintained during the insertion process.

an array S, we sort $S[1 \ldots 5], S[6 \ldots 10], \ldots, S[n - 5 + 1 \ldots n]$. Notice that this requires the application of $n/5$ sorting routines. However, each sorting routine only requires constant time (why?). Once the array is sorted within these segments of size 5, we gather the medians of each of these segments. So we now have a set of $n/5$ medians. Notice that after the initial local sort step, the first median is in $S[3]$ (this is the median of $S[1 \ldots 5]$), the next median is in $S[8]$ (the median of $S[6 \ldots 10]$), and so on. We now (recursively) find the median of these $n/5$ median values. This median of medians, which we denote as AM, is an approximate median of the entire set S. Once we have this approximation, we compare all elements of S with AM and create three buckets: namely, those elements less than AM, those elements equal to AM, and those elements greater than AM (see Figure 9-6). Finally, we determine which of these three buckets contains the k-th element and solve the problem on that bucket, recursively if necessary. (Notice that if the k-th element falls in the second bucket, then, since all elements have equal value, we have identified the requested element.)

Function Selection(*k*, *S*, *lower*, *upper*)

Input: An array *S*, positions *lower* and *upper*, and a value *k*.

Output: The *k*-th smallest item in *S*[*lower*, . . . , *upper*].

Local variables:

    n, the size of the subarray;

    M, used for medians of certain subarrays of *S*;

    smallList, *equalList*, *bigList*: linked lists used to partition *S*;

    smallList_array, *bigList_array*: arrays used for recursive function calls;

    j, an index variable;

    AM, an approximation of the median of *S*

Action:

    If $|upper - lower| < 50$, then

    {This is the base case of recursion.}

        SelectionSort (*S*, *lower*, *upper*)

        return *S*[*lower* + *k* − 1];

    End If

    Else {This is the recursive case.}

        1. $n = (upper - lower) + 1$

        2. Sort disjoint subarrays of size 5 or less. That is, independently sort
           S[*lower*, . . . , *lower* + 4], . . . , *S*[*lower* + 5($\lceil n/5 \rceil$ − 1), . . . , *upper*]

        3. For j = 1 to $\lceil n/5 \rceil$, do
           Assign the *j*-th median to *M*[*j*]. That is, *M*[*j*] = *S*[*lower* + 5*j* − 3]

        4. $AM = Selection(\lceil |M|/2 \rceil, M, 1, \lceil n/5 \rceil)$, the median of *M*

        5. Create empty lists *smallList*, *equalList*, and *bigList*

        6. For *j* = 1 to *n*, do
           Copy *S*[*lower* + *j* − 1] to

$$\begin{cases} smallList \text{ if } S[lower + j - 1] < AM \\ equalList \text{ if } S[lower + j - 1] = AM \\ bigList, \text{ otherwise} \end{cases}$$

        End For

        7. If $k \le |smallList|$, then
           CreateArray(*smallList*,*smallList_array*)
           return *Selection*(*k*, *smallList_array*, 1, |*smallList*|)
        Else if $k \le |smallList| + |equalList|$ then return *AM*
        Else
           CreateArray(*bigList*, *bigList_array*)
           return *Selection*(*k* − |*smallList*| − |*equalList*|,
                    bigList_array, 1, |*bigList*|)

    End Else {This is the recursive case.}

End Selection

We now present a discussion of the correctness of this algorithm, which will be followed by an analysis of its running time. Consider the lists *smallList*, *equalList*, and *bigList*. These lists contain members of *S* such that if *x* ∈ *smallList*, *y* ∈ *equalList*, and *z* ∈ *bigList*, then *x* < *y* < *z*. Therefore,

■ if $k \leq |smallList|$, then the entries of *smallList* include the k smallest entries of S, so the algorithm correctly returns *Selection(k, smallList_array, 1, |smallList|)*;

■ if $|smallList| < k \leq |smallList| + |equalList|$, then the k-th smallest entry of S belongs to *equalList*, each entry of which has a key value equal to *AM*, so the algorithm correctly returns *AM*.

■ if $|smallList| + |equalList| < k$, then the k-th smallest member of S must be the $(k - |smallList| - |equalList|)$-th smallest member of *bigList*, so the algorithm correctly returns *Selection(k - |smallList| - |equalList|, bigList_array, 1, |bigList|)*.

Analysis of Running Time: The base case of the recursive algorithm calls for sorting a list with length of at most 50. Therefore, the running time of the base case is $\Theta(1)$. This is due to the fact that any polynomial time algorithm, such as the $\Theta(n^2)$ time selection sort, will run in constant time on a fixed number of input items. We remark that the criterion value 50 is rather arbitrary; for analysis of our algorithm, any fixed positive integer will suffice.

We now consider the remainder of the algorithm.

■ Step 1 clearly requires $\Theta(1)$ time.

■ Step 2 calls for sorting $\Theta(n)$ sublists of the input list, where each sublist has at most five entries. Since 5 is a constant, we know that each sublist can be sorted in constant time. Therefore, the time to complete these $\Theta(n)$ sorts, each of which requires $\Theta(1)$ time, is $\Theta(n)$.

■ Step 3 gathers the medians of each sublist, which requires making a copy of $\lceil n/5 \rceil$ elements, each of which can be retrieved in $\Theta(1)$ time. Therefore, the running time for this step is $\Theta(n)$.

■ Step 4 requires the application of the entire procedure on an array with $\lceil n/5 \rceil$ elements. Therefore, this step requires $T(\lceil n/5 \rceil)$ time. We can simplify notation by saying that there is a constant c_0 such that this step requires less than $c_0 T(n/5)$ time. Further, we can assume that $c_0 T(n/5) \leq c_0 T(n/2)$.

■ Step 5 calls for the creation of several lists, which requires $\Theta(1)$ time in most modern programming languages.

■ Step 6 consists of copying each of the n input elements to exactly one of the three lists created in Step 4. Therefore, the running time for this step is $\Theta(n)$.

■ Step 7 determines which of the three lists needs to be inspected and makes a recursive call. The running time for this step is a function of the input value k as well as the order of the initial set of data. Due to these complexities, analysis of the running time of this step is a bit more involved. Three basic cases must be considered, each of which we evaluate separately. Namely, the requested element could be in *smallList*, *equalList*, or *bigList*.

■ We first consider the case where the requested element is in *smallList*, which occurs when $k \leq |smallList|$. Let's consider just how large *smallList* can be. That is, what is the maximum number of elements that can be in *smallList*? The maximal size of *smallList* can be determined as follows:

a. Consider the maximum number of elements that can be less than AM (the median of the medians). At most $\lfloor |M|/2 \rfloor = \lfloor \lceil n/5 \rceil /2 \rfloor$ members of M are less than AM. For simplicity, and since our analysis is based on asymptotic behavior, let's say that at most $n/10$ (median) elements are less than AM.

b. Notice that each $m \in M$ comes from a sublist of the input list S. In the $n/10$ sublists in which $m < AM$, possibly all 5 members could be less than AM; however, in the $n/10$ sublists in which $m \geq AM$, at most 2 members apiece could be less than AM.

Therefore, at most

$$\frac{5n}{10} + \frac{2n}{10} = \frac{7n}{10}$$

elements of the input list S can be sent to *smallList*. Equivalently, we can say that there is a constant c_1 such that the recursive call to *Selection(k, smallList_array, 1, |smallList|)* requires at most $c_1 T(7n/10)$ time.

■ If $|smallList| < k$ and $|smallList| + |equalList| \geq k$, then the required element is in *equalList*, and this step requires only $\Theta(1)$ time, since the required element is equal to AM. (Notice at most one of the elements in *equalList* must be examined.)

■ If $|smallList| + |equalList| < k$, then the required element is in *bigList*. Consider the maximum number of elements that can appear in *bigList*. An argument similar to the one given above for the size of *smallList* can be used to show that *bigList* has at most $7n/10$ entries. Thus, we can say there is a constant c_2 such that the recursive call of the *Selection* routine requires at most $c_2 T(7n/10)$ time.

Therefore, there is a constant c_3 such that Step 7 uses at most $c_3 T(7n/10)$ time.

Finally, consider the total running time $T(n)$ for the selection algorithm we have presented. There are constants c, C_0, and C_1, such that the running time of this algorithm is given by

$T(n) \leq cn$ for $1 \leq n \leq 50$;

$T(n) \leq C_0 T(7n/10) + C_1 n$ for $n > 50$.

An upper bound on the right side of the recursion relation is $C_2[T(7n/10) + n]$, where $C_2 = \max\{C_0, C_1\}$. Since $T(n) = C_2[T(7n/10) + n]$ reflects a geometric series that resolves as $T(n) = \Theta(n)$ (see Exercises in Chapter 2, "Induction and Recursion"), we have $T(n) = O(n)$. Since we also must examine every entry of the input list (because were we to overlook an entry, it is possible that the entry overlooked has the "answer"), any selection algorithm must take $\Omega(n)$ time. Therefore, our algorithm takes $\Theta(n)$ time on a RAM, and this is optimal.

Parallel Machines: Notice that a lower bound on the time required to perform a selection on a parallel machine is based on the communication diameter of the machine, not the bisection width. Therefore, one might hope to construct an algorithm that runs in time proportional to the communication diameter of the given parallel model.

Consider applying the algorithm we have just presented on a PRAM. Notice that the independent sorting of Step 2 can be performed in parallel in $\Theta(1)$ time. Step 3 requires that the median elements are placed in their proper positions, which can be done quite simply on a PRAM in $\Theta(1)$ time. Step 4 is a recursive step that requires time proportional to $T(n/5)$. Step 5 requires constant time. Step 6 is interesting. The elements can be ordered and rearranged by performing a parallel prefix operation to number the elements in each list, in order to obtain the locations to write them into. That is, for each of the elements of S, we assign (by keeping a running count) its position in the appropriate of *smallList*, *equalList*, or *bigList* and copy the element of S into its assigned position in the appropriate one of these auxiliary lists. Therefore, this step can be performed in $O(\log n)$ time. Now consider the recursion in Step 7. Again, the running time of this step is no more than $T(7n/10)$. Therefore, the running time for the algorithm can be expressed as $T(n) = T(7n/10) + T(n/5) + O(\log n)$, which is asymptotically equivalent to $T(n) = T(7n/10) + O(\log n)$, which resolves to $T(n) = O(\log^2 n)$. It should be noted that the running time of this algorithm can be reduced to $O(\log n \log \log n)$ by applying some techniques that are outside the scope of this text. In addition, the problem can also be solved by first sorting the elements in $\Theta(\log n)$ time and then selecting the required element in $\Theta(1)$ time. This $\Theta(\log n)$ time sorting routine is also outside the scope of this book.

Consider the selection problem on a mesh of size n. Since the communication diameter of a mesh of size n is $\Theta(n^{1/2})$, and since it will be shown later in this chapter that sorting can be performed on the mesh in $\Theta(n^{1/2})$ time, we know that the problem of selection can be solved in optimal $\Theta(n^{1/2})$ time on a mesh of size n.

QUICKSORT (PARTITION SORT)

QuickSort is an efficient and popular sorting algorithm that was originally designed for the RAM by C.A.R. Hoare. It is a beautiful algorithm that serves as an excellent example of the divide-and-conquer paradigm. It is also a good example of an algorithm without a deterministic running time, in the sense that expected and worst-case running times are not the same. Depending on the arrangement of the n input items, QuickSort has a $\Theta(n)$ best-case running time and a $\Theta(n^2)$ worst-case running time on a RAM. However, the reason that QuickSort is so popular on the RAM is that it has a very fast, $\Theta(n \log n)$ expected-case running time. One must take care with QuickSort, however, as it can have a rather slow $\Theta(n^2)$ running time for important input sets, including nearly ordered or nearly reverse ordered data.

The basic algorithm consists of the three standard divide-and-conquer steps:

- **Divide:** Divide the n input items into three lists, denoted as *smallList*, *equalList*, and *bigList*, where all items in *smallList* are less than all items in *equalList*, all items in *equalList* have the same value, and all items in *equalList* are less than all items in *bigList*.

■ **Conquer:** Recursively sort *smallList* and *bigList*.

■ **Stitch:** *Concatenate smallList, equalList,* and *bigList.*

The reader should note the similarity of the divide step of QuickSort with the divide step of the Selection algorithm discussed earlier in this chapter (see Figure 9-7). Also note that the Conquer step does not require processing the *equalList*, as its members all have the same value.

QuickSort is naturally implemented with data arranged in queue structures. Since a queue can be efficiently and naturally implemented as a linked list, we will compare the QuickSort and MergeSort algorithms. Consider the divide (split) step. MergeSort requires a straightforward division of the elements into two lists of equal size, while QuickSort requires some intelligent reorganization of the data. However, during the stitch step, Merge-Sort requires an intricate combination of the recursively sorted sublists, while QuickSort merely requires concatenating sublists. Thus, MergeSort is referred to as an *easy split-hard join* algorithm, while QuickSort is referred to as a *hard split-easy join* algorithm. That is, it appears that MergeSort is more efficient than QuickSort in the divide stage, but less efficient than QuickSort in the stitch stage.

Notice that in MergeSort, comparisons are made between items in different lists during the merge operation. In QuickSort, however, notice that comparisons are made between

$q \rightarrow 5 \rightarrow 8 \rightarrow 1 \rightarrow 2 \rightarrow 6 \rightarrow 7 \rightarrow 4 \rightarrow 9 \rightarrow 3 \rightarrow|$

(a) Initial unsorted list

smallList $\rightarrow 1 \rightarrow 2 \rightarrow 4 \rightarrow 3 \rightarrow|$

equalList $\rightarrow 5 \rightarrow|$

bigList $\rightarrow 8 \rightarrow 6 \rightarrow 7 \rightarrow 9 \rightarrow|$

(b) Three lists after the partitioning based on the value of 5

smallList $\rightarrow 1 \rightarrow 2 \rightarrow 3 \rightarrow 4 \rightarrow|$

equalList $\rightarrow 5 \rightarrow|$

bigList $\rightarrow 6 \rightarrow 7 \rightarrow 8 \rightarrow 9 \rightarrow|$

(c) Three lists after *smallList* and *bigList* recursively sorted

$q \rightarrow 1 \rightarrow 2 \rightarrow 3 \rightarrow 4 \rightarrow 5 \rightarrow 6 \rightarrow 7 \rightarrow 8 \rightarrow 9 \rightarrow|$

(d) Completed list after the three sorted sublists are concatenated

Figure 9-7 An example of QuickSort on a linked list.

elements during the divide stage. The reason that no comparisons are made during the stitch step in QuickSort is because the divide step guarantees that if element x is sent to list *smallList*, element y is sent to list *equalList*, and element z is sent to *bigList*, then $x < y < z$.

Typically, the input data is divided into three lists by first using a small amount of time to determine an element that has a high probability of being a good approximation to the median element. We use the term *splitValue* to refer to the element that is selected for this purpose. This value is then used much in the same way as *AM* is used during the selection algorithm. Every element is sent to one of three lists, corresponding to those elements less than *splitValue* (list *smallList*), those elements equal to *splitValue* (list *equalList*), and those elements greater than *splitValue* (list *bigList*). After recursively sorting *bigList* and *smallList*, the three lists can simply be concatenated.

We mentioned above that depending on the order of the input, QuickSort could turn out to be a relatively slow algorithm. Consider the split step. Suppose that *splitValue* is chosen such that only a constant number of elements are either greater than or equal to *splitValue* or less than or equal to *splitValue*. This would create a situation where all but a few items wind up in either *smallList* or *bigList*, respectively. If this scenario continues throughout the recursion, it is easy to see that the analysis of running time would obey the recurrence $T(n) = T(n - c) + \Theta(n)$, for some constant c, which sums as an arithmetic series to $T(n) = \Theta(n^2)$. Of course, we hope that the splitting item is chosen (recursively) to be close to the median. This would result in a running time given by $T(n) = 2T(n/2) + \Theta(n)$, which gives $T(n) = \Theta(n \log n)$. Notice, unfortunately, that this worst-case running time of $\Theta(n^2)$ easily occurs if the data is nearly ordered or nearly reverse-ordered. Therefore, the user must be very careful in applying QuickSort to data for which such situations might arise.

We now present details of a list-based QuickSort algorithm on a RAM. We start with a top-down description of the algorithm.

Subprogram QuickSort(*q*)
Input: A list *q*.
Output: The list *q*, with the elements sorted.
Procedure: Use QuickSort to sort the list.
Local variables:
     splitValue, key used to partition the list;
     smallList, equalList, bigList, sublists for partitioning
Action:
     If *q* has at least two elements, then {Do work.}
         Create empty lists *smallList, equalList*, and *bigList*
         {Divide: Partition the list.}
         splitValue = findSplitValue(q);
         splitList(q, smallList, equalList, bigList, splitValue);
         {Conquer: Recursively sort sublists.}
         QuickSort(smallList);
         QuickSort(bigList);
         {Stitch: Concatenate sublists.}
         Concatenate(smallList, equalList, bigList, q)
     End If
   End Sort

We reiterate that it is not necessary to sort *equalList* in the "Conquer" section of the algorithm since all members of *equalList* have identical key fields. Now let's consider the running time of QuickSort:

- It takes $\Theta(1)$ time to determine whether or not a list has at least two items. Notice that a list having fewer than two items serves as the base case of recursion, requiring no further work since such a list is already sorted.
- Constructing three empty lists requires $\Theta(1)$ time using a modern programming language.
- Consider the time it takes to find the splitter. Ideally, we want the splitter to be the median element, so that *smallList* and *bigList* are of approximately the same size, which will serve to minimize the overall running time of the algorithm. The splitter can be chosen in as little as $\Theta(1)$ time, if one just grabs an easily accessible item, or in as much as $\Theta(n)$ time, if one wants to determine the median precisely (see the selection algorithm in the previous section). Initially, we will consider using a unit-time algorithm to determine the splitter. We realize that this could lead to a bad split and, if this continues recursively, to a very slow algorithm. Later in the chapter we will discuss improvements in choosing the splitter and the effect that such improvements have on the overall algorithm.
- Splitting the list requires $\Theta(1)$ time per item, which results in a $\Theta(n)$ time algorithm to split the n elements into the three aforementioned lists. The algorithm follows.

Subprogram splitList(*A, smallList, equalList, bigList, splitValue*)
Input: List *A*, partition element *splitValue*.
Output: Three sublists corresponding to items of *A* less than, equal to, and greater than *splitValue*.
Local variable: *temp*, a pointer used for dequeing and enqueing
Action:
    While not *empty(A)*, do
        getfirst(A, temp);
        If *temp.key* < *splitValue*, then
            putelement(temp, smallList)
        Elsc If *temp.key* = *splitValue*, then
            putelement(temp, equalList)
            Else *putelement(temp, bigList)*
    End While
End *SplitList*

Notice that for the sake of efficiency, it is important to be able to add an element to a list in $\Theta(1)$ time. Many designers make the mistake of adding a new element to the end of a list without keeping a tail pointer. Since elements are added to lists without respect to order, it is critical that elements be added efficiently to the lists. In a queue, elements can be added quite simply to the back of a list in $\Theta(1)$ time per element, resulting in a $\Theta(n)$-time split procedure.

Let's resume a discussion of the running time of QuickSort, though we will defer a detailed analysis until the next section. In the *best case*, every element of the input list goes into *equalList*, with *smallList* and *bigList* remaining empty. If this is the case, then the algorithm makes one pass through the data, places all of the items in a single list, has recursive calls that use $\Theta(1)$ time, and concatenates the lists in $\Theta(1)$ time. This results in a total running time of $\Theta(n)$.

Without loss of generality, let's now consider the case where all of the elements are distinct. Given this scenario, the *best-case* running time will occur when an even split occurs. That is, when one item is placed in *equalList*, $\lfloor n/2 \rfloor$ items in either *smallList* or *bigList*, and $\lceil n/2 \rceil - 1$ items in *bigList* or *smallList*, respectively. In this situation, the running time of the algorithm, $T(n)$, is given (approximately) as follows.

$$T(1) = \Theta(1)$$
$$T(n) = 2T(n/2) + \Theta(n)$$

Recall from the presentation of MergeSort that this recurrence results in a running time of $T(n) = \Theta(n \log n)$. So, in the best case, the running time of QuickSort is asymptotically optimal. In the next section, we will show that on average the running time is $\Theta(n \log n)$. This is a very important result with practical implications. It is one of the reasons that QuickSort comes packaged with so many computing systems as one of the built-in sorting routines.

Now consider the worst-case scenario. Suppose that either the maximum or minimum element in the list is chosen as *splitValue*. Therefore, after assigning elements to the three lists, one of the lists will have $n-1$ items in it, one will be empty, and *equalList* will have only the splitter in it. In this case, the running time of the algorithm obeys the recurrence $T(n) = T(n - 1) + \Theta(n)$, which has a solution of $T(n) = \Theta(n^2)$. That is, if one gets very unlucky at each stage of the recursion, the running time of QuickSort could be as bad as $\Theta(n^2)$. One should be concerned about this problem in the event that such a running time is not acceptable. Further, if one anticipates data sets that have large segments of ordered data, one may want to avoid a straightforward implementation of QuickSort. The scenario of a bad split at every stage of the recursion could also be realized with an input list that does not have large segments of ordered data (see the Exercises). Later in this chapter, we discuss techniques for minimizing the possibility of a $\Theta(n^2)$-time QuickSort algorithm.

Array Implementation: In this section, we discuss the application of QuickSort to a set of data stored in an array. The astute reader might note that with modern programming languages, one very rarely encounters a situation where the data to be sorted is maintained in a static array. However, an efficient static array implementation of QuickSort is important for "dusty deck" codes that must be maintained in their original style. This includes old scientific software written in languages such as FORTRAN. In addition, there are other reasons why we present this *unnatural implementation of QuickSort*. The first is historic. When algorithms texts first appeared, the major data structure was a static array. For this reason, QuickSort has been presented in many texts predominantly from the array point of view. Although this is unfortunate, we do believe that for historic reasons, it is also important to include an array implementation of QuickSort in this book. Finally, while the linked list implementation that we presented in the preceding section is straightforward in its design, implementation, and analysis, the array implementation is quite complex and very counterintuitive. The advantage of this is that it allows us to present some interesting analysis techniques and to discuss some interesting algorithmic issues in terms of optimization.

The input to the QuickSort routine consists of an array *A* containing *n* elements to be sorted. We will assume that *A* contains the keys to be compared. Note that the data associated with each element could be maintained in other fields if the language allows an array of records or could be maintained in other (parallel) arrays. The latter situation was common in the 1960s and 1970s, especially with languages such as FORTRAN. Also notice that the major problem with a static array is partitioning the elements. We assume that additional data structures cannot be allocated in a dynamic fashion. Therefore, we assume that any rearrangement must take place within the given array *A*. Again, this situation may seem strange to students of computer science who grew up (in computing) in the 1980s or later. However, we reiterate that there are situations and languages for which this scenario is critical.

So let's consider the basic QuickSort algorithm as implemented on an array *A*, where we wish to sort the elements *A*[*left* . . . *right*], where *left* ≤ *right* are integers that serve as pointers into the array.

Subprogram QuickSort (*A*, *left*, *right*)
Input: An array *A*.
Output: The array *A* with elements sorted by the QuickSort method.
If *left* < *right*, then
      Partition(*A*, *left*, *right*, *partitionIndex*)
      QuickSort(*A*, *left*, *partitionIndex*)
      QuickSort(*A*, *partitionIndex*+1, *right*)
End If
End QuickSort

Notice that the basic algorithm is similar to the generic version of QuickSort presented previously. That is, we need to partition the elements and then sort each of the subarrays. For purposes of our discussion in this section, we view the array as being horizontal. In order to work more easily with an array, we will partition it into only two subarrays under a relaxed criterion that requires all elements in the left subarray to be *less than* or *equal to* all elements in the right subarray. We then recursively sort the left subarray and the right subarray. Notice that the concatenation step comes for free since concatenating two adjacent subarrays does not require any work. Specifically, we have the following:

1. **Divide:** *A*[*left* . . . *right*] is partitioned into two *nonempty* subarrays *A*[*left* . . . *p*] and *A*[*p* + 1 . . . *right*] such that all elements in *A*[*left* . . . *p*] are less than or equal to all elements in *A*[*p*+1 . . . *right*].

2. **Conquer:** Recursively sort the two subarrays, *A*[*left* . . . *p*] and *A*[*p* + 1 . . . *right*].

3. **Stitch:** Requires no work since the data is in an array that is already correctly joined.

So, given the basic algorithm, we only need to fill in the algorithm for the partition routine (see Figure 9-8). We need to point out that this routine is specific to array implementations. Over the years, we have watched numerous programmers (predominantly students) try to implement this routine on a linked list because they did not understand the fundamentals of QuickSort and did not realize that this array implementation is unnatural. The (standard) partition routine that we are about to present *should only be used with an array*.

5	8	1	2	6	7	4	9	3

(a) The initial unordered array is given.

3	4	1	2	6	7	8	9	5

(b) The data is shown after partitioning has been
performed with respect to the value of 5. Notice that
⟨3,4,1,2⟩ are all less than or equal to 5 and
⟨6,7,8,9,5⟩ are all greater than or equal to 5.

1	2	3	4	5	6	7	8	9

(c) The array is presented after the recursive sorting
on each of the two subarrays. Notice that this results
in the entire array being sorted.

Figure 9-8   An example of QuickSort on an array of
size 9.

This partition routine works as follows. First, choose a partition value. Next, partition the array into two subarrays so that all elements in the left subarray are less than or equal to the partition value, while all elements in the right subarray are greater than or equal to this value. This is done by marching through the array from left to right in search of an element that is *greater than or equal to* the partition value, and similarly, from right to left in search of an element that is *less than or equal to* the partition value. If such elements are found, they are swapped, and the search continues until the elements discovered are in their proper subarrays. Refer again to Figure 9-8. Pseudocode follows.

Subprogram Partition(*A*, *left*, *right*, *partitionIndex*)
Input: A subarray *A*[*left*, . . . , *right*].
Output: An index, *partitionIndex*, and the subarray *A*[*left*, . . . , *right*] partitioned
          so that all elements in *A*[*left*, . . . , *partitionIndex*] are less than or equal to
          all elements in *A*[*partitionIndex* + 1, . . . , *right*].
Local variables: *splitValue*; indices *i, j*
Action:
       splitValue ← *A*[*left*] {A simple choice of splitter.}
       i ← *left* − 1
       j ← *right* + 1
       While *i* < *j*, do
              Repeat *j* ← *j* − 1 until *A*[*j*] ≤ *splitValue*
              Repeat *i* ← *i* + 1 until *A*[*i*] ≥ *splitValue*
              If *i* < *j*, then *SWAP*(*A*[*i*], *A*[*j*])
              Else *partitionIndex* ← *j*
       End While
End Partition

We now present an example of the partition routine. Notice that the marching from left to right is accomplished by the movement of index *i*, while the marching from right to left is accomplished by the movement of index j. It is important to note that each is look-ing for an element that could be on the other side. That is, i will stop at any element *greater than or equal to* the splitter element, and j will stop at any element *less than or equal to* the splitter element. The reader should note that this guarantees the algorithm will terminate without allowing either index to move off of the end of the array, so there is no infinite loop.

EXAMPLE (SEE FIGURE 9-9)

Illustration of Partition: Initially, the *splitValue* is chosen to be $A[1] = 5$, the first elementof the array, i is set to $left-1 = 0$, and j is set to $right + 1 = 9$, as shown in Figure 9-9a.

Since $i < j$, the algorithm proceeds by decrementing j until an element is found that is less than or equal to 5. Next, i is incremented until an element is encountered that is greater than or equal to 5. At the end of this first pair of index updates, we have $i = 1$ and $j = 7$, as shown in Figure 9-9b.

Since $i < j$, we swap elements $A[1]$ and $A[7]$. This results in the configuration of the array shown in Figure 9-9c.

Since $i < j$, the algorithm proceeds by decrementing j until an element is found that is less than or equal to 5. Next, i is incremented until an element is encountered that is greater than or equal to 5. At the end of this pair of index updates, we have $i = 4$ and $j = 6$, as shown in Figure 9-9d.

Since $i < j$, we swap elements $A[4]$ and $A[6]$. This results in the configuration of the array shown in Figure 9-9e.

Since $i < j$, the algorithm continues. First, we decrement j until an element (4) is found that is less than or equal to 5. Next, we increment i until an element (6) is found that is greater than or equal to 5. At the end of this pair of index updates, we have $i = 6$ and $j = 5$ (see Figure 9-9f).

Since $i \geq j$, the procedure terminates with the *partitionIndex* set to $j = 5$. This means that QuickSort can be called recursively on $A[1 \ldots 5]$ and $A[6 \ldots 8]$.

Analysis of QuickSort: In this section, we consider the time and space requirements for the array version of QuickSort, as implemented on a RAM.

Time: Notice that the running time is given by $T(n) = T(n_L) + T(n_R) + \Theta(n)$, where $\Theta(n)$ is the time required for the partition and concatenation operations, $T(n_L)$ is the time required to sort recursively the left subarray of size n_L, and $T(n_R)$ is the time required to sort recur-sively the right subarray of size n_R, where $n_L + n_R = n$.

Consider the best-case running time. That is, consider the situation that will result in the minimum running time of the array version of QuickSort as presented. Notice that in order to minimize the running time, we want $T(n_L) = \Theta(T(n_R))$, which occurs if $n_L = \Theta(n_R)$. In fact, it is easy to see that the running time is minimized if we partition the array into two approximately equally sized pieces at every step of the recursion. This basically results in

(a)

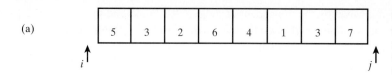

Figure 9-9a-f   An example of the *Partition* routine of QuickSort on an array of eight items.

(b)

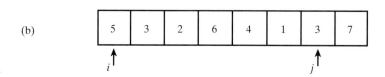

(c)

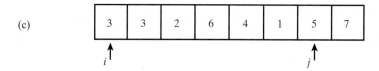

(d)

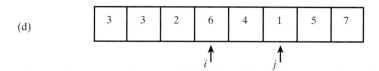

(e)

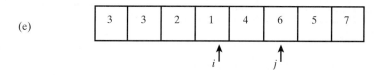

(f)

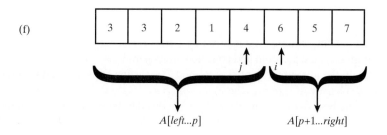

$A[left...p]$ $A[p+1...right]$

the recurrence $T(n) = 2T(n/2) + \Theta(n)$, which has a solution of $T(n) = \Theta(n \log n)$. This situation will occur if every time the partition element is selected, it is the median of the elements being sorted.

Consider the worst-case running time. Notice that the running time is maximized if either n_L or n_R is equal to $n - 1$. That is, the running time is maximized if the partition is such that the subarrays are of size 1 and $n - 1$. This would yield a recurrence of $T(n) = T(n - 1) + \Theta(n)$, which resolves to $T(n) = \Theta(n^2)$. While this situation can occur in a variety of ways, notice that this situation easily occurs for data that is ordered or reverse-ordered. The user should be very careful of this since sorting data that is nearly ordered can occur frequently in a number of important situations.

Finally, consider the expected running time. As it turns out, the expected-case running time is asymptotically equivalent to the best-case running time. That is, given a set of elements with distinct keys arbitrarily distributed throughout the array, we expect the running time of QuickSort to be $\Theta(n \log n)$. The proof of this running time is a bit complex, though very interesting. We present this proof later in this chapter.

A summary of the running times for the array version of QuickSort is presented in the following table.

Scenario	Running Time
Best-Case	$\Theta(n \log n)$
Worst-Case	$\Theta(n^2)$
Expected-Case	$\Theta(n \log n)$

Space: In this section, we consider the *additional* space used by the array version of Quick-Sort as implemented on a RAM. This may seem like a trivial issue since the routine does not use anything more than a few local variables. That is, there are no additional arrays, no dynamic allocation of memory, and so on. However, notice that the routine is recursive. This means that the system will create a system stack entry for each procedure call pushed onto the system stack.

Consider the best-case space scenario. This occurs when both procedure calls are placed on the stack, the first is popped off and immediately discarded, and the second is popped off and evaluated. In this case, there need never be more than two items on the stack: the initial call to QuickSort and one additional recursive call. Notice that this situation occurs when the array is split into pieces of size 1 and $n - 1$. Furthermore, the recursive calls must be pushed onto the system stack so that the subarray of size 1 is sorted first. This procedure call terminates immediately since sorting an array of size 1 represents the base case of the QuickSort routine. Next, the system stack is popped and the procedure is invoked to sort the subarray of size $n - 1$. The system stack is prevented from growing to more than two calls via minor modification in the code that replaces a (tail-end) recursive call by either an increment to *left* or a decrement to *right*, and a branch.

Now let's consider the worst-case space scenario. This situation is almost identical to the best-case space scenario. The only difference is that the procedure calls are pushed onto the system stack in the reverse order. That is, the procedure call to sort the subarray of size 1 is pushed on before the procedure call to sort the subarray of size $n - 1$. In this situation, the procedure will first be invoked to evaluate the subarray of size $n - 1$, and after that routine is complete, the system stack will be popped and the subarray of size 1 will be sorted. In this situation, the system stack will need to store $\Theta(n)$ procedure calls.

It is interesting to note that both the best-case and worst-case space situations occur with the $\Theta(n^2)$ worst-case running time.

Consider the expected-case space scenario. This occurs with the expected-case $\Theta(n \log n)$ running time, where no more than $\Theta(\log n)$ procedure calls are ever on the system stack at any one time. Again, this can be seen in conjunction with the expected-case analysis that will follow.

A summary of space requirements for the array version of QuickSort is presented in the table below.

Scenario	Extra Space
Best-Case	$\Theta(1)$
Worst-Case	$\Theta(n)$
Expected-Case	$\Theta(\log n)$

Expected-Case Analysis of QuickSort: In this section, we consider the expected-case running time of QuickSort. The analysis is intricate and is suitable only for a reader who has a solid mathematical background. We will make a variety of assumptions, most of which serve only to simplify the analysis. Our first major assumption is that the array consists of n *distinct keys, randomly distributed*. In terms of fundamental notation, we let $k(i)$ be the expected number of key comparisons required to sort i items. QuickSort is a comparison-based sort, and our analysis will focus on determining the number of times QuickSort compares two elements during the sorting procedure. The reader should note that $k(0) = 0$, $k(1) = 0$, and $k(2) = 3.5$. That is, an array with one (or fewer) element(s) is already sorted and does not require any keys to be compared. An array of size 2 requires (on average) 3.5 comparisons to be sorted by the array version of QuickSort that we have presented. The reader should verify this.

We now consider some assumptions that apply to the partition routine. Assume that we are required to sort $A[1 \ldots n]$:

■ According to the partition routine, we will use $A[1]$ as the partition element.

■ As we are assuming distinct keys, if the partition element (originally $A[1]$) is the i-th largest element in $A[1 \ldots n]$ and $i > 1$, then at the end of the partition, the smallest $i - 1$ elements will be stored in $A[1 \ldots i - 1]$. We can make a simple modification to the code so that at the end of the partition routine, the splitter is placed in position i, and *partitionIndex* is set to i. Notice that this modification requires $\Theta(1)$ time.

■ Therefore, notice that it suffices to have the recursive calls performed on $A[1 \ldots (i - 1)]$ and $A[(i + 1) \ldots n]$.

Consider the number of comparisons that are made in the partition routine:

■ Notice that it takes $\Theta(n)$ comparisons to partition the n elements. The reader should verify this.

■ Based on our notation and the recursive nature of QuickSort, we note that, on average, it takes $k(i - 1)$ and $k(n - i)$ comparisons to sort each subarray, respectively.

We should point out that since we assume unique input elements and that all arrangements of the input data are equally likely, then it is equally likely that the *partitionIndex* returned is any of the elements of $\{1, \ldots, n\}$. That is, the *partitionIndex* will wind up with any value from 1 through and including n with probability $1/n$. Finally, we present details for determining the expected-case running time of QuickSort.

We have $k(n) = (n + 1) + \dfrac{1}{n}\displaystyle\sum_{i=1}^{n} [k(i - 1) + k(n - i)]$, where

- $k(n)$ is the expected number of key comparisons,
- $(n + 1)$ is the number of comparisons required to partition n data items, to partition n data items, assuming that Partition is modified in such a way as to prevent i and j from crossing,
- $1/n$ is the probability of the input $A[1]$ being the i-th largest entry of A,
- $k(i - 1)$ is the expected number of key comparisons to sort $A[1 \ldots i - 1]$, and
- $k(n - i)$ is the expected number of key comparisons to sort $A[i + 1 \ldots n]$.

So,

$$k(n) = (n + 1) + \frac{1}{n}\sum_{i=1}^{n} [k(i - 1) + k(n - i)]$$

$$= n + 1 + \frac{1}{n}\begin{bmatrix} k(0) & + k(n - 1) \\ +k(1) & + k(n - 2) \\ +\ldots & + \ldots \\ +k(n - 1) & + k(0) \end{bmatrix}$$

$$= n + 1 + \frac{2}{n}\sum_{i=1}^{n-1} k(i).$$

(Note that we used the fact that $k(0) = 0$.)

Therefore, we now have

$$k(n) = n + 1 + \frac{2}{n}[k(n - 1) + k(n - 2) + k(n - 3) + \ldots + k(1)].$$

Notice that this means that

$$k(n - 1) = n + \frac{2}{n - 1}[k(n - 2) + k(n - 3) + \ldots + k(1)].$$

In order to simplify the equation for $k(n)$, let's define

$$S = [k(n - 2) + k(n - 3) + \ldots + k(1)].$$

By substituting into the previous equations for $k(n)$ and $k(n - 1)$, we obtain

$$k(n) = n + 1 + \frac{2}{n}[k(n - 1) + S] \text{ and } k(n - 1) = n + \frac{2}{n - 1}S.$$

Therefore, $S = \dfrac{n - 1}{2}(k(n - 1) - n)$.

So,

$$k(n) = n + 1 + \frac{2}{n}\left[k(n-1) + \frac{n-1}{2}(k(n-1) - n)\right]$$

$$= \frac{n+1}{n}k(n-1) + 2.$$

Hence, $\dfrac{k(n)}{n+1} = \dfrac{2}{n+1} + \dfrac{k(n-1)}{n}.$

In order to simplify, let's define

$$X(n) = \frac{k(n)}{n+1}.$$

Therefore,

$$\frac{k(n-1)}{n} = X(n-1).$$

So,

$$X(n) = \frac{2}{n+1} + X(n-1) = \frac{2}{n+1} + \frac{2}{n} + X(n-2) =$$

$$\frac{2}{n+1} + \frac{2}{n} + \frac{2}{n-1} + X(n-3) = \dots$$

The reader should be able to supply an induction argument from which it can be concluded that

$$X(n) = \frac{2}{n+1} + \frac{2}{n} + \frac{2}{n-1} + \dots + \frac{2}{4} + X(2)$$

$$= 2\left(\frac{1}{4} + \frac{1}{5} + \dots + \frac{1}{n+1}\right) + C, \left(C = X(2) \text{ \{A constant.\}} = \frac{k(2)}{3} = \frac{3.5}{3} = \frac{7}{6}\right)$$

$$= C + 2\sum_{i=4}^{n+1}\frac{1}{i} = \Theta(\log n).$$

So, $k(n) = (n+1)X(n) = \Theta(n \log n)$ expected-case number of comparisons.

It is easily seen that the expected-case number of data moves (swaps) is $O(n \log n)$, as the number of data moves is no more than the number of comparisons. Therefore, the expected-case running time of QuickSort is $\Theta(n \log n)$. The argument given above requires little modification to show that our queue-based implementation of QuickSort also has an expected-case running time of $\Theta(n \log n)$.

Improving QuickSort: In this section, we discuss some improvements that can be made to QuickSort. First, we consider modifications targeted at improving the running time. (It is important to note that the modifications we suggest should be evaluated experimentally on the computer systems under consideration.) One way to avoid the possibility of a bad splitter is to sample more than one element. For example, choosing the median of some small number of keys as the splitter might result in a small (single-digit) percentage improvement in overall running time for large input sets. As an extreme case, one might use the selection algorithm presented earlier in this chapter to choose the splitter as the median value in the list. Notice that this raises the time from $\Theta(1)$ to $\Theta(n)$ to choose the splitter. However, because the selection of a splitter is bundled into the $\Theta(n)$ time partition routine, this increased running time will have no effect on the asymptotic running time of QuickSort. Of course, it will often have a significant effect on the real running time of QuickSort.

If one is really concerned about trying to avoid the worst-case running time of Quick-Sort, it might be wise to reduce the possibility of having to sort mostly ordered or reverse-ordered data. As strange as it may seem, a reasonable way to do this is first to randomize your input data. That is, *take your set of input data and randomly permute it.* This will have the effect of significantly reducing the possibility of taking ordered sequences of significant length as input.

After experimentation, the reader will note that QuickSort is very fast for large values of n, but slow (relatively) for small values of n. The reader might perform an experiment comparing QuickSort to SelectionSort, InsertionSort, and other sorting methods for various values of n. One of the reasons that QuickSort is slow for small n is that there is significant overhead to recursion. This overhead does not exist for straight-sorting methods, like InsertionSort and SelectionSort, which are constructed as tight, doubly nested loops. Therefore, one might consider a *hybrid* approach to QuickSort that exploits an asymptotically inferior routine, which is only applied in a situation where it is better in practice. Such a hybrid sort can be constructed in several ways. The most obvious is to use QuickSort (recursively) only as long as $right - left \geq m$, for some experimentally determined m. That is, one uses the basic QuickSort routine of partitioning and calling QuickSort recursively on both the left and right subarrays. However, the base case changes from a simple evaluation of $left < right$ to $right - left < m$. In the case that $right - left < m$, then one applies the straight-sorting routine that was used to determine the cutoff value of m. Possibilities include SelectionSort and InsertionSort, with SelectionSort typically being favored.

Consider an alternative approach. Sort the data recursively, so long as $right - left \geq m$. Whenever a partition is created such that $right - left < m$, however, simply ignore that partition. Then at the end of the entire QuickSort procedure, notice that every element is within m places of where it really belongs. At this point, one could run InsertionSort on the entire set of data. Notice that InsertionSort runs in $O(mn)$ time, where n is the number of elements in the array, and m is the maximum distance any element must move. Therefore, for m small, this is a very fast routine. In fact, for m constant, this implementation of InsertionSort requires only $\Theta(n)$ time. Further, compared to the previous hybrid approach, this approach has an advantage in that only one additional procedure call is made, compared to the $O(n)$ procedure calls that could be made if small subarrays are immediately sorted. Hence, this version of a hybrid QuickSort is generally preferred.

We now consider improvements in the space requirements of QuickSort. Recall that the major space consideration is the additional space required for the system stack. One might consider unrolling the recursion and rewriting QuickSort in a nonrecursive fashion, which requires maintaining your own stack. This can be used to save some real space, but it does not have a major asymptotic benefit. Another improvement we might consider is to maintain the stack only with jobs that need to be done and not jobs representing tail-end recursion that are simply waiting for another job to terminate. However, in terms of saving significant space, one should consider pushing the jobs onto the stack in an intelligent fashion. That is, one should always push the jobs onto the stack so that the smaller job (that is, the job sorting the smaller of the two subarrays) is evaluated first. This helps to avoid the $\Theta(n)$ worst-case space problem, which can be quite important if you are working in a relatively small programming environment.

Parallel Models: There have been numerous attempts to parallelize QuickSort for a variety of machines and models of computation. One parallelization that is particularly interesting is the extension of QuickSort, by Bruce Wagar, to *HyperQuickSort*, a QuickSort-based algorithm targeted at medium- and coarse-grained parallel computers. In this section, we first describe the *HyperQuickSort* algorithm for a medium-grained hypercube and then present an analysis of its running time.

HYPERQUICKSORT

1. Initially, it is assumed that the n elements are evenly distributed among the 2^d nodes so that every node contains $N = n/2^d$ elements.

2. Each node sorts its N items independently using some $\Theta(N \log N)$ time algorithm.

3. Node 0 determines the median of its N elements, denoted as *Med*. This takes $\Theta(1)$ time since the elements in the node have just been sorted.

4. Node 0 broadcasts *Med* to all 2^d nodes in $\Theta(d)$ time by a straightforward hypercube broadcast routine.

5. Every node logically partitions its local set of data into two groups, X and Y, where X contains those elements less than or equal to *Med* and Y contains those elements greater than *Med*. This requires $\Theta(\log N)$ time via a binary search for *Med* among the values of the node's data.

6. Consider two disjoint subcubes of size 2^{d-1}, denoted as L and U. For simplicity, let L consist of all nodes with a 0 as the most significant bit of its address and let R consist of all nodes with a 1 as the most significant bit of its address. Note that the union of L and U is the entire hypercube of size 2^d. So every node of the hypercube is a member of either L or U. Each node that is a member of L sends its set Y to its adjacent node in U. Likewise, each node in U sends its set X to its adjacent node in L. Notice that when this step is complete, all elements less than or equal to *Med* are in L, while all elements greater than *Med* are in U. This step requires $\Theta(N)$ time for the transmission of the data.

7. Each node now *merges* the set of data just received with the one it has kept (*i.e.*, a node in L merges its own set X with its U-neighbor's set X, a node in U merges its own set Y with its L-neighbor's set Y). Therefore, after $\Theta(N)$ time for merging two sets of data, every node again has a sorted set of data.

8. Repeat steps 3–7 on each of L and U simultaneously, independently, recursively, and in parallel until the subcubes consist of a single node, at which point the data in the entire hypercube is sorted. For example, during the first recursive call, work on L will involve two subcubes of size 2^{d-1}, one of which has leading address bits of 00 and the other of which has leading address bits of 01. Similarly, work on R will involve two subcubes of size 2^{d-1}, one with leading bits 10 and the other with leading bits 11.

The time analysis embedded in the presentation above is not necessarily correct as the algorithm continues to iterate (recurse) over steps 3–7 due to the fact that after some time the data may become quite unbalanced. That is, pairs of processors may require $\omega(N)$ time to transmit and merge data. As a consequence, when the algorithm terminates, all processors may not necessarily have N items.

Assuming that the data is initially distributed in a random fashion, Wagar has shown that the expected-case running time of this algorithm is

$$\Theta\left(N \log N + \frac{d(d+1)}{2} + dN\right).$$

The $N \log N$ term represents the sequential running time from Step 2, the $(d(d+1))/2$ term represents the broadcast step used in Step 4, and the dN term represents the time required for the exchanging and merging of the sets of elements.

In the next section, we will consider a medium-grained implementation of bitonic sort. We will see that bitonic sort offers the advantage that, throughout the algorithm, all nodes maintain the same number of elements per processor. However, given good recursive choices of splitting elements, HyperQuickSort offers the advantage that it is more efficient than bitonic sort.

BITONIC SORT (REVISITED)

In Chapter 4, we presented some motivation, history, and a detailed description of Bitonic Sort. In addition, we presented an analysis of the algorithm for several models of computation. To recap, given a set of n elements, we showed that Bitonic Sort will run in $\Theta(\log^2 n)$ time on a PRAM of size n, in $\Theta(\log^2 n)$ on a hypercube of size n, and in $\Theta(n \log^2 n)$ time on a RAM. In this section, we consider Bitonic Sort on a medium-grained hypercube, as a means of comparison to the HyperQuickSort routine presented in the last section. We then consider Bitonic Sort on a mesh of size n.

Our initial assumptions are the same as they were for HyperQuickSort. Assume that we are initially given n data elements evenly distributed among the 2^d processors (nodes) so that each processor contains $N = n/2^d$ items. Suppose that each processor sorts its initial set of data in $\Theta(N \log N)$ time. Once this is done, we simply follow the data movement and general philosophy of the fine-grained Bitonic Sort algorithm, as previously presented. The major modification is to accommodate the difference between processors performing a comparison and exchange of two items (fine-grained model), and a comparison and exchange of $2N$ items (medium-grained model).

Suppose processor A and processor B need to order their $2N$ items in the medium-grained model so that the N smaller items will reside in processor A and the N larger items will reside in processor B. This can be accomplished as follows. In $\Theta(N)$ time, processors A and B exchange data so that each processor has the complete set of $2N$ items. Each processor now merges the two sets of items in $\Theta(N)$ time simultaneously. Finally, processor A retains the N smallest items (discarding the N largest items) and processor B retains the N largest items (discarding the N smallest items).

The running time of Bitonic Sort on a medium-grained hypercube consists of the initial $\Theta(N \log N)$ sequential sort, followed by the $d(d + 1)/2$ steps of Bitonic Sort, each of which now requires $\Theta(N)$ time, resulting in a total running time of

$$\Theta\left(N \log N + \frac{d(d + 1)}{2} N \right).$$

As mentioned previously, the reader should note two major differences when considering whether to use Bitonic Sort or HyperQuickSort on a medium-grained hypercube. The first difference is the improvement in running time of HyperQuickSort over Bitonic Sort by a relatively small factor. The second difference concerns the placement of the data when the algorithm terminates. In Bitonic Sort, the data is distributed evenly among the processors, while this is not the case with HyperQuickSort.

Bitonic Sort on a Mesh: In this section, we present a straightforward implementation of the fine-grained Bitonic Sort algorithm on a fine-grained mesh computer. After the presentation of the algorithm, we discuss details of the implementation and the effect that such details have on the running time of the algorithm.

Initially, let's assume that a set of n data elements is given, arbitrarily distributed one per processor on a mesh of size n. In order to perform sorting on a distributed-memory parallel machine, we must define the ordering of the processors since the elements are sorted with respect to the ordering of the processors. Initially, we assume that the processors are ordered with respect to *shuffled row-major* indexing scheme, as shown in Figure 9-10.

Figure 9-10 The *shuffled-row major index scheme* as applied to a mesh of size 16. It is important to note that on a mesh of size n, this indexing continues recursively within each quadrant.

(Note that for a machine with more than 16 processors, this ordering holds recursively within each quadrant.)

At the end of this section, we will discuss a simple way to adapt Bitonic Sort to whatever predefined processor ordering is required/utilized. Recall that Bitonic Sort is a variant of MergeSort. Viewed in a bottom-up fashion, initially bitonic sequences of size 2 are bitonically merged into sorted sequences of size 4. Then bitonic sequences of size 4 are bitonically merged into sorted sequences of size 8, and so on. At each stage, the sequences being merged are independent and the merging is performed in parallel on all such sequences. In addition, recall that the concatenation of an increasing sequence with a decreasing sequence will form a bitonic sequence. Therefore, we must be careful when merging a bitonic sequence into a sorted sequence as to whether it is merged into an increasing or a decreasing sequence. The reader may wish to review the section on Bitonic Sort before proceeding with the remainder of this section.

In the example presented below, notice that we exploit the shuffled row-major indexing scheme. Therefore, sequences of size 2 are stored as 1×2 strings, sequences of size 4 are stored as 2×2 strings, sequences of size 8 are stored as 2×4 strings, and so on. A critical observation is that if a comparison and (possible) exchange must be made between data that reside in two processors, then those processors always *reside in either the same row or in the same column*. This is due to the properties of the shuffled row-major indexing scheme coupled with the fact that Bitonic Sort only compares entries that differ in one bit of their indexing.

Consider the example of Bitonic Sort on a mesh of size 16, as presented in Figure 9-11. This example shows how to sort the initial set of arbitrarily distributed data into increasing order with respect to the shuffled row-major ordering of the processors. The first matrix shows the initial set of arbitrarily distributed data. Notice that a sequence of size 1 is sorted into either increasing or decreasing order. Therefore, initially, there are $n/2$ bitonic sequences of size 2 (in the form of 1×2 strings), each of which must be bitonically merged. This is accomplished by a single comparison, representing the base case of the Bitonic Sort, resulting in the second matrix. Notice that some of the sequences are sorted into increasing order and some into decreasing order. Next, we take this matrix and wish to merge bitonic sequences of size 4 (in the form of 2×2 strings) into sorted order. This is accomplished by first performing a comparison-exchange operation between items that are two places apart in the indexing, followed by recursively sorting each of the 1×2 strings independently. The fourth matrix shows the result of this sorting. Notice that each of the four quadrants has data in sorted order with respect to the shuffled row-major indexing. (The northwest and southwest quadrants are in increasing order, while the northeast and southeast quadrants are in decreasing order.) The example continues, showing the details of combining 2×2 strings into sorted 2×4 strings, and finally combining the two 2×4 strings into the final sorted 4×4 string.

Analysis of Running Time: Recall from the detailed analysis of Bitonic Sort presented in Chapter 4 that Bitonic Sort is based on MergeSort. Therefore, it requires $\Theta(\log n)$ parallel merge operations (that is, complete passes through the data), merging lists of size 1 into lists of size 2, then lists of size 2 into lists of size 4, and so forth. However, the merge operation is not the standard merge routine that one learns in a second semester computer science course, but rather the more complex bitonic merge. Further, the time for each bitonic merge requires a slightly

Example:

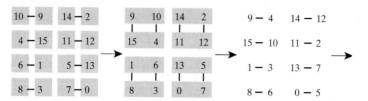

initially ordered   Now sorted into
into 1×1 sections   1×2 sections

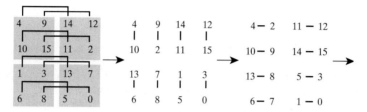

Now sorted into
2×2 sections

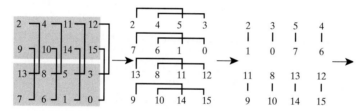

Now sorted into
2×4 sections

1 — 0	5 — 4	
2 — 3	7 — 6	
9 — 8	13 — 12	
11 — 10	14 — 15	

0	1	4	5
2	3	6	7
8	9	12	13
10	11	14	15

Now sorted into
4×4 sections

Figure 9-11 An example of *Bitonic Sort* on a mesh of size 16. The elements are sorted into a shuffled-row major order, as given in Figure 9-10. The initial data is given in the top-left matrix. After applying a comparison-exchange operation between the indicated elements (e.g., 10–9, 14–2, 4–15, . . .), the matrix has been ordered into disjoint 1 × 2 segments, as indicated in the next matrix. The interpretation of the figure continues in this manner.

more complex analysis than that of determining the time for a traditional merge. For example, merging pairs of elements into ordered lists of size 2 requires one level of comparison-exchange operations (which can be thought of as one parallel comparison-exchange operation). This is the base case. Merging bitonic sequences of size 2 into ordered lists of size 4 requires an initial comparison-exchange level (that is, $n/2$ comparison-exchange operations), followed by applying the Bitonic Sort routine for sequences of size 2 to each of the resulting subsequences. Therefore, the total number of comparison-exchange levels is $1 + 1 = 2$. The time to merge bitonic sequences of size 4 into ordered sequences of size 8 requires one comparison-exchange level to divide the data, followed by two (parallel) comparison-exchange levels to sort each of the bitonic subsequences of size 4. Therefore, the total number of comparison-exchange levels to merge a bitonic sequence of size 8 into an ordered sequence is three ($1 + 2 = 3$). In general, the time to merge two bitonic sequences of size $n/2$ into an ordered sequence of size n is $\log_2 n$.

Recall that in order to use the bitonic merge unit to create a sorting routine/network, you must apply the basic MergeSort scenario. That is, sorting an arbitrary sequence of n items requires us first to sort (in parallel) two subsequences of size $n/2$, then to perform a comparison-exchange on items $n/2$ apart, and then to merge recursively each subsequence of size $n/2$. Therefore, the total number of comparison-exchange levels (or parallel comparison-exchange operations) is

$$\sum_{i=1}^{\log_2 n} i = \frac{(\log_2 n)(\log_2 n + 1)}{2} = \frac{\log^2(n)}{2} + \frac{\log(n)}{2}.$$

The reader should refer to the section on Bitonic Sort for the original presentation of this analysis.

Now consider a mesh implementation. Suppose that each of the $\Theta(\log^2 n)$ comparison-exchange levels is implemented by a rotation (either a column rotation or a row rotation, as appropriate). The running time of the algorithm on a mesh of size n would then be $\Theta(n^{1/2} \log^2 n)$. However, if you look closely at the data movement operations that are required in order to perform the comparison-exchange operations, you will notice that during the first iteration, when creating the 1×2 lists, the data items are only one link apart. When creating the 2×2 lists, the data items are again only one link apart. When creating the 2×4 and 4×4 lists, the data items are either one or two links apart, and so forth. Therefore, if one is careful to construct modified row and column rotations that allow for simultaneous and disjoint rotations within segments of a row or column, respectively, the running time can be improved significantly. With this optimized rotation scheme, the time to sort n items on a mesh of size n is given by the recurrence $T(n) = T(n/2) + \Theta(n^{1/2})$, where $T(n/2)$ is the time to sort each of the subsequences of size $n/2$, and $\Theta(n^{1/2})$ is the time required to perform a set of $n/2$ comparison-exchange operations (that is, one level of comparison-exchange operations). Therefore, the running time of this algorithm is $\Theta(n^{1/2})$, which is optimal for a mesh of size n, due to the communication diameter. While the algorithm is optimal for this architecture, notice that the cost of the algorithm is $\Theta(n^{3/2})$, which is far from optimal. We leave as an exercise the possibility of modifying this architecture and algorithm to achieve a cost-optimal sorting algorithm on a mesh.

Sorting Data with Respect to Other Orderings: How would you handle the situation of sorting a set of data on a fine-grained mesh into an ordering other than shuffled row-major? For example, given a set of n data items, initially distributed in an arbitrary fashion one per processor on a mesh of size n, how would you sort the data into row-major or snake-like order? If one is only concerned about asymptotic complexity, the answer is quite simple: perform two sorting operations. The first operation will sort data in terms of a known sorting algorithm into the indexing order required by that algorithm. For example, one could use Bitonic Sort and sort data into shuffled row-major order. During the second sort, each processor would generate a *sort key* that corresponds to the desired destination address with respect to the desired indexing scheme (such as row major or snake-like ordering).

Suppose that one wants to sort the 16 data items from the previous example into row-major order. One could first sort the data into shuffled row-major order and then re-sort the items so that they are appropriately ordered. For example, during the second sort, keys would be created so that processor 0 would send its data to processor 0, processor 1 would send its data to processor 1, processor 2 would send its data to processor 4, processor 3 would send its data to processor 5, processor 4 would send its data to processor 2, and so on (see Figure 9-12). The combination of these two sorts would result in the data being sorted according to row-major order in the same asymptotically optimal $\Theta(n^{1/2})$ time. Notice that this algorithm assumes that the destination addresses can be determined in $O(n^{1/2})$ time, which is sufficient for most well-defined indexing schemes.

CONCURRENT READ/WRITE

In this section, we discuss an important application of sorting that is concerned with porting PRAM algorithms to other architectures. The PRAM is the most widely studied parallel model of computation. As a result, a significant body of algorithmic literature exists for that architecture. Therefore, when one considers developing an efficient algorithm for a non-PRAM-based parallel machine, it is often constructive to consider first the algorithm that would result from a direct simulation of the PRAM algorithm on the target architecture. In order to simulate the PRAM, one must be able to simulate the concurrent read and concurrent write capabilities of the PRAM on the target machine.

A **concurrent read** (in its more general form, an **associative read**) can be used in a situation where a set of processors must obtain data associated with a set of keys, but where there need not be *a priori* knowledge as to which processor maintains the data associated with any particular key.

For example, processor P_i might need to know the data associated with the key "blue," but might not know which processor P_j in the system is responsible for maintaining the information associated with the key "blue." In fact, all processors in the system might be requesting one or more pieces of data associated with keys that are not necessarily distinct.

A **concurrent write** (in its more general form, an **associative write**) may be used in a situation where a set of processors P_i must update the data associated with a set of keys, but again P_i does not necessarily know which processor is responsible for maintaining the data associated with the key.

5	2	10	6
12	8	4	0
14	1	11	13
15	7	3	9

(a) Initial data

0_0	1_1	4_2	5_3
2_4	3_5	6_6	7_7
8_8	9_9	12_{10}	13_{11}
10_{12}	11_{13}	14_{14}	15_{15}

(b) Sorted data with keys
for re-sorting

0_0	1_1	2_4	3_5
4_2	5_3	6_6	7_7
8_8	9_9	10_{12}	11_{13}
12_{10}	13_{11}	14_{14}	15_{15}

(c) Resorted data with keys

Figure 9-12 An example of sorting data on a mesh into row-major order by two applications of sorting into shuffled-row major order. The initial unordered set of data is given in (a). After applying a shuffled-row major sort, the data appears as in (b). Note that in the lower-right corner of each item is the index where that item should be placed with respect to shuffled-row major order. The items are then sorted into shuffled-row major order with respect to these indices with the results appearing in (c).

As one can see, these concurrent read/write operations generalize the CR/CW operations of a PRAM by making them *associative*, in other words by locating data with respect to a key rather than by an address. In order to maintain consistency during concurrent read and concurrent write operations, we will assume that there is at most one *master record*, stored in some processor, associated with each unique key. In a concurrent read, every processor generates one *request record* corresponding to each key that it wishes to receive information about, though the total number of request records generated by any processor is no more than some fixed constant. A concurrent read permits multiple processors to request information about the same key. A processor requesting information about a nonexistent key will receive a null message at the end of the operation.

Implementation of a Concurrent Read: A relatively generic implementation of a concurrent read operation on a parallel machine with n processors follows.

1. Every processor creates C_1 *master records* of the form [Key, Return Address, data, "MASTER"], where C_1 is the maximum number of keyed master records maintained by any processor, and Return Address is the index of the processor that is creating the record. (Processors maintaining less than C_1 master records will create dummy records so that all processors create the same number of master records.)

2. Every processor creates C_2 *request records* of the form [Key, Return Address, data, "REQUEST"], where C_2 is the maximum number of request records generated by any processor, and Return Address is the index of the processor that is creating the record. (Processors making fewer than C_2 requests will create dummy request records so that all processors create the same number of request records.) Notice that the data fields of the request records are presently undefined.

3. *Sort* all $(C_1 + C_2)n$ records together by the Key field. In case of ties, place records with the flag "MASTER" before records with the flag "REQUEST."

4. Use a *broadcast* within ordered intervals to propagate the data associated with each master record to the request records with the same Key field. This allows all request records to find and store their required data.

5. Return all records to their original processors by *sorting* all records on the Return Address field.

Therefore, the time to perform a concurrent read, as described, is bounded by the time to perform a fixed number of sort and interval operations (see Figure 9-13).

Implementation of Concurrent Write (Overview):   The implementation of the concurrent write is quite similar to that of the concurrent read. In general, it consists of a sort step to group records with similar keys together, followed by a semigroup operation within each group to determine the value to be written to the master record, followed by a sort step to return the records to their original processors. Again, it is assumed that there is at most one *master record*, stored in some processor, associated with each unique key. When processors generate *update records*, they specify the key of the record and the piece of information they wish to update. If two or more update records contain the same key, then a master record will be updated with, for example, the minimum data value of these records. (In other circumstances, one could replace the minimum operation with any other commutative, associative, binary operation.) Therefore, one can see that the implementation of the concurrent write is nearly identical to the implementation just described for the concurrent read.

Concurrent Read/Write on a Mesh: A mesh of size n can simulate any PRAM algorithm that works with n data items on n processors by using a concurrent read and concurrent write to simulate every step of the PRAM algorithm. Suppose that the PRAM algorithm of interest runs in $T(n)$ time. Then by simulating every read and write step of the PRAM algorithm by a $\Theta(n^{1/2})$ time concurrent read and concurrent write, respectively, the running time of the PRAM algorithm as ported to a mesh of size n is $O(T(n)n^{1/2})$, which is often quite good. In fact, it is often not more than some polylogarithmic factor from optimal.

| [red,0,10,M],[blue,0,?,R] | [–,1,–1,M],[blue,1,?,R] | [blue,2,30,M],[red,2,?,R] | [green,3,40,M],[blue,3,?,R] |

(a) The initial data is given where each processor maintains one master record (signified by an "M" in the fourth field) and generates one request record (with an "R" in the fourth field).

| [blue,2,30,M],[blue,0,?,R] | [blue,1,?,R],[blue,3,?,R] | [green,3,40,M],[red,0,10,M] | [red,2,?,R],[–,1,–1,M] |

(b) After sorting all of the data together based on the key (first) field, with ties broken in favor of master records, we arrive at the situation shown here.

| [blue,2,30,M],[blue,0,30,R] | [blue,1,30,R],[blue,3,30,R] | [green,3,40,M],[red,0,10,M] | [red,2,10,R],[–,1,–1,M] |

(c) A segmented broadcast is then performed so that the information maintained in the master records is propagated to the appropriate request records.

| [red,0,10,M],[blue,0,30,R] | [–,1,–1,M],[blue,1,30,R] | [blue,2,30,M],[red,2,10,R] | [green,3,40,M],[blue,3,30,R] |

(d) The data is resorted based on the return address (second) field.

Figure 9-13   An example of a concurrent read on a linear array of size 4.

CHAPTER NOTES

Divide-and-conquer is a paradigm central to the design and analysis of both parallel and sequential algorithms. An excellent reference, particularly for sequential algorithms, is *Introduction to Algorithms* by T.H. Cormen, C.E. Leiserson, & R.L. Rivest (McGraw-Hill Book Company, New York, 1989). A nice text focusing on algorithms for the hypercube, which includes some divide-and-conquer algorithms, is *Hypercube Algorithms for Image Processing and Pattern Recognition* by S. Ranka and S. Sahni (Springer-Verlag, New York, 1990). More general references for theoretical parallel algorithms that exploit the divide-and-conquer paradigm are *Parallel Algorithms for Regular Architectures* by R. Miller and Q.F. Stout (The MIT Press, 1996), and *Introduction to Parallel Algorithms and Architectures: Arrays, Trees, Hypercubes*, by F.T. Leighton (Morgan Kaufmann Publishers, San Mateo, CA, 1992). Details of advanced PRAM algorithms, including a $\Theta(\log n)$ time sorting algorithm, can be found in *An Introduction to Parallel Algorithms* by J. Já Já, (Addison Wesley, 1992).

The QuickSort algorithm was originally presented by in "QuickSort," by C.A.R. Hoare, *Computer Journal*, 5(1), 1962, 10–15. Wagar's HyperQuickSort algorithm was originally presented in, "HyperQuickSort: A fast algorithm sorting algorithm for hypercubes," by B. Wagar in *Hypercube Multiprocessors, 1987*, 292–299.

EXERCISES

1. We have shown that QuickSort has a $\Theta(n^2)$ running time if its input list is sorted or nearly sorted. Other forms of input can also produce a $\Theta(n^2)$ running time. For example, let $n = 2^k$ for some positive integer k and suppose
   - the input list has key values $x_1, x_2, \ldots, x_n$;
   - the subsequence $O = <x_1, x_3, x_5, \ldots, x_{n-1}>$ of odd-indexed keys is decreasing;
   - the subsequence $E = <x_2, x_4, x_6, \ldots, x_n>$ of even-indexed keys is increasing;
   - $x_{n-1} > x_n$ (therefore, every member of O is greater than every member of E);
   - queues are used for the lists, with the partitioning process enqueueing new items to *smallList*, *equalList*, and *bigList*; and
   - the split value is always taken to be the first key in the list.

   Show that under these circumstances, the running time of QuickSort will be $\Theta(n^2)$.

2. In our sequential implementation of QuickSort, the "conquer" part of the algorithm consists of two recursive calls. The order of these calls clearly does not matter in terms of the correctness of the algorithm. However, the order of these recursive calls does affect the size of the stack needed to keep track of the recursion. Show that if one always pushes the jobs onto the stack so that the larger job is processed first, then the stack must be able to store n items.

3. Suppose that in a parallel computer with n processors, processor P_i has data value x_i, $i \in \{1, \ldots, n\}$. Further, suppose that $i \neq j \Rightarrow x_i \neq x_j$. Describe an efficient algorithm so that each processor P_i can determine the rank of its data value x_i. That is, if x_i is the k-th largest member of $\{x_j\}_{j=1}^{n}$, then processor P_i will store the value k at the end of the algorithm. Analyze the running time of your algorithm in terms of operations discussed in this chapter. Your analysis may be quite abstract. For example, you may express the running time of your algorithm in terms of the running times of the operations you use.

4. Suppose that you implement a linked-list version of QuickSort on a RAM using predefined ADTs (abstract data types). Further, suppose the ADT for inserting an element into a list is actually written so that it traverses a list from the front to the end and then inserts the new element at the end of the list. Give an analysis of the running time of QuickSort under this situation.

5. Suppose you are given a singly-linked list on a RAM and mistakenly implement the array version of QuickSort to perform the partition step. Give the running time of the partition step and use this result to give the running time of the resulting version of the QuickSort algorithm.

6. Describe and analyze the running time of Bitonic Sort given a set of n data items arbitrarily distributed n/p per processor on a hypercube with p processors where $n \gg p$ (where n is much larger than p).

7. Prove that algorithm Partition is correct.

8. Modify QuickSort so that it recursively sorts as long as the size of the subarray under consideration is greater than some constant C. Suppose that if a subarray of size C or less is reached, then the subarray is not sorted. As a final postprocessing step, suppose that this subarray of size at most C is then sorted by

a) InsertionSort

b) BubbleSort

c) SelectionSort

Given the total running time of the modified QuickSort algorithm. Prove that the algorithm is correct.

9. Let S be a set of n distinct real numbers and let k be a positive integer with $1 < k < n$. Give a $\Theta(n)$ time RAM algorithm to determine the middle k entries of S. The input entries of S should not be assumed ordered; however, if the elements of S are such that $s_1 < s_2 < \ldots < s_n$, then the output of the algorithm is the (unsorted) set

$$\left\{ s_{\frac{n-k}{2}}, s_{\frac{n-k}{2}+1}, \ldots, s_{\frac{n+k}{2}-1} \right\}$$

Since the running time of the algorithm should be $\Theta(n)$, sorting S should not be part of the algorithm.

10. Analyze the running time of the algorithm you presented in response to the previous query as adapted in a straightforward fashion for

a) a PRAM and

b) for a mesh.

11. Develop a version of MergeSort for a linear array of $\Theta(\log n)$ processors to sort n data items, initially distributed $\Theta(n/\log n)$ items per processor. Your algorithm should run in $\Theta(n)$ time (which is cost-optimal). Show that it does so.

12. Analyze the running time of a concurrent read operation involving $\Theta(n)$ items on a mesh of size n.

13. Given a set of n data items distributed on a mesh of size m so that each processor contains n/m items, what is the best lower bound to sort these items? Justify your answer. Provide an algorithm that matches these bounds.

14. Given a set of n input elements, arbitrarily ordered, prove that any sorting network has a depth of at least $\log_2 n$.

15. Prove that the number of comparison units in any sorting network on n inputs is $\Omega(n \log n)$.

16. Suppose that you are given a sequence of arcs of a circle $R = \langle r_1, r_2, \ldots, r_n \rangle$, and that you are required to find a point on the circle that has maximum overlap. That is, you are required to determine a (not necessarily unique) point q that has a maximum number of arcs that overlap it. Suppose that no arc is contained in any other arc, that no two arcs share a common endpoint, that the endpoints of the arcs are given completely sorted in clockwise order, and that the tail point of an arc only appears following the head of its arc. Give efficient algorithms to solve this problem on the following architectures. Discuss the time-, space-, and cost-complexity.

a) RAM

b) PRAM

c) Mesh

17. Give an efficient algorithm to compute the parallel prefix of n values, initially distributed one per processor in the base of a pyramid computer. Discuss the time- and cost-complexity of your algorithm. You may assume processors in the base mesh are in shuffled row major order, with data distributed accordingly.

10

Computational Geometry

Computational Geometry

The field of computational geometry is concerned with problems involving geometric objects such as points, lines, and polygons. Computational geometry has a widespread usage in many applications, including the design and analysis of models that represent physical systems such as cars, buildings, airplanes, and so on. In fact, in Chapter 7, "Parallel Prefix," we presented a solution to *dominance*, a fundamental problem in computational geometry. In this chapter, we consider several additional problems from this important and interesting field. Many of the problems in this chapter were chosen so that we could continue our exploration of the divide-and-conquer solution strategy.

CONVEX HULL

The first problem we consider is that of determining the *convex hull* of a set of points in the plane. The convex hull is an extremely important geometric structure that has been studied extensively. It can be applied to problems in image processing, feature extraction, layout and design, molecular biology, geographic information systems, and so on. In fact, the convex hull of a set *S* often gives a good approximation of *S* with significantly reduced data. Further, the convex hull of a set *S* is often used as an intermediate step in order to obtain additional geometrical information about *S*.

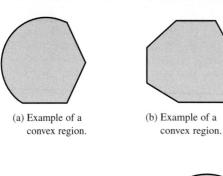

(a) Example of a   (b) Example of a
    convex region.   convex region.

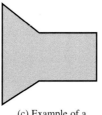

(c) Example of a   (d) Example of a   **Figure 10-1**   Examples of convex and non-
    nonconvex region.   nonconvex region.   convex regions.

DEFINITIONS

A set R is *convex* if and only if for every pair of points $x, y \in R$, the line segment $\overline{xy}$ is contained in R (see Figure 10-1). Let S be a set of n points in the plane. The convex hull of S is the smallest convex polygon P containing all n points of S. A solution to the *convex hull problem* consists of determining a minimal ordered list of points of S that define the boundary of the convex hull of S. This ordered list of points is referred to as *hull(S)*. Each point in *hull(S)* is called an *extreme point* of the convex hull and each pair of adjacent extreme points is referred to as an *edge* of the convex hull (see Figure 10-2).

The reader may wish to consider an intuitive construction of the convex hull. Suppose that each of the planar points in S is represented as a (headless) nail sticking out of a board. Now, take an infinitely elastic rubberband and stretch it in all directions. Lower the rubberband over the nails so that all the nails are enclosed within the rubberband. Finally, let the rubberband go so that it is restricted from collapsing only by the nails in S that it contacts. Then the polygon P, determined by the rubberband and its interior, represents the convex hull of S. The nails that cause the rubberband to change direction are the *extreme points* of the convex hull. Further, adjacent extreme points define the *edges* of the convex hull.

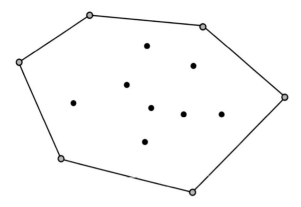

Figure 10-2   The convex hull. The set S of n points in the plane is represented by circles, some of which are black and some of which are gray. The *extreme points of S* are represented by the gray points. The set of such extreme points is denoted as *hull(S)*. Each pair of adjacent extreme points represents an *edge* of the convex hull.

Notice that a solution to the convex hull problem requires presenting a set of points in a predefined order. Therefore, we first consider the relationship between the convex hull problem and the sorting problem.

Theorem: Sorting is linear-time transformable to the convex hull problem.

Proof: Given a set of n positive real numbers, $x_1, x_2, \ldots, x_n$, a convex hull algorithm can be used to sort them with only linear overhead, as follows. Corresponding to each number x_i is the point (x_i, x_i^2). Notice that these n points all lie on the parabola $y = x^2$. The convex hull of this set consists of a list of the points sorted by x-coordinate. One linear-time pass through the list will enable us to read off the values of x_i in order.

Implications of Theorem: Based on this theorem, we know that we cannot solve the convex hull problem faster than we can solve the problem of sorting for a set of points presented in arbitrary order. So given an arbitrary set of n 2-dimensional points, solving the convex hull problem requires $\Omega(n \log n)$ time on a RAM.

GRAHAM'S SCAN

In this section, we present a traditional sequential solution to the convex hull problem, known as *Graham's scan*. It is important to note that this solution is not based on divide-and-conquer. For that reason, the reader interested primarily in divide-and-conquer might wish to skip this section. For those who continue, you may note that this algorithm is dominated by sort and scan operations. The *Graham scan* procedure is quite simple. A description follows (see Figure 10-3.)

1. Select the lowest (and in the case of ties, leftmost) point in S and label this point 0.

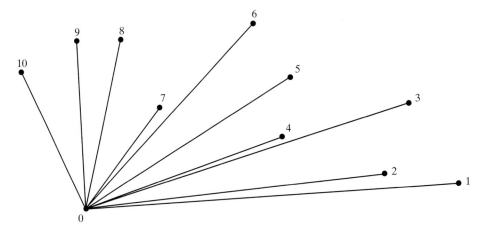

Figure 10-3 *Graham's scan* is a technique for determining the convex hull of a set of points. The lowest point is chosen as point 0 and the remaining points are sorted into counterclockwise order with respect to the angles they make with a horizontal line through point 0. Graham's scan examines the points in the order listed.

2. Sort the remaining $n - 1$ points of S by angle in $[0, \pi)$ with respect to the origin (point 0). For any angle that includes multiple points, remove all duplicates, retaining only the point at the maximum distance from point 0. Without loss of generality, we will proceed under the assumption that the set S has n distinct points.

3. Now consider the points $[1, \ldots, n - 1]$ in sequence. We build the convex hull up in an iterative fashion. At the i-th iteration, we consider point $S(i)$. For $i = 1$, we have point $S(1)$ initially considered an "active point" (*i.e.*, it is an extreme point of the two element set $S(0, \ldots, 1)$). For $1 < i < n$, we proceed as follows. Assume the active points prior to the i-th iteration are $S(0), S(j_1), \ldots, S(j_k)$, where $0 < j_1 < \ldots < j_k < i$.

   a) Suppose that the path from $S(j_{k-1})$ to $S(j_k)$ to $S(i)$ turns toward the left at $S(j_k)$ in order to reach $S(i)$, as shown in Figure 10-4. Then the point $S(i)$ is an extreme point of the convex hull with respect to the set of points $S(0, \ldots, i)$, and it remains active. Further, all of the currently active points in $S(0, \ldots, i - 1)$ remain active (those points that were extreme points of $S(0, \ldots, i - 1)$ will remain extreme points of $S(0, \ldots, i)$).

   b) Suppose that the path from $S(j_{k-1})$ to $S(j_k)$ to $S(i)$ turns toward the right at $S(j_k)$ in order to reach $S(i)$, as shown in Figure 10-5. Then the point $S(i)$ is an extreme point of the convex hull with respect to the set of points $S(0, \ldots, i)$, and it remains active. However, we now know that some of the currently active points in $S(0, \ldots, i - 1)$ are not extreme points in $S(0, \ldots, i)$ and must be eliminated (that is, become inactive). This elimination is performed by working backwards through the ordered list of currently active points and eliminating each point that continues to cause point $S(i)$ to be reached via a right turn with respect to the currently active points in $S(0, \ldots, i - 1)$. In fact, we only need work backwards through the ordered list of currently active points until we reach an active point that is not eliminated.

Figure 10-4 A path from $S(j_{k-1})$ to $S(j_k)$ to $S(i)$ that makes a left turn at $S(j_k)$.

Figure 10-5 A path from $S(j_{k-1})$ to $S(j_k)$ to $S(i)$ that makes a right turn at $S(j_k)$.

c) Suppose that $S(j_{k-1})$, $S(j_k)$, and $S(i)$ are collinear (that is, the path from $S(j_{k-1})$, to $S(j_k)$ to $S(i)$ does not turn, or turns exactly half a revolution, at $S(j_k)$ in order to reach $S(i)$). Then one of these three points is between the other two and can be eliminated since it cannot be an extreme point in $S(0, \ldots, i)$. Indeed, since we previously saw to it that active members of $S(1 \ldots n)$ have unique angles with respect to $S(0)$ and the active points are ordered with respect to these angles, the point that is eliminated is $S(j_k)$ (see Figure 10-6).

Consider the example presented earlier in Figure 10-3. We are required to enumerate the convex hull of S, a set consisting of 11 points. Details of the algorithm, as applied to this specific example, follow:

(a) Scan the list of points in order to determine the lowest point. Label this lowest point 0. Note: if there is more than one lowest point, choose the leftmost one.

(b) Sort the remaining $n - 1$ points by angle with respect to a horizontal line through point 0.

(c) The points are now ordered in counterclockwise fashion with respect to point 0, as shown in Figure 10-3. Initially, all n points are candidates as extreme points of $hull(S)$.

(d) The point labeled 0 must be an extreme point (hull vertex), as it is the lowest point in the set S. We proceed to visit successive points in order, applying the "right-turn test" described in the algorithm given above.

(e) The first stop on our tour is point number 1, which is accepted since points 0 and 1 form a convex set.

(f) Now consider point number 2. Notice that the turn from point 0 to 1 to 2 is a left turn. Therefore, points 0, 1, and 2 are extreme points with respect to $S(0, \ldots, 2)$.

Figure 10-6   A path from $S(j_{k-1})$ to $S(j_k)$ to $S(i)$ that is straight. That is, all three points are collinear.

(g) Now consider point number 3. Notice that the turn from point 1 to 2 to 3 is a right turn. Therefore, we begin to work backwards from the preceding point. That is, point number 2 must be eliminated. Next, consider the turn from point 0 to 1 to 3. This is a left turn. Therefore, point number 1 remains, and this backward scan to eliminate points is complete. So points 0, 1, and 3 are the extreme points representing the convex hull of $S(0, \ldots, 3)$.

(h) Now consider point number 4. Notice that the turn from point 1 to 3 to 4 is a left turn. Therefore, no points are eliminated, and we know that points 0, 1, 3, and 4 are extreme points of $S(0, \ldots, 4)$.

(i) Now consider point number 5. Notice that the turn from point 3 to 4 to 5 is a right turn. Therefore, we begin to work backwards from the preceding point. That is, point number 4 is eliminated. Next, consider the turn from point 1 to 3 to 5. Notice that this is a left turn. Therefore, the points 0, 1, 3, and 5 are the extreme points representing the convex hull of $S(0, \ldots, 5)$.

(j) Now consider point number 6. Notice that the turn from point 3 to 5 to 6 is a right turn. Therefore, we begin to work backwards from the preceding point. That is, point number 5 is eliminated. Next, consider the turn from point 1 to 3 to 6. This is a left turn. Therefore, the points 0, 1, 3, and 6 are the extreme points representing the convex hull of $S(0, \ldots, 6)$.

(k) Now consider point number 7. Notice that the turn from point 3 to 6 to 7 is a left turn. Therefore, no points are eliminated, and we know that points 0, 1, 3, 6, and 7 are extreme points of $S(0, \ldots, 7)$.

(l) Now consider point number 8. Notice that the turn from 6 to 7 to 8 is a right turn. Therefore, we begin to work backwards from the preceding point. That is, point number 7 is eliminated. Now consider the turn from point 3 to 6 to 8. This is a left turn. Therefore, the points 0, 1, 3, 6, and 8 are the extreme points representing the convex hull of $S(0, \ldots, 8)$.

(m) Now consider point number 9. Notice that the turn from point 6 to 8 to 9 is a right turn. Therefore, we begin to work backwards from the preceding point. That is, point number 8 is eliminated. Now consider the turn from point 3 to 6 to 9. This is a left turn. Therefore, the points 0, 1, 3, 6, and 9 are the extreme points representing the convex hull of $S(0, \ldots, 9)$.

(n) Now consider point number 10. Notice that the turn from point 6 to 9 to 10 is a left turn. Therefore, no points are eliminated, and we know that points 0, 1, 3, 6, 9, and 10 are extreme points of $S(0, \ldots, 10)$. The solution is now complete.

Analysis on a RAM: Let's consider the running time and space requirements of Graham's scan on a RAM. The first step of the algorithm consists of determining point 0, the lowest point in the set S (in the case of ties, the leftmost of these lowest points). Assuming that S contains n points, the lowest point can be determined in $\Theta(n)$ time by a simple scan through the data. The remaining $n - 1$ points of S can then be sorted with respect to point 0 (and a horizontal line through it) in $\Theta(n \log n)$ time. Next, the algorithm considers the points in order and makes decisions about eliminating points. Notice that each time a new point i is encountered, it will be an extreme point of $S(0, \dots , i)$; this is because we are traversing the points in order according to their angles with respect to $S(0)$, and we have eliminated (Step 3c above) all but one member of any set in $S \setminus \{S(0)\}$ that has the same angle with $S(0)$. Each time a new point is visited, $\Theta(1)$ work is necessary in order to

1. include the new point in the data structure if it is active, and
2. stop any backwards search that might arise.

The remainder of the time spent in the tour is accounted for when considering the total number of points that can be eliminated, since with a judicious choice of data structures, such as a separate array or a stack, no point is ever considered once it has been eliminated. It is important to consider the analysis from a global perspective. Since no point is ever eliminated more than once, the total time required for the loop in Step 3 is $\Theta(n)$, though the analysis is a bit different than some of the straightforward deterministic analyses presented earlier in the book. Therefore, the running time of Graham's scan on a RAM is a worst-case optimal $\Theta(n \log n)$, which is dominated by the sort performed in Step 2.

Next we consider the space required in addition to that which is necessary in order to maintain the initial set of points. Notice that this algorithm does not rely on recursion, so we need not worry about the system stack. It does, however, require a separate data structure that in the worst case might require a copy of every point. That is, it is possible to construct situations where $\Theta(n)$ points are in the convex hull. Therefore, if an additional stack or array is used, the additional space will be $\Theta(n)$. However, if one maintains the points in a pointer-based data structure, it is possible to avoid making copies of the points. Of course, the penalty one pays for this is the additional $\Theta(n)$ pointers.

Parallel Implementation: Consider parallel implementations of Graham's scan. Notice that Steps 1 and 2, which require computing a semigroup operation and sorting the data, can be done efficiently on most parallel models. However, Step 3 is another matter. One might try to remove concave regions in parallel and hope that (reminiscent of our pointer jumping algorithms) the number of such parallel removals will be polylogarithmic in the number of points. However, consider the situation where the first $n-1$ points form a convex set, but when the last point is added to this set, then $\Theta(n)$ points must be removed. It is not clear that such a situation can be easily parallelized.

Jarvis's March: An alternative convex hull algorithm is *Jarvis's march*, which works by a *package wrapping* technique. To illustrate this, find a piece of string of sufficient length.

Hold one end of the string fixed at the lowest point (point number 0) and then wrap the string around the nails representing the points in a counterclockwise fashion. This can be done by iteratively adding the point with the least polar angle with respect to a horizontal line through the most recently added point. Since all the remaining points are considered at each iteration, the total running time of this algorithm is $O(nh)$, where h is the number of vertices (extreme points) on $hull(S)$. Therefore, when the number of extreme points is $o(\log n)$, Jarvis' march is asymptotically faster than Graham's scan.

DIVIDE-AND-CONQUER SOLUTION

In this section, we focus on divide-and-conquer solutions to the convex hull problem. Initially, we present a generic divide-and-conquer solution. An analysis is then presented for both a RAM and a mesh implementation. At the conclusion of this section, we present a divide-and-conquer algorithm, complete with analysis, for the PRAM.

Generic Divide-and-Conquer Solution to the Convex Hull Problem: Assume that we are required to enumerate the extreme points of a set S of n planar points. We will enumerate the points so that the rightmost point is labeled 1 (in the case of ties, the lowest rightmost point is labeled 1). The numbering of the extreme points is given in a counterclockwise fashion. Notice that for algorithmic convenience, the first enumerated extreme point determined by this algorithm differs in position from the first enumerated extreme point derived from Graham's scan (leftmost-lowest point). The basic algorithm follows:

1. If $n \leq 2$, then **return**. In this case, both of the points are extreme points of the given set. If $n > 2$, then we continue with Step 2.
2. *Divide* the n points by x-coordinate into two sets, A and B, each of size approximately $n/2$. The division of points is done so that all points in A are to the left of all points in B. That is, A is linearly separable from B by a vertical line (see Figure 10-7).
3. *Recursively* compute $hull(A)$ and $hull(B)$. See Figure 10-8.
4. Stitch $hull(A)$ and $hull(B)$ together to determine $hull(S)$. This is done as follows (see Figure 10-9).
   a) Find the upper and lower common tangent lines (often referred to as the *lines of support*) between $hull(A)$ and $hull(B)$.
   b) Discard the points inside the quadrilateral formed by the four points that determine these two lines of support.
   c) Renumber the extreme points so that they remain ordered with respect to the defined enumeration scheme. This is necessary since the algorithm is recursive in nature.

Notice that Step 2 requires us to divide the input points into disjoint sets A and B in such a fashion that

- every point of A is left of every point of B, and
- both A and B have approximately $n/2$ members.

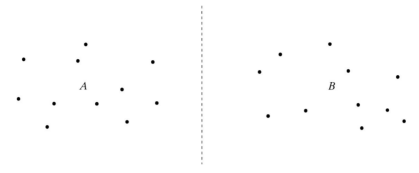

Figure 10-7 A set of *n* planar points evenly divided into two sets *A* and *B* by an *x*-coordinate. All points in *A* lie to the left of every point in *B*.

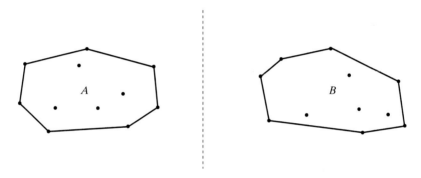

Figure 10-8 An illustration of the situation after *hull(A)* and *hull(B)* have been determined from input shown in Figure 10-7.

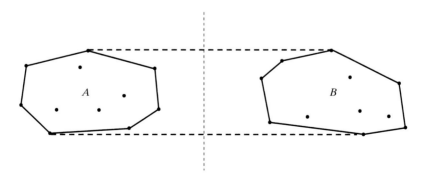

Figure 10-9 The stitch step. In order to construct *hull(S)* from *hull(A)* and *hull(B)*, the upper common tangent line and lower common tangent line between *hull(A)* and *hull(B)* are determined.

Unfortunately, if we are overly strict in our interpretation of "approximate," these requirements might not be met. Such a situation might occur when the median x-coordinate is shared by a large percentage of the input points. For example, suppose five of 100 input points have an x-coordinate less than 0, 60 input points have an x-coordinate equal to 0, and 35 input points have an x-coordinate greater than 0. The requirement that every point of A is to the left of every point of B makes it likely that either $|A| = 5$ and $|B| = 95$ or $|A| = 65$ and $|B| = 35$. This is not really a problem since the recursion will quickly rectify the imbalance due to the fact that at most two points with the same x-coordinate can be extreme points of a convex hull. Thus, when we determine the vertical line of separation between A and B, we can arbitrarily assign any input points that fall on this line to A.

This algorithm is a fairly straightforward adaptation of divide-and-conquer. The interesting step is that of determining the lines of support. It is important to note that the lines of support are not necessarily determined by easily identified special points. For example, the lines of support are not necessarily determined by the topmost and bottommost points in the two convex hulls, as illustrated in Figure 10-10. Considerable thought is required in order to construct an efficient algorithm to determine these four points and hence the two tangent lines.

Since the convex hulls of A and B are linearly separable by a vertical line, there are some restrictions on possibilities of points that determine the upper tangent line. For example, consider a_l, a leftmost point of A and a_r, a rightmost point of A. Similarly, consider b_l, a leftmost point of B, and b_r, a rightmost point of B. It is then easy to show that the upper common tangent line is determined by an extreme point of $hull(A)$ on or above $\overline{a_l a_r}$ (the edges of $hull(A)$ on or above $\overline{a_l a_r}$ are referred to as the *upper envelope* of A) and an extreme point of $hull(B)$ on or above $\overline{b_l b_r}$ (on the upper envelope of B). Similarly, the lower common tangent line is determined by an extreme point of $hull(A)$ on or below $\overline{a_l a_r}$ and an extreme point of $hull(B)$ on or below $\overline{b_l b_r}$. Therefore, without loss of generality, we focus

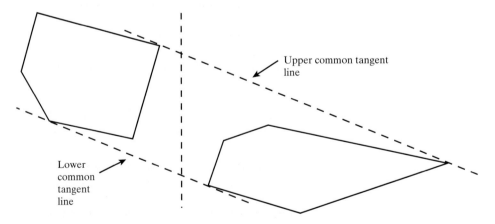

Figure 10-10 An illustration of the common tangent lines between linearly separable convex hulls. The upper common tangent line between *hull*(A) and *hull*(B) does not necessarily include the topmost extreme points in either set. A similar remark can be made about the lower common tangent line.

on determining the upper common tangent line, and note that determining the lower common tangent line is similar.

The extreme point $p \in hull(A)$ that determines the upper common tangent line has the property that if x and y are, respectively, its left and right neighbors among the extreme points of $hull(A)$ (one or both of x and y may not exist), then every extreme point of $hull(B)$ lies on or below $\overrightarrow{xp}$, while at least one extreme point of $hull(B)$ lies on or above $\overrightarrow{py}$. See Figure 10-11. Notice that the mirror image scenario is valid in terms of identifying the right common tangent point, that is, the upper common tangent point in $hull(B)$.

Convex Hull Algorithm on a RAM: In this section, we consider the implementation details and running time of the divide-and-conquer algorithm just presented on a RAM. In order to partition the points with respect to x-coordinates, a $\Theta(n \log n)$-time sorting procedure can be used. In fact, it is important to notice that this single sort will serve to handle the partitioning that is required at every level of the recursion. That is, sorting is only performed once for partitioning, not at every level of recursion. Now let's consider the stitch step. The necessary points can be identified in $\Theta(\log n)$ time by a clever "teeter-totter" procedure. Basically, the procedure performs a type of binary search in which endpoints of a line segment (one from $hull(A)$ and the other from $hull(B)$) are adjusted in a binary-type iterative fashion. Once the extreme points are identified, then with an appropriate choice of data structures, the points can be reordered and renumbered in $\Theta(n)$ time. This eliminates the points inside the quadrilateral determined by the lines of support. Therefore, the running time of the algorithm is given by $T(n) = \Theta(n \log n) + R(n)$, where $\Theta(n \log n)$ is the time required for the initial sort, and $R(n)$ is the time required for the recursive procedure. Notice that $R(n) = 2 R(n/2) + \Theta(n)$, where $\Theta(n)$ time is required to stitch two convex hulls

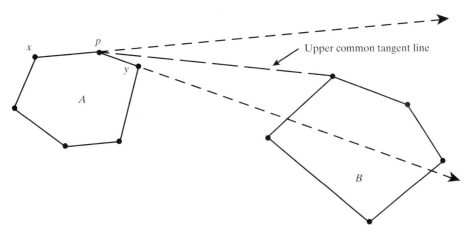

Figure 10-11 Constructing the upper common tangent lines. The upper common tangent line includes the extreme point $p \in hull(A)$ with the following properties. Let the next extreme point in counterclockwise order be called x and the previous extreme point in counterclockwise order be called y. Then every extreme point of $hull(B)$ lies on or below $\overrightarrow{xp}$, while at least one extreme point of $hull(B)$ lies on or above $\overrightarrow{py}$.

($\Theta(\log n)$ time to identify the tangent line and $\Theta(n)$ time to reorder the points). Therefore, the running time of the entire algorithm is $\Theta(n \log n)$, which is asymptotically optimal.

Convex Hull Algorithm on a Mesh: In this section, we discuss a mesh implementation and provide an analysis of our divide-and-conquer solution to the convex hull problem. Specifically, given n points, arbitrarily distributed one point per processor on a mesh of size n, we will show that the convex hull of the set S of planar points can be determined in optimal $\Theta(n^{1/2})$ time.

The basic algorithm follows. First, sort the points into shuffled row-major order. This results in the first $n/4$ points (with respect to x-coordinate ordering) being mapped to the northwest quadrant, the next $n/4$ points being mapped to the northeast quadrant, and so forth, as shown in Figure 10-12. Notice that with this indexing scheme, the partitioning holds recursively within each quadrant.

Since this algorithm is recursive, we now need only discuss the binary search routine. Notice that due to the mesh environment and the way in which we have partitioned the data, we will perform simultaneous binary searches between $S1$ and $S2$, as well as between $S3$ and $S4$. We will then perform a binary search between $S1 \cup S2$ and $S3 \cup S4$. Therefore, we only need to describe the binary search between $S1$ and $S2$, with the others being similar. In fact, we will only describe the binary search that will determine the upper common tangent line between $S1$ and $S2$.

Notice that it takes $\Theta(n^{1/2})$ time to broadcast a query from $S1$ to $S2$ and then report the result back to all processors in $S1$. So, in $\Theta(n^{1/2})$ time, we can determine whether or not some line from $S1$ goes above all of the points in $S2$ or whether there is at least one point in $S2$ that is above the query line. If we continue performing this binary search in a natural way, the running time of this convex hull algorithm will be $\Theta(n^{1/2} \log n)$.

However, if we first perform a query from $S1$ to $S2$, and then one from $S2$ to $S1$, notice that half of the data from $S1$ and half the data from $S2$ can be logically eliminated. In fact, this is the precise feature that a binary search exploits. The reader should note that while logically eliminating during this back-and-forth binary search both common tangent points remain in the active sets.

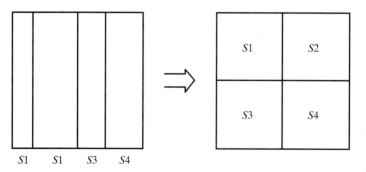

Figure 10-12 Dividing the n planar points in S so that each of the four linearly separable sets of points is stored in a different quadrant of the mesh. Notice that the vertical slabs of points in the plane need not cover the same area of space. They simply must contain the same number of points.

R_1 R_2 R_3 R_4 R_5

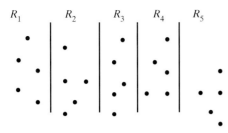

Figure 10-13 An illustration of partitioning the set S of n planar points into $n^{1/2}$ linearly separable sets, each with $n^{1/2}$ points. The sets are denoted as $R_1, R_2, \ldots, R_{n^{1/2}}$.

So, if the logically active data is compressed in $\Theta(n^{1/2})$ time, then each iteration of the binary search will take time proportional to the square root of the number of items remaining. Therefore, such a dual binary search with compression will run in $B(n) = B(n/2) + \Theta(n^{1/2}) = \Theta(n^{1/2})$ time. Therefore, the total running time of the divide-and-conquer-based binary search on a mesh of size n is the $\Theta(n^{1/2})$ time for the initial sort plus $T(n) = T(n/4) + B(n) = T(n/4) + \Theta(n^{1/2}) = \Theta(n^{1/2})$ time for the remainder of the algorithm. Hence, the total running time to determine the convex hull on a mesh of size n is $\Theta(n^{1/2})$, which is optimal for this architecture.

Convex Hull Algorithm on a PRAM: In this section, we present a divide-and-conquer algorithm to solve the convex hull problem on a PRAM. The algorithm follows the spirit of the divide-and-conquer algorithm that we have presented; however, the individual steps have been optimized for the PRAM. The algorithm follows:

1. *Partition* the set S of n planar points into $n^{1/2}$ sets, denoted $R_1, R_2, \ldots, R_{n^{1/2}}$. The partitioning is done so that all points in region R_i are to the left of all points in region R_{i+1} for all i (see Figure 10-13). This partitioning is most simply accomplished by sorting, as previously described.

2. *Recursively* (and in parallel) solve the convex hull problem for every R_i, $i \in \{1, \ldots, n^{1/2}\}$. At this point, $hull(R_i)$ is now known for every R_i.

3. *Stitch* the $n^{1/2}$ convex hulls together in order to determine $hull(S)$. This is done by the **combine** routine that we define below.

Combine: The input to the combine routine is the set of convex hulls, $hull(R_1)$, $hull(R_2)$, $\ldots$, $hull(R_{n^{1/2}})$, each represented by $O(n^{1/2})$ extreme points. Notice that $hull(R_1) \le hull(R_2) \le \ldots \le hull(R_{n^{1/2}})$, where we use "$A \le B$" to mean that "all points in A are to the left of all points in B." The combine routine will produce $hull(S)$. As we have done previously, we will only consider the upper envelopes of $hull(R_i)$, $1 \le i \le n^{1/2}$, and we will describe an algorithm to merge these $n^{1/2}$ upper envelopes in order to produce the upper envelope of $hull(S)$. The procedure for determining the lower envelope is analogous. The algorithm follows:

1. Assign $n^{1/2}$ processors to each set R_i of points. For each R_i, determine the $n^{1/2} - 1$ tangent lines between $hull(R_i)$ and every distinct $hull(R_j)$. Notice that a total of $n^{1/2} \times (n^{1/2} - 1) = O(n)$ such upper tangent lines are determined. These tangent lines are computed as follows:

   a) Let $T_{i,j}$ denote the (upper) common tangent line between $hull(R_i)$ and $hull(R_j)$, $i \neq j$.

   b) For each R_i, use the k-th processor that was assigned to it to determine the upper tangent line between $hull(R_i)$ and $hull(R_k)$, $i \neq k$. Each of these upper tangent lines can be determined by a single processor in $O(\log n)$ time by invoking the "teeter-totter" algorithm outlined earlier. In fact, all $\Theta(n)$ tangent lines can be determined simultaneously in $O(\log n)$ time on a CREW PRAM.

2. Let V_i be the tangent line with the smallest slope in $\{T_{i,1}, T_{i,2}, \ldots, T_{i,i-1}\}$. That is, with respect to R_i, V_i represents the tangent line of minimum slope that "comes from the left." Let v_i be the point of contact of V_i with $hull(R_i)$.

3. Let W_i be the tangent line with the largest slope in $\{T_{i,i+1}, T_{i,i+2}, \ldots, T_{i,n^{1/2}}\}$. That is, with respect to R_i, W_i represents the tangent line of a maximum slope that "comes from the right." Let w_i be the point of contact of W_i with $hull(R_i)$.

4. Notice that both V_i and W_i can be found in $O(\log n)$ time by the $n^{1/2}$ processors assigned to R_i. This only requires that the $n^{1/2}$ processors perform a minimum or maximum operation, respectively.

5. If the angle of intersection between V_i and W_i is less than or equal to 180° (see Figure 10-16), or if w_i is to the left of v_i (see Figure 10-17), then none of the points representing the upper envelope of $hull(R_i)$ belong to $hull(S)$; otherwise, all points on the upper hull of $hull(R_i)$ from v_i to w_i, inclusive, belong to $hull(S)$ (see Figures 10-14 and 10-15). Notice that this operation is performed in $\Theta(1)$ time.

6. Finally, compress all of the extreme points of $hull(S)$ into a compact region in memory in $O(\log n)$ time by performing parallel prefix computations.

The running time of the **combine** routine is dominated by the time required to determine the common tangent lines and the time required to organize the final results. Therefore, the running time for the combine routine is $\Theta(\log n)$.

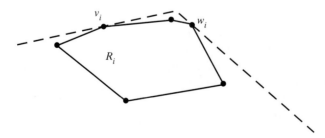

Figure 10-14 Suppose that v_i is to the left of w_i and that the angle above the intersection of their tangents exceeds 180°. Then all of the extreme points of R_i between (and including) v_i and w_i are extreme points of S.

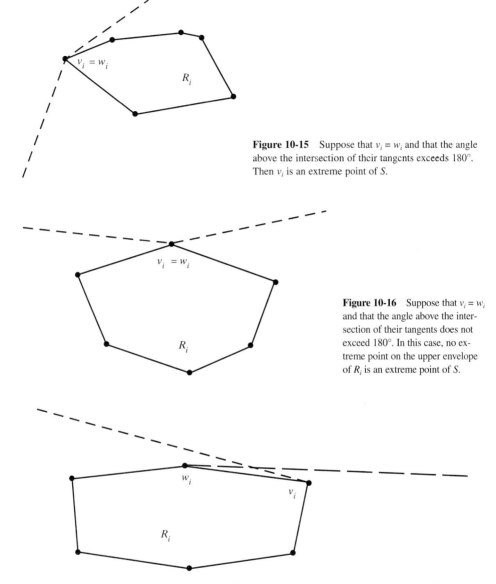

Figure 10-15   Suppose that $v_i = w_i$ and that the angle above the intersection of their tangents exceeds 180°. Then v_i is an extreme point of S.

Figure 10-16   Suppose that $v_i = w_i$ and that the angle above the intersection of their tangents does not exceed 180°. In this case, no extreme point on the upper envelope of R_i is an extreme point of S.

Figure 10-17   Suppose that w_i is to the left of v_i. Then no extreme point on the upper envelope of R_i is an extreme point of S.

PRAM Analysis: While it is beyond the scope of this text, we have mentioned that sorting can be performed on a PRAM in $\Theta(\log n)$ time. Therefore, the running time of this convex hull algorithm is given by $T(n) = S(n) + R(n)$, where $S(n) = \Theta(\log n)$ is the time required for the initial sort, and $R(n) = R(n^{1/2}) + C(n)$ is the time required for the recursive part of the algorithm, including the $C(n) = O(\log n)$ time combine routine. Hence, the running time for this convex hull algorithm is $\Theta(\log n)$. Further, this results in an optimal total cost of $\Theta(n \log n)$.

SMALLEST ENCLOSING BOX

In this section, we consider the problem of determining a smallest enclosing "box" of a set of points. That is, given a set S of n planar points, determine a (not necessarily unique) minimum-area enclosing rectangle of S. This problem has applications in layout and design. Since a rectangle is convex, it follows from the definition of convex hull that any enclosing rectangle of S must enclose $hull(S)$. One can show that for a minimum-area enclosing rectangle, each of its edges must intersect an extreme point of $hull(S)$ and one of the edges of the rectangle must be collinear with a pair of adjacent extreme points of $hull(S)$ (see Figure 10-18).

A straightforward solution to the smallest enclosing box problem consists of the following steps:

1. Identify the extreme points of the set S of n planar points.
2. Consider every pair of adjacent extreme points in $hull(S)$. For each such pair, find the three maximum points, as shown in Figure 10-18, and as described below.
   a) Given a line collinear with $\overline{xx'}$, the point E associated with $\overline{xx'}$ is the last point of $hull(S)$ encountered as a line perpendicular to $\overline{xx'}$ passes through $hull(S)$ from left to right.
   b) Similarly, the point N associated with $\overline{xx'}$ is the last point encountered as a line parallel to $\overline{xx'}$, originating at $\overline{xx'}$, passes through $hull(S)$.
   c) Finally, the point W associated with $\overline{xx'}$ is the last point of $hull(S)$ encountered as a line perpendicular to $\overline{xx'}$ passes through $hull(S)$ from right to left.
3. For every adjacent pair of extreme points, x and x', determine the area of the minimum enclosing box that has an edge collinear with $\overline{xx'}$.
4. A smallest enclosing box of S is one that yields the minimum area over all of the rectangles just determined. Therefore, identify a box that corresponds to the minimum area with respect to those values determined in Step 3.

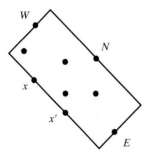

Figure 10-18   A *smallest enclosing box* of a set S planar points. A not necessarily unique minimum-area enclosing rectangle of S includes three edges, each of which is collinear with an extreme point of $hull(S)$, and one edge that is collinear with an edge of $hull(S)$.

RAM: We have shown that the convex hull of a set S of n planar points can be determined in $\Theta(n \log n)$ on a RAM. Further, given m enumerated extreme points, for each pair of adjacent extreme points, one can determine the other three critical points by a binary search type of procedure in $\Theta(\log m)$ time. Therefore, the time required to determine the m restricted minimum-area rectangles is $\Theta(m \log m)$. Once these m rectangles have been determined, a minimum-area rectangle over this set can be determined in $\Theta(m)$ time by a simple scan. Therefore, the running time for the entire algorithm on a RAM is $\Theta(n \log n + m \log m) = \Theta(n \log n)$, since $m = O(n)$.

PRAM: Consider the same basic strategy as just presented for the RAM. Notice that the m restricted minimum-area rectangles can be determined simultaneously in $\Theta(\log m)$ time on a PRAM. Further, a semigroup operation can be used to determine the minimum of these in $\Theta(\log m)$ time. Therefore, the running time of the entire algorithm, including the time to determine the extreme points of the convex hull, is $\Theta(\log n + \log m) = \Theta(\log n)$ on a PRAM.

Mesh: Given a mesh of size n, we have shown how to enumerate the m extreme points of $hull(S)$ in $\Theta(n^{1/2})$ time. In order to arrive at an asymptotically optimal algorithm for this architecture, we need to be able to design a $\Theta(n^{1/2})$-time algorithm to generate the m rectangles. Once we have generated the rectangles, we know that a straightforward $\Theta(n^{1/2})$ time semigroup operation can be used to identify one of these of minimum area rectangles. So, how do we determine all m minimum-area rectangles simultaneously in $\Theta(n^{1/2})$ time?

Recall that the extreme points of $hull(S)$ have been enumerated. Each point is incident on two hull edges. Each such edge has an *angle of support* that it makes with $hull(S)$. These angles are all in the range of $[0,2\pi)$, where the angle is viewed with respect to the points of S (see Figure 10-19). Consider the situation in which every edge $\overline{xx'}$ is trying to determine its point N. This corresponds to the situation in which every edge $\overline{xx'}$ is searching for the extreme point of $hull(S)$ that has an angle of support that differs from that of $\overline{xx'}$ by π. In order for edge $\overline{xx'}$ to determine its other two points, E and W, it is simply searching for points bounded by hull edges with angles of support that differ from that of $\overline{xx'}$ by $\pi/2$ and $3\pi/2$, respectively. Therefore, these simultaneous searches can simply be performed by a fixed number of sort-based routines and ordered interval broadcasts. We

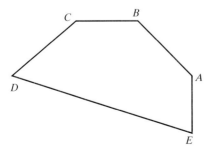

Figure 10-19   An illustration of *angles of support*. The *angle* of incidence of hull edge EA is $\pi/2$, of $\overline{AB}$ is $3\pi/4$, of $\overline{BC}$ is π, and so forth. An angle of support of extreme point A is in $[\pi/2, 3\pi/4]$. An angle of support of extreme point B is in $[3\pi/4, \pi]$, and so forth.

leave the details to the reader, though we should point out that these operations are essentially performed by concurrent read operations. Therefore, the running time of this algorithm, including the time to identify the extreme points of $hull(S)$, is $\Theta(n^{1/2})$.

ALL-NEAREST NEIGHBOR PROBLEM

In this section, we consider another fundamental problem in computational geometry. Suppose you have a set S of n planar points and for every point in S you want to know its nearest neighbor with respect to the other points in S. That is, you are required to determine for every point $p \in S$, a point $\overline{p}$, such that $dist(p,\overline{p})$ is the minimum $dist(p,q)$, $p \neq q$, $q \in S$. For this reason, the problem is often referred to as the *all-nearest neighbor problem*.

An optimal $\Theta(n \log n)$ time algorithm for the RAM typically consists of constructing the *Voronoi diagram* of S and then traversing this structure. The *Voronoi diagram* of a set of planar points consists of a collection of n convex polygons, where each such polygon C_i represents the region of 2-dimensional space such that any point in C_i is closer to $p_i \in S$ than to any other point in S. The Voronoi diagram is a very important structure in computational geometry. Unfortunately, a detailed discussion of its construction, either sequentially or in parallel, is beyond the scope of this book.

In this section, we will concentrate on an interesting divide-and-conquer solution to the all-nearest neighbor problem for the mesh. Notice that an optimal $O(n^{1/2})$-time algorithm on a mesh of size n carries with it a cost of $O(n^{3/2})$. Since $\Theta(n^2)$ operations are required to compute distances between all pairs of points, notice that this algorithm must be smarter (more efficient) than such a brute-force algorithm. In the remainder of this section, we concentrate on a $\Theta(n^{1/2})$-time mesh algorithm (optimal for this architecture).

We consider an algorithm that partitions the points into disjoint sets of points, solves the problem recursively within each set of points, and then stitches the partial results together in an efficient fashion. We prevent the stitching process from becoming the dominant step by partitioning in such a way that almost all of the points within each partition know their final answer after the recursive solution. We can accomplish this by partitioning the plane into linearly separable vertical slabs, solving the problem recursively within each vertical slab, then repartitioning the plane into linearly separable horizontal slabs, and solving the problem recursively within each horizontal slab. We can then exploit a theorem from computational geometry that states that there are no more than some fixed number of points in each rectangle formed by the intersection of a horizontal and vertical slab that could have a nearest neighbor somewhere other than in its horizontal or vertical slab (see Figure 10-20).

We now give an outline of the algorithm.

1. Solve the problem recursively in vertical slabs, as follows:
    a) Sort the n points in S by x-coordinate, creating four vertical slabs.
    b) Solve the all-nearest neighbor problem recursively (Steps 1-3) within each vertical slab.
2. Solve the problem recursively in horizontal slabs, as follows:

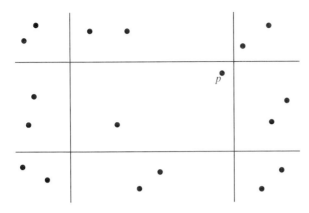

Figure 10-20 The nearest neighbor of p is neither in the same horizontal nor on the same vertical slab as p.

    a) Sort the n points in S by y-coordinate, creating four horizontal slabs.

    b) Solve the all-nearest neighbor problem recursively (Steps 1-3) within each horizontal slab.

3. Sort the n points of S with respect to the identity of their boxes. The identity of a specific box is given as the concatenation of the label of the vertical slab and the label of the horizontal slab.

    a) For the points in each box, it is important to note that a result from computational geometry shows that at most two points closest to each corner of the box could be closer to a point outside the box than to any point found so far. Notice that there are no more than $8 \times 16 = 128$ such corner points.

    b) Each of these corner points can now be passed through the mesh so that they can view (and be viewed by) all n points. After this traversal, each of these corner points will know its nearest neighbor. Hence, the solution will be complete.

Running Time: The running time of this algorithm on a mesh of size n is given as $T(n) = 2T(n/4) + \Theta(n^{1/2})$. Using the *Master Method*, we can determine that this recurrence has a solution of $T(n) = \Theta(n^{1/2})$, which is optimal for this architecture. However, we should point out that the cost of this algorithm is $\Theta(n^{3/2})$. Since the problem can be solved sequentially in $\Theta(n \log n)$ time, it should not be a great surprise that we are able to design a time-optimal solution on a mesh of size n.

ARCHITECTURE-INDEPENDENT ALGORITHM DEVELOPMENT

A number of interesting problems in computational geometry lend themselves to *architecture-independent algorithm development*. That is, we can state an algorithm to solve the problem that may be implemented on a variety of architectures. It should be noted that such algorithms are often stated at a very high level. This is because they usually involve basic operations such as sorting, prefix, semigroup operations, computation of the convex hull, and so forth. These are operations for which implementation details may be quite different on different architectures. Nevertheless, these operations may be regarded as fundamental abstract operations in the sense that efficient implementations are known on popular models of computation. Suppose problem X can be solved by an algorithm consisting of the computation of a convex hull, followed by a prefix computation, followed by a semigroup operation. A straightforward implementation of this algorithm on a given model Y results in a running time that is the sum of the times for these three fundamental operations as implemented on model Y.

Algorithms discussed for the remainder of this chapter will be presented in an architecture-independent style. In the exercises that follow, the reader will be asked to analyze the running times of these algorithms on a variety of architectures.

LINE INTERSECTION PROBLEMS

Suppose we are given a set L of n line segments in the Euclidean plane. The segments may be arbitrary, or we may have additional knowledge, such as that every member of L is either horizontal or vertical. Common *line intersection problems* include the following:

1. *Intersection Query:* Determine if there is a pair of members of L that intersect.
2. *Intersection Reporting:* Find and report all pairs of members of L that intersect.

An easy, though perhaps inefficient, method of solving the intersection query problem is to solve the intersection reporting problem and then observe whether or not any intersections are reported. We might hope to obtain an asymptotically faster solution to the intersection query problem that does not require us to solve the intersection reporting problem.

An obvious approach to both problems is based on an examination of each of the $\Theta(n^2)$ pairs of members of L. It is easy to see how such an approach yields an $O(n^2)$-time RAM algorithm for the intersection query problem, and a $\Theta(n^2)$-time RAM algorithm for the intersection reporting problem. In fact, other solutions are more efficient:

■ Consider the intersection query problem. In $\Theta(n)$ time, create two records for each member of L, one for each endpoint. Let each record have an indicator as to whether the endpoint is a *left* or *right* endpoint (lower corresponds to *right* in the case of a vertical segment). In $\Theta(n \log n)$ time, sort these $2n$ records into ascending order by the x-coordinate of their endpoints, using the *left/right* switch as the secondary key, with *right* $<$ *left*, and y-coordinates as the tertiary key. Now perform a *plane sweep* operation, which allows us to "sweep the plane" from left to right, maintaining an ordered data structure T of nonintersecting members of L not yet eliminated from consideration as possible members of an intersecting pair. Assume that T is a data structure such as a red-black tree in which insert, retrieve, and delete operations can be done in sequential $O(\log n)$ time. As we move the vertical "sweep line" from left to right and encounter a left endpoint of a member s of L, we insert s into T, and then determine if s intersects either of its at most two neighbors in T; if we find an inter-

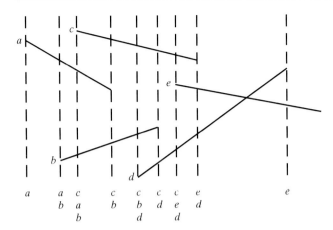

Figure 10-21 Illustration of a *plane sweep* operation to solve the intersection query problem. The line segments are labeled by left endpoint. As a sweep of all the endpoints is performed from left to right, when a left endpoint is encountered, the line segment is inserted into the list at the appropriate ordered position (top to bottom) and is tested for intersection with its neighbors in the test. The currently active ordered list of line segments is shown beneath each endpoint. When a right endpoint is encountered, an evaluation of an intersection is made before removing that point from the ordering. Here, when the left endpoint of *e* is encountered, the *d-e* intersection is detected.

section, we report its existence and halt. As the sweep line encounters a right endpoint of a member s of L, we remove s from T, and, as above, determine if s intersects either of its at most two neighbors in T. If we find an intersection, we report its existence and halt; otherwise, we continue the plane sweep (see Figure 10-21).

■ Consider the intersection reporting problem. One can construct an algorithm with an *output-sensitive* running time for the RAM, which is asymptotically faster under certain conditions than the straightforward $\Theta(n^2)$ time required for the brute force algorithm. The term *output-sensitive* refers to the fact that the amount of output is a parameter of the running time. That is, if there are k intersections, a RAM algorithm for this problem can be constructed to run in $O((n + k)\log n)$ time. Thus, if $k = o(n^2/\log n)$, such an algorithm is asymptotically faster than one that examines all pairs. Such an algorithm can be obtained by making minor modifications to the solution above for the intersection query problem. The most important change is that instead of halting upon discovering an intersection, we list the intersection and continue the plane sweep to the right.

OVERLAPPING LINE SEGMENTS

In Chapter 7, we examined the following:

■ *the coverage query problem*, in which we determine whether or not a given fixed interval $[a,b]$ is covered by the union of an input set of intervals, and

■ *the maximal overlapping point problem*, where we determine a point of the real line that is covered by the largest number of members of an input set of intervals.

Such problems fall within the scope of computational geometry. Another problem in computational geometry that is concerned with overlapping line segments is the *minimal-cover* problem, which can be expressed as follows. Given an interval $[a,b]$ and a set of n intervals $S = \{[a_i,b_i]\}_{i=1}^{n}$, find a minimal-membership subset S' of S such that $[a,b]$ is contained in the union of the members of S', if such a set exists, or report that no such set exists. Another version of this problem uses a circle and circular arcs instead of intervals.

An application of this problem is in minimizing the cost of security. The interval $[a,b]$ (respectively, a circle) might represent a borderline (respectively, a convex perimeter) to be guarded, and the members of S might represent sectors that can be watched by individual guards. A positive solution to the problem then represents a minimal cost solution, including a listing of the responsibilities of the individual guards, for keeping the entire borderline or perimeter under surveillance.

Efficient solutions exist for both the interval and circular versions of these problems, which are quite similar. The circular version seems to be the one that has appeared most often in the literature. For the student's convenience, however, the interval version will be the one we work with, as some of its steps are easier to state than their analogs in the circular version of the problem.

We discuss a *greedy* algorithm, that is, an algorithm marked by steps designed to reach as far as possible towards a solution. The algorithm is greedy in that it starts with a member of S that covers a and extends maximally to the right. (If no such member of S exists, then the algorithm terminates and reports that the requested coverage does not exist.) Further, once a member $s \in S$ is selected, a maximal *successor* for s is determined (in other words, a member of S that intersects with s and extends maximally to the right). This procedure continues until either b is covered (a success) or a successor cannot be found (a failure). Thus, a high-level view of this algorithm is as follows:

- Find a member $s \in S$ that covers a and has a maximal right endpoint. If no such member of S exists, report *failure* and halt.
- While *failure* has not been reported and $s = [a_i, b_i]$ does not cover b, assign to s a member of $S\setminus\{s\}$ that has a maximal right endpoint among those members of $S\setminus\{s\}$ that contain b_i. If no such member of $S\setminus\{s\}$ exists, report *failure* and halt.

At the end of these steps, if failure has not been reported, the selected members of S form a minimal-cardinality cover of $[a,b]$. See Figure 10-22, in which the intervals of S have been raised vertically in the Euclidean plane for clear viewing but should be thought of as all belonging to the same Euclidean line.

The approach outlined above seems inherently sequential. We can make some changes so that the resulting algorithm can be implemented in parallel, yet uses key ideas mentioned above:

1. For each $t \in S$, find its maximal successor, if one exists.
2. For each $t \in S$, take the union of t and its successor as a chain of at most two connected intervals. Then take the union of this chain of at most two intervals and its

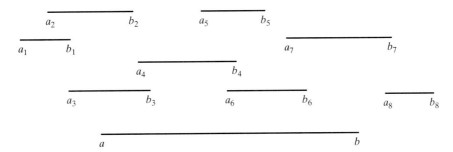

Figure 10-22   A minimal-cardinality cover of [*a*,*b*] consists of arcs 3, 4, 6, and 7.

final arc's successor's chain of at most two intervals to produce a chain of at most four. Repeat this doubling until the chain starting with *t* either does not have a successor chain or covers *b*.

3. Use a minimum operation to find a chain that covers [*a*,*b*] with a minimal number of intervals.

As is so often the case, "find" operations, including those mentioned above, are typically facilitated by having the data appropriately sorted. In the case of the intervals that we are concerned with, we basically want to have this data ordered from left to right. However, since the data consists of intervals rather than single values, some thought must be given to what such an ordering means. Our primary concern is to order the intervals in such a way as to enable an efficient solution to the problem at hand. The ordering that we use is embedded in the algorithm given below, which relies on a postfix operation of the ordered intervals in order to determine maximal overlap of [*a*,*b*] with a minimum number of intervals:

1. Sort the interval records by left endpoint, breaking ties in favor of maximal right endpoints.

2. We observe that if $\{[a_i, b_i], [a_j, b_j]\} \subset S$ and $[a_i, b_i] \subset [a_j, b_j]$, then any connected chain of members of *S* of minimal-cardinality among those chains that start with $[a_i, b_i]$ and cover [*a*, *b*], will have at least as many members as a connected chain of members of *S* of minimal-cardinality among those chains that start with $[a_j, b_j]$ and cover [*a*, *b*]. Therefore, we can remove all such nonessential intervals $[a_i, b_i]$ by performing a simple prefix operation on the ordered set of interval data. Without loss of generality, we will proceed under the assumption that no remaining member of *S* is a subset of another remaining member of *S*.

3. For each remaining $[a_i, b_i] \in S$, create two records. The first set of records, called *successor records*, consists of two components, namely, the index *i* of the interval and the index *j* of the successor of the interval. For each interval $[a_i, b_i] \in S$, we initialize its successor record to (*i*, *i*) with the interpretation that initially every interval is its own successor. Notice that during the procedure, the first component of these records does not change, while the second component will eventually point to the successor of interval $[a_i, b_i]$. The second set of records, referred to as *information*

records, contains connectivity information. The components of the information records are the following:

■ The first two components are the left and right endpoints, respectively, of the connected union of members of S represented by the record's chain of intervals.

■ The third and fourth components represent the indices of the leftmost and rightmost members of the record's chain, respectively.

■ The fifth component is the index of the successor to the rightmost interval in the record's chain (the successor to the interval indexed by the fourth component).

■ The sixth component is the number of members of S in the arc's chain.

For each record $[a_i, b_i] \in S$, we initialize an information record to $(a_i, b_i, i, i, i, 1)$.

4. Sort the information records into ascending order by the second component.

5. In this step, we use the first four components of the information records. Determine the successor of each member of S as follows. Let the operation $\circ$ be defined by the formula:

$$(a_i, b_j, i, j) \circ (a_k, b_m, k, m) = \begin{cases} (a_i, b_m, i, m) \text{ if } a_i \leq a_k \leq b_i \leq b_j < b_m \\ \quad \text{and } b \notin [a_i, b_j]; \\ (a_i, b_j, i, j) \text{ otherwise.} \end{cases}$$

Thus, $A \circ B$ represents $[a_i, b_j] \cup [a_k, b_m]$, provided these arcs intersect, $b \notin [a_i, b_j]$, and $[a_k, b_m]$ extends $[a_i, b_i]$ to the right more than does $[a_j, b_j]$; otherwise, $A \circ B = A$. Use a parallel postfix operation with operation $\circ$ to compute, for each information record representing $[a_i, b_i]$, the transitive closure of $\circ$ on all records representing arc i up through and including the information record representing arc n. Since the intervals are ordered by their right endpoints, it follows that the fourth component of the postfix information record representing arc $[a_i, b_i]$ is the index of the successor of the chain initiated by $[a_i, b_i]$.

6. For all $i \in \{1, 2, \ldots, n\}$, copy the fourth component of the postfix information record created in the previous step, representing $[a_i, b_i]$, to the second component of the successor record representing $[a_i, b_i]$, so that the successor record for $[a_i, b_i]$ will have the form (i, s_i), where s_i is the index of the successor of $[a_i, b_i]$.

7. For all $i \in \{1, 2, \ldots, n\}$, compute the chain of intervals v_i obtained by starting with $[a_i, b_i]$ and adding successors until either b is covered or we reach an interval that is its own successor. This can be done via a parallel postfix computation in which we define the $\cdot$ operation by the formula

$$(a_i, b_j, i, j, k, c) \cdot (a_m, b_q, m, q, r, s) = \begin{cases} (a_i, b_q, i, q, r, c + s) \text{ if } k = m; \\ (a_i, b_j, i, j, k, c) \text{ otherwise.} \end{cases}$$

8. A minimum operation on $\{v_i\}_{i=1}^{n}$, in which we seek the minimal sixth component such that the interval determined by the first and second components contains $[a, b]$, determines whether or not a minimal-cardinality covering of $[a, b]$ by members of S exists, and, if so, its cardinality. If j is an index such that v_j yields a minimal-cardinality covering of $[a, b]$ by members of S, the members of S that make up this covering can

be listed by a parallel prefix operation that marks a succession of successors starting with $[a_j, b_j]$.

CHAPTER NOTES

The focus of this chapter is on efficient sequential and parallel solutions to fundamental problems in the field of computational geometry. The reader interested in a more comprehensive exploration of computational geometry is referred to *Computational Geometry* by F.P. Preparata & M.I. Shamos (Springer-Verlag, 1985). In fact, the proof that sorting is linear-time transformable to the convex hull problem comes from this source. The reader interested in parallel implementations of solutions to problems in computational geometry is referred to S.G. Akl & K.A. Lyons' *Parallel Computational Geometry* (Prentice Hall, 1993).

The Graham scan algorithm was originally presented in "An efficient algorithm for determining the convex hull of a finite planar set," by R.L. Graham in *Information Processing Letters* 1, 1972, 132–133. The Jarvis march algorithm was originally presented by R.A. Jarvis in the paper "On the identification of the convex hull of a finite set of points in the plane," *Information Processing Letters* 2, 1973, 18–21. These algorithms are also presented in a thorough fashion in *Introduction to Algorithms* by T.H. Cormen, C.L. Leiserson, and R.L. Rivest (McGraw Hill Book Company, 1990).

The generic divide-and-conquer solution to the convex hull problem presented in this chapter is motivated by the material presented in *Parallel Algorithms for Regular Architectures* by R. Miller & Q.F. Stout (The MIT Press, 1996). The "teeter-totter" binary search algorithm referred to when describing an intricate binary search for determining common tangent lines was originally presented by M.H. Overmars and J. van Leeuwen in "Maintenance of configurations in the plane," in the *Journal of Computer and Systems Sciences*, Vol. 23, 1981, 166–204. The interesting divide-and-conquer algorithm for the PRAM was first presented by M. Atallah and M. Goodrich in "Efficient parallel solutions to some geometric problems," in the *Journal of Parallel and Distributed Computing* 3, 1986, 492–507. One might note that this algorithm exploits the CR capabilities of a CREW PRAM. We should point out that an optimal time $\Theta(\log n)$ EREW PRAM algorithm to solve the convex hull problem has been presented by R. Miller & Q.F. Stout in "Efficient parallel convex hull algorithms," in *IEEE Transactions on Computers*, 37 (12), 1988. However, the presentation of the Miller and Stout algorithm is beyond the scope of this book.

The notion of angles of support is interesting in that it allows multiple parallel searches to be implemented by a series of sort steps. Details of the mesh convex hull algorithm that relies on angles of support can be found in *Parallel Algorithms for Regular Architectures*.

The reader interested in learning more about the Voronoi diagram and its application to problems involving proximity might consult *Computational Geometry* by F.P. Preparata & M.I. Shamos (Springer-Verlag, 1985). Details of the all-nearest neighbor algorithm for the mesh can be found in *Parallel Algorithms for Regular Architectures*.

A RAM algorithm for the circular version of the cover problem was presented by C.C. Lee and D.T. Lee in "On a Cover-Circle Minimization Problem," in *Information Processing Letters* 18, 1984, 180–185. A CREW PRAM algorithm for the circular version of this problem appears in "Parallel Circle-Cover Algorithms," by A.A. Bertossi in *Information Processing Letters* 27, 1988, 133–139. The algorithm by Bertossi was improved independently in each of the following papers:

- M.J. Atallah and D.Z. Chen, "An optimal parallel algorithm for the minimum circle-cover problem," *Information Processing Letters* 32, 1989, 159–165.
- L. Boxer and R. Miller, "A parallel circle-cover minimization algorithm," *Information Processing Letters* 32, 1989, 57–60.
- D. Sarkar and I. Stojmenovic, "An optimal parallel circle-cover algorithm," *Information Processing Letters* 32, 1989, 3–6.

The exercises below include questions concerning the *all maximal equally spaced collinear points problem*. This and several related problems were studied in the following papers:

- A.B. Kahng and G. Robins, "Optimal algorithms for extracting spatial regularity in images," *Pattern Recognition Letters* 12, 1991, 757–764.
- L. Boxer and R. Miller, "Parallel algorithms for all maximal equally spaced collinear sets and all maximal regular coplanar lattices," *Pattern Recognition Letters* 14, 1993, 17–22.

These problems have considerable practical value, as the presence of the regularity amidst seeming or expected chaos is often meaningful. For example, the members of S might represent points observed in an aerial or satellite photo, and the maximal equally spaced collinear sets might represent traffic lights, military formations, property or national boundaries in the form of fence posts, and so forth. The paper of Kahng and Robins presents a RAM algorithm for the all maximal equally spaced collinear sets problem that runs in optimal $\Theta(n^2)$ time. This algorithm seems to be essentially sequential. The Boxer and Miller paper shows how a rather different algorithm can be implemented in efficient to optimal time on parallel architectures.

EXERCISES

Many of the exercises in this section can be considered for a variety of models of computation.

1. Given a set S of n planar points, construct an efficient algorithm to determine whether or not there exist three points in S that are collinear.

2. Given a set of n line segments in the plane, prove that there may be as many as $\Theta(n^2)$ intersections.

3. Show that the algorithm sketched in this chapter to solve the intersection query problem runs in $\Theta(n \log n)$ time on a RAM.

4. Given a set of n line segments in the plane that have a total of k intersections, show that a RAM algorithm can solve the intersection reporting problem, reporting all intersections, in $O((n+k) \log n)$ time.

5. Given a convex polygon with n vertices, construct an efficient algorithm to determine the area of the polygon. Input to the problem consists of the circularly ordered edges (equivalently, vertices) of the polygon.

6. Given a polygon with n vertices, construct an efficient algorithm to determine whether or not the polygon is simple.

7. Given two simple polygons, each consisting of n vertices, give an efficient algorithm to determine whether or not the polygons intersect.

8. Given a simple polygon P and a point p, give an efficient algorithm to determine whether or not p is contained in P.

9. Give an efficient algorithm to determine the convex hull of a simple polygon.

10. On a fine-grained parallel computer, a very different approach can be taken to the intersection reporting problem. Suppose input to a PRAM, mesh, or hypercube of n processors consists of the n line segments in the Euclidean plane. In the case of a mesh or hypercube, assume the segments are initially distributed one per processor. Provide a solution to the intersection reporting problem that is optimal in the worst case, and prove the optimality, for each of these architectures. Hints: This can be done with an algorithm that seems simpler to describe than the RAM algorithm described in the text. Also, the processors of a hypercube may be renumbered in a circular fashion.

11. In this chapter, we sketched an algorithm to solve the following problem: For a set of n intervals and a range $[a,b]$, determine a minimal-cardinality subset of the intervals that cover $[a,b]$ or to show, when appropriate, that no such cover exists. Prove the algorithm runs in

   ■ $\Theta(n \log n)$ time on a RAM;

   ■ $\Theta(\log n)$ time on a CREW PRAM;

   ■ $\Theta(n^{1/2})$ time on a mesh of n processors, assuming the intervals are initially distributed one per processor.

12. In the Graham scan procedure given in this chapter, prove that both the point chosen as the origin and the last point encountered in the tour must be extreme points of the convex hull.

13. Given a set S of n planar points, prove that a pair of farthest neighbors (a pair of points at a maximum distance over all pairs of points in S) must be chosen from the set of extreme points.

14. Given two sets of points, P and Q, give an efficient algorithm to determine whether P and Q are *linearly separable*. That is, give an efficient algorithm to determine whether or not it is possible to define a line l with the property that all points of P lie on one side of l while all points of Q lie on the other side of l.

15. In this problem, we consider the *all maximal equally spaced collinear points problem* in the Euclidean plane R^2: Given a set S of n points in R^2, identify all of the maximal equally spaced collinear subsets of S that have at least three members. A collinear set $\{p_1, p_2, \ldots, p_k\}$ (assume the points are numbered according to their order on their common line) is *equally-spaced* if all the line segments $\overline{p_i p_{i+1}}$, $i \in \{1, 2, \ldots, k-1\}$, have the same length. Assume that we are given a set S of n points in R^2, where each point is represented by its Cartesian coordinates (see Figure 10-23).

a) Show that $O(n^2)$ is an upper bound for the output of this problem. Hint: Show that every pair of distinct points $\{p,q\} \subset S$ can be a consecutive pair of at most one maximal equally spaced collinear subset of S.

b) Show that $\Omega(n^2)$ is a lower bound for the worst-case output of this problem. Hint: Let n be a square and let S be the square of integer points $S = \{(a,b) \mid 1 \le a \le n^{1/2}, 1 \le b \le n^{1/2}\}$. Let $S' \subset S$ be defined by

$$S' = \left\{ (a,b) \;\middle|\; \frac{n^{1/2}}{3} \le a \le \frac{2n^{1/2}}{3}, \frac{n^{1/2}}{3} \le b \le \frac{2n^{1/2}}{3} \right\}.$$

Show that if $\{p,q\} \subset S', p \ne q$, then $\{p,q\}$ is a consecutive pair in a maximal equally spaced collinear subset C of S such that $|C| \ge 3$. Together with the previous exercise, this shows the worst-case output for this problem is $\Theta(n^2)$.

c) Consider the following algorithm, which can be implemented on a variety of architectures (the details of implementing some of the steps will vary with the architecture).

i) Form the set P of all ordered pairs $(p,q) \subset S$ such that $p < q$ in the lexicographic order of points in R^2.

ii) Sort the members of P in ascending order with respect to all the following keys:

a) Slope of the line determined by a member of P as the primary key (use ∞ for a vertical segment);

b) Length of the line segment determined by a member of P as the secondary key;

c) Lexicographic order of the endpoints of P as the tertiary key.

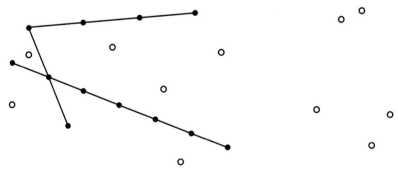

Figure 10-23 The *all maximal equally spaced collinear points problem*. An illustration of three equally spaced collinear line segments.

iii) Use a parallel postfix operation on P to identify all maximal equally spaced collinear subsets of S. The operation is based on the formation of quintuples and a binary operation specified as follows. Initial quintuples are of the form $(p, q, length, 2, true)$, where the first two components are the endpoints (members of S) in an equally spaced collinear set; the third is the length of segments that make up the current equally spaced collinear set; the fourth component is the number of input points in the equally spaced collinear set; and the fifth component is true or false according to whether the first component is the first point in an equally spaced collinear set. The binary operation is defined by

$$(a, b, c, d, u) \otimes (e, f, g, h, v) = \begin{cases} (a, f, c, d + h - 1, u) \text{ if} \\ \quad (b = e) \text{ and } (c = g) \\ \quad\quad\quad \text{and} \\ (\{a, b, f\} \text{ is a collinear set}); \\ (a, b, c, d, u) \text{ otherwise.} \end{cases}$$

and in the former case, set $v = false$.

iv) A postfix operation on the members of P is used to enumerate members of each equally spaced collinear set of more than two points. This operation is based on members of P with a postfix quintuple having the fifth component $true$ and the fourth component greater than two.

Analyze the running time of this algorithm for each of a RAM, a CREW PRAM of n^2 processors, and a mesh of n^2 processors. In the case of the mesh, assume that the members of S are initially distributed so that no processor has more than one member of S. Formation of the set P can thus be done on the mesh by appropriate row and column rotations, and/or random-access write operations. The details are left to the reader.

11

Image Processing

Image Processing

In this chapter, we consider some fundamental problems in image processing, an important and challenging area of computer science. Due to the fact that the mesh computer is well matched to image-based problems, the focus of this chapter is on algorithms and paradigms for the mesh. Many of the algorithms presented in this chapter are based on divide-and-conquer since this is a natural match to image problems on a mesh computer. Even though the focus of this chapter is a bit different from those of the preceding chapters, please note that we will present algorithms for the RAM, as appropriate.

PRELIMINARIES

In this chapter, we consider the input to the problems to be an $n \times n$ digitized black/white picture. That is, the input can be viewed as a matrix (mesh) of data in which every element is either a 1 (black) or a 0 (white). These "picture elements" are typically referred to as *pixels*. The interpretation of the image is that it is a black image on a white background, and the set of black pixels can be referred to as a *digital image*. The terminology and assumptions that we use in this chapter represent the norm in the field of image processing.

Readers must be very careful to recalibrate their expectations. In most of the preceding chapters, the input was of size n, whereas in this chapter the input is of size n^2. Therefore, a linear time sequential algorithm will run in $\Theta(n^2)$ time, not in $\Theta(n)$ time. If the input data is to be sorted on a RAM, then an optimal worst-case comparison-based sequential sorting algorithm will take $\Theta(n^2 \log n)$ time, not $\Theta(n \log n)$ time.

Since we want to map the image directly onto the mesh, we assume that pixel $p_{i,j}$ is mapped to mesh processor $P_{i,j}$ on a mesh of size n^2. Again, we need to recalibrate. Given a mesh of size n^2, the communication diameter and bisection width are both $\Theta(n)$. So, for any problem that might require pixels at opposite ends of the mesh to be combined in some way, a lower bound on the running time of an algorithm to solve such a problem is given as $\Omega(n)$.

There is an important mesh result concerned with determining the transitive closure of a matrix that we will use in this chapter. Let G be a directed graph with n vertices, represented by an adjacency matrix A. That is, $A(i, j) = 1$ if and only if there is a directed edge in G from i to j. Otherwise, $A(i, j) = 0$. The *transitive closure* of A, which is typically written as A^*, is an $n \times n$ matrix such that $A^*(i, j) = 1$ if and only if there is a directed path in G from vertex i *to* vertex j. $A^*(i, j) = 0$ otherwise.

It is important to note that both A and A^* are binary matrices. That is, A and A^* are matrices in which all entries are either 0 or 1. Consider the effect of "multiplying" matrix A by itself, where the usual method of matrix multiplication is modified by replacing addition ($+$) with OR ($\vee$) and multiplication ($\times$) with AND ($\wedge$). Notice that an entry $A^2(i, j) = 1$ if and only if

- $A(i, j) = 1$, or
- $A(i, k) = 1$ AND $A(k, j) = 1$ for some k.

That is, $A^2(i, j) = 1$ if and only if there is a path of length no more than two from i to j. Now consider the matrix A^3, which can be computed in a similar fashion from A and A^2. Notice that $A^3(i, j) = 1$ if and only if there is a path from i to j that consists of three or fewer edges. Continuing this line of thought, notice that the matrix A^n is such that $A^n(i, j) = 1$ if and only if there is a path from i to j that consists of n or fewer edges. That is, A^n contains information about the existence of every directed path in the graph G. The matrix A^n, which is often referred to as the *connectivity matrix*, represents the transitive closure of A. That is, $A^* = A^n$.

Consider a sequential solution to the problem of determining the transitive closure of an $n \times n$ matrix A. Based on the preceding discussion, it is clear that the transitive closure can be determined by multiplying A by itself n times. Since the traditional matrix multiplication algorithm on two $n \times n$ matrices takes $\Theta(n^3)$ time, we know that the transitive closure of A can be determined in $O(n \times n^3) = O(n^4)$ time. So the question is, can we do better? Well, consider matrix A^2. Once we have A^2, we could either multiply it by A to arrive at A^3, or we could multiply $A^2 \times A^2$ to arrive at A^4. Clearly, we are better off squaring the current matrix if our motivation is to try and reach A^n as quickly as possible. In fact, notice that if we overshoot A^n, it doesn't matter. The reader should verify that $A^{n+c} = A^n$ for any positive integer $c > 0$. Therefore, if we perform $\Theta(\log n)$ matrix multiplication operations, each time squaring the resulting matrix, we can reduce the natural running time of transitive closure from $O(n^4)$ down to $O(n^3 \log n)$.

Define a Boolean matrix A_k so that $A_k(i, j) = 1$ if and only if there is a path from vertex i to vertex j using no intermediate vertex with label greater than k. Notice that this is a nonstandard interpretation of a Boolean matrix. Given this matrix, an algorithm can be designed that will iteratively transform $A_0 = A$ to $A_n = A^n = A^*$ through a series of intermediate matrix computations A_k, $0 < k < n$. Based on our discussion, we define $A_k(i, j) = 1$ if and only if

- there is a path from i to j using no intermediate vertex greater than $k - 1$, or
- there is a path from i to k using no intermediate vertex greater than $k - 1$ and there is a path from k to j using no intermediate vertex greater than $k - 1$.

We now present *Warshall's algorithm* for determining the transitive closure of a Boolean matrix:

> For $k = 1$ to n, do
> > For $i = 1$ to n, do
> > > For $j = 1$ to n, do
> > > > $A_k(i, j) = A_{k-1}(i, j) \vee [A_{k-1}(i, k) \wedge A_{k-1}(k, j)]$

While the running time of Warshall's algorithm on a RAM is $\Theta(n^3)$, notice that the algorithm requires $\Theta(n^2)$ additional memory. This is due to the fact that at the k-th iteration of the outermost loop, it is necessary to keep the previous iteration's matrix A_{k-1} in memory.

F. L. Van Scoy has shown that given an $n \times n$ adjacency A matrix mapped onto a mesh of size n^2 such that $A(i, j)$ is mapped to processor $P_{i,j}$, the transitive closure of A can be determined in $\Theta(n)$ optimal time. Details of this algorithm are presented in Chapter 12.

Notes on Terminology: Since pixels are mapped to processors of a fine-grained mesh in a natural fashion, we tend to think about pixels and processors as coupled when designing mesh algorithms. Therefore, when there is no confusion, we will use the terms "pixel" and "processor" interchangeably in describing fine-grained mesh algorithms.

COMPONENT LABELING

In this section, we consider the problem of uniquely labeling every maximally connected component in an image. Efficient algorithms to solve the *component labeling problem* serve as fundamental tools to many image processing tasks. Given a digitized black-and-white picture, viewed as a black image on a white background, one of the early steps in image processing is to label uniquely each of the distinct figures (*i.e.,* components) in the picture. Once the figures are labeled, then one can process the image at a higher level in an effort to recognize shapes and to develop relationships among objects.

It is often convenient to recast the component-labeling problem in graph theoretic terms. Consider every black pixel to be a vertex. Consider that an edge exists between every pair of vertices represented by neighboring black pixels. We assume that pixels are *neighbors* if and only if they are directly above, below, left of, or right of each other. (This notion of neighbors is called *4-adjacency* in the literature.) In particular, pixels that are diagonally adjacent are not considered neighbors for the purpose of this presentation, though such an interpretation does not typically affect the asymptotic analysis of component-labeling algorithms. The goal of a component-labeling algorithm is to label uniquely every maximally connected set of pixels (vertices). Although the label chosen for every component is irrelevant, in this book we will choose to label every component with the minimum

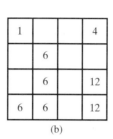

Figure 11-1 (a) A digitized 4 × 4 picture. The interpretation is that it is a black image on a white background. (b) The same 4 × 4 picture with its maximally connected components labeled under a 4-adjacency definition of connectedness. Each component is labeled with the pixel of minimum label in its components, where the pixel labels are taken to be the row-major labeling with values $[1, \ldots, 16]$.

(a)

(b)

label over any pixel (vertex) in the figure (component). This is a fairly standard means of labeling components (see Figure 11-1).

RAM: Initially, let's consider a sequential algorithm to label the maximally connected components of an $n \times n$ digitized black-and-white picture. Suppose we use a straightforward propagation-based algorithm. Initialize the *component label* for every pixel to *nil*. Initialize the *vertex label* for every pixel to the concatenation of its row and column indices. Now traverse the image in row-major order. When a black pixel is encountered that has not previously been assigned a component label, assign that pixel's vertex label as its component label. Next use backtracking to propagate this component label to all of its black neighbors (which recursively propagate the label to all of their black neighbors, and so on).

Let's consider the running time of this simple propagation algorithm. Every pixel is visited once during the row-major scan. Now consider the backtracking phase of the algorithm, in which both black and white pixels can be visited. The black pixels can be visited as the propagation continues and the white pixels serve as stopping points to the backtracking. Fortunately, every component is only labeled once, and if backtracking is done properly, every black pixel is only visited a fixed number of times during a given backtracking/propagation phase. That is, when a black pixel is visited, no more than three of its neighbors need to be considered (why?), and in the recursion, control returns to the pixel those three times at most before it returns control to whichever pixel examined it. A white pixel can only be visited by four of its neighbors during some propagation phase, each time returning control immediately. Therefore, the running time of the algorithm is linear in the number of pixels, which is $\Theta(n^2)$.

Mesh: Now let's consider a mesh algorithm to solve the component-labeling problem. Assume that we are given an $n \times n$ digitized black-and-white picture mapped in a natural fashion onto a mesh of size n^2 so that pixel $p_{i,j}$ is mapped to processor $P_{i,j}$. The first algorithm we might consider is a direct implementation of the sequential propagation algorithm. If we implement the algorithm directly, then clearly the running time remains at $\Theta(n^2)$, which is unacceptable. Therefore, let's consider the natural parallel variant of propagation. Parallel propagation consists of every black pixel continually exchanging its current component label with each of its black neighbors (at most four). During each such exchange, a processor accepts the minimum of its current label and that of its black neighbors as its new component label. The effect is that the minimum vertex/processor label in a component is propagated throughout the component in the minimum time required (that is, using the minimum number of communication links required), assuming that all messages must remain within a component. In fact, this label reaches every processor in its component in the minimum time necessary to broadcast the label between them, assuming that all messages must remain within the component. Therefore, if all the (maximally) connected components (figures) are relatively small, this is an effective algorithm. If every figure is enclosed in some $k \times k$ region, then the running time of the algorithm is $\Theta(k^2)$. This is efficient if $k^2 = O(n)$. In fact, if we regard k as constant, then the running time is $\Theta(1)$ (see Figure 11-2).

Now let's consider the worst-case running time of this parallel propagation algorithm. Suppose we have a picture that consists of a single figure. Further, suppose that the internal diameter (the maximum distance between two black pixels, assuming that one travels only between pixels that are members of the figure) is large. For example, consider Figure 11-3, which includes a "spiral" on the left and a "snake" on the right.

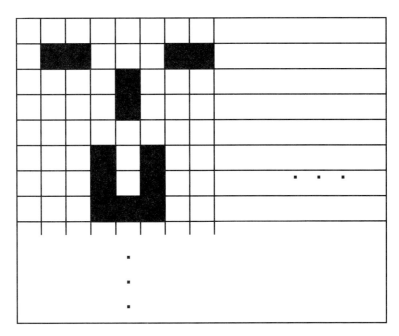

Figure 11-2 Each connected component is confined to a 3×3 region. In such situations, the mesh propagation algorithm is run in $\Theta(1)$ time.

 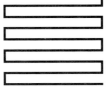

Figure 11-3 Two problematic figures. A "spiral" is shown on the left and a "snake" is shown on the right.

We see that it is easy to construct figures that have internal diameters of $\Theta(n^2)$. Therefore, this propagation algorithm will run in $\Theta(n^2)$ time on such figures. So our parallel propagation algorithm has a running time of $\Omega(1)$ and $O(n^2)$. For many situations, we might be willing to accept such an algorithm if we know *a priori* that these troublesome situations (*i.e.*, the worst-case running time) will not occur. There may be situations in which, even if such an image might occur, we know that no figure of interest could have such characteristics, and we could then modify the algorithm so that it terminates after some more reasonable predetermined amount of time. Unfortunately, there are many situations in which we care about minimizing the general worst-case running time.

We will now consider a divide-and-conquer algorithm to solve the general component-labeling problem on a mesh. This divide-and-conquer algorithm is fairly traditional and exhibits an asymptotically optimal worst-case running time:

1. **Divide** the image into four subimages, each of size $(n/2) \times (n/2)$.
2. **Recursively** label each of the independent subimages.
3. **Stitch** the independently labeled subimages together in order to obtain a labeled image.

As with many divide-and-conquer algorithms, the stitch step is crucial. Notice that once each $(n/2) \times (n/2)$ subproblem has been solved, there are only $O(n)$ labels in each such submesh that might be incorrect globally. That is, for every (global) component completely contained within its $(n/2) \times (n/2)$ region, the recursive label must be correct in a global sense. Only those local components (components of one of the $(n/2) \times (n/2)$ regions) with a pixel on an edge between two subproblems might need to be relabeled (see Figure 11-4). Therefore, while the initial problem had $\Theta(n^2)$ pieces of data (pixels), after the recursive solutions were obtained, there are only $O(n)$ critical pieces of information (that is, information that is necessary in order to obtain the final result). We can stitch the partial results together as follows.

	4	4			20	20	
			16	27			32
							54
		39					54
		39	39	57	57		54

Figure 11-4 An 8×8 image after labeling each of its 4×4 quadrants. Notice that the component labels come from the shuffled row-major indexing scheme. The global components that are completely contained in a quadrant (components 4 and 20) do not need to be considered further. The remaining components are required for a global relabeling procedure. The labels shown use the shuffled row-major order of the processors, starting with processor 1 (not 0).

First, each processor P containing a black pixel on the border of one of the $(n/2) \times (n/2)$ regions examines its neighbors that are located in a distinct $(n/2) \times (n/2)$ region. For each such border processor P, there are either one or two such neighbors. For each neighboring black pixel in a different region, processor P generates a record containing the identity and current component label of both P and the neighboring pixel. Notice that there are at most two records generated by any processor containing a border vertex. However, also notice that for every record generated by one processor, a "mirror image" record is generated by its neighboring processor. Next, compress these $O(n)$ records into an $n^{1/2} \times n^{1/2}$ region within the $n \times n$ mesh. In the $n^{1/2} \times n^{1/2}$ region, use these $O(n)$ unordered edge records to solve the component-labeling problem on the underlying graph.

Notice that the stitch step can perform the compression operation by sorting the necessary records in $\Theta(n)$ time. Once the critical data is compressed to an $n^{1/2} \times n^{1/2}$ region, we can perform a logarithmic number of iterations to merge components together until they are maximally connected. Each such iteration involves a fixed number of sort-based operations, including concurrent reads and writes. Therefore, each iteration is performed in $\Theta(n^{1/2})$ time. Hence, the time required for computing maximally connected components within the $n^{1/2} \times n^{1/2}$ region is $\Theta(n^{1/2} \log n)$. Completing the stitch step involves a complete $\Theta(n)$ time concurrent read so that every pixel in the image can determine its new label. Since the compression and concurrent read steps dominate the running time of the stitch routine, the running time of the algorithm is given as $T(n^2) = T(n^2/4) + \Theta(n)$, which sums to $T(n^2) = \Theta(n)$. Notice that this is a time-optimal algorithm for a mesh of size n^2. However, the total cost of such an algorithm is $\Theta(n^3)$, while the problem has a lower bound of $\Omega(n^2)$ total cost.

We now consider an interesting alternative to the stitch step. In the approach that we presented, we reduced the amount of data from $\Theta(n^2)$ to $O(n)$, compressed the $O(n)$ data, and then spent time leisurely working on it. Instead, we can consider creating a cross-product with the reduced amount of critical data. That is, once we have reduced the data to $O(n)$ critical pieces, representing an undirected graph, we can create an adjacency matrix. Notice that the adjacency matrix will easily fit into the $n \times n$ mesh. Once the adjacency matrix is created, we can perform the $\Theta(n)$ time transitive closure algorithm of Van Scoy mentioned at the beginning of the chapter in order to determine maximally connected components. The minimum vertex label can be chosen as the label of each connected component, and a concurrent read by all pixels can be used for the final relabeling. Although the running time of this algorithm remains at $\Theta(n)$, it is instructive to show different approaches to dealing with a situation in which one can drastically reduce the size of the set of data under consideration.

CONVEX HULL

In this section, we consider the problem of marking the extreme points of the convex hull for every labeled set of pixels in a given image. Suppose that we have a mesh of size n^2 and that we associate every processor $P_{i,j}$ with the lattice point (i,j). Suppose that every processor contains a label in the range of $0 \ldots n^2$, where the interpretation is that 0 represents the background (a white pixel) and that values in the range of $1 \ldots n^2$ represent labels of foreground pixels (or nonwhite pixels). Further, we assume that all pixels with the same label are members of the same set of points and we want to determine the convex hull for every distinctly labeled set of points.

Notice that a maximal set of points with the same label need not be a connected component. In fact, the sets might be intertwined and their convex hulls might overlap, as shown in Figure 11-5.

We have discussed the general convex hull problem for a variety of models in a preceding chapter. Clearly, the image input considered in this section can be simply and efficiently converted to the more general form of 2-dimensional point data input. From such input, the algorithms of the previous chapter can be invoked in a straightforward fashion. Our goal in this section, however, is to introduce some new techniques, which will result in a greatly simplified routine for the mesh, given lattice input as imposed on the mesh. The premise of the algorithm is first to determine the extreme points for every set as restricted to each row. Once this is done, we will show that there are not too many possible extreme points for any given set. Within each such set, every row-restricted extreme point can consider all other row-restricted extreme points of its set and determine whether or not it is contained in some triangle formed by the remaining points, in which case it is not an extreme point. Further, if no such triangle can be found, then it is an extreme point. The algorithm follows.

Initially in every row, we wish to identify the extreme points for every labeled set. In a given row, the extreme points of each set are simply the (at most two) outermost points of the set. This identification can be done by a simple row rotation, simultaneously for all rows, so that every processor can view all of the data within its row and decide whether or not it is an extreme point for its labeled set.

Next, sort all of these row-restricted extreme points by label so that after the sort is complete, adjacent elements are stored in adjacent processors. Although there are $O(n^2)$ such points, it is important to note that for any label, there are at most $2n$ such points (at most

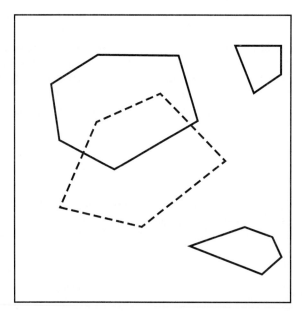

Figure 11-5   A illustration of overlapping convex hulls of labeled (not necessarily connected) sets of pixels.

two points per each row). Notice that all of the row-restricted extreme points for a given set are now in a contiguous set of processors. Therefore, we can perform rotations within such ordered intervals. These rotations are similar to row and column rotations but work within intervals that might cover fractions of one or more rows. Thus, simultaneously for all intervals (that is, labeled sets), rotate the set of row-restricted extreme points. During the rotation, suppose a processor is responsible for lattice point X. Then as a new lattice point Y arrives, the processor responsible for X performs the following operations:

- ■ If no other point is stored in the processor, then the processor stores Y.
- ■ Suppose the processor has previously stored one other point, say, U. Then the processor will store Y. However, if X, Y, and U are on the same line, then the processor eliminates the interior point of these three.
- ■ Suppose the processor has previously stored two other points, U and V, before Y arrives.
  a) If X is in the triangle determined by U, V, and Y, then the processor determines that X is not an extreme point.
  b) Otherwise, if Y is on a line segment determined by X and either U or V, then of the three collinear points X is not interior (otherwise, the previous case would apply). Discard the interior of the three collinear points, Y or U (respectively, Y or V).
  c) Otherwise, the processor should eliminate whichever of U, V, and Y is inside the triangle formed by X and the other two.

If after the rotation, the processor responsible for row-restricted extreme point X has not eliminated this point, X is an extreme point.

A final concurrent read can be used to send the row-restricted extreme points back to their originating processors (corresponding to their lattice points) and the extreme points can then be marked.

Running time: The analysis of running time is straightforward since no recursion is involved. The algorithm consists of a fixed number of $\Theta(n)$-time rotations and sort-based operations. Therefore, the running time of this algorithm is $\Theta(n)$. Notice that the cost of the algorithm is $\Theta(n^3)$ and we know that the problem can be solved sequentially in $\Theta(n^2 \log n)$ time by the traditional convex hull algorithm on arbitrary point data.

DISTANCE PROBLEMS

In this section, we consider problems that involve distances between labeled sets of pixels and within connected components. The first problem is concerned with determining for every labeled set of pixels its nearest distinctly labeled set of pixels. For this problem, we again assume a labeled set of (not necessarily connected) pixels. The second problem is concerned with distances within a connected component. For this problem, we assume that one special pixel in each connected component is "marked," and that every pixel needs to find its minimal internal distance to this marked pixel.

All-Nearest Neighbor Between Labeled Sets: In this section, we consider the *all-nearest neighbor between labeled sets problem*. Assume that the input consists of a labeled set of pixels. That is, assume that every processor $P_{i,j}$ is associated with the lattice point (i,j) on a mesh of size n^2. As we did in the previous section, assume that every processor contains a label in the range of $0 \ldots n^2$, where the interpretation is that 0 represents the background (a white pixel) and that values in the range of $1 \ldots n^2$ represent labels of foreground pixels (nonwhite pixels). Recall pixels in the same labeled set are not necessarily connected.

The problem we are concerned with is determining for every labeled set of pixels the label of a nearest distinctly labeled set of pixels. Algorithmically, we can first determine for every pixel the label and distance to a nearest distinctly labeled pixel. This solves the problem for pixels. In order to solve the problem for every labeled set, we can then determine the minimum of these pixels' nearest-pixel distances over all pixels within a labeled set. Details of the algorithm follow.

For every labeled processor, we first find its nearest distinctly labeled processor. To do this, we exploit the fact that the pixels are laid out on a grid and that we are using the Euclidean distance as a metric. Suppose that p and q are labeled pixels that are in the same column. Further, let r be a nearest distinctly labeled pixel to p in the same row as p, as shown in Figure 11-6. Notice that this means that with respect to p's row, either p or r is a nearest distinctly labeled pixel to q. We refer to this observation as "work-reducing." To find a nearest distinctly labeled processor, follow these steps:

1. Perform parallel row rotations of every row so that every processor p finds at most two nearest processors in its row with distinct foreground labels. Notice that if processor p maintains a foreground pixel then the identity of this pixel corresponds to one of the at most two foreground pixels in its row with distinct labels that the processor p will identify. Call these processors r_1, r_2, where the labels of the foreground pixels maintained in r_1 and r_2 are distinct. We need two such processors if the row has foreground pixels with distinct labels, as, say, r_1 may have the same label as a processor in the column of p.

2. Perform parallel column rotations of every column. Every processor p sends its information (labels and positions) and the information associated with its row-restricted nearest dis-

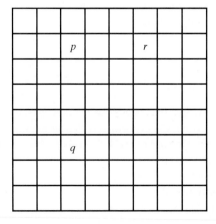

Figure 11-6   The *all-nearest-neighbor-between-labeled-sets problem*. Suppose p, q, and r are labeled pixels. If r is a closest distinctly labeled pixel in row 2 to p, then either p or r is a closest distinctly labeled pixel to q among those in row 2.

tinctly labeled processors r_1 and r_2. During the rotation, every processor is able to determine a nearest distinctly labeled processor, using the work-reducing observation.

3. Sort all of the near neighbor information by initial pixel (set) label.

4. Within every labeled set of data, perform a semigroup operation (in particular, a minimum operation) and broadcast so that every pixel knows the label of a nearest distinctly labeled set to its set.

5. Finally, use a concurrent read so that the initial set of pixels can determine the final result.

Running Time: On an $n \times n$ mesh, the running time of this algorithm is $\Theta(n)$. This is due to the fact that the algorithm is dominated by a row rotation, column rotation, semigroup operation, and sort-based operations. Again, the cost of the algorithm is $\Theta(n^3)$, which is suboptimal, as the problem can be solved in $\Theta(n^2 \log n)$ time on a RAM.

Minimum Internal Distance Within Connected Components: In this section, we consider the *all-points minimal internal distance problem*. The input to this problem is a set of figures (that is, maximally connected components that have been properly labeled) and one *marked* pixel per figure. The problem requires us to determine the minimum internal distance from every black pixel to the unique marked pixel in its figure.

Let's first consider a simple propagation algorithm over a single figure. Assume the *marked* processor is labeled X. The processor associated with X assigns its distance to 0, since it is the *marked* processor. All other processors in the figure assign their initial distance to ∞. Now every black processor exchanges distance information with its neighboring black processors. A given processor with current distance of s to the marked processor will receive at most four additional pieces of distance information denoted as a, b, c, and d. This processor will now set $s = \min(s, \min(a, b, c, d) + 1)$. The algorithm continues until no distances in the figure change. Notice that the algorithm will terminate immediately after information from the *marked* processor X reaches the processor(s) at maximal internal distance from it. As with propagation algorithms discussed earlier, this algorithm is quite efficient for figures with a small internal diameter, but can be quite bad for figures with large internal diameters. In fact, if we consider a spiral- or snake-like figure, we see that this algorithm has a running time of $O(n^2)$ on a mesh of size n^2.

We now consider a significantly more complicated algorithm based on divide-and-conquer, which exhibits a $\Theta(n)$ worst-case running time. This algorithm involves both data reduction and the application of a generalized transitive closure algorithm, which was mentioned earlier.

The algorithm consists of two *phases*. The first phase of the algorithm can be viewed as exploiting a bottom-up divide-and-conquer strategy. During the i-th stage of the first phase, the objective is to determine correctly the internal distance from every black pixel on the border of a $2^i \times 2^i$ region

a) to every other border pixel, and

b) to the marked pixel.

The assumption in determining this information during the i-th stage is that the image is restricted to the $2^i \times 2^i$ region. Notice that pixels within a figure might not even be connected within the $2^i \times 2^i$ region, and these will have a final result of ∞ after performing the required computations during the i-th stage. Further, notice that the marked pixel of a figure can only be in one of the $2^i \times 2^i$ regions. Therefore, after stage $\log_2 n - 1$, three of the four $(n/2) \times (n/2)$ regions will have every entry between a border pixel and the marked pixel set to ∞.

The first stage of this bottom-up phase is stage 0, in which every pixel has a distance of ∞ to the marked pixel, with the exception of the marked pixel itself, which has a distance of 0. The final stage of this phase is stage $\log_2 n$ in which the (at most) $4n - 4$ outer pixels of the $n \times n$ mesh obtain the correct internal distance from their pixels to each other as well as to the marked pixel.

The second phase of this algorithm consists of using the information determined during the first phase to determine recursively the correct internal distances for all remaining pixels. This is accomplished by a divide-and-conquer algorithm that can be viewed as top-down. That is, the correct outer border pixel distances for the entire $n \times n$ mesh are used to determine the correct outer border pixel distances for each of the four $(n/2) \times (n/2)$ regions, which can be used to determine the correct outer border pixel distances for each of the sixteen $(n/4) \times (n/4)$ regions, and so on.

Before we give details of each phase of the algorithm, we will take the unorthodox approach of discussing the running time. It will be shown that each stage i of the first phase can be performed in time $\Theta(2^i)$. Therefore, the running time of the first phase of the algorithm is given by $T(n^2) = T(n^2/4) + \Theta(2^{\log_2 n})$, which is $T(n^2) = T(n^2/4) + \Theta(n)$. Therefore, the running time of the first phase of the algorithm is $T(n^2) = \Theta(n)$. We will also show that the time for each stage of the second phase can be performed by following the same steps as in the first phase, but with a slightly different set of input. So, the running time for the second phase, which uses the first phase as a subroutine, is given by $T(n^2) = T(n^2/4) + \Theta(n)$, which yields $T(n^2) = \Theta(n)$. Therefore, the algorithm that we are discussing is asymptotically optimal for the model and input under discussion.

We now discuss some of the details of the two phases of the algorithm. First, we consider the i-th phase of the first stage. We show how to determine properly the restricted internal distances from the outer pixels of the $2^i \times 2^i$ region to the marked pixel. Assume that for each of the $(2^i/2) \times (2^i/2)$ subsquares of the region, the problem for the first phase has been solved recursively. Then we need to show how to combine the distance results from each of the four $(2^i/2) \times (2^i/2)$ regions into the required result for the $2^i \times 2^i$ region. At the end of stage $i - 1$, we assume that each of the four subsquares not only has the correct restricted internal distance from every outer pixel to the marked pixel, but also from every outer pixel to every other outer pixel. Notice that there is room to store this as a matrix within each of the four $(2^i/2) \times (2^i/2)$ subsquares. The algorithm performed at the i-th phase simply consists of combining all of this internal distance information in an appropriate way. This is done by combining the four internal distance matrices into one distance matrix. This matrix contains restricted internal distances between the outer border elements of the four subsquares and also to the marked pixel (see Figure 11-7).

Now in order to consider the $2^i \times 2^i$ region, we simply have to modify the matrix to include a distance of 1 (instead of ∞) between those outer black pixels in a $(2^i/2) \times (2^i/2)$ subsquare that have a neighboring black pixel in an adjacent $(2^i/2) \times (2^i/2)$ subsquare. Once the distance matrix is initialized, a generalized transitive closure algorithm can be run to determine the necessary distances. Notice that if we define $S_k(i,j)$ to be the minimal internal distance from vertex i to vertex j using no intermediate vertex with label greater than k, then

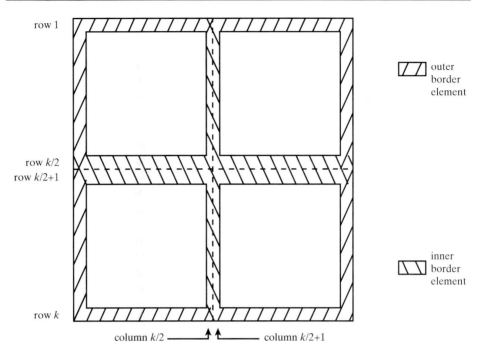

Figure 11-7 An illustration of the possible border elements in a $k \times k$ submesh.

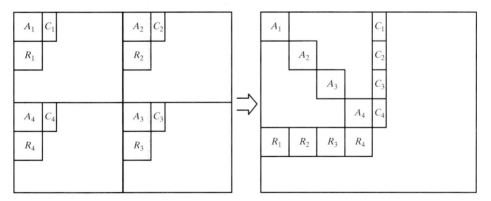

Figure 11-8 A mapping that shows how to rearrange the distance matrices from recursive solutions in an effort to solve the *all-points minimal internal distance problem*.

$S_{k+1}(i,j) = \min\{S_k(i,j), S_k(i,k+1) + S_k(k+1,j)\}$. Notice that the matrices can be moved into their proper location, as shown in Figure 11-8, in $\Theta(2^i)$ time. Further, the necessary edges can be added in $\Theta(2^i)$ time, and the transitive closure and final random access read can also be performed in $\Theta(2^i)$ time. Therefore, the running time of phase 1 is as claimed.

Consider phase 2 of the algorithm. We need to show that, given the final matrices and distances involving the outer border elements of the $(n/2) \times (n/2)$ regions (computed while determining the final correct distances for the outer border elements of the $n \times n$

mesh), we can continue to pass this information on down to recursively smaller and smaller subsquares. This is fairly straightforward since all we are required to do is to run the phase 1 algorithm on each subsquare with the final outer border distance information included. Therefore, this phase can be completed in the time claimed.

HAUSDORFF METRIC FOR DIGITAL IMAGES

Let A and B be nonempty, closed, bounded subsets of a Euclidean space R^k. The *Hausdorff metric*, $H(A,B)$, is used to measure how well the elements of each such pair of sets approximates the other. In general, the Hausdorff metric provides the following properties:

- $H(A,B)$ is small if every point of A is close to some point of B and every point of B is close to some point of A.
- $H(A,B)$ is large if some point of A is far from every point of B, or some point of B is far from every point of A.

Formally, we can define the Hausdorff metric as follows. Let d be the Euclidean metric for R^k. For $x \in R^k$, $\phi \neq Y \subset R^k$, define $d(x, Y) = \min\{d(x,y)|y \in Y\}$. Let $H^*(A, B) = \max\{d(a, B)|a \in A\}$, where $H^*(A, B)$ is said to be the "one-way" or "nonsymmetric" Hausdorff distance. (Please note that $H^*(A, B)$ is not truly a "distance" in the sense of a metric function.) Then the Hausdorff metric (which is indeed a metric function) is defined by $H(A, B) = \max\{H^*(A, B), H^*(B, A)\}$. This definition is equivalent to the statement that $H(A, B) = \varepsilon$ if ε is the minimum of all positive numbers r for which each of A and B is contained in the r-neighborhood of the other, where the r-neighborhood of Y in R^k is the set of all points in R^k that are less than r distant from some point in Y. See Figure 11-9 for an example of $H(A, B)$.

Suppose that A and B are finite sets of points in R^2 or R^3. Further, suppose that these points represent black pixels corresponding to digital images. That is, suppose A and B represent distinct digital images in the same dimensional space. Then in order to determine

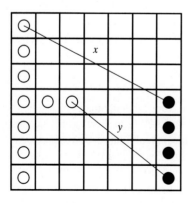

○ A
● B

Figure 11-9 An example of the Hausdorff metric. The distances x and y, respectively, mark a furthest member of A from B and a furthest member of B from A. $H(A,B) = \max\{x, y\}$.

whether or not the probability is high that A and B represent the same physical object, one might consider the result of applying a rigid motion M (translation, rotation, and/or reflection) to B and evaluating the result of $H(A, M(B))$. If for some M, $H(A, M(B))$ is small, then in certain situations, there is a good chance that A and B represent the same physical object; but if no rigid motion translates B close to A in the Hausdorff sense, it is unlikely that A and B represent the same object.

It is interesting to note that two sets in a Euclidean space can occupy approximately the same space and yet have very different geometric features. Although better image recognition might result from a metric that reflects geometric as well as positional similarity, such metrics are often much more difficult to work with, both conceptually and computationally.

A simple, although inefficient, algorithm for computing the Hausdorff metric for two digital images A and B, each contained in an $n \times n$ digital picture, is described below. The algorithm is a straightforward implementation of the definition of the Hausdorff metric as applied to digital images.

1. For every (black) pixel $a \in A$, compute $d(a, B) = \min\{d(a, b) | b \in B\}$. On a RAM, this takes $O(n^4)$ time, since each of A and B has $O(n^2)$ black pixels.
2. Compute $H^*(A, B) = \max \{d(a, B) | a \in A\}$ by a semigroup operation. This takes $\Theta(n^2)$ time on a RAM.
3. Interchange the roles of A and B and repeat steps 1 and 2. Now $H^*(B, A)$ is known.
4. Compute $H(A, B) = \max\{H^*(A, B), H^*(B, A)\}$. This takes $\Theta(1)$ time.

Thus, the algorithm above has running times dominated by its first step and takes $O(n^4)$ time on a RAM. Clearly, the running time of the RAM algorithm leaves much to be desired. Indeed, a simple and more efficient algorithm for computing the Hausdorff metric between two digital images on a RAM can be given using techniques presented in this chapter. We leave this problem as an exercise.

We now consider metrics related to the Hausdorff metric for measuring the difference between two *fuzzy sets*. "Fuzzy set" generalizes the notion of a set; as implemented in a digital picture, a fuzzy set is not necessarily a binary image. A fuzzy set is defined to be a function $f: S \rightarrow [0,1]$ such that the domain, S, is nonempty. S is called the *support set* of f. For $s \in S$, the value $f(s)$ is the "degree of membership" or the "membership value" of s in S. $T \subset S$ is a *crisp set* or an "ordinary set" for the fuzzy set f if $T = f^{-1}(\{1\}) = \{s \in S | f(s) = 1\}$ and $f(S) \subset \{0,1\}$. Thus, as implemented in a digital picture, a crisp set is a digital image (the set of 1 pixels) in a support set S consisting of an $n \times n$ grid of pixels. In a more general fuzzy set (not necessarily a binary digital image), membership values could represent color codes for a colored picture or local physical information for a map, such as land elevation, temperature or other meteorological data, etc.

Let F be a family of fuzzy sets defined on the nonempty support set S such that

■ S is a metric space (this is a technical requirement; for purposes of our discussion, the reader unfamiliar with such notions can assume S is a subset of a Euclidean space, such as a grid of pixels);

- There is a finite set of membership values $T = \{t_1, t_2, \ldots, t_m\} \subset [0,1]$ such that for every $f \in F$, $f(S) \subset T$;
- For every $f \in F$ and $t_k \in T$, the set $f^{-1}([t_k,1]) = \{s \in S | t_k \leq f(s) \leq 1\}$ is bounded and closed in S;
- $1 \in T$;
- For every $f \in F$, there exists $s \in S$ such that $f(s) = 1$.

Then the formula

$$D(f, g) = \frac{\sum_{k=1}^{m} t_k H\{f^{-1}([t_k,1]), g^{-1}([t_k,1])\}}{\sum_{k=1}^{m} t_k} \quad \text{for all } f, g \in F$$

defines a metric. The reader should examine the formula above carefully. At first, it may look quite complex, but it is in fact rather simple and can be computed efficiently. We leave it as an exercise to develop an efficient algorithm to compute this formula.

CHAPTER NOTES

This chapter focuses on fundamental problems in image analysis for the RAM and mesh. These problems serve as a nice vehicle to present interesting paradigms. Many of the mesh algorithms presented in this chapter are derived from algorithms presented by R. Miller & Q.F. Stout in *Parallel Algorithms for Regular Architectures* (The MIT Press, 1996). These algorithms include the component-labeling algorithm, the all-nearest-neighbor-between-labeled-sets algorithm, and the minimum internal distance within connected components algorithm. The book by R. Miller and Q.F. Stout also contains details of some of the data movement operations that were presented and utilized in this chapter, including rotation operations based on ordered intervals and so on. The ingenious algorithm used to compute the transitive closure of an $n \times n$ matrix on a RAM was devised by S. Warshall in his paper "A theorem on Boolean matrices," in the *Journal of the ACM* 9, 1962, 11–12. Further, in 1980, F.L. Van Scoy ("The parallel recognition of classes of graphs," *IEEE Transactions on Computers* 29, 1980, 563–570) showed that the transitive closure of an $n \times n$ matrix could be computed in $\Theta(n)$ time on an $n \times n$ mesh.

For more information about the Hausdorff metric, the reader is referred to *Hyperspaces of Sets*, by S.B. Nadler, Jr. (Marcel Dekker, New York, 1978). The reader interested in additional information on Hausdorff metrics for fuzzy sets is referred to L. Boxer, "On Hausdorff-like metrics for fuzzy sets" in *Pattern Recognition Letters* 18, 1997, 115–118, and related papers including B.B. Chaudhuri and A. Rosenfeld's "On a metric distance between fuzzy sets" in *Pattern Recognition Letters* 17, 1996, 1157–1160; M.L. Puri and D.A. Ralescu's *"Differentielle d'un fonction floue"* in *Comptes Rendes Acad. Sci. Paris, Serie I* 293, 1981, 237–239; and A. Rosenfeld's "'Continuous' functions on digital pictures" in *Pattern Recognition Letters* 4, 1986, 177–184.

EXERCISES

1. Given an $n \times n$ digitized image, give an efficient algorithm to determine both i) the number of black pixels in the image, and ii) the number of white pixels in the image. Present an algorithm and analysis for both the RAM and mesh.

2. Let A be the adjacency matrix of a graph G with n vertices. For integer $k > 0$, let A^k be the k-th power of A, as discussed in the chapter.

   a. Prove that for $i \neq j$, $A^k[i,j] = 1$ if and only if there is a path in G from vertex i to vertex j that has at most k edges, for $1 \leq k \leq n$.

   b. Prove that $A^{n+c} = A^n$ for any positive integer c.

3. Given an $n \times n$ digitized image in which each pixel is associated with a numerical value, provide an efficient algorithm that will set to zero (0) all of the pixel values that are below the median pixel value of the image. Present analysis for both the RAM and mesh.

4. Given an $n \times n$ digitized image, provide an efficient algorithm that will set each pixel to the average of itself and its eight (8) nearest neighbors. Present analysis for both the RAM and mesh.

5. Given a labeled $n \times n$ digitized image, give an efficient algorithm to count the number of connected components in the image. Present analysis for both the RAM and mesh.

6. Given a labeled $n \times n$ digitized image and a single "marked" pixel somewhere in the image, give an efficient algorithm that will mark all other pixels in the same connected component as the "marked" pixel. Present analysis for both the RAM and mesh.

7. Given a labeled $n \times n$ digitized image, give an efficient algorithm to determine the number of pixels in every connected component. Present analysis for both the RAM and mesh.

8. Given a labeled $n \times n$ digitized image and one "marked" pixel per component, give an efficient algorithm for every pixel to determine its Euclidean distance to its marked pixel. Present analysis for both the RAM and mesh.

9. Given a labeled $n \times n$ digitized image, give an efficient algorithm to determine a minimum-enclosing box of every connected component. Present analysis for both the RAM and mesh.

10. Give an efficient algorithm for computing $H(A, B)$, the Hausdorff metric between A and B, where each of A and B is an $n \times n$ digital image. Hint: the algorithm presented in the text may be improved upon by using row and column rotations similar to those that appeared in our algorithm for the all-nearest-neighbor-between-labeled-sets problem, modified to allow that a pixel could belong to both A and B. Show that your algorithm can be implemented in worst case times of $\Theta(n^2)$ for the RAM and $\Theta(n)$ for the mesh.

11. Let F be a family of fuzzy sets with support set S consisting of an $n \times n$ grid of pixels. Present an algorithm and analysis for the RAM and mesh to compute the distance formula $D(f, g)$ described above for members of F. Your algorithm should run in $O(mn^2)$ time on a RAM and in $O(mn)$ time on the mesh. Assume $m = O(n^2)$.

12. Suppose A and B are sets of black pixels for distinct $n \times n$ digital pictures. Let $f: A \to B$ be a function, *i.e.*, for every (black) pixel $a \in A$, $f(a)$ is a (black) pixel in B. Using the 4-adjacency notion of neighboring pixels, we say f is (*digitally*) *continuous* if for every pair of neighboring black pixels $a_0, a_1 \in A$, either $f(a_0) = f(a_1)$ or $f(a_0)$ and $f(a_1)$ are neighbors in B. Prove that the following are equivalent:

- $f: A \to B$ is a digitally continuous function.

- For every connected subset A_0 of A, the image $f(A_0)$ is a connected subset of B.

- Using the Euclidean metric (in which 4-connected neighboring pixels are at distance one apart and non-neighboring pixels are at distance greater than one), for every $\varepsilon \geq 1$, there is a $\delta \geq 1$ such that if $a_0, a_1 \in A$ and $d(a_0, a_1) \leq \delta$, then $d[f(a_0), f(a_1)] \leq \varepsilon$.

13. Refer to the previous exercise. Let A and B be sets of black pixels within respective $n \times n$ digital pictures. Let $f: A \to B$ be a function. Suppose the value of $f(a)$ can be computed in $\Theta(1)$ time for every $a \in A$. Present an algorithm to determine whether or not the function f is digitally continuous (and, in the case of the mesh, let every processor know the result of this determination), and give your analysis for the RAM and mesh. Your algorithm should take $\Theta(n^2)$ time on a RAM and $\Theta(n)$ time on an $n \times n$ mesh.

14. *Conway's Game of Life* can be regarded as a population simulation that is implemented on an $n \times n$ digitized picture A. The focus of the "game" is the transition between a "parent generation" and a "child generation"; the child generation becomes the parent generation for the next transition. In one version of the game, the transition proceeds as follows:

- If in the parent generation $A[i, j]$ is a black pixel and exactly two or three of its nearest 8-neighbors are black, then in the child generation $A[i, j]$ is a black pixel (life is propagated under "favorable" living conditions). However, if $A[i, j]$ in the parent generation is a black pixel with less than two black 8-neighbors ("loneliness") or more than three black 8-neighbors ("overcrowding"), then in the child generation $A[i, j]$ is a white pixel.

■ If in the parent generation $A[i,j]$ is a white pixel, then in the child generation $A[i,j]$ is a black pixel if and only if exactly three of its nearest 8-neighbors are black.

Present and analyze an algorithm to compute the child generation matrix A from the parent generation matrix for one transition for the RAM and the mesh. Your algorithm should run in $\Theta(n^2)$ time on the RAM and in $\Theta(1)$ time on the mesh.

12

Graph Algorithms

Graph Algorithms

In this chapter, we focus on algorithms and paradigms to solve fundamental problems including graphs. We will present efficient solutions to problems such as determining the connected components of a graph, constructing a minimal-cost spanning tree of a connected graph, and determining shortest paths between vertices in a graph. The algorithms will be presented for the sequential model (RAM), the PRAM, and the mesh. In this way, we will be able to present a variety of techniques and paradigms. Some of the material presented in this chapter will rely on algorithms presented earlier in the book. As appropriate, we will review some of this material.

Many important real-world problems can be expressed in terms of graphs, including problems involving telephone connections, power grids, the scheduling or routing of airplanes, and so on. Graphs are often used in the following ways.

- To represent a set of locations with distances or costs between the locations. This can arise in transportation systems (airline, bus, or train systems) where the costs can be distance, time, or money.
- To represent the connectivity in networks of objects. Such networks can be internal to devices (VLSI design of computer chips) or among higher-level devices (telephone or computer networks).
- To represent problems concerned with network flow capacity, which is important in the water, gas, and electric industries, to name a few.
- To represent an ordered list of tasks, such as the tasks that must be completed in order to construct a building or to solve a problem on a computer.

One of the first uses of graphs dates back to 1736, when Leonhard Euler considered the town of Königsberg, in which the Pregel River flows around the island of Kneiphof, as shown in Figure 12-1. Notice that the Pregel River borders on four land regions in this area, which are connected by seven bridges, as shown in Figure 12-2. Euler considered the problem of whether or not it is possible to start on one of the four land areas, cross every bridge exactly once, and return to the original land area. In fact, for this situation, which is represented in the graph in Figure 12-3, Euler was able to prove that such a tour was not possible. The generalization of this problem has become known as the *Euler tour*. That is, an Euler tour of a connected, directed graph is a cycle (the path starts

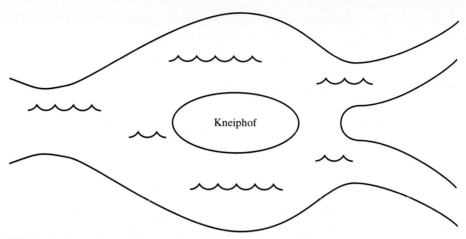

Figure 12-1 In 1736, Leonhard Euler graphed the town of Königsberg where the Pregel River flows around the island of Kneiphof.

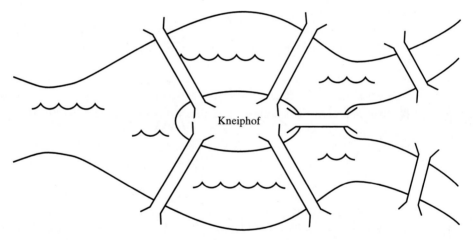

Figure 12-2 The seven bridges in the area of Kneiphof and the Pregel River that Euler considered in terms of navigating the town of Königsberg.

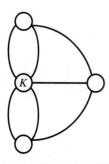

Figure 12-3 A graph with four vertices and seven edges representing Königsberg. Euler considered this graph in terms of whether or not it was possible to start on one of the four land masses (vertices), cross every bridge exactly once, and return to the original land area. The generalization of this problem is now known as the *Euler tour problem*.

and ends at the same vertex) that traverses each edge of the graph exactly once, although it may visit a vertex more than once.

TERMINOLOGY

Let $G = (V, E)$ be a graph consisting of a set V of vertices and a set E of edges. The edges, which connect members of V, can either be directed or undirected, resulting in either a *directed graph (digraph)* or an *undirected graph*, respectively. That is, given a directed graph $G = (V, E)$, an edge $(a, b) \in E$ represents a directed connection from vertex a to vertex b, where both $a, b \in V$. Given an undirected graph, an edge $(a, b) \in E$ represents an undirected connection between a and b. Typically, we do not permit *i) self-edges*, in which an edge connects a vertex to itself, nor *ii)* multiple occurrences of an edge (resulting in a *multigraph*). See Figure 12-4 for examples of directed and undirected graphs.

The number of vertices in $G = (V, E)$ is written as $|V|$ and the number of edges is written as $|E|$. However, for convenience, whenever the number of vertices or number of edges

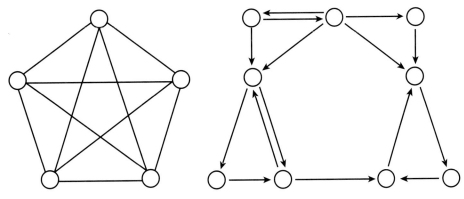

(a) A complete graph with five vertices.   (b) For some pairs of vertices (u,v), a path from u to v does not exist.

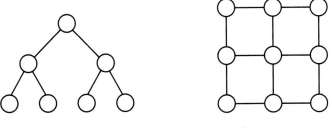

(c) An undirected tree with seven vertices.   (d) A mesh.

Figure 12-4   Four sample graphs. Notice that graphs (a), (c), and (d) are undirected graphs, while graph (b) is a directed graph.

is represented inside of asymptotic notation, we will typically avoid the absolute value signs since there is no ambiguity. For example, an algorithm that runs in time linear in the sum of the vertices and edges will be said to run in $\Theta(V + E)$ time.

In any description of a graph, we assume that there is a unique representation of the vertices and edges. That is, no vertex will have more than one identity and no edge will be represented more than once. Given a directed graph, the maximum number of edges is $|V|(|V| - 1)$, while for an undirected graph, the maximum number of unique edges is $|V|(|V| - 1)/2$. Therefore, the number of edges in a graph $G = (V, E)$ is such that $|E| = O(V^2)$. A *complete graph* $G = (V, E)$ is one in which all possible edges are present. A *sparse graph* is one in which there are not very many edges, while a *dense graph* is one in which a high percentage of the possible edges are present. Alternately, a graph is typically termed *sparse* if $|E|/|V|^2$ is very small, while a graph is typically referred to as *dense* if $|E|/|V|^2$ is moderate-sized.

Vertex b is said to be *adjacent* to vertex a if and only if $(a, b) \in E$. At times, adjacent vertices will be described as *neighbors*. An edge $(a, b) \in E$ is said to be *incident* on vertices a and b. In a *weighted graph*, every edge $(a, b) \in E$ will have an associated weight or cost (see Figure 12-5).

A *path* in a graph $G = (V, E)$ is a sequence of vertices $v_1, v_2, \ldots, v_k$ such that $(v_i, v_{i+1}) \in E$ for all $1 \le i \le k - 1$. The *length* of such a path is defined to be the number of edges on the path, which in this case is $k - 1$. A *simple path* is defined to be a path in which all vertices are unique. A *cycle* is a path of length 3 or more in which $v_1 = v_k$. A graph is called *acyclic* if it has no cycles. A *directed acyclic graph* is often referred to as a *dag*.

An undirected graph is called *connected* if and only if there is at least one path from every vertex to every other vertex. Given a graph $G = (V, E)$, a subgraph S of G is such that $S = (V', E')$, where V' is a subset of V and E' is a subset of those edges in E that contain vertices only in V'. The *connected components* of an undirected graph $G = (V, E)$ correspond to the maximally connected subgraphs of G (see Figure 12-6).

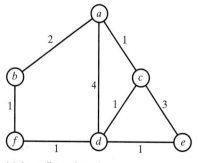

(a) An undirected graph.

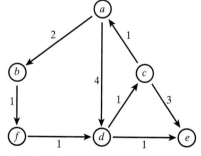

(a) A directed graph.

Figure 12-5   Notice in (a) that there are eight pairs of neighboring (adjacent) vertices. Also notice in (a) that the entire graph is connected since there is a path between every pair of vertices. In graph (b), however, paths are not formed between every pair of vertices. In fact, notice that vertex e is isolated in that e does not serve as the source of any nontrivial path. Notice in (a) that a minimum-weight path from a to e is $\langle a, c, d, e \rangle$, which has a total weight of 3, while in (b) a minimum-weight path from a to e is either $\langle a, d, e \rangle$, or $\langle a, b, f, d, e \rangle$.

A directed graph is called *strongly connected* if and only if there is at least one path from every vertex to every other vertex. If a directed graph is not strongly connected but the underlying graph in which all directed edges are replaced by undirected edges is connected, then the original directed graph is called *weakly connected* (see Figure 12-7). As

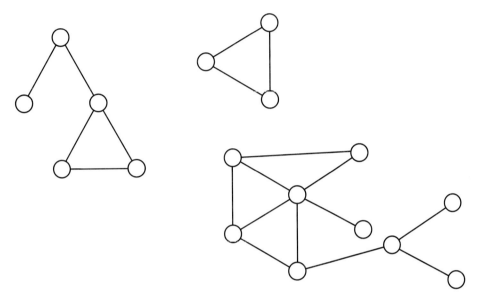

Figure 12-6   An undirected graph with three connected components.

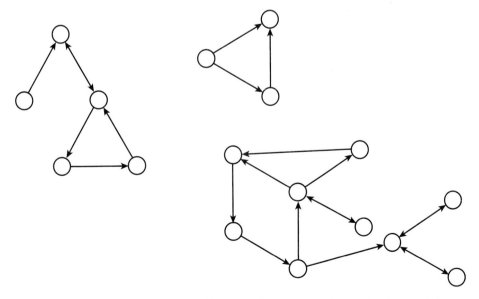

Figure 12-7   A directed graph with three weakly connected components and seven strongly connected components.

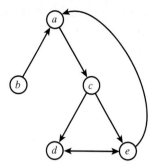

Figure 12-8 A directed graph. The in-degree of $\langle a, b, c, d, e\rangle$, is $\langle 2, 0, 1, 2, 2\rangle$, respectively, and the out-degree of $\langle a, b, c, d, e\rangle$ is $\langle 1, 1, 2, 1, 2\rangle$, respectively.

a point of information, note that a *tree* in which all edges point away from the root is a directed acyclic graph.

Given an undirected graph, the *degree of a vertex* is the number of edges incident on the vertex, and the *degree of the graph* is the maximum degree of any vertex in the graph. Given a directed graph, the *in-degree* of a vertex is the number of edges that point to it and the *out-degree* of a vertex is the number of edges that point away from it (see Figure 12-8).

Frequently, it makes sense to assign weights to the edges or vertices in a graph. A graph $G = (V, E)$ is called an *edge-weighted graph* if there is a weight $W(v_i, v_j)$ associated with every edge $(v_i, v_j) \in E$. In the case of edge-weighted graphs, the *distance* (or *shortest path*) between vertices v_i and v_j is defined as the sum over the edge weights in a v_i-to-v_j path of minimum total weight. The *diameter* of such a graph is defined to be the maximum of the distances between all pairs of vertices. Notice that for many applications, it makes sense to consider all edges in an (otherwise) unweighted graph as having a weight of 1.

REPRESENTATIONS

There are several ways to represent a graph. In this book, we will consider three of the most common: namely, an adjacency list, an adjacency matrix, and a set of arbitrarily distributed edges. It is important to note that in some cases, the user may have a choice of representations and can therefore choose a representation for which the computational resources are optimized. In other situations, the user may be given the graph in a particular form and may need to design and implement efficient algorithms to solve problems on the structure.

Adjacency Lists

The *adjacency-list representation* of a graph $G = (V, E)$ typically consists of $|V|$ linked lists, one corresponding to each vertex $v_i \in V$. For each such vertex v_i, its linked list contains an entry corresponding to each edge $(v_i, v_j) \in E$. In order to navigate efficiently through a graph, the headers of the $|V|$ linked lists are typically stored in an array or linked list, which we call *Adj*, as shown in Figure 12-9. In this chapter, unless otherwise specified, we will assume an array implementation of *Adj* so that we can refer to the adjacency list associated with vertex $v_i \in V$ as $Adj(v_i)$. It is important to note that the vertices stored in each adjacency list, which represent the edges in the graph, are typically stored in arbitrary order.

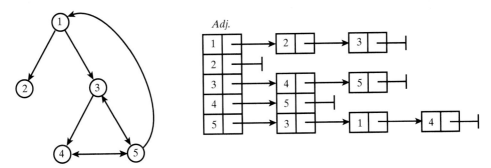

Figure 12-9 A directed graph and its adjacency list representation.

	1	2	3	4	5
1	0	1	1	0	0
2	0	0	0	0	0
3	0	0	0	1	1
4	0	0	0	0	1
5	1	0	1	1	0

Figure 12-10 An adjacency matrix representation of the graph presented in Figure 12-9.

If the graph $G = (V, E)$ is a directed graph, then the total number of entries in all adjacency lists is $|E|$, since every edge $(v_i, v_j) \in E$ is represented in $Adj(v_i)$. However, if the graph $G = (V, E)$ is an undirected graph, then the total number of entries in all adjacency lists is $2|E|$, since every edge $(v_i, v_j) \in E$ is represented in both $Adj(v_i)$ and $Adj(v_j)$. Notice that regardless of the type of graph, an adjacency-list representation has the feature that the space required to store the graph is $\Theta(V + E)$. Assuming that one must store some information about every vertex and about every edge in the graph, this is an optimal representation.

Suppose the graph $G = (V, E)$ is weighted. Then the elements in the individual adjacency lists can be modified to store the weight of each edge or vertex, as appropriate. For example, given an edge-weighted graph, an entry in $Adj(v_i)$ corresponding to edge $(v_i, v_j) \in E$ can store the identity of v_j, a pointer to $Adj(v_j)$, the weight $W(v_i, v_j)$, other miscellaneous fields required for necessary operations, and a pointer to the next record in the list.

While the adjacency list representation is robust, in that it can be modified to support a wide variety of graphs and is efficient in storage, it does have the drawback of not being able to identify quickly whether or not a given edge (v_i, v_j) is present. In the next section, we consider a representation that will overcome this deficiency.

Adjacency Matrix

An adjacency matrix is presented in Figure 12-10 that corresponds to the adjacency list presented in Figure 12-9. Given a graph $G = (V, E)$, the adjacency matrix A is a $|V| \times |V|$ matrix in which entry $A(i, j) = 1$ if $(v_i, v_j) \in E$ and $A(i, j) = 0$ otherwise. Thus, row i of the adjacency matrix contains all information in $Adj(v_i)$ of the corresponding adjacency list. Notice that the matrix contains a single bit at each of the $\Theta(V^2)$ positions. Further, if the graph is undirected, there is no need to store all of the entries $A(i, j)$ for which either $i > j$ or $i < j$, since $A(i, j) = A(j, i)$. That is, given an undirected graph, one only needs to maintain either the upper triangular or lower triangular portion of the adjacency matrix. Given an edge-weight graph, each entry $A(i, j)$ will be set to the weight of edge (v_i, v_j) if the edge exists and will be set to 0 otherwise. Given either a weighted or unweighted graph that is either directed or undirected, the total space required by an adjacency matrix is $\Theta(V^2)$.

The adjacency matrix has the advantage of providing direct access to information concerning the existence or absence of an edge. Given a dense graph, the adjacency matrix also has the advantage that it requires only one bit per entry, as opposed to the additional pointers required by the adjacency list representation. However, for relatively small (typically sparse) graphs, the adjacency list has the advantage of requiring less space and providing a relatively simplistic manner in which to traverse a graph. For an algorithm that requires the examination of all vertices and all edges, an adjacency list implementation can provide a sequential algorithm with running time $\Theta(V + E)$, while an adjacency matrix representation would result in a sequential running time of $\Theta(V^2)$. Thus, the algorithm based on the adjacency list might be significantly more efficient.

Unordered Edges

A third form of input that we discuss in this book is that of unordered edges, which provides the least amount of information and structure. Given a graph $G = (V, E)$, *unordered edge* input is such that the $\Theta(E)$ edges are distributed in an arbitrary fashion throughout the memory of the machine. On a sequential computer, one will typically restructure this information in order to create adjacency-list or adjacency-matrix input. However, on parallel machines, it is not always economical or feasible to perform such a conversion.

FUNDAMENTAL ALGORITHMS

In this section, we consider fundamental algorithms for traversing and manipulating graphs. It is often useful to be able to visit the vertices of a graph in some well-defined order based on the graph's topology. We first consider sequential approaches to this concept of *graph traversal*. The two major techniques we consider, breadth-first search and depth-first search, both have the property that they begin with a specified vertex and then visit all other vertices in a deterministic fashion. In the presentation of both of these algorithms, the reader will notice that we keep track of the vertices as they are visited. Following the presentations of fundamental sequential traversal methods, several fundamental techniques will be presented for the PRAM and mesh. In particular, for the PRAM we discuss list ranking via pointer jumping, Euler tour techniques, and tree contraction, while for both the PRAM and mesh we discuss algorithms for obtaining the transitive closure of a Boolean matrix.

Breadth-First Search

The first algorithm we consider for traversing a graph on a RAM is called *breadth-first search*, which is sometimes referred to as *BFS*. The general flow of a BFS traversal is first to visit a predetermined "root" vertex r, then visit all vertices at distance 1 from r, then visit all vertices at distance 2 from r, and so forth. This is a standard sequential technique for traversing a graph $G = (V, E)$. Algorithmically, the search procedure follows:

- Start at a *root* vertex $r \in V$,
- add neighboring vertices to a queue as they are encountered, and
- process the queue in a standard FIFO (first-in, first-out) order.

So, initially all vertices $v \in V$ are marked as *unvisited*, and the queue is initialized to contain only a root vertex $r \in V$. The algorithm then proceeds by removing the root from the queue (the queue is now empty), determining all neighbors of the root, and placing each of these neighbors into the queue. In general, each iteration of the algorithm consists of

- removing the next vertex $v \in V$ from the queue,
- examining all neighbors of v in G to determine those that have not yet been marked (those that have not yet been visited in the breadth-first search),
- marking each of these previously unvisited neighbors as visited, and
- inserting these previously unvisited neighbors of v into the queue (specifically, inserting them at the end of the queue).

This process of removing an element from the queue and inserting its unvisited neighbors into the queue continues until the queue is empty. Once the queue is empty at the conclusion of a remove-explore-insert step, all vertices reachable from the root vertex $r \in V$ (*i.e.*, all vertices in the same component of G as r) have been visited. Further, if the vertices are output as they are removed from the queue, the resulting list corresponds to a breadth-first search tree over the graph $G = (V, E)$ with root $r \in V$ (see Figure 12-11).

We now present an algorithm that will implement a sequential breadth-first search of a graph and record the distance from the root to every reachable vertex (see Figure 12-12). The reader should note that our algorithm is presented as a graph traversal, that is, a procedure that visits every vertex of the root's component. This procedure is easily modified to solve the query problem by returning to the calling routine with the appropriate information when a vertex is reached that is associated with the requested key.

```
        BFSroutine(G, r)
        CreateEmptyQueue(Q)                   {Initialize the queue.}
        For all vertices v ∈ V, do
            visited(v) ← false                {Initialize every vertex to "unvisited".}
            dist(v) ← ∞                        {Initialize all distances.}
            parent(v) ← nil                   {Initialize parents of all vertices.}
        End For
{*}     visited(r) ← true                     {Initialize information about the root
        dist(r) ← 0                            vertex—it is visited, it has distance
        PlaceInQueue(Q, r)                     0 from itself, and it goes into the queue.}
        While NotEmptyQueue(Q), do
            v ← RemoveFromQueue(Q)            {Take first element from queue: v.}
            For all vertices w ∈ Adj(v), do   {Examine all neighbors of v.}
                If visited(w) = false then    {Process those neighbors not previously visited.}
```

$visited(w) \leftarrow true$ {Mark neighbor as visited.}
$parent(w) \leftarrow v$ {The BFS parent of w is v.}
$dist(w) \leftarrow dist(v) + 1$ {The distance from w to r is one more than
                                         the distance from its parent (v) to r.}

   PlaceInQueue (Q, w) {Place w at the end of the queue.}
      End If
   End For
End While

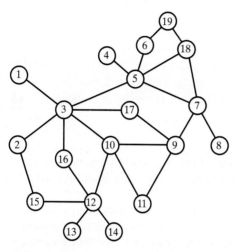

(a) A given graph G.

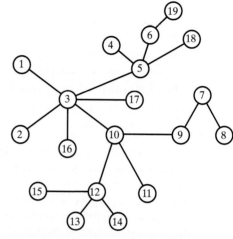

(b) This tree is associated with a traversal $\langle 10, 3, 12, 11, 9, 5, 17, 16, 2, 1, 15, 13, 14, 7, 4, 6, 18, 8, 19 \rangle$ of G, though other traversals of G would also yield this tree.

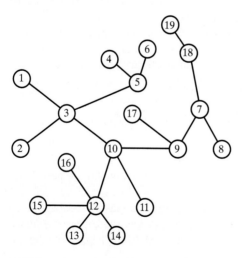

(c) This tree is associated with a traversal $\langle 10, 9, 12, 11, 3, 17, 7, 13, 14, 15, 16, 2, 1, 5, 18, 8, 6, 4, 19 \rangle$ of G, though other traversals of G would also yield this tree.

Figure 12-11   An example of a breadth-first search traversal. Depending on the order in which the vertices given graph (a) are stored in the associated data structure, a BFS initiated at vertex 10 could yield a variety of breadth-first search trees, including those given in (b) and (c).

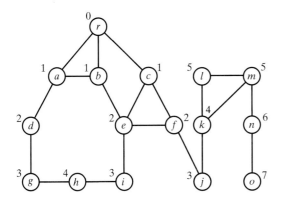

Figure 12-12   An undirected connected graph with distances from the root vertex *r* recorded next to the vertices. One possible traversal of the vertices in this graph by a breadth-first search is ⟨*r, c, b, a, e, f, d, i, j, g, h, k, l, m, n, o*⟩.

Notice that the steps in which we compute the parent of a vertex *v* and the distance of *v* from the root are not necessary to the graph traversal. We have included these steps as they are useful to other problems we discuss below.

Given a connected undirected graph $G = (V, E)$, a call to BFSroutine(G, r) for any $r \in V$ will visit every vertex and every edge. In fact, a careful examination shows that every edge will be visited exactly twice and that every vertex will be considered at least once. Therefore, assuming that inserting and removing items from a queue are performed in $\Theta(1)$ time, the sequential running time for this BFSroutine on a connected undirected graph is $\Theta(V + E)$.

Now suppose that the undirected graph $G = (V, E)$ is not necessarily connected, but that you want to use a variant of BFSroutine in order to visit all vertices of *G*. A simple extension can be made to BFSroutine. See Figure 12-13 while considering the algorithm below.

```
BFS-all-undirected (G = (V, E))
CreateEmptyQueue(Q)                  {Initialize the queue.}
For all vertices v ∈ V, do
       visited(v) ← false           {Initialize every vertex to "unvisited."}
       dist(v) ← ∞                  {Initialize all distances.}
       parent(v) ← nil              {Initialize parents of all vertices.}
End For
For all v ∈ V, do                   {Consider all vertices in the graph.}
     If not visited (v), then
       BFSroutine (G, v) at line {*} {Perform a BFS starting at every vertex that
                                      has not been previously visited—call
                                      BFSroutine, but jump immediately to line {*}.}
End For
```

Notice that given an undirected graph $G = (V, E)$, the procedure BFS-all-undirected will visit all vertices and traverse all edges in the graph in $\Theta(V + E)$ time on a sequential machine.

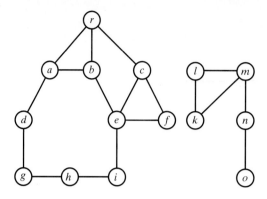

Figure 12-13   An undirected graph that is not connected. The two connected components can be labeled in time linear in the number of vertices plus the number of edges by a simple extrapolation of the breadth-first search algorithm.

Depth-First Search

The second algorithm we consider for traversing a graph is called *depth-first search*, which is sometimes referred to as *DFS*. The philosophy of DFS is to start at a predetermined "root" vertex r and *recursively* visit a previously unvisited neighbor v of r, one by one, until all neighbors of r are marked as visited. This is a standard sequential technique for traversing a graph $G = (V, E)$. Algorithmically, the search procedure follows:

1. Start at a root vertex $r \in V$,
2. consider a previously unvisited neighbor v of r,
3. recursively visit v, and then
4. continue with another previously unvisited neighbor of r.

The algorithm is recursive in nature. Given a graph $G = (V, E)$, choose an initial vertex $r \in V$, which we again call the root, and mark r as visited. Next, find a previously unvisited neighbor of r, say, v. Recursively perform a depth-first search on v and then return to consider any other neighbors of r that have not been visited (see Figure 12-14). A simple recursive presentation of this algorithm is given below.

```
{Assume that visited ← false for all v ∈ V prior to this routine being called.}
DFSroutine (G, r)
visited(r) ← true              {Mark r as being visited.}
For all vertices v ∈ Adj(r), do   {Consider all neighbors of r in turn.}
    If not visited(v), do          {If a given neighbor has not been visited,
        parent(v) ← r                  then mark its parent as being r and
        DFSroutine (G, v)              recursively visit this neighbor.}
        visited(v) ← true
    End If
End For
```

As in a breadth-first search graph traversal, the step in which we compute a vertex's parent is not necessary to a depth-first search graph traversal, but it is included for its usefulness

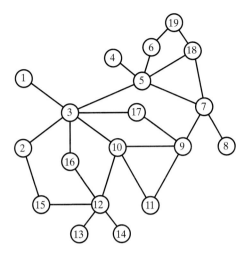

(a) A given graph G.

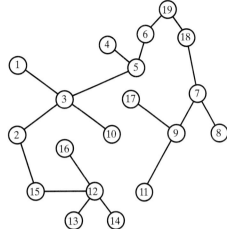

(b) This tree is associated with a traversal ⟨10, 3, 1, 2, 15, 12, 13, 14, 16, 5, 4, 6, 19, 18, 7, 8, 9, 11, 17⟩ of G, though other traversals of G would also yield this tree.

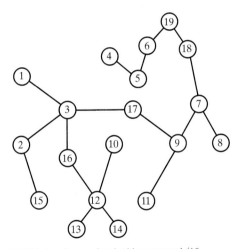

(c) This tree is associated with a traversal ⟨10, 12, 16, 3, 17, 9, 11, 7, 18, 19, 6, 5, 4, 8, 1, 2, 15, 14, 13⟩ of G, though other traversals of G would also yield this tree.

Figure 12-14   An example of a depth-first search traversal. (Notice that the graph given in (a) is identical to the graph utilized in Figure 12-11.)

in a number of related problems. Also, as with a breadth-first search, we have presented depth-first search as a graph traversal algorithm that can be modified by the insertion of a conditional exit instruction if a traditional search is desired that stops upon realizing success.

Depth-first search is an example of a standard "backtracking" algorithm. That is, when considering a given vertex *v*, the algorithm considers all of *v*'s "descendants" before backtracking to the parent of v in order to allow its parent to continue with the traversal. Now consider the analysis of DFSroutine on a sequential platform. Notice that every vertex is initialized to unvisited and that every vertex is visited exactly once during the search. Also notice that every directed edge in a graph is considered exactly once. (Every undirected edge would be considered twice, once from the point of view of each incident vertex.) Therefore, the running time of DFSroutine on a graph $G(V, E)$ is $\Theta(V + E)$, which is the same as the running time of BFSroutine.

Discussion of Depth-First and Breadth-First Search

A *depth-first search tree* $T = (V, E')$ of a graph $G = (V, E)$ is formed during a depth-first search of the graph G, as follows. An edge $(u, v) \in E$ is a member of E' if and only if one of its vertices is the parent of the other vertex. Given a depth-first search tree $T = (V, E')$ of G, it should be noted that if an edge $(u, v) \in E$ is not in E', then either

- u is a descendant of v in T and v is not the parent of u, or
- v is a descendant of u in T and u is not the parent of v

See Figure 12-15.

Each vertex v in a depth-first search tree of G can be given a time stamp corresponding to when the vertex was first encountered and another time stamp corresponding to when the search finished examining all of v's neighbors. These time stamps can be used in higher-level graph algorithms to solve interesting and important problems. Problems typically solved through a depth-first search include labeling the strongly connected components of a directed graph, performing a topological sort of a directed graph, determining articulation points and biconnected components, and labeling connected components of undirected graphs, to name a few.

A *breadth-first search tree* is similarly formed from the edges joining parent and child vertices in a BFS of a graph $G = (V, E)$. Given a breadth-first search tree $T = (V, E')$ of G, it should be noted that if an edge $(u, v) \in E$ is not in E', then u is not a descendant of v in T and v is not a descendant of u in T (see Figure 12-16).

The vertices in a breadth-first search tree $T = (V, E')$ of $G = (V, E)$ are at minimum distance from the root $r \in V$ of the tree. That is, the distance of $u \in V$ in T from r is the length

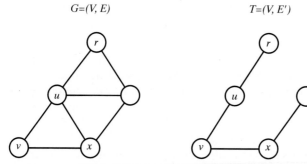

$G = (V, E)$ \qquad $T = (V, E')$

Figure 12-15 A depth-first search tree $T = (V, E')$ of a graph $G = (V, E)$. An edge $(u, v) \in E$ is a member of E' if and only if one of its vertices is the parent of the other vertex. Edge $(u, x) \in E$ is not in E', corresponding to the fact that one of its vertices is an ancestor but not the parent of the other.

$G = (V, E)$ $T = (V, E')$

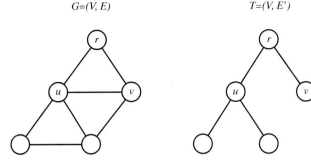

Figure 12-16 A breadth-first search tree $T = (V, E')$ of $G = (V, E)$. If an edge $(u, v) \in E$ is not in E', then u is not a descendant of v in T and v is not a descendant of u in T.

of the shortest path in G from u to r. This is a useful property when we consider certain minimal path-length problems, including the *single-source shortest-path problem*. Such searches, however, are not useful when one is considering weighted paths (as when solving the minimal-weight spanning tree problem). A breadth-first search of a graph can be used to solve a number of problems, including determining whether or not a graph is bipartite.

Fundamental PRAM Graph Techniques

In this section, we will present some techniques amenable to managing pointer-based graph structures on a PRAM. The working assumption in this section is that the data structure is arbitrarily distributed throughout the shared memory of the PRAM. We briefly review the pointer jumping technique, which was introduced in Chapter 8. We will then present the Euler tour technique, discuss the consequences of list ranking and Euler tour, and then present a critical tree-based contraction technique.

List Ranking via Pointer Jumping: Assume that we have a linked list L stored in the shared memory of a PRAM. Let $L(i)$ represent the contents of the i-th item and $next(i)$ be a pointer to $L(i + 1)$. We assume that the last element in the list has $next(i) = nil$. The *list ranking problems* requires that every element i in the list determine its distance, $dist(i)$, to the end of the list. The following algorithm solves the list ranking problem via pointer jumping, where it is assumed that each of the n processors knows the location in memory of a unique list element.

```
Forall L(i), do                          {Assume there are n elements.}
    If next(i) = nil, then dist(i) ← 0   {Initialize all distance values.}
    If next(i) ≠ nil, then dist(i) ← 1
    orig_next(i) ← next(i)               {Store original next pointers.}
End Forall
For ⌈log₂ n⌉ iterations, do              {Prepare to pointer-jump until done.}
    Forall L(i), do
        If next(i) ≠ nil, then           {For elements with successors,
            dist(i) ← dist(i) +             perform the pointer jumping
            dist(next(i))                   step of the algorithm.}
```

{*} $next(i) \leftarrow next(next(i))$
                    End If
                End Forall
            End For-do
            Forall $L(i)$, do
                    $next(i) \leftarrow orig\_next(i)$ {Restore original pointer values.}
            End Forall

The operation used in Step {*} of this algorithm (replacing a pointer by the pointer's pointer) is called the *pointer jumping step* of the algorithm. When the algorithm terminates, $dist(i)$ is the rank of the i-th item in the list, for all i. A proof is straightforward, and we have previously discussed the analysis of this algorithm, which has a running time of $\Theta(\log n)$. The cost of an algorithm that runs in $\Theta(\log n)$ time with $\Theta(n)$ processors is $\Theta(n \log n)$, which is suboptimal for this problem since we know that a linear-time sequential traversal can be used to solve the problem in $\Theta(n)$ time on a RAM. We note that it is possible to construct an EREW PRAM algorithm to solve the list ranking problem in $\Theta(\log n)$ time using only $\Theta(n/\log n)$ processors. While the algorithm is beyond the scope of this book, an outline of the algorithm follows:

1. Reduce the size of the linked list L from n nodes to $O(n/\log n)$ nodes. Call the new list R.

2. Apply the previous pointer-jumping algorithm to R in order to compute the rank of all nodes in R. Transfer the ranks of all nodes in R to their corresponding nodes in the original list L.

3. Rank all nodes in L that do not have a rank (that were not members of R).

Euler Tour Technique: Given a tree $T = (V, E)$ represented by an undirected graph, we let $T' = (V, E')$ be a directed graph obtained from T in which every undirected edge $(u, v) \in E$ is replaced by two directed edges, $(u, v), (v, u) \in E'$. An *Euler circuit* of T' is a cycle of T' that traverses every directed edge exactly once. An Euler circuit of $T' = (V, E')$ can be defined by specifying a successor function $next(e)$ for every edge $e \in E'$, so that a circuit is defined using all edges in E'. This can be accomplished as follows. Suppose that for a given vertex $v \in V$, the set of neighbors D of v is enumerated as $\langle v_0, v_1, \ldots, v_{d-1} \rangle$. Then we define $next((v_i, v)) = (v, v_{(i+1) \bmod d})$. Notice that we do not generally traverse all edges incident on a given vertex consecutively; an edge (u, v) is followed by the edge determined by the $next$ function as determined by $adj(v)$, not $adj(u)$ (see Figure 12-17). It follows that on a RAM, an Euler circuit of T can be listed in $\Theta(E)$ time. Straightforward applications of list ranking and Euler tour include the following:

1. A tree T can be rooted. That is, all vertices v can determine $parent(v)$.
2. The vertices can be assigned labels corresponding to the postorder number of the vertex.
3. The level of every vertex can be determined.
4. The preorder number of every vertex can be determined.
5. The number of descendants of every vertex can be determined.

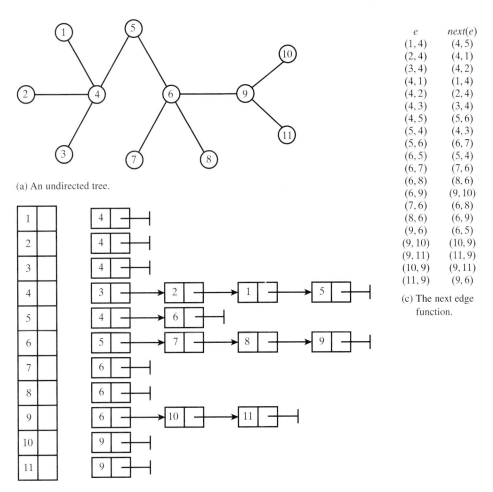

(a) An undirected tree.

(b) An adjacency representation.

e	next(e)
(1, 4)	(4, 5)
(2, 4)	(4, 1)
(3, 4)	(4, 2)
(4, 1)	(1, 4)
(4, 2)	(2, 4)
(4, 3)	(3, 4)
(4, 5)	(5, 6)
(5, 4)	(4, 3)
(5, 6)	(6, 7)
(6, 5)	(5, 4)
(6, 7)	(7, 6)
(6, 8)	(8, 6)
(6, 9)	(9, 10)
(7, 6)	(6, 8)
(8, 6)	(6, 9)
(9, 6)	(6, 5)
(9, 10)	(10, 9)
(9, 11)	(11, 9)
(10, 9)	(9, 11)
(11, 9)	(9, 6)

(c) The next edge function.

Figure 12-17   An undirected tree $T = (V, E)$ is presented in (a) along with an adjacency representation of the graph in (b). In (c), the next edge function is given for the Euler tour of the graph, which is a function of the adjacency representation. Notice that since an adjacency representation is not unique, if the representation given in (b) is changed, the next function in (c) would also change. By starting at any directed edge in the graph $T' = (V, E')$ (every undirected edge $(u, v) \in E$ is replaced by two directed edges, $(u, v),(v, u) \in E'$), and following the next function, an Euler tour can be achieved.

Tree Contraction: In this section, we consider a procedure for contracting a tree, initially presented as a pointer-based data structure on a PRAM. The tree contraction problem has wide applicability, including providing an efficient solution to the expression evaluation problem. The *expression evaluation problem* requires the evaluation of an expression stored in an *expression tree*, where an expression tree is typically presented as a binary tree in which every node is either a leaf node containing a value or an internal node containing an operator ($+$, $-$, $\times$, $\div$, and so forth), as shown in Figure 12-18.

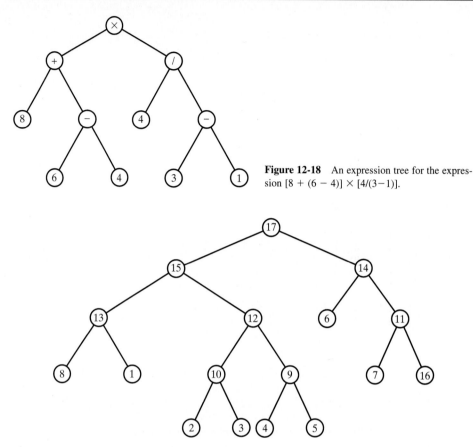

Figure 12-18 An expression tree for the expression $[8 + (6 - 4)] \times [4/(3-1)]$.

Figure 12-19 Input to a tree contraction algorithm is a rooted binary tree in which each vertex has either two children or none at all. Further, it is assumed that the leaves have been consecutively labeled from left to right, with the exception of the leftmost and rightmost leaves.

Tree contraction consists of successively compressing leaf nodes with their respective parents until the tree collapses into a single vertex. When considering the expression evaluation problem, notice that when a leaf is compressed with a parent, the appropriate arithmetic operation is performed, so that partial results are provided in an iterative fashion until the tree finally collapses, at which point the complete expression has been evaluated.

For the purpose of the PRAM algorithm that we present, we will make several assumptions about the tree that is given as input. It should be noted that some of these assumptions are not critical and that the problem could be solved within the same time bounds if these restrictions were removed. We simply impose these restrictions to facilitate a clean presentation. We assume that the input is a rooted binary tree $T = (V, E)$ in which each vertex is either a leaf node or an internal node with two children. The root is denoted as r. The vertices are assumed to be labeled with integers in such a fashion that the interior leaves are labeled consecutively from left to right, as shown in Figure 12-19. (Do not confuse the labels of the vertices with the contents of the vertices, which are either operators, for interior vertices, or values, for leaf vertices.) We also assume that every vertex v knows the location of *parent(v)*, *sibling(v)*, *left_child(v)*, and *right_child(v)*. Notice that the root will have *parent(v)* = *nil*, and the leaves will have *left_child(v)* = *nil* and *right_child(v)* = *nil*.

The *collapse* or *rake* operation applied to a leaf node *v* consists of removing *v* and *parent(v)* from the tree and connecting *sibling(v)* to *parent(parent(v))*, as shown in Figure 12-20. The tree contraction algorithm consists of collapsing leaf nodes in an iterative and parallel fashion so that approximately half of the leaf nodes disappear each time through the loop. This results in an algorithm that runs in $\Theta(\log n)$ time. See Figure 12-21 for an example. The algorithm follows:

> Given a tree $T = (V, E)$, assume that the *m* leaves are labeled consecutively from left to right, excluding the leftmost and rightmost leaves (the exterior leaves).
>
> Let *Active* = $(1, 2, \ldots, m)$ be an ordered list of the interior leaf labels. Notice that *Active* does not include the label of the leftmost or rightmost leaf.
>
> For $\lceil \log_2(n + 1) \rceil$ iterations, do
>> Apply the collapse operation to all leaf nodes with odd indexed entries in *Active* that are left children. That is, apply collapse simultaneously to nodes that are left children from the set of first, third, fifth, ... , elements in *Active*.
>
> Apply the collapse operation to the remaining leaf nodes that correspond to odd indexed entries in *Active*.
>
> Update *Active* by removing the indices of the odd indexed leaves that were just collapsed and then compressing the array *Active*.
>
> End For

Notice that at the end of the algorithm, the input tree $T = (V, E)$ with root vertex *r* has been reduced to three vertices; namely, the root and two children. We remark without proof that this algorithm can be implemented on an EREW PRAM in $O(\log n)$ time.

Finally, we should note that if one is interested in compressing a tree in which a root has not been identified and the vertices have not been labeled, efficient PRAM procedures exist to identify a root and label the vertices. The algorithms to solve the latter two problems rely on an efficient solution to the *Euler tour problem*, which can be solved

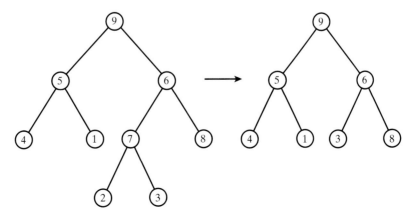

Figure 12-20 An example of a collapse operation applied to vertex number 2.

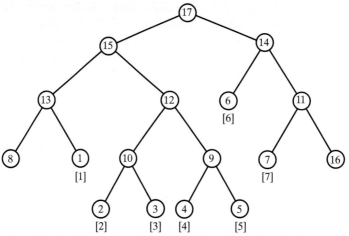

(a) The initial tree.

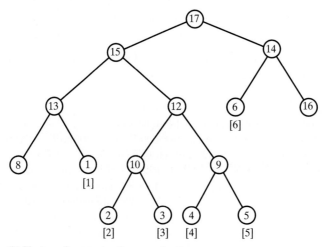

(b) The tree after a contraction on vertex 7.

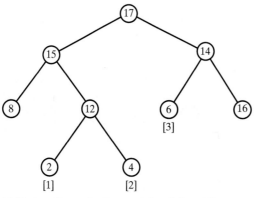

(c) The tree after contraction on vertices 1, 3, and 5.

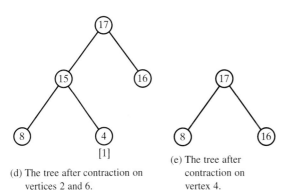

Figure 12-21 An example of tree contraction. Indices of nodes in the array *Active* are shown below the nodes (these are updated following compression of *Active* as the steps are executed). The initial tree is given in (a). The tree is shown in (b) after performing contraction on vertex 7 during the first iteration of the algorithm. The tree is shown in (c) after performing contraction on vertices 1, 3, and 5 to finish the first iteration of the algorithm. The tree is shown in (d) after performing tree contraction on vertices 2 and 6 to initiate the second iteration of the algorithm. The tree is shown in (e) after performing tree contraction on vertex 4 to conclude the algorithm (after the third iteration).

(d) The tree after contraction on vertices 2 and 6.

(e) The tree after contraction on vertex 4.

by using list ranking as a subroutine. It should be noted that a solution to the Euler tour problem can also be used to determine preorder, postorder, and inorder numbering of the vertices of a tree.

Computing the Transitive Closure of an Adjacency Matrix

In this section, we review both a sequential and mesh implementation of a transitive closure algorithm. The solution to this problem is critical to a variety of efficient solutions to fundamental graph problems. Assume that an $n \times n$ adjacency matrix representation of a directed graph $G = (V, E)$ is given, where $n = |V|$. In such a representation, $A(i,j) = 1$ if and only if there is an edge from v_i to v_j in E, and $A(i,j) = 0$ if $(v_i, v_j) \notin E$. The transitive closure of A is represented as a Boolean matrix $A^*_{n \times n}$ in which $A^*(i,j) = 1$ if and only if there is a path in G from v_i to v_j. $A^*(i,j) = 0$ if no such path exists. As we have previously discussed, one way to obtain the transitive closure of an adjacency matrix A is to multiply A by itself n times. This is not very efficient, however. Alternatively, one could perform $\lceil \log_2 n \rceil$ operations of squaring the matrix: $A \times A = A^2$, $A^2 \times A^2 = A^4$, and so on until a matrix A^m is obtained where $m \geq n$. Sequentially, this squaring procedure would result in a $\Theta(n^3 \log n)$ time algorithm, while on a mesh of size n^2, the procedure would run in $\Theta(n \log n)$ time. The reader should verify both of these results.

Consider the Boolean matrix $A_k(i,j)$ representing G, with the interpretation that $A_k(i,j) = 1$ if and only if there is a path from v_i to v_j that only uses $\{v_1, \ldots, v_k\}$ as intermediate vertices. Notice that $A_0 = A$ and that $A_n = A^*$. Further, notice that there is a path from v_i to v_j using intermediate vertices $\{v_1, \ldots, v_k\}$ if and only if either there is a path from v_i to v_j using intermediate vertices $\{v_1, \ldots, v_{k-1}\}$ or there is a path from v_i to v_k using intermediate vertices $\{v_1, \ldots, v_{k-1}\}$ and a path from v_k to v_j also using only intermediate vertices $\{v_1, \ldots, v_{k-1}\}$. This observation forms the foundation of *Warshall's algorithm*, which can be used to compute the transitive closure of A on a sequential machine in $\Theta(n^3)$ time. The sequential algorithm follows.

For $k = 1$ to n, do
    For $i = 1$ to n, do
        For $j = 1$ to n, do
            $A_k(i, j) \leftarrow A_{k-1}(i, j) \vee [A_{k-1}(i, k) \wedge A_{k-1}(k, j)]$
        End For j
    End For i
End For k

Now we consider an implementation of Warshall's algorithm on a mesh computer. Suppose A is stored in an $n \times n$ mesh such that processor $P_{i,j}$ stores entry $A(i,j)$. Further, suppose that at the end of the algorithm processor $P_{i,j}$ is required to store entry $A^*(i,j) = A_n(i,j)$. This can be accomplished with some interesting movement of data that adheres to the following conditions:

1. Entry $A_k(i,j)$ is computed in processor $P_{i,j}$ at time $3k + |k - i| + |k - j| - 2$.
2. For all k and i, the value of $A_k(i,k)$ moves in a horizontal lock-step fashion (in row i) away from processor $P_{i,k}$.
3. For all k and j, the value of $A_k(k,j)$ moves in a vertical lock-step fashion (in column j) away from processor $P_{k,j}$.

See Figure 12-22 for an illustration of this data movement. Notice from condition 1 that the algorithm runs in $\Theta(n)$ time. The reader is advised to spend some time with small examples of the mesh implementation of Warshall's algorithm in order to be comfortable with the fact that the appropriate items arrive at the appropriate processors at the precise time that they are required. Therefore, there is no congestion or bottleneck in any of the rows or columns.

Finally, it should be noted that the data movement associated with the mesh transitive closure algorithm can be used to provide solutions to many recurrences of the form

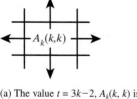

(a) The value $t = 3k-2$, $A_k(k, k)$ is computed in processor $P_{k,k}$.

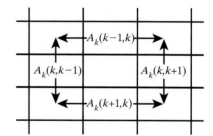

(b) The values $A_k(k - 1, k)$, $A_k(k, k + 1)$, $A_k(k + 1, k)$, and $A_k(k, k - 1)$ are computed in processors $P_{k-1,k}$, $P_{k,k+1}$, $P_{k+1,k}$, and $P_{k,k-1}$, respectively,

Figure 12-22 Data movement of van Scoy's implementation of Warshall's transitive closure algorithm on a mesh. $A_k(k, k)$ is computed at time $t = 3k - 2$ in processor $P_{k,k}$. During the next time step, this value is transmitted to processors $P_{k,k+1}$, $P_{k,k-1}$, $P_{k+1,k}$, and $P_{k-1,k}$, as shown in (a). At time $t + 1$, the values $A_k(k - 1, k)$, $A_k(k, k + 1)$, $A_k(k + 1, k)$, and $A_k(k, k - 1)$ are computed in processors $P_{k-1,k}$, $P_{k,k+1}$, $P_{k+1,k}$, and $P_{k,k-1}$, respectively, as shown in (b). The arrows displaying data movement in (b) show the direction that this information begins to move during time step $t + 2$.

$f_k(i,j) = g(f_{k-1}(i,j), f_{k-1}(i,k), f_{k-1}(k,j))$ or $f_k(i,j) = g(f_{k-1}(i,j), f_k(i,k), f_k(k,j))$. As with the previous algorithm, the initial value $f(i,j)$ will be stored in processor $P_{i,j}$ and the final value $f_n(i,j)$ will be computed in processor $P_{i,j}$.

The mesh algorithm for the (generalized) transitive closure can be used to solve the connected component labeling problem, the all-pairs shortest-path problem, and to determine whether or not a graph is a tree, to name a few. The first two algorithms will be discussed in more detail later in the chapter.

CONNECTED COMPONENT LABELING

In this section, we consider the problem of labeling the connected components of an undirected graph. The labeling should be such that if vertex v is assigned a label $label(v)$, then all vertices that v is connected to are also assigned a component label of $label(v)$.

RAM: A simple sequential algorithm can be given to label all of the vertices of an undirected graph. Such an algorithm consists of applying the breadth-first search procedure to a given vertex. During the breadth-first search, the label corresponding to the initial vertex is propagated. Once the breadth-first search is complete, a search is made for any unlabeled vertex. If one is found, then the BFS is repeated, labeling the next component, and so on. An algorithm follows.

1. Given a graph $G = (V, E)$, where $V = \{v_1, v_2, \ldots, v_n\}$.
2. Assign $label(v_i) = nil$ for all $v_i \in V$ {Initialize the labels of all vertices representing each vertex as currently unvisited.}
3. For $i = 1$ to n, do
4.   If $label(v_i) = nil$, then   {Check if vertex has been visited/labeled so far. If not, then initiate a search, during
5.   BFSroutine(G, v_i)   which we set $label(v) = i$ to every vertex visited.}
6.   End If
7. End For

The algorithm is straightforward. Since the graph is undirected, every invocation of the BFSroutine will visit and label all vertices that are connected to the given vertex. Due to the For-loop, the algorithm will consider every connected component. The total running time for all applications of step 4 is $\Theta(V)$. Further, the running time for step 5 in aggregate is $\Theta(V + E)$ since every vertex and every edge in the graph is visited within the context of one and only one breadth-first search. Hence, the running time of the algorithm is $\Theta(V + E)$, which is optimal in the size of the graph.

PRAM: The problem of computing the connected components of a graph $G = (V, E)$ is considered a fundamental problem in the area of graph algorithms. Unfortunately, an efficient parallel strategy for performing a breadth-first search or a depth-first search of a graph on a PRAM is not known. For this reason, the connected component problem has generated a lot of interest for people working on PRAM algorithms. Several efficient algorithms have been presented with slightly different running times and on a variety of PRAM models. The basic strategy of these algorithms consists of processing the graph for $O(\log V)$ stages. During each stage, the vertices are organized as a forest of directed trees, where each vertex is in one tree and has a link (a directed edge or pointer) to its parent in that tree. All vertices in such a tree are in the same connected component of the graph. The algorithm repeatedly combines trees containing vertices in the same connected component. However, until the algorithm terminates, there is no guarantee that every such tree represents a maximally connected component.

Initially, there are $|V|$ directed trees, each consisting of a vertex pointing to itself. Refer to the example presented in Figure 12-23. During the i-th stage of the algorithm, trees from stage $i - 1$ are *hooked* or *grafted* together and compressed by a pointer-jumping operation so that the trees do not become unwieldy. Each such compressed tree is referred to as a *supervertex*. When the algorithm terminates, each supervertex corresponds to a maximally connected component in the graph and takes the form of a *star*, a directed tree in which all vertices point directly to the root vertex. It is the implementation of hooking that is critical to designing an algorithm that runs in $O(\log V)$ stages. We will present an algorithm for an arbitrary CRCW PRAM that runs in $O(\log V)$ time using $\Theta(V + E)$ processors.

Define $index(v_i) = i$ to be the index of vertex v_i. Define $root(v_i)$ as a pointer to the root of the tree (or supervertex) that v_i is a currently a member of. Then we can define the hooking operation $hook(v_i, v_j)$ as an operation that attaches $root(v_i)$ to $root(v_j)$, as shown in Figure 12-24.

We can determine for each vertex $v_i \in V$, whether or not v_i belongs to a star via the following procedure:

1. Determine the Boolean function $star(v_i)$ for all $v_i \in V$, as follows.
2. For all vertices v_i, do in parallel
3. $star(v_i) \leftarrow true$
4.   If $root(v_i) \neq root(root(v_i))$, then
5. $star(v_i) \leftarrow false$
6. $star(root(v_i)) \leftarrow false$
7. $star(root(root(v_i))) \leftarrow false$
8.   End If
9. $star(v_i) \leftarrow star(root(v_i))$
10. End For

See Figure 12-25 for an example that shows the necessity of Step 9. It is easily seen that this procedure requires $\Theta(1)$ time.

The basic component labeling algorithm follows:

We wish to label the connected components of an undirected graph $G = (V, E)$.
Assume that every edge between vertices v_i and v_j is represented by a pair of
    unordered edges (v_i, v_j) and (v_j, v_i).
Recall that we assume an arbitrary CRCW PRAM. That is, if there is a write
    conflict, one of the writes will arbitrarily succeed.
For all $v_i \in V$, set $root(v_i) = v_i$ {Initialize supervertices.}
For all $(v_i, v_j) \in E$, do   {Loop uses arbitrary CRCW property.}
   If $index(v_i) > index(v_j)$, then   {Hook larger indexed vertices into
     $hook(v_i, v_j)$ smaller indexed vertices.}
End for all edges
Repeat

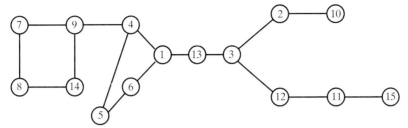

(a) The initial undirected graph $G = (V,E)$.

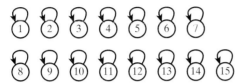

(b) The initial forest consisting of a distinct tree representing every vertex in V.

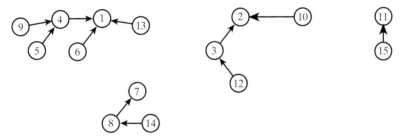

(c) The result of every vertex in V attaching to its minimum-labeled neighbor.

(d) The four disjoint subgraphs resulting from the compression given in (c).

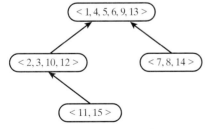

(e) The result from each of these four supervertices choosing its minimum-labeled neighbor.

$$< 1, 2, 3, 4, 5, 6, 7, 8, 9, 10, 11, 12, 13, 14, 15 >$$

(f) The final stage of the algorithm in which all vertices in the connected graph have been compressed into a single supervertex.

Figure 12-23   A general description of a parallel component labeling algorithm. The initial undirected graph $G = (V,E)$ is given in (a). In (b), the initial forest is presented. The initial forest consists of a distinct tree representing every vertex in V. The graph presented in (c) shows the result of every vertex in V attaching to its minimum-labeled neighbor. The graph that results from the compression of these four disjoint subgraphs is given in (d). Notice that four supervertices are generated. The directed graph in (e) shows the result from each of these four supervertices choosing its minimum-labeled neighbor. Finally, (f) shows the result from the final stage of the algorithm in which all vertices in the connected graph have been compressed into a single supervertex. Note that when we present supervertices, the first vertex (minimum label) in the list will serve as the label for the supervertex.

Determine $star(v_i)$ for all $v_i \in E$
For all edges $(v_i,v_j) \in E$, do
    if v_i is in a star   {Hook vertices in star to
    and $index(root(v_i)) > index(root(v_j))$ neighbors with lower-indexed
    then $hook(v_i,v_j)$ roots.}
Determine $star(v_i)$ for all $v_i \in V$
For all vertices v_i, do
    if v_i is not in a star, then
        $root(v_i) \leftarrow root(root(v_i))$ {This is the pointer jumping.}
until no changes are produced by the steps of the Repeat loop

While it is beyond the scope of this book, it can be shown that the algorithm above is correct for an arbitrary CRCW PRAM. Critical observations can be made, such as

- at any time during the algorithm, the structure defined by the set of root pointers corresponds to a proper (upward) directed forest, as no vertex ever has a root with a larger index, and
- when the algorithm terminates, the forest defined by the root pointers consists of stars.

Given an arbitrary CRCW PRAM with $\Theta(V + E)$ processors, every computational step in the algorithm defined above requires $\Theta(1)$ time. Therefore, we only need to determine the number of iterations required of the main loop before the algorithm naturally terminates with stars corresponding to every connected component. It can be shown that each

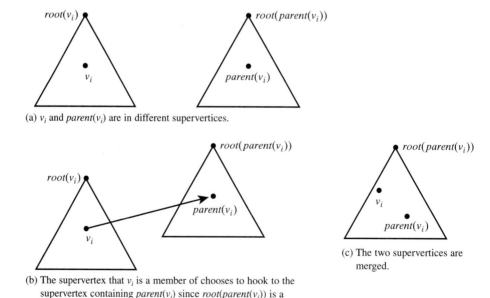

(a) v_i and $parent(v_i)$ are in different supervertices.

(b) The supervertex that v_i is a member of chooses to hook to the supervertex containing $parent(v_i)$ since $root(parent(v_i))$ is a minimum label over all of the supervertices to which members of the supervertex labeled $root(v_i)$ are connected.

(c) The two supervertices are merged.

Figure 12-24   A demonstration of the hooking operation.

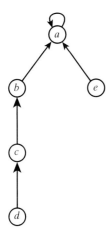

Figure 12-25 Computing the star function in parallel. Arrows represent *root* pointers. Step 3 initializes *star(v_i)* ← *true* for all vertices. Steps 5 through 7 change *star(a)*, *star(b)*, *star(c)*, and *star(d)* to *false*. However, Step 9 is required to change *star(e)* to *false*.

pass through the loop reduces the height of a nonstar tree by a fixed fraction. Therefore, the algorithm will terminate after $O(\log V)$ steps, yielding an algorithm with total cost of $O((V + E) \log V)$, which is not optimal. In fact, slightly more efficient algorithms are possible, but they are beyond the scope of this book.

Mesh: Recall that a single step of a PRAM computation with n processors operating on a set of n data items can be simulated on a mesh of size n in $\Theta(n^{1/2})$ time by a sort-based associative read and associative write operation. Therefore, given a graph $G = (V, E)$ represented by a set of $|E|$ unordered edges, distributed arbitrarily one per processor on a mesh of size $|E|$, the component labeling algorithm can be solved in $\Theta(E^{1/2} \log E)$ time. Notice that this is at most a factor of $\Theta(\log E)$ from optimal on a mesh of size $|E|$. However, it is often convenient to represent dense graphs by an adjacency matrix. So consider the situation in which a $|V| \times |V|$ adjacency matrix is distributed in a natural fashion on a mesh of size $|V|^2$. Then by applying the time-optimal transitive closure algorithm followed by a simple row or column rotation, the component labeling algorithm can be solved in $\Theta(V)$ time, which is optimal for this combination of architecture and graph representation.

MINIMUM-COST SPANNING TREES

Suppose we want to run cable on a college campus so that every building can reach every other building by some path. Further, suppose we want to minimize the total amount of cable that we lay. Viewing the buildings as vertices and the cables between buildings as edges, then this cabling problem is reduced to determining a spanning tree covering the buildings on campus in which the total length of cable that is laid is at a minimum. This example can be expressed in terms of a minimum-cost spanning tree.

Given a connected undirected graph $G = (V, E)$, we define a *spanning tree* $T = (V, E')$, where $E' \subseteq E$, to be a connected acyclic graph. The reader should verify that in order for T to have the same vertex set as the connected graph G, and for T not to contain any cycles, it must contain exactly $|V| - 1$ edges. Suppose that for every edge $e \in E$, there exists a *weight w(e)*, where such a weight might represent, for example, the cost, length, or time required to traverse the edge. Then a *minimum-cost spanning tree T* (sometimes referred to as a *minimal spanning tree, minimum-weight spanning tree, minimum spanning tree, or MST*), is a spanning tree over G in which the weight of the tree is minimized with respect to every spanning tree of G. The weight of a tree $T = (V, E')$ is defined intuitively to be

$$w(T) = \sum_{e \in E'} w(e).$$

RAM: In this section, we consider three traditional algorithms for determining a minimum-cost spanning tree of a connected, weighted, undirected graph $G = (V, E)$ on a RAM. All three algorithms use a *greedy* approach to solving the problem. At any point during these algorithms, a set of edges E' exists that represents a subset of some minimal spanning tree of G. At each step of these algorithms, a "best" edge is selected from those that remain, based on certain properties, and added to the working minimal spanning tree. One of the critical properties of any edge that is added to E' is that it is *safe, i.e.*, that the updated edge set E' will continue to represent a subset of some minimal spanning tree.

Kruskal's Algorithm

The first algorithm we consider is *Kruskal's algorithm*. In this greedy algorithm, E' will always represent a forest over all vertices V in G. Furthermore, this forest will always be a subset of some minimum spanning tree. Initially, we set $E' = \varnothing$, which represents the forest of isolated vertices. We also sort the edges of the graph into increasing order by weight. At each step in the algorithm, the next smallest weight edge from the ordered list is chosen and that edge is added to E', so long as it does not create a cycle. The algorithm follows:

Kruskal's MST Algorithm
The input consists of a connected, weighted, undirected graph $G = (V, E)$ with
    weight function w on the edges $e \in E$.
$E' \leftarrow \varnothing$
For each $v \in V$, create $Tree(v) = \{v\}$. That is, every vertex is currently its own tree.
Sort the edges of E into nondecreasing order by the weight function w.
While there is more than one distinct tree, consider each $(u, v) \in E$ by sorted order.
    If $Tree(u) \neq Tree(v)$, then
        $E' \leftarrow E' \cup \{(u, v)\}$
        Merge $Tree(u)$ and $Tree(v)$
    End If
End While

    The analysis of this algorithm depends on the data structure used to implement the graph $G = (V, E)$, which is critical to the time required to perform a sort operation, the time necessary to execute the function $Tree(u)$, and the time required for the merge operation over two trees in the forest. Suppose that each tree is implemented as a linked list with a header element. The header element will contain the name of the tree, the number of vertices in the tree, a pointer to the first element in the list, and a pointer to the last element in the list. Assuming that the vertices are labeled by integers in $1 \ldots |V|$, the name of a tree will correspond to the minimum vertex in the

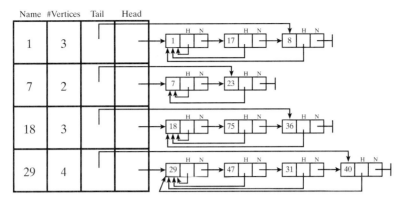

Figure 12-26   A representation of a data structure that allows for an efficient implementation of Kruskal's algorithm. H is a pointer to the head of the list. N is a pointer to the next element in the list.

tree. Suppose that every list element contains a pointer to the next element in the list and a pointer to the head of the list (see Figure 12-26). With such a data structure, notice that $Tree(u)$ can be determined in $\Theta(1)$ time, and that two trees T_1 and T_2 can be merged in $\Theta(\min(|T_1|,|T_2|))$ time.

Given the data structures described, it takes $\Theta(1)$ time to set $E' \leftarrow \varnothing$, $\Theta(E \log E)$ time to sort the edges, and $\Theta(V)$ time to create the initial forest of isolated elements. The reader should verify that the union operation is invoked exactly $|V| - 1$ times. The difficult part of the analysis is in determining the total time for the $|V| - 1$ merge operations. We leave it as an exercise to show that in the worst case, the time to perform all merge operations is $\Theta(V \log V)$. Therefore, the running time of the algorithm, as described, is $O(E \log E)$, which is $O(E \log V)$.

An alternative implementation to our presentation of Kruskal's algorithm follows. Suppose that instead of initially sorting the edges into decreasing order by weight, we place the weighted edges into a heap, and that during each iteration of the algorithm, we simply extract the minimum weighted edge left in the heap. Recall that this heap can be constructed in $\Theta(E \log E) = \Theta(E \log V)$ time, and a heap extraction can be performed in $\Theta(\log E) = \Theta(\log V)$ time. Therefore, the heap-based (or priority queue-based) variant of this algorithm requires $\Theta(E \log V)$ time to set up the initial heap and $\Theta(\log V)$ time to perform the operation required during each of the $\Theta(E)$ iterations. Therefore, a heap-based approach results in a total running time of $\Theta(E \log V)$, including the merge operations.

Prim's Algorithm

The second algorithm we consider is *Prim's algorithm* for determining a minimum-cost spanning forest of a weighted, connected, undirected graph $G = (V, E)$, with edge weight function w. The approach taken in this greedy algorithm is to add continually edges to $E' \subseteq E$ so that E' always represents a tree with the property that it is a subtree of some minimum spanning tree of G. Initially, an arbitrary vertex $r \in V$ is chosen to be the root of the tree that will be grown. Next, an edge (r, u) is used to initialize E', where (r, u) has minimal weight among edges incident on r. As the algorithm continues, an edge of minimum weight between some vertex in the current tree, represented by E', and some vertex not in the current tree, is chosen and added to E'. The algorithm follows:

Prim's MST Algorithm

1. The input consists of a connected, weighted, undirected graph $G = (V, E)$ with weight function w on the edges $e \in E$.
2. Let vertex set $V = \{v_1, \ldots, v_n\}$.
3. Let the root of the tree be $r = v_1$.
4. Initialize $NotInTree = \{v_2, \ldots, v_n\}$.
5. For all $v \in NotInTree$, initialize $smalledge(v) \leftarrow \infty$.
6. Set $smalledge(r) \leftarrow 0$ since r is in the tree.
7. Set $parent(r) \leftarrow nil$ since r is the root of the tree.
8. For all $v \in Adj(r)$, do
9. $parent(v) \leftarrow r$
10. $smalledge(v) \leftarrow w(r, v)$
11. End For all $v \in Adj(r)$
12. While $NotInTree \neq \varnothing$, do
13. $u \leftarrow ExtractMin(NotInTree)$
14.   Add $(u, parent(u))$ to E' and remove u from $NotInTree$.
15.   forall $v \in Adj(u)$, do
16.   If $v \in NotInTree$ and $w(u, v) < smalledge(v)$, then
17. $parent(v) \leftarrow u$
18. $smalledge(v) \leftarrow w(u, v)$
19.   End If
20.   End forall
21. End While-Do

The structure *NotInTree* is most efficiently implemented as a priority queue since the major operations include finding a minimum weight vertex in *NotInTree* and removing it from *NotInTree*. Suppose that *NotInTree* is implemented as a heap. Then the heap can be initialized (lines 4-11) in $\Theta(V \log V)$ time. The loop (lines 12–21) is executed $V - 1$ times. Therefore, the $O(\log V)$ time *ExtractMin* operation is invoked $\Theta(V)$ times. Thus, the total time to perform all *ExtractMin* operations is $\Theta(V \log V)$.

Now consider the time required to perform the operations specified in lines 17 and 18. Since every edge in a graph is determined by two vertices, lines 17 and 18 of the program can be invoked at most twice for every edge. Therefore, these assignments are performed $\Theta(E)$ times at most. However, notice that line 18 requires the adjustment of an entry in the priority queue, which requires $O(\log V)$ time. Therefore, the running time for the entire algorithm is $\Theta(V \log V + E \log V)$, which is $\Theta(E \log V)$. Notice that this is the same asymptotic running time as Kruskal's algorithm. However, by using Fibonacci heaps instead of traditional heaps, it should be noted that the time required to perform Prim's algorithm on a RAM can be reduced to $\Theta(E + V \log V)$.

Sollin's Algorithm

Finally, we mention *Sollin's algorithm*. In this greedy algorithm, E' will always represent a forest over all vertices V in G. Initially, $E' = \varnothing$, which represents the forest of isolated vertices. At each step in the algorithm, every tree in the forest nominates one edge to be considered for inclusion in E'. Specifically, every tree nominates an edge of minimal weight between a vertex in its tree and a vertex in a distinct tree. So during the i-th iteration of the algorithm, the $|V| - (i - 1)$ trees represented by E' generate $|V| - (i - 1)$, not necessarily distinct edges to be considered for inclusion. The minimal weight edge will then be selected from these nominees for inclusion in E'. The sequential algorithm and analysis is left as an exercise.

PRAM: In this section, we consider the problem of constructing a minimum-cost spanning tree for a connected graph represented by a weight matrix on a CREW PRAM. Given a connected graph $G = (V, E)$, we assume that the weights of the edges are stored in a matrix W. That is, entry $W(i, j)$ corresponds to the weight of edge $(i, j) \in E$. Since the graph is not necessarily complete, we define $W(i, j) = \infty$ if the edge $(i, j) \notin E$. Since we assume that self-edges are not present in the input, we should note that $W(i, i) = \infty$ for all $1 \le i \le n$. Notice that we use ∞ to represent nonexistent edges since the problem is one of determining a *minimum*-weight spanning tree.

The algorithm we consider is based on Sollin's algorithm, as previously described. Initially, we construct a forest of isolated vertices, which are then repeatedly merged into trees until a single tree (a minimum spanning tree) remains. The procedure for merging trees at a given stage of the algorithm is to consider one candidate edge e_i from every tree T_i. The candidate edge e_i corresponds to an edge of minimum weight connecting a vertex of T_i to a vertex in some T_j where $i \ne j$. All candidate edges are then added to the set of edges representing a minimum weight spanning tree of G, as we have done with previously described minimum spanning tree algorithms.

During each of the merge steps, we must collapse every tree in the forest into a virtual vertex (that is, a supervertex). Throughout the algorithm, every vertex must know the identity of the tree that it is a member of so that candidate edges can be chosen in a proper fashion during each iteration of the algorithm. We will use the component labeling technique, described earlier in this chapter, to accomplish this task.

Without loss of generality, we assume that every edge has a unique weight. Notice that in practice, ties in edge weight can be broken by appending unique edge labels to every weight. The basic algorithm follows:

The input consists of a connected, weighted, undirected graph $G = (V, E)$ with weight function w on the edges $e \in E$.
Let weight matrix W be used to store the weights of the edges, where
$W(i, j) = w(i, j)$.
Let vertex set $V = \{v_1, \ldots, v_n\}$.
Let $G' = (V, E')$ represent a minimum spanning tree of G that is under construction.
Initially, set $E' = \varnothing$.
Initially, set the forest of trees $F = \{T_1, \ldots, T_n\}$, where $T_i = \{v_i\}$. That is, every vertex is its own tree.
While $|F| > 1$, do
    For all $T_i \in F$, determine $Cand_i$, an edge of minimum weight between a vertex in T_i and a vertex in T_j, where $i \ne j$.
    For all i, add $Cand_i$ to E'.
    Combine all trees in F that are in the same connected component with respect to the edges just added to E'. Assuming that r trees remain in the forest, relabel these virtual vertices (connected components) so that $F = \{T_1, \ldots, T_r\}$.
    Relabel the edges in E so that the vertices correspond to the appropriate

virtual vertices. This can be accomplished by reducing the weight matrix W
so that it contains only information pertaining to the r virtual vertices.
End While

Consider the running time of the algorithm as described. Since the graph G is connected, we know that every time through the While loop, the number of trees in the forest
will be reduced by at least half. That is, every tree in the forest will hook up with at least
one other tree. Therefore, the number of iterations of the While loop is $O(\log V)$. The operations described inside of the While loop can be performed by invoking procedures to sort
edges based on vertex labels, performing parallel prefix in order to determine candidate edges,
and applying the component-labeling algorithm in order to collapse connected components
into virtual vertices. Since each of these procedures can be performed in time logarithmic
in the size of the input, the running time for the entire algorithm as given is $O(\log^2 V)$.

Mesh: The mesh algorithm we discuss in this section is identical in spirit to that just presented for the PRAM. Our focus in this section is on the implementation of the specific
steps of the algorithm. We assume that the input to the problem is a weight matrix W rep-
resenting a graph $G = (V,E)$ where $|V| = n$. Initially, $W(i,j)$, the weight of edge $(i,j) \in E$,
is stored in mesh processor $P_{i,j}$. Again we assume that $W(i,j) = \infty$ if the edge does not exist
or if $i = j$. We also assume, without loss of generality, that the edge weights are unique.

Initially, we define the forest $F = \{T_1, \ldots, T_n\}$, where $T_i = (\{v_i\}, \phi)$. During each of
the $\lfloor \log_2 V \rfloor$ iterations of the algorithm, the number of virtual vertices (supervertices) in the
forest is reduced by at least half. The reader might also note that at any point during the
course of the algorithm, only a single minimum-weight edge needs to be maintained between any two virtual vertices. We need to discuss the details of reducing the forest during a generic iteration of the algorithm. Suppose that the forest F currently has r virtual
vertices. Notice that at the start of an iteration of the While loop, as given in the previous
section, every virtual vertex is represented by a unique row and column in an $r \times r$ weight
matrix W. As shown in Figure 12-27, entry $W(i,j)$, $1 \le i, j \le r$, denotes the weight and
identity of a minimum-weight edge between virtual vertex i and virtual vertex j.

In order to determine the candidate edge for every virtual vertex i, $1 \le i \le r$, simply per-

	1	2	3	$\cdots$	r
1	$(\infty,\text{-})$	$(W(1,2),e_{1,2})$	$(W(1,3),e_{1,3})$	$\cdots$	$(W(1,r),e_{1,r})$
2	$(W(2,1),e_{2,1})$	$(\infty,\text{-})$	$(W(2,3),e_{2,3})$	$\cdots$	$(W(2,r),e_{2,r})$
3	$(W(3,1),e_{3,1})$	$(W(3,2),e_{3,2})$	$(\infty,\text{-})$	$\cdots$	$(W(3,r),e_{3,r})$
$\vdots$					
r	$(W(r,1),e_{r,1})$	$(W(r,2),e_{r,2})$	$(W(r,3),e_{r,3})$	$\cdots$	$(\infty,\text{-})$

Figure 12-27   The $r \times r$ matrix W as distributed one entry per processor in a natural fashion on an $r \times r$ submesh. Notice that each entry in processor $P_{i,j}$, $1 \le i, j \le r$, contains the record $(W(i,j),e_{i,j})$, which represents the minimum weight of any edge between virtual vertices (super-vertices) v_i and v_j, as well as information about one such edge $e_{i,j}$ to which the weight corre-sponds. In this situation, the "edge" $e_{i,j}$ is actually a record containing information identify-ing its original vertices and its current virtual vertices.

form a row rotation simultaneously over all rows of W, where the rotation is restricted to the $r \times r$ region of the mesh currently storing W. The edge in E that this virtual edge represents can be conveniently stored in the rightmost column of the $r \times r$ region since there is only one such edge per row, as shown in Figure 12-28. Based on the virtual vertex indices of these edges being added to E', an adjacency matrix can be created in the $r \times r$ region that represents the connections being formed between the current virtual vertices, as shown in Figure 12-29. Warshall's algorithm can then be applied to this adjacency matrix in order to determine the connected com-

	1	2	3	4	5	6
1	∞	98	17	36	47	58 / $17, e_{1,3}$
2	98	∞	38	89	21	39 / $21, e_{2,5}$
3	17	38	∞	97	27	73 / $17, e_{3,1}$
4	36	89	97	∞	18	9 / $9, e_{4,6}$
5	47	21	27	18	∞	47 / $18, e_{5,4}$
6	58	39	73	9	47	∞ / $9, e_{6,4}$

Figure 12-28 A sample 6×6 weight matrix in which, for simplicity's sake, only the weights of the records are given. Notice that the processors in the last column also contain a minimum-weight edge and its identity after the row rotation.

	1	2	3	4	5	6
1	0	0	1	0	0	0
2	0	0	0	0	1	0
3	1	0	0	0	0	0
4	0	0	0	0	0	1
5	0	0	0	1	0	0
6	0	0	0	1	0	0

Figure 12-29 The 6×6 adjacency matrix corresponding to the minimum-weight edges selected by the row rotations as shown in Figure 12-28.

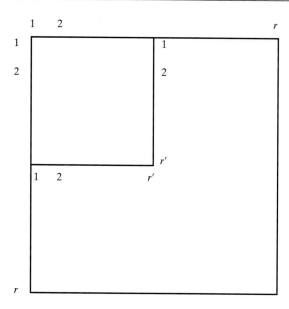

Figure 12-30   A concurrent write is used within the $r \times r$ region of the mesh to compress and update the r' rows and columns corresponding to the r' supervertices. This results in the creation of an $r' \times r'$ weight matrix in the upper-left regions of the $r \times r$ region so that the algorithm can proceed to the next stage.

ponents. That is, an application of Warshall's algorithm will determine which trees in F have just been combined using the edges in E'. The rows of the matrix can now be sorted according to their new virtual vertex number. Next, in a similar fashion, the columns of the matrix can be sorted with respect to the new virtual vertex numbers. Now within every interval of rows, a minimum weight edge can be determined to every other new virtual vertex by a combination of row and column rotations. Finally, a concurrent write can be used to compress the $r \times r$ matrix to an $r' \times r'$ matrix, as shown in Figure 12-30.

Notice that each of the critical mesh operations working in an $r \times r$ region can be performed in $O(r)$ time. Since the size of the matrix is reduced by at least a constant factor after every iteration, the running time of the algorithm is $\Theta(n)$, which includes the time to perform a final concurrent read to mark all of the edges in the minimum spanning tree that was determined.

SHORTEST-PATH PROBLEMS

In this section, we consider problems involving shortest paths within graphs. Specifically, we consider two fundamental problems, defined as follows:

1. **Single-Source Shortest-Path Problem:** Given a weighted, directed graph $G = (V, E)$, a solution to the *single-source shortest-path problem* requires that we determine a shortest (minimum-weight) path from *source vertex* $s \in V$ to every other vertex $v \in V$. Notice that the notion of a minimum-weight path generalizes that of a shortest path in that a shortest path (a path containing a minimal number of edges) can be regarded as a minimum-weight path in a graph in which all edges have weight 1.

2. **All-Pairs Shortest-Path Problem**: Given a weighted, directed graph $G = (V, E)$, a
   solution to the *all-pairs shortest-path problem* requires the determination of a shortest (minimum weight) path between every pair of distinct vertices $u, v \in V$.

For problems involving shortest paths, several issues must be considered, such as whether
or not negative weights and/or cycles are permitted in the input graph. It is also important to
decide whether the total weight of a minimum-weight path will be presented as the sole result
or if a representation of a path that generates such a weight is also required. Critical details
such as these, which often depend on the domain of the problem, have a great effect on the algorithm that is to be developed and utilized. In the remainder of this section, we consider some
of the more popular variants of shortest-path problems as a way to introduce critical paradigms.

RAM: For the RAM, we will consider the single-source shortest-path problem in which
we need to determine the weight of a shortest path from a unique source vertex to every other
vertex in the graph. Further, we assume that the result must contain a representation of an appropriate shortest path from the source vertex to every other vertex in the graph. Assume that
we are given a weighted, directed graph $G = (V, E)$, in which every edge $e \in E$ has an associated weight $w(e)$. Let $s \in V$ be the known source vertex. The algorithm that we present will
produce a *shortest-path tree* $T = (V', E')$, rooted at s, where $V' \subseteq V$, $E' \subseteq E$, V' is the set of
vertices reachable from s, and for all $v \in V'$, the unique simple path from s to v in T is a
minimum-weight path from s to v in G. It is important to emphasize that "shortest" paths
(minimum-weight paths) are not necessarily unique and that shortest-path trees (trees representing minimum-weight paths) are also not necessarily unique. See Figure 12-31, which shows
two shortest path trees for the given graph G.

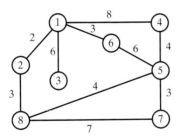

(a) A weighted, undirected graph $G = (V, E)$.

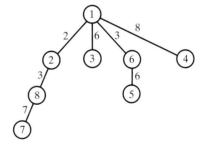

(b) A shortest-path tree. Notice the path $\langle 1, 2, 8, 7 \rangle$ of
weight 12 chosen between source vertex 1 and sink
vertex 7.

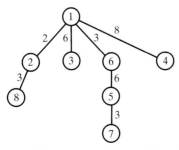

(c) A different shortest-path tree. Notice that
the path $\langle 1, 6, 5, 7 \rangle$ chosen between vertices 1 and 7 is also of total weight 12.

Figure 12-31   A demonstration that shortest paths and
shortest-path trees are not necessarily unique.

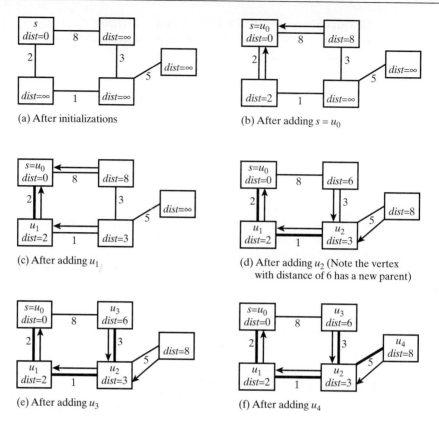

Figure 12-32   A demonstration of the progress of Dijkstra's algorithm, through the iterations of its While loop, for constructing a shortest-path tree. The vertices are numbered $u_0, u_1, \ldots$, in the order in which they are inserted into the tree. Arrows represent parent pointers. Dark edges are those inserted into the tree.

We consider *Dijkstra's algorithm* for solving the single-source shortest-path problem on a weighted, directed graph $G = (V, E)$ where all of the edge weights are nonnegative. Let $s \in V$ be the predetermined source vertex. The algorithm will create and maintain a set V' of vertices that, when complete, is used to represent the final shortest-path tree T. When a vertex v is inserted into V', it is assumed that the edge $(parent(v), v)$ is inserted into E'.

Initially, every vertex $v \in V$ is assumed to be at distance $dist(v) = \infty$ from the source vertex s, with the exception of all vertices directly connected to s by an edge. Let u be a neighboring vertex of s. Then, since $(s, u) \in E$, we initialize the distance from s to u to be $dist(u) = w(s, u)$, the weight of the edge originating at s and terminating at u.

The algorithm consists of continually identifying a vertex that has not been added to V', which is at minimum distance from s. Suppose the new vertex to be added to V' is called x. Then after adding x to V', all vertices t for which $(x, t) \in E$, are examined. If the current minimum distance from s, which is maintained in $dist(t)$, can now be improved based on the fact that x is in V', then $dist(t)$ is updated, and $parent(t)$ is set to x (see Figure 12-32).

The algorithm follows:

The algorithm takes a weighted, directed graph $G = (V,E)$ as input.

Initialize the vertices and edges in the shortest-path tree $T = (V',E')$ that this algorithm produces to be empty sets. That is, set $V' \leftarrow \varnothing$ and $E' \leftarrow \varnothing$.

Initialize the set of available vertices to be added to V' to be the entire set of vertices. That is, set $Avail \leftarrow V$.

For every vertex $v \in V$, do

    Set $dist(v) \leftarrow \infty$. That is, the distance from every vertex to the source is initialized to be infinity.

    Set $parent(v) \leftarrow nil$. That is, the parent of every vertex is initially assumed to be nonexistent.

End do

Set $dist(s) \leftarrow 0$. That is, the distance from the source to itself is 0. This step is critical to seeding the While loop that follows.

$GrowingTree \leftarrow true$

While $Avail \neq \varnothing$, and $GrowingTree$, do

    Determine $u \in Avail$, where $dist(u)$ is a minimum over all distances of vertices in $Avail$. {Note the first pass through the loop yields $u = s$.}

    If $dist(u)$ is finite, then

        $V' \leftarrow V' \cup \{u\}$ and $Avail \leftarrow Avail \setminus \{u\}$. That is, add u to the shortest-path tree and remove u from $Avail$.

        If $u \neq s$, then $E' \leftarrow E' \cup \{(parent(u),u)\}$. That is, add $(parent(u),u)$ to the edge set of T.

        For every vertex $v \in Adj(u)$, do {Check to see if neighboring vertices should be updated.}

            If $dist(v) > dist(u) + w(u, v)$, then {Update distance and parent information since a shorter path is now possible.}

                $dist(v) \leftarrow dist(u) + w(u,v)$

                $parent(v) \leftarrow u$

            End If $dist(v) > dist(u) + w(u,v)$

        End For

    End If $dist(u)$ is finite

    Else $GrowingTree \leftarrow false$ {This is the finished component of source vertex.}

End While

The algorithm is greedy in nature in that at each step the best local choice is taken and that choice is never undone. Dijkstra's algorithm relies on an efficient implementation of a priority queue, since the set $Avail$ of available vertices is continually queried in terms of minimum distance. Suppose that the priority queue of $Avail$ is maintained in a simple linear array. Then a generic query to the priority queue will take $\Theta(V)$ time. Since there are $\Theta(V)$ such queries, the total time required for querying the priority queue is $\Theta(V^2)$. Since each vertex is inserted into the shortest-path tree exactly once, this means that every edge in E is examined exactly twice in terms of trying to update distance information to neighboring vertices. Therefore, the total time to update distance and parent information is $\Theta(E)$, the running time of the algorithm is $\Theta(V^2 + E)$, or $\Theta(V^2)$, since $E = O(V^2)$.

Notice that this algorithm is efficient for dense graphs. That is, if $E = \Theta(V^2)$, then the algorithm has an efficient running time of $\Theta(E)$. However, if the graph is sparse, then this implementation is not necessarily efficient. In fact, for a sparse graph, one might implement the priority queue as a binary heap or a Fibonacci heap in order to achieve a slightly more efficient running time.

PRAM and Mesh: For both of these parallel models of computation, we consider the all-pairs shortest-path problem, given a weight matrix as input. Specifically, suppose we are given a weighted, directed graph $G = (V, E)$ as input, where $|V| = n$, and every edge $(u,v) \in E$ has an associated weight $w(u,v)$. Further, assume that G is represented by an $n \times n$ weight matrix W, where $W(u,v) = w(u,v)$ if $(u, v) \in E$ and $W(u,v) = \infty$ otherwise.

Let $W_k(u,v)$ represent the weight of a minimum-weight path from vertex u to vertex v, assuming that the intermediate vertices traversed on the path from u to v are indexed in $\{1, 2, \ldots, k\}$. Then the matrix W_n will contain the final weights representing a directed minimum-weight path between every pair of vertices. That is, $W_n(u,v)$ will contain the weight of a minimum-weight directed path with source u and sink v, if such a path exists. $W_n(u,v)$ will have a value of ∞ if a $u \to v$ path does not exist.

Notice that we have recast the all-pairs shortest-path problem as a variant of the transitive closure problem discussed earlier in this chapter in the section "Computing the Transitive Closure of an Adjacency Matrix." Given a mesh of size n^2 in which processor $P_{i,j}$ stores weight information concerning a path from vertex i to vertex j, we can represent the computation of W as

$$W_k(i, j) = \min[W_{k-1}(i, j), W_{k-1}(i, k) + W_{k-1}(k, j)].$$

Therefore, we can apply van Scoy's implementation of Warshall's algorithm, as described earlier in this chapter, in order to solve the problem on a mesh of size n^2 in optimal $\Theta(n)$ time. Notice that if the graph is dense (that is, $E = \Theta(V^2)$), then the weight matrix input is an efficient representation.

On a PRAM, notice that we can also implement Warshall's algorithm for computing the transitive closure of the input matrix W. Recall that we can multiply two matrices in $\Theta(\log n)$ time on a PRAM containing $n^3/\log n$ processors. Given an $n \times n$ matrix as input on a PRAM, we know that we can determine W_n by performing $\Theta(\log n)$ such matrix multiplications. Therefore, given an $n \times n$ weight-matrix as input, the running time to solve the all-pairs shortest-path problem on a PRAM with $n^3/\log n$ processors is $O(\log^2 n)$.

CHAPTER NOTES

In this chapter, we have considered algorithms and paradigms to solve fundamental graph problems on a RAM, PRAM, and mesh computer. For the reader interested in a more in-depth treatment of sequential graph algorithms, please refer to the following sources:

- *Graph Algorithms* by S. Even (Computer Science Press, 1979).
- *Data Structures and Network Algorithms* by R.E. Tarjan (Society for Industrial and Applied Mathematics, 1983).

■ "Basic Graph Algorithms" by S. Khuller and B. Raghavachari, in the *Handbook of Algorithms and Theory of Computation*, M. Atallah, ed. (CRC Press, New York, 1999).

For the reader interested in a survey of PRAM graph algorithms, complete with an extensive citation list, please refer to

■ "A survey of parallel algorithms and shared memory machines" by R.M. Karp and V. Ramachandran in the *Handbook of Theoretical Computer Science: Algorithms and Complexity*, A.J. vanLeeuwen, ed. (Elsevier, New York, 1990, pp. 869–941).

The depth-first search procedure was developed by J.E. Hopcroft and R.E. Tarjan. Early citations to this work include

■ "Efficient algorithms for graph manipulation" by J.E. Hopcroft and R.E. Tarjan, *Communications of the ACM*, 16:372–378, 1973, and

■ "Depth-first search and linear graph algorithms" by R.E. Tarjan, *SIAM Journal on Computing*, 1(2), June, 1972, 146–160.

Warshall's innovative and efficient transitive closure algorithm was first presented in "A theorem on Boolean matrices" by S. Warshall in the *Journal of the ACM* 9, 1962, 11–12. An efficient mesh implementation of Warshall's algorithm is discussed in detail in *Parallel Algorithms for Regular Architectures* by R. Miller and Q.F. Stout (The MIT Press, Cambridge, 1996).

An in-depth presentation of tree contraction for the PRAM can be found in *An Introduction to Parallel Algorithms* by J. Já Já (Addison Wesley, 1992). This book also contains details of PRAM algorithms for additional problems discussed in this chapter, including component labeling and minimum spanning trees. The PRAM component-labeling algorithm presented in this chapter comes from a combination of the algorithms presented in these sources:

■ "A survey of parallel algorithms and shared memory machines" by R.M. Karp and V. Ramachandran in the *Handbook of Theoretical Computer Science: Algorithms and Complexity*, A.J. vanLeeuwen, ed., (Elsevier, New York, 1990, pp. 869–941), and

■ "Introduction to Parallel Connectivity, List Ranking, and Euler Tour Techniques" by S. Baase in *Synthesis of Parallel Algorithms*, J.II. Reif, ed. (Morgan Kaufmann Publishers, San Mateo, CA, 1993, pp. 61–114).

The sequential minimum spanning tree algorithm presented in this chapter combines techniques presented in *Data Structures and Algorithms in Java* by M.T. Goodrich and R. Tamassia (John Wiley & Sons, Inc., New York, 1998), with those presented in *Introduction to Algorithms* by T.H. Cormen, C.E. Leiserson, and R.L. Rivest (McGraw-Hill Book Company, New York, 1989). The minimum spanning tree algorithm for the PRAM was inspired by the one presented in *An Introduction to Parallel Algorithms* by J. Já Já (Addison Wesley, 1992), while the MST algorithm for the mesh was inspired by the one that appears in *Parallel Algorithms for Regular Architectures* by R. Miller and Q.F. Stout (The MIT Press, Cambridge, 1996).

The reader interested in exploring additional problems involving shortest paths, as well as techniques and algorithms for solving such problems, is referred to the following sources:

- *Introduction to Algorithms* by T.H. Cormen, C.E. Leiserson, and R.L. Rivest (McGraw-Hill Book Company, New York, 1989).

- *An Introduction to Parallel Algorithms* by J. Já Já (Addison Wesley, 1992).

- *Parallel Algorithms for Regular Architectures* by R. Miller and Q.F. Stout (The MIT Press, Cambridge, 1996).

EXERCISES

1. Suppose a graph G is represented by unordered edges. Give efficient algorithms for the following:

   a. Construct an adjacency list representation of G. Analyze the running time of your algorithm for the RAM and for a PRAM with $|V| + |E|$ processors.

   b. Construct an adjacency matrix representation of G. Analyze the running time of your algorithm for the RAM, for a PRAM of $\Theta(V^2)$ processors, and for a mesh of $\Theta(V^2)$ processors. For the mesh, assume an initial distribution so that no processor has more than one edge, and include appropriate data movement operations in your algorithm.

2. Give an efficient RAM algorithm to compute the height of a nonempty binary tree. The *height* is the maximum number of edges between the root node and any leaf node. (Hint: recursion makes this a short problem.) What is the running time of your algorithm?

3. Prove that if v_0 and v_1 are distinct vertices of a graph $G = (V, E)$ and a path exists in G from v_0 to v_1, then there is a simple path in G from v_0 to v_1. (Hint: this can be done using mathematical induction on the number of edges in a shortest path from v_0 to v_1.)

4. A graph $G = (V, E)$ is *complete* if an edge exists between every pair of vertices. Given an adjacency list representation of G, describe an algorithm that determines whether or not G is complete. Analyze the algorithm for the RAM and for a CREW PRAM with $n = |V|$ processors.

5. Suppose the graph $G = (V, E)$ is represented by an adjacency matrix. Let $n = |V|$. Give an algorithm that determines whether or not G is complete (see the previous exercise for the definition). Analyze the algorithm for the RAM, for an arbitrary CRCW PRAM with n^2 processors, and for an $n \times n$ mesh (for the mesh, at the end of the algorithm, every processor should know whether or not G is complete).

6. Let v_0, v_1 be vertices of a graph $G = (V, E)$. Suppose we want to determine whether or not these two vertices are in the same component of G. One way to answer this query is by executing a component-labeling algorithm and then comparing the component labels of v_0 and v_1. However, simpler algorithms (perhaps not asymptotically faster) can determine whether two vertices belong to the same component. Give such an algorithm and its running time on a RAM.

7. The *distance* between two vertices in the same component of a graph is the number of edges in a shortest path connecting the vertices. The *diameter* of a connected graph

is the maximum distance between a pair of vertices of the graph. Give an algorithm to find the maximal diameter of the components of a graph. Analyze the algorithm's running time for the PRAM and the mesh.

8. Let $G = (V, E)$ be a connected graph. Suppose there is a Boolean function *has-Trait(vertex)* that can be applied to any vertex of G in order to determine in $\Theta(1)$ RAM time whether or not the vertex has a certain trait.

   ■ Given a graph represented by adjacency lists, describe an efficient RAM algorithm to determine whether or not there are adjacent vertices with the trait tested for by this function. Give an analysis of your algorithm.

   ■ Suppose instead that the graph is represented by an adjacency matrix. Describe an efficient RAM algorithm to determine whether or not there are adjacent vertices with the trait tested for by this function. Give an analysis of your algorithm.

9. A *bipartite graph* is an undirected graph $G = (V, E)$ with subsets V_0 and V_1 of V such that $V_0 \cup V_1 = V$, $V_0 \cap V_1 = \varnothing$, and every member of E joins a member of V_0 to a member of V_1. Let $T = (V, E')$ be a minimum spanning tree of a connected bipartite graph G. Show that T is also a bipartite graph.

10. Suppose G is a connected graph. Give an algorithm to determine whether or not G is a bipartite graph (see the previous problem). Analyze the algorithm's running time for the RAM, PRAM, and mesh.

11. Let $S = \{I_i = [a_i, b_i]\}_{i=1}^{n}$ be a set of intervals on the real line. An *interval graph* $G = (V, E)$ is determined by S as follows. $V = \{v_i\}_{i=1}^{n}$ and for distinct indices i and j, there is an edge from v_i to v_j if and only if $I_i \cap I_j \neq \varnothing$. Give an algorithm to construct an interval graph from a given set S of intervals and analyze the algorithm's running time for a RAM. Note: there is a naive algorithm that runs in $\Theta(n^2)$, where $n = |V|$. You should be able to give a more sophisticated algorithm that runs in $\Theta(n \log n + E)$ time.

12. Let $G = (V, E)$ be a connected graph. We say $e \in E$ is a *bridge* of G if the graph $G_e = (V, E \setminus \{e\})$ is disconnected. It is easy to see that if G represents a traffic system, its bridges represent potential bottlenecks. Thus, it is useful to be able to identify all bridges in a graph.

   a. A naive (nonoptimal) algorithm may be given to identify all bridge edges as follows. Every edge e is regarded as a possible bridge, and the graph G_e is tested for connectedness. Show that such an algorithm runs on a RAM in $O(E(V + E))$ time.

   b. Let T be a minimal spanning tree for G. Show that every bridge of G must be an edge of T.

   c. Use the result of part b to obtain an algorithm for finding all bridges of G that runs on a RAM in $O(V(V + E))$ time.

13. Let $G = (V, E)$ be a connected graph. An *articulation point* is a vertex of G whose removal would leave the resulting graph disconnected. That is, v is an articulation point

of G if and only if the graph $G_v = (V \setminus \{v\}, E_v)$, where $E_v = E \setminus \{e \in E | e$ is incident on $v\}$, is a disconnected graph. Thus, an articulation point plays a role among vertices analogous to that of a bridge among edges.

a. Suppose that $|V| > 2$. Show that at least one vertex of a bridge of G must be an articulation point of G.

b. Let $v \in V$ be an articulation point of G. Must there be a bridge of G incident on v? If so, give a proof; if not, give an example.

c. Let G be a connected graph for which there is a positive number C such that no vertex has degree greater than C. Let $v \in V$ be a vertex of G. Give an algorithm to determine whether or not v is an articulation point. Discuss the running time of implementations of your algorithm on the RAM, CRCW PRAM, and mesh.

14. Suppose $T = (V, E)$ is a tree. What is the asymptotic relationship between $|E|$ and $|V|$? Explain.

15. Let $\otimes$ be an associative binary operation that is commutative and that can be applied to data stored in the vertices of a graph $G = (V, E)$. Assume a single computation using $\otimes$ requires $\Theta(1)$ time. Suppose G is represented in memory by unordered edges. How can we perform an efficient RAM semigroup computation based on $\otimes$, on the vertices of G? Give the running time of your algorithm.

16. Let $\otimes$ be an associative binary operation that is commutative and that can be applied to the edges of a tree $T = (V, E)$. Assume a single computation using $\otimes$ requires $\Theta(1)$ time. How can we perform an efficient RAM semigroup computation on the edges of T? Give the running time of your algorithm. (Note that your algorithm could be used for such purposes as totaling the weights of the edges of a weighted tree.)

17. Suppose an Euler tour of a tree starts at the root vertex. Show that for every nonroot vertex v of the tree, the tour uses the edge $(parent(v), v)$ before using any edge from v to a child of v.

18. Suppose it is known that a graph $G = (V, E)$ is a tree with root vertex $v_* \in V$, but the identity of the parent vertex $parent(v)$ is not known for $v \in V \setminus \{v_*\}$. How can every vertex v determine $parent(v)$? What is the running time of your algorithm on a RAM?

19. Give an efficient RAM algorithm to determine for a binary tree $T = (V, E)$, with root vertex $v_* \in V$, the number of descendants of every vertex. What is the running time of your algorithm?

20. Suppose $T = (V, E)$ is a binary tree with root vertex $v_* \in V$. Let T' be the graph derived from T as described in the Euler tour section of the chapter. Is a *preorder* (respectively, *inorder* or *postorder*) traversal of T' an Euler tour (see Figure 12-33)? What is the running time on a RAM of a preorder (respectively, inorder or postorder) traversal?

21. Prove that the time required for all $|V| - 1$ merge operations in Kruskal's algorithm, as outlined in the text, is $\Theta(V \log V)$ in the worst case on a RAM.

22. Analyze the running time of Sollin's algorithm as described in the text.

23. Given a labeled $n \times n$ digitized image, and one "marked" pixel per component, provide an efficient algorithm to construct a minimum-distance spanning tree within every component with respect to using the "marked" pixel as the root. Present analysis for the RAM.

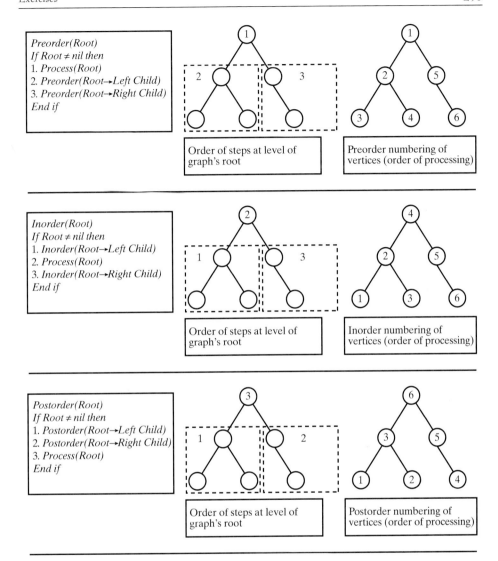

Figure 12-33 Tree traversals. Steps of each recursive algorithm are shown at the top level of recursion; also, the order in which the vertices are processed by each algorithm.

13

Numerical Problems

Numerical Problems

With the exception of Chapter 6, most of this book has been concerned with "non-numerical" problems and algorithms. That is not to say that we have avoided doing arithmetic. Rather, we have concentrated on problems in which algorithms do not require the intensive use of floating point calculations or the unusual storage required for very large integers. It is important to realize that a stable, accurate, and efficient use of numerically intensive calculations plays an important role in scientific and technical computing. As we have mentioned previously, *computational science and engineering* is an emerging discipline that unites computer technology and mathematics with disciplinary research in chemistry, biology, physics, and other scientific fields. Computational science and engineering focuses on scientific problems in an effort to gain an improved understanding of the problem area, often through simulation and modeling. In this chapter, we examine algorithms for some fundamental numerical problems.

In most of our previous discussions, we have used n as a measure of the size of a problem, in the sense of how much data is processed by an algorithm (or how much storage is required by the data processed). This is not always the case for the problems discussed in this chapter. For example, the value of x^n can be determined with only $\Theta(1)$ data items. However, the value of n will still play a role in determining the running time and memory usage of the algorithms discussed. The focus of this chapter is on RAM algorithms, but several of the exercises focus on the design and analysis of parallel algorithms to solve numerical problems.

PRIMALITY

Given an integer $n > 1$, suppose we wish to determine if n is a *prime number*; that is, if the only positive integer factors of n are 1 and n. This problem, from the area of mathematics known as *number theory*, was once thought to be largely of theoretical interest. However, modern encryption techniques, such as those of importance to e-commerce, depend on factoring large integers. This is one of the many reasons why there has been a renewed interest in number theory.

Our analysis of any solution to the primality problem depends in part on assumptions that we should re-examine. For most of this book, we have assumed that operations such as computing the quotient of two numbers or the square root of a number can be done in $\Theta(1)$ time. This assumption is appropriate if we assume the operands have magnitude that is bounded both above and below. However, researchers are now considering the primality problem for numbers with thousands of decimal digits. For such numbers n, computations of n/u (where u is a smaller integer) and $n^{1/2}$ (with accuracy, say, to some fixed number of decimal places) take time that is a function of the number of digits in n. That is, for significantly large values of n, we must revert to the proper assumption that arithmetic operations require $O(\log n)$ time. (Magnitudes of numbers considered are bounded by available memory. However, when we allow the possibility of integers with hundreds or thousands of decimal digits and observe that the time to perform arithmetic operations depends on the number of digits in the operands, it seems more appropriate to say such operations take $\Theta(\log n)$ time than to say they take $\Theta(1)$ time.) In the following, we say "n is bounded" if there is a positive integer C such that $n < C$ (hence, the number of digits of n is bounded), while "n is arbitrary" means n is not bounded; and we speak of "bounded n" and "arbitrary n" models, respectively.

We observe that n is prime if and only if the only integral factorization $n = u \times v$ of n with integers $1 \leq u \leq v$ is $u = 1$, $v = n$. This naturally suggests a RAM algorithm in which we test every integer u from 2 to $n - 1$ to see if u is a factor of n. Such an algorithm runs in $O(n)$ time under the bounded n model; or $O(n \log n)$ time under the arbitrary n model. However, we can improve the running time of our algorithm by observing that any factorization $n = u \times v$ of n with integers $1 \leq u \leq v$ must satisfy $1 \leq u \leq n^{1/2}$. Thus, we obtain the following RAM algorithm.

Procedure Primality(*n*, *nIsPrime*, *factor*)
Input: *n*, a positive integer.
Output: *nIsPrime*, true or false according to whether *n* is prime;
        factor, the smallest prime factor of *n* if *n* is not prime.
Local variable: *Root_n*, integer approximation of $n^{1/2}$
Action:
    factor = 2;
    Root_n = $\lfloor n^{1/2} \rfloor$;
    nIsPrime $\leftarrow$ *true*;
    repeat
        If *n/factor* = $\lfloor n/factor \rfloor$, then *nIsPrime* $\leftarrow$ *false*
        Else *factor* $\leftarrow$ *factor* + 1;
    until (not *nIsPrime*) or (*factor* > *Root_n*);

It is easily seen that this algorithm takes $O(n^{1/2})$ time under the bounded n model and $O(n^{1/2} \log n)$ time under the arbitrary n model. Notice that worst-case running times — $\Theta(n^{1/2})$ under the bounded n model and $\Theta(n^{1/2} \log n)$ time under the arbitrary n model — are achieved when n is prime.

Notice that exploring nonprime values of *factor* in the algorithm above is unnecessary, since if n is divisible by a composite integer $u \times v$, it follows that n is divisible by u. Therefore, if we have in memory a list of the prime integers that are at most $n^{1/2}$ and use only these values for *factor* in the algorithm above, we obtain a faster algorithm. It is known that the number $\pi(n)$ of prime numbers that are less than or equal to n satisfies $\pi(n) = \Theta(n/\log n)$. This follows from the Prime Number Theorem, which states that

$$\lim_{n \to \infty} \left[\frac{\pi(n)}{n/\ln n} \right] = 1.$$

Thus, we modify the previous algorithm as follows:

Procedure Primality(n, *prime*, *nIsPrime*, *factor*)
Input: n, a positive integer;
        prime, an array in which consecutive entries are successive primes
        including all primes $\leq n^{1/2}$, and the next prime.
Output: *nIsPrime*, true or false according to whether n is prime;
        factor, the smallest prime factor of n if n is not prime.
Local variables: i, an index;
        Root_n, integer approximation of $n^{1/2}$
Action:
    $i = 1$; {Set index for first entry of *prime*.}
    $Root\_n, = \lfloor n^{1/2} \rfloor$;
    nIsPrime $\leftarrow$ *true*;
    repeat
        factor = *prime*[i];
        If $n/factor = \lfloor n/factor \rfloor$, then *nIsPrime* $\leftarrow$ *false*
        Else $i \leftarrow i + 1$;
    until (not *nIsPrime*) or (*prime*[i] > *Root_n*);

In light of the asymptotic behavior of the function $\pi(n)$, it is easily seen that this RAM algorithm runs in $O(n^{1/2}/\log n)$ time under the bounded n model and in $O(n^{1/2})$ time under the arbitrary n model.

In the Exercises, the reader is asked to devise a parallel algorithm for the primality problem.

GREATEST COMMON DIVISOR

Another problem concerned with factoring integers is the *greatest common divisor (gcd)* problem. Given positive integers n_0 and n_1, we wish to find the largest positive integer, denoted

(n_0, n_1), that is a factor of both n_0 and n_1. We will find it useful to define $(0,n) = (n,0) = n$ for all positive integers n.

The greatest common divisor is used in the familiar process of "reducing a fraction to its lowest terms." This can be important in computer programming when calculations originating with integer quantities must compute divisions without roundoff error. For example, we would store 1/3 as the pair (1,3) rather than as 0.333 . . . 33.

The *Euclidean algorithm,* a classical solution to this problem, is based on the following observation. Suppose there are integers q and r (*quotient* and *remainder,* respectively) such that

$$n_0 = q \times n_1 + r$$

Then any common factor of n_0 and n_1 must also be a factor of r. Therefore, if $n_0 \geq n_1$ and $q = \lfloor n_0/n_1 \rfloor$, we will have $n_1 > r \geq 0$ and $(n_0, n_1) = (n_1, r)$. These observations give us the following recursive algorithm:

Function *gcd(n0, n1)* {Greatest common divisor of arguments.}
Input: Nonnegative integers $n0, n1$.
Local variables: integer *quotient, remainder*
Action:
     If $n0 < n1$, then *swap(n0, n1)*;
     If $n1 = 0$, return $n0$
     Else
          quotient $\leftarrow \lfloor n0 / n1 \rfloor$;
          remainder $\leftarrow n0 - n1 \times quotient$;
          return gcd($n1$, *remainder*)
     End Else

In terms of the variables discussed above, we easily see that the running time of this algorithm $T(n_0, n_1)$, satisfies the recursive relation

$$T(n_0, n_1) = T(n_1, r) + \Theta(1)$$

It is perhaps not immediately obvious how to solve this recursion, but we can make use of the following.

Lamé's Theorem: The number of division operations needed to find gcd(n_0, n_1), for integers satisfying $n_0 \geq n_1 \geq 0$, is no more than five times the number of decimal digits of n_1.

It follows that if we use the bounded n model discussed above for the primality problem, our implementation of the Euclidean algorithm on a RAM requires $T(n_0, n_1) = O(\log(\min\{n_0, n_1\}))$ time for positive integers n_0, n_1.

The Euclidean algorithm seems inherently sequential. In the exercises, a very different approach is suggested that can be parallelized efficiently.

INTEGRAL POWERS

Let x be a real (*i.e.*, floating point) number and let n be an integer. Often we consider the computation of x^n to be a constant-time operation. This is a reasonable assumption to make if the absolute value of n is bounded by some constant. For example, we might assume that the computation of x^n requires $\Theta(1)$ time for $|n| \leq 100$. However, if we regard n as an unbounded parameter of this problem, it is clear that the time to compute x^n is likely to be related to the value of n.

We can easily reduce this problem to the assumption that $n \geq 0$ since an algorithm to compute x^n for an arbitrary integer n can be constructed as follows:

1. Compute *temp* $= x^{|n|}$.
2. If $n \geq 0$, return *temp* else return 1 / *temp*.

Notice that Step 2 requires $\Theta(1)$ time. Therefore, the running time of the algorithm is dominated by the computation of a nonnegative power. Thus, without loss of generality in the analysis of the running time of an algorithm to solve this problem, we will assume that $n \geq 0$. A standard, brute-force algorithm is given below for computing a simple power function on a RAM.

Function power(x, n) {Return the value of x^n.}
Input: x, a real number;
     n, a nonnegative integer.
Output: x^n.
Local variables: *product*, a partial result
              counter, the current power
Action:
    product $= 1$;
    If $n > 0$, then
        For *counter* $= 1$ to n, do
            product $=$ *product* $\times x$
        End For
    End If
    Return *product*

The reader should verify that the running time of the RAM algorithm given above is $\Theta(n)$, and that this algorithm requires $\Theta(1)$ extra space.

Now let's consider computing x^{19} for any real value x. The brute-force algorithm given above requires 19 multiplications. However, by exploiting the concept of recursive doubling that has been used throughout the book, observe that we can compute x^{19} much more efficiently, as follows:

1. Compute (and save) $x^2 = x \times x$.
2. Compute (and save) $x^4 = x^2 \times x^2$.
3. Compute (and save) $x^8 = x^4 \times x^4$.

4. Compute (and save) $x^{16} = x^8 \times x^8$.
5. Compute and return $x^{19} = x^{16} \times x^2 \times x$.

Notice that this procedure requires a mere six multiplications, although we pay a (small) price in requiring extra memory.

In order to generalize from our example, we remark that the key to our recursive doubling algorithm is in the repeated squaring of powers of x instead of the repeated multiplication by x. The general recursive doubling algorithm follows.

Function power(x, n) {Return the value of x^n.}
Input: x, a real number;
         n, a nonnegative integer.
Output: x^n
Local variables: *product*, a partial result
                 counter, *exponent*: integers
                 $p[0 \ldots \lfloor \log_2 n \rfloor]$, an array used for certain powers of x

                 $q[0 \ldots \lfloor \log_2 n \rfloor]$, an array used for powers of 2
Action:
     product = 1;
     If $n > 0$, then
         $p[0] = x$;
         $q[0] = 1$;
         For *counter* = 1 to $\lfloor \log_2 n \rfloor$, do
             $q[counter] = 2 \times q[counter - 1]$; $\{= 2^{counter}\}$
             $p[counter] = (p[counter - 1])^2$ $\{p[i] = x^{q[i]} = x^{2^i}\}$
         End For
         exponent = 0;
         For *counter* = $\lfloor \log_2 n \rfloor$ downto 0, do
             If *exponent*+$q[counter] \leq n$, then
                 exponent = *exponent* + $q[counter]$;
                 product = *product* $\times$ $p[counter]$
             End If *exponent*+$q[counter] \leq n$
         End For
     End If $n > 0$
     Return *product*

The reader should be able to verify that this algorithm runs in $\Theta(\log n)$ time on a RAM, using $\Theta(\log n)$ extra space. The reader will be asked to consider parallelizing this RAM algorithm as an exercise.

EVALUATING A POLYNOMIAL

Let $f(x)$ be a polynomial function,

$$f(x) = a_n x^n + a_{n-1} x^{n-1} + \ldots + a_1 x + a_0$$

for some set of real numbers $\{a_i\}_{i=0}^n$, with $a_n \neq 0$ if $n > 0$. Then n is the *degree* of $f(x)$. As was the case in evaluating x^n, a straightforward algorithm for evaluating $f(t)$, for a given real number t, does not yield optimal performance. Consider the following naive algorithm.

> *evaluation* = 0.
> For $i = 0$ to n, do
>   If $a_i \neq 0$, then *evaluation* = *evaluation* + $a_i \times x^i$.
> Return *evaluation*.

It is clear that the For loop dominates the running time. If we use the brute-force linear time algorithm to compute x^n, then the algorithm presented above for evaluating a polynomial will run on a RAM in

$$\Theta\left(\sum_{i=1}^{n} i \right) = \Theta(n^2)$$

worst-case time. Even if we use our recursive doubling $\Theta(\log n)$-time algorithm for computing x^n, this straightforward algorithm for evaluating a polynomial will run on a RAM in

$$\Theta\left(\sum_{i=1}^{n} \log i \right) = \Theta(n \log n)$$

worst-case time. However, we can do better than this.

Notice that $a_3 x^3 + a_2 x^2 + a_1 x + a_0 = ((a_3 x + a_2)x + a_1)x + a_0$. For example,

$$10x^3 + 5x^2 - 8x + 4 = ((10x + 5)x - 8)x + 4.$$

This illustrates a general principle that by grouping expressions appropriately we can reduce the number of arithmetic operations to a number linear in n, the degree of the polynomial. This observation is the basis for *Horner's Rule* and a corresponding algorithm, given below.

Function HornerEvaluate(a, x)
{Evaluate the polynomial represented by the coefficient array a at the input
  value x.}
Input: Array of real coefficients $a[0 \ldots n]$, real number x.
Output: Value $f(x) = \displaystyle\sum_{i=0}^{n} a[i] \times x^i$.
Local variables: i, an index variable; *result* to accumulate the return value
Action:
    result = $a[n]$;
    If $n > 0$, then
        For $i = n$ downto 1, do
            result = *result* $\times$ x + $a[i - 1]$
        End For
    End If
    Return *result*

The reader should verify that the algorithm given above implements Horner's Rule on a RAM in $\Theta(n)$ time. This polynomial evaluation method appears to be inherently sequential. That is, it is difficult to see how Horner's method might be recognizable if modified for efficient implementation on a fine-grained parallel computer. In the exercises, the reader is asked to consider other approaches to constructing an efficient parallel algorithm to evaluate a polynomial.

APPROXIMATION BY TAYLOR SERIES

Recall from calculus that a function that is sufficiently differentiable can be approximately evaluated by using a *Taylor polynomial* (*Taylor series*). In particular, let $f(x)$ be continuous everywhere on a closed interval $[a, b]$ and n times differentiable on the open interval (a, b) containing values x and x_0, and let $\{p_k\}_{k=0}^{n-1}$ be the set of polynomial functions defined by

$$p_k(x) = \sum_{i=0}^{k} \frac{f^{(i)}(x_0)}{i!}(x - x_0)^i$$

where $f^{(i)}$ denotes the i-th order derivative function and $i!$ denotes the factorial function. Then the error term in approximating $f(x)$ by $p_{n-1}(x)$ is

$$\varepsilon_n(x) = f(x) - p_{n-1}(x) = \frac{f^{(n)}(\tau)}{n!}(x - x_0)^n$$

for some τ between x and x_0. (Actually, this term is the *truncation error* in such a calculation, so called because it is typically due to replacing an exact value of an infinite computation by the approximation obtained via truncating to a finite computation. By contrast, a *roundoff error* occurs whenever an exact calculation yields more nonzero decimal places than can be stored. In the remainder of this section, we will consider only truncation errors.)

Often, we do not know the exact value of τ in the error term. If we knew the value of τ, we could compute the error and adjust our calculation by its value to obtain a net truncation error of 0. However, we can often obtain a useful upper bound on the magnitude of the error. Such a bound may provide us with information regarding how hard we must work in order to obtain an acceptable approximation.

For example, we may have an error tolerance $\varepsilon > 0$. This means we wish to allow no more than ε of error in our approximation. The value of ε may give us a measure of how much work (how much computer time) is necessary to compute an acceptable approximation. Therefore, we may wish to express our running time as a function of ε. Notice that this is significantly different from the analysis of algorithms presented in previous chapters. We are used to the idea that the larger the value of n, the larger the running time of an algorithm. However, in a problem in which error tolerance determines running time, it is usually the case that the smaller the value of ε, the larger the running time; that is, the smaller the error we can tolerate, the more we must work to obtain a satisfactory approximation. It is difficult to give an analysis for large classes of functions. This is due to the fact that the rate of convergence of a Taylor series for the function $f(x)$ that it represents depends on the nature of $f(x)$ and the interval $[a, b]$ on which the approximation is desired. Of course, the analysis also depends on the error tolerance. Below, we present examples to illustrate typical methods.

EXAMPLE

Give a polynomial of minimal or nearly minimal degree that will approximate the exponential function e^x to d decimal places of accuracy on the interval $[-1, 1]$, for some positive integer d.

Solution: Let's take $x_0 = 0$ and observe that $f^{(i)}(x) = e^x$ for all i. Our estimate of the truncation error then becomes

$$\varepsilon_n(x) = \frac{e^\tau}{n!} x^n$$

Notice that e^x is a positive and increasing (since its first derivative is always positive) function. Therefore, its maximum absolute value on any interval is at the interval's right endpoint. Thus, on the interval $[-1, 1]$, we have

$$|\varepsilon_n(x)| \le \frac{e^1}{n!} 1^n = \frac{e}{n!} < \frac{2.8}{n!}$$

(Note the choice of 2.8 as an upper bound for e is somewhat arbitrary; we could have used 3 or 2.72 instead.) The requirement of approximation accurate to d decimal places means we need to have $|\varepsilon_n(x)| \le 0.5 \times 10^{-d}$. Therefore, it suffices to take

$$\frac{2.8}{n!} \le 0.5 \times 10^{-d} \Leftrightarrow \frac{2.8 \times 10^d}{0.5} \le n! \Leftrightarrow$$

$$5.6 \times 10^d \le n! \tag{13.1}$$

in order that the polynomial

$$p_{n-1}(x) = \sum_{i=0}^{n-1} \frac{x^i}{i!}$$

approximate e^x to d decimal places of accuracy on the interval $[-1, 1]$.

We would prefer to solve inequality (13.1) for n in terms of d, but it doesn't appear to be easy to do so. However, it is not hard to see from inequality (13.1) that $n = o(d)$ (see the Exercises). This is important because we know that on a RAM, for example, n as a measure of the degree of a polynomial is also the measure of the running time in evaluating the polynomial.

For a given value of d, let n_d be the smallest value of n satisfying inequality (13.1). Simple calculations based on inequality (13.1) yield the following values:

d	n_d
1	5
2	6
3	8
4	9
5	10

Thus, if $d = 3$, the desired approximating polynomial for e^x on $[-1, 1]$ is

$$p_{n_d-1}(x) = \sum_{i=0}^{7} \frac{x^i}{i!}.$$

EXAMPLE

Give a polynomial of minimal or nearly minimal degree that will approximate the trigonometric function $\sin x$ to d decimal places of accuracy on the interval $[-\pi, \pi]$ for some positive integer d.

Solution: Let's take $x_0 = 0$ and observe that $f^{(i)}(0) \in \{-1, 0, 1\}$ for all i. If the latter claim is not obvious to the reader, it is a good exercise in mathematical induction. Our estimate of the truncation error then becomes

$$|\varepsilon_n(x)| \leq \left| \frac{1}{n!} x^n \right| \leq \frac{\pi^n}{n!} < \frac{3.2^n}{n!}$$

As in the previous example, accuracy to d decimal places implies an error tolerance of $|\varepsilon_n(x)| \leq 0.5 \times 10^{-d}$. Hence, it suffices to take

$$\frac{3.2^n}{n!} \leq 0.5 \times 10^{-d} \Leftrightarrow$$

$$2 \times 10^d \leq \frac{n!}{3.2^n} \tag{13.2}$$

If we take the minimal value of n that satisfies inequality (13.2) for a given d, we have $n = o(d)$ (see the Exercises).

For a given value of d, let n_d be the smallest value of n satisfying inequality (13.2). Simple calculations based on inequality (13.2) yield the following values:

d	n_d
1	10
2	12
3	14
4	15
5	17

Thus, for $d = 2$ we can approximate $\sin x$ on the interval $[-\pi, \pi]$ to two decimal places of accuracy by the polynomial

$$p_{n_d - 1}(x) = 0 + \frac{1x}{1!} + \frac{0x^2}{2!} + \frac{-x^3}{3!} + \frac{0x^4}{4!} + \frac{1x^5}{5!}$$

$$+ \frac{0x^6}{6!} + \frac{-1x^7}{7!} + \frac{0x^8}{8!} + \frac{1x^9}{9!} + \frac{0x^{10}}{10!} + \frac{-1x^{11}}{11!}$$

$$= x - \frac{x^3}{6} + \frac{x^5}{120} - \frac{x^7}{5,040} + \frac{x^9}{362,880} - \frac{x^{11}}{39,916,800}$$

TRAPEZOIDAL INTEGRATION

A fundamental theorem of calculus is that if $F'(x) = f(x)$ for every $x \in [a,b]$, then

$$\int_a^b f(x)dx = F(b) - F(a).$$

Unfortunately, for many important functions $f(x)$, the corresponding antiderivative function $F(x)$ is difficult to evaluate for a given value of x. As an example, consider the function $f(x) = x^{-1}$ with

$$F(x) = \ln x = \int_1^x f(t)dt.$$

For such functions, it is important to have approximation techniques in order to evaluate definite integrals.

One of the best-known approximation techniques for definite integrals is *Trapezoidal Integration*, in which we use the relationship between definite integrals and the area between the graph and the x-axis to approximate a slab of the definite integral with a trapezoid. We will not bother to prove the following statement, as its derivation can be found in many calculus or numerical analysis textbooks.

Theorem: Let $f(x)$ be a function that is twice differentiable on the interval $[a, b]$ and let n be a positive integer. Let

$$h = \frac{b - a}{n}$$

and let x_i, $i \in \{1, 2, \ldots, n - 1\}$, be defined by $x_i = a + ih$. Let

$$t_n = h\left[\frac{f(a) + f(b)}{2} + \sum_{i=1}^{n-1} f(x_i)\right].$$

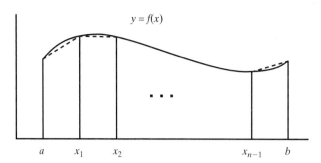

Figure 13-1 Trapezoidal integration. The dashed lines represent the tops of the trapezoids. The area under each small arc is approximated by the area of a trapezoid. It is often much easier to compute the area of a trapezoid than the area under an arc. The total area of the trapezoids serves as an approximation to the total area under the curve.

Then t_n is an approximation to

$$\int_a^b f(x)dx,$$

with the error in the estimate given by

$$\varepsilon_n = t_n - \int_a^b f(x)dx = \frac{(b-a)^3 f''(\eta)}{12n^2} \tag{13.3}$$

for some $\eta \in (a,b)$.

The reader may wish to consider Figure 13-1 in order to recall the principles behind Trapezoidal Integration.

The value of η in equation (13.3) is often unknown to us, but an upper bound for $|f''(\eta)|$ is often sufficient, as what we hope to achieve is that $|\varepsilon_n|$ be small.

If we assume that for $x \in [a, b]$, each value of $f(x)$ can be computed on a RAM in $\Theta(1)$ time, then it is easy to see that t_n can be computed on a RAM in $\Theta(n)$ time (see the Exercises). We expect that the running time of an algorithm will be a factor of the quality of the approximation, much as was the case of computing the Taylor series to within a predetermined error.

EXAMPLE

For some positive integer d, compute ln 2 to d decimal places via trapezoidal integration. Give an analysis of the running time of your algorithm in terms of d.

Solution: Since

$$\ln 2 = \int_1^2 x^{-1}dx$$

we take $f(x) = x^{-1}, f'(x) = -x^{-2}, f''(x) = 2x^{-3}, f^{(3)}(x) = -6x^{-4}, [a, b] = [1, 2]$. Notice $f''(x) > 0$ on $[1, 2]$, and f'' is a decreasing function (since its derivative, $f^{(3)}(x)$, is negative for all $x \in [1, 2]$). Therefore, f'' attains its maximum absolute value on $[1, 2]$ at the left endpoint. It follows that

$$|\varepsilon_n| \leq \frac{(2-1)^3 f''(1)}{12n^2} = \frac{1 \times 2(1)^{-3}}{12n^2} = \frac{1}{6n^2}$$

Since we wish to attain d decimal place accuracy, we want $|\varepsilon_n| \leq 0.5 \times 10^{-d}$, so it suffices to take

$$\frac{1}{6n^2} \leq 0.5 \times 10^{-d} \Leftrightarrow \frac{10^d}{3} \leq n^2 \Leftrightarrow$$

$$\frac{10^{d/2}}{3^{1/2}} \leq n \tag{13.4}$$

If we choose the smallest value of n satisfying the latter inequality, we conclude that the running time of our approximation of ln 2 via trapezoidal integration as discussed above is exponential in the number of decimal places of accuracy, $\Theta(10^{d/2})$.

We remark that it is not unusual to find that the amount of work required is exponential in the number of decimal places of accuracy required. In these situations, trapezoidal integration may not be a very good technique to use for computing approximations that are required to be extremely accurate. Another way of looking at this analysis is to observe that using an error tolerance of $\varepsilon = 0.5 \times 10^{-d}$, we have $d = -\log_{10}(2\varepsilon)$. Further, if we substitute this into inequality (13.4), we conclude that the minimal value of n satisfying the inequality is $\Theta(1/\varepsilon^{1/2})$.

Notice also, for example, that for $d = 6$ (for many purposes, a highly accurate estimate), the minimum value of n to satisfy inequality (13.4) is $n = 578$. While this indicates an unreasonable amount of work for a student in a calculus class using only pencil, paper, and a calculator, it is still a small problem for a modern computer.

Other methods of "numerical integration," including Simpson's method, tend to converge faster (though not asymptotically so) to the definite integral represented by the approximation. Fortunately, for many purposes, only a small number of decimal places of accuracy are required. Also, it may be that another technique, such as using a Taylor series, is more efficient for computing the value of a logarithm.

CHAPTER NOTES

The primality problem and the greatest common divisor problem are taken from number theory, a branch of mathematics devoted to fundamental properties of numbers, particularly (although not exclusively) integers.

We have used the Prime Number Theorem concerning the asymptotic behavior of the function $\pi(n)$, the number of primes less than or equal to the positive integer n. This theorem is discussed in the following sources:

■ T.M. Apostol, *Introduction to Analytic Number Theory* (Springer-Verlag, New York, 1976).

■ K.H. Rosen, *Elementary Number Theory and its Applications* (Addison-Wesley Publishing, Reading, MA, 1993).

The latter also discusses the Euclidean algorithm for the greatest common divisor problem and contains a proof of Lamé's Theorem.

Other problems we have discussed in this chapter are taken from *numerical analysis*, an area of applied mathematics and computing that is concerned with computationally intensive problems involving numerical algorithms, approximation, error analysis, and related issues. Problems in numerical analysis have applications in branches of mathematics that derive from calculus (differential equations, probability, and statistics) and linear algebra (matrix multiplication, solution of systems of linear equations, and linear programming) and their application areas. For an introduction to the field, the reader is referred to the following:

■ N.S. Asaithambi, *Numerical Analysis: Theory and Practice* (Saunders College Publishing, Fort Worth, 1995).

■ R.L. Burden and J.D. Faires, *Numerical Analysis* (PWS-Kent Publishing Company, Boston, 1993).

■ S. Yakowitz and Ferenc Szidarovszky, *An Introduction to Numerical Computations* (Macmillan Publishing Company, New York, 1989).

We have discussed approximation problems with regard to the algorithmic efficiency of our solutions in terms of error tolerance, sometimes expressed in terms of the number of decimal places of accurate calculation. It is tempting to say this is rarely important, that most calculations require only a small number of decimal places of accuracy. One should note, however, that there are situations in which very large numbers of accurate decimal places are required. As an extreme example, some mathematicians are interested in computing the value of π to thousands of decimal places. While these examples involve techniques beyond the scope of this book (because, for example, ordinary treatment of real numbers allows for the storage of only a few decimal places), the point is that interest exists in computations with more than "ordinary" accuracy.

EXERCISES

1. Devise a parallel algorithm to solve the primality problem for the positive integer n. At the end of the algorithm, every processor should know whether n is prime and, if so, what the smallest prime factor of n is. Use the bounded n model and assume your computer has $\lfloor n^{1/2} \rfloor$ processors, but that a list of primes is not already stored in memory. Analyze the running time of your algorithm on each of the following platforms: CREW PRAM, EREW PRAM, Mesh, and hypercube.

2. Suppose you modify the algorithm of the previous exercise as follows: assume a list of primes p satisfying $p \leq \lfloor n^{1/2} \rfloor$ is distributed one prime per processor. How many processors are needed to store the primes? Analyze the running time of the resulting

algorithm on each of the following platforms: CREW PRAM, EREW PRAM, Mesh, and hypercube.

3. Consider the problem of computing (n_0, n_1) for nonnegative integers n_0 and n_1, where $n_0 \geq n_1$. Assume a list of primes p satisfying $p \leq \lfloor (n_1)^{1/2} \rfloor$ is kept in memory (for a parallel model of computation, assume these primes are distributed one prime per processor). Devise an algorithm for computing (n_0, n_1) efficiently based on finding, for each prime p in this list, the maximal nonnegative integer k such that p^k is a common factor of n_0 and n_1. Assume that multiplication and division operations can be done in $\Theta(1)$ time. For parallel machines, at the end of the algorithm, every processor should have the value of (n_0, n_1). Analyze the running time of such an algorithm for the RAM, CREW PRAM, EREW PRAM, Mesh, and hypercube.

4. Decide whether or not our $\Theta(\log n)$-time algorithm for computing x^n is effectively parallelizable. That is, either give a version of this algorithm for a PRAM that runs in $o(\log n)$ time and show that it does so, or argue why it is difficult or impossible to do so.

5. Show that a RAM algorithm to evaluate a polynomial of degree n must take $\Omega(n)$ time; hence, our $\Theta(n)$ time algorithm is optimal.

6. Devise an algorithm for the evaluation of a polynomial of degree n on a PRAM. This will be somewhat easier on a CREW PRAM than on an EREW PRAM, but in either case, you should be able to achieve $\Theta(\log n)$ time using $\Theta(n/\log n)$ processors, hence an optimal cost of $\Theta(n)$.

7. Modify your algorithm from the previous exercise to run on a mesh or hypercube of size n. Assume the coefficients of the polynomial are distributed $\Theta(1)$ per processor. Analyze the running time for each of these architectures.

8. Show that for any $x \in [-1, 1]$, the value of e^x can be computed to within 0.5×10^{-d} for positive integer d (that is, to d-decimal place accuracy) in $o(d)$ time on a RAM. You may use inequality (13.1).

9. Show that inequality (13.2) implies $n = o(d)$ and use this result to show that the function $\sin x$ can be computed for any $x \in [-\pi, \pi]$ to d-decimal place accuracy in $o(d)$ time on a RAM.

10. Show that if we assume the value of $f(x)$ can be computed in $\Theta(1)$ time for all $x \in [a, b]$, then the trapezoidal integration estimate t_n can be computed on a RAM in $\Theta(n)$ time.

11. Analyze the running time of using trapezoidal integration to compute

$$\int_0^1 e^{-x^2} dx$$

to d decimal places, as an asymptotic expression in d. To simplify the problem, you may assume (possibly incorrectly) that for all $x \in [0, 1]$, e^x can be computed with sufficient accuracy in $\Theta(1)$ time.

Bibliography

1. A.V. Aho, J.E. Hopcroft, and J.D. Ullman, *The Design and Analysis of Computer Algorithms*, Addison Wesley, Reading, MA, 1974.

2. S.G. Akl and K.A. Lyons, *Parallel Computational Geometry*, Prentice Hall, Upper Saddle River, NJ, 1993.

3. G.S. Almasi and A. Gottlieb, *Highly Parallel Computing*, The Benjamin/Cummings Publishing Company, New York, NY, 1994.

4. G. Amdahl, "Validity of the single processor approach to achieving large scale computing capabilities," *AFIPS Conference Proceedings*, Vol. 30, Thomson Information Publishing Group, Stamford, CT, 1967, pp. 483–485.

5. T.M. Apostol, *Introduction to Analytic Number Theory*, Springer-Verlag, New York, NY, 1976.

6. N.S. Asaithambi, *Numerical Analysis: Theory and Practice*, Saunders College Publishing, Fort Worth, TX, 1995.

7. M.J. Atallah and D.Z. Chen, "An optimal parallel algorithm for the minimum circle-cover problem," *Information Processing Letters* 32, 1989, pp. 159–165.

8. M. Atallah and M. Goodrich, "Efficient parallel solutions to some geometric problems," *Journal of Parallel and Distributed Computing* 3, 1986, pp. 492–507.

9. S. Baase, "Introduction to parallel connectivity, list ranking, and Euler tour techniques," in *Synthesis of Parallel Algorithms*, J. H. Reif, ed., Morgan Kaufmann Publishers, San Mateo, CA, 1993, pp. 61–114.

10. K.E. Batcher, "Sorting networks and their applications," *Proc. AFIPS Spring Joint Computer Conference* 32, 1968, pp. 307–314.

11. J.L. Bentley, D. Haken, and J.B. Saxe, "A general method for solving divide-and-conquer recurrences," *SIGACT News*, 12(3), 1980, pp. 36–44.

12. A.A. Bertossi, "Parallel circle-cover algorithms," *Information Processing Letters* 27, 1988, pp. 133–139.

13. G.E. Blelloch, *Vector Models for Data-Parallel Computing*, The MIT Press, Cambridge, MA, 1990.

14. G. Brassard and P. Bratley, *Algorithmics: Theory and Practice*, Prentice Hall, Upper Saddle River, NJ, 1988.

15. L. Boxer, "On Hausdorff-like metrics for fuzzy sets," *Pattern Recognition Letters* 18, 1997, pp. 115–118.

16. L. Boxer and R. Miller, "A parallel circle-cover minimization algorithm," *Information Processing Letters* 32, 1989, pp. 57–60.

17. L. Boxer and R. Miller, "Parallel algorithms for all maximal equally-spaced collinear sets and all maximal regular coplanar lattices," *Pattern Recognition Letters* 14, 1993, pp. 17–22.

18. R.L. Burden and J.D. Faires, *Numerical Analysis*, PWS-Kent Publishing Company, Boston, MA, 1993.

19. B.B. Chaudhuri and A. Rosenfeld, "On a metric distance between fuzzy sets," *Pattern Recognition Letters* 17, 1996, pp. 1157–1160.

20. T.H. Cormen, C.E. Leiserson, and R.L. Rivest, *Introduction to Algorithms*, McGraw-Hill, New York, NY, 1989.

21. S. Even, *Graph Algorithms,* Computer Science Press, New York, NY, 1979.

22. M.J. Flynn, "Very high-speed computing systems," *Proceedings of the IEEE*, 54 (12), 1966, pp. 1901–1909.

23. M.J. Flynn, "Some computer organizations and their effectiveness," *IEEE Transactions on Computers*, C-21, 1972, pp. 948–960.

24. M.T. Goodrich and R. Tamassia, *Data Structures and Algorithms in JAVA,* John Wiley & Sons, Inc., New York, NY, 1998.

25. R.L. Graham, "An efficient algorithm for determining the convex hull of a finite planar set," *Information Processing Letters* 1, 1972, pp. 132–133.

26. R.L. Graham, D.E. Knuth, and O. Patashnik, *Concrete Mathematics*, Addison Wesley, Reading, MA, 1989.

27. C.A.R. Hoare, "Quicksort," *Computer Journal* 5(1), 1962, pp. 10–15.

28. J.E. Hopcroft and R.E. Tarjan, "Effective algorithms for graph manipulation," *Communications of the ACM* 16, 1973, pp. 372–478.

29. E. Horowitz, S. Sahni, and S. Rajasekaran, *Computer Algorithms in C++,* Computer Science Press, New York, NY, 1997.

30. J. Já Já, *An Introduction to Parallel Algorithms*, Addison Wesley, Reading, MA, 1992.

31. R.A. Jarvis, "On the identification of the convex hull of a finite set of points in the plane," *Information Processing Letters* 2, 1973, pp. 18–21.

32. A.B. Kahng and G. Robins, "Optimal algorithms for extracting spatial regularity in images," *Pattern Recognition Letters* 12, 1991, pp. 757–764.

33. R.M. Karp and V. Ramachandran, "A survey of parallel algorithms and shared memory machines," in *Handbook of Theoretical Computer Science: Algorithms and Complexity*, A.J. vanLeeuwen, ed., Elsevier, New York, NY, 1990, pp. 869–941.

34. S. Khuller and B. Raghavachari, "Basic graph algorithms," in *Handbook of Algorithms and Theory of Computation,* M. Atallah, ed., CRC Press, New York, NY, 1999.

35. D.E. Knuth, *Fundamental Algorithms*, Volume 1 of *The Art of Computer Programming*, Addison Wesley, Reading, MA, 1968.

36. D.E. Knuth, *Seminumerical Algorithms*, Volume 2 of *The Art of Computer Programming*, Addison Wesley, Reading, MA, 1969.

37. D.E. Knuth, *Sorting and Searching*, Volume 3 of *The Art of Computer Programming*, Addison Wesley, Reading, MA, 1973.

38. D.E. Knuth, "Big omicron and big omega and big theta," *ACM SIGACT News* 8(2), 1976, pp. 18–23.

39. C.C. Lee and D.T. Lee, "On a cover-circle minimization problem," *Information Processing Letters* 18, 1984, pp. 180–185.

40. F.T. Leighton, *Introduction to Parallel Algorithms and Architectures: Arrays, Trees, Hypercubes*, Morgan Kaufmann Publishers, San Mateo, CA., 1992.

41. S.B. Maurer and A. Ralston, *Discrete Algorithmic Mathematics*, Addison Wesley, Reading, MA, 1991.

42. R. Miller and Q.F. Stout, "Efficient parallel convex hull algorithms," *IEEE Transactions on Computers* 37 (12), 1988.

43. R. Miller and Q.F. Stout, *Parallel Algorithms for Regular Architectures: Meshes and Pyramids*, The MIT Press, Cambridge, MA, 1996.

44. R. Miller and Q.F. Stout, "Algorithmic techniques for networks of processors," in *Handbook of Algorithms and Theory of Computation*, M.J. Atallah, ed., CRC Press, New York, NY, 1999, pp. 46–1:46–19.

45. S.B. Nadler, Jr., *Hyperspaces of Sets*, Marcel Dekker, New York, NY, 1978.

46. M.H. Overmars and J. van Leeuwen, "Maintenance of configurations in the plane," *Journal of Computer and Systems Sciences* 23, 1981, pp. 166–204.

47. M.L. Puri and D.A. Ralescu, *"Differentielle d'un fonction floue,"* *Comptes Rendes Acad. Sci. Paris, Serie* I 293, 1981, pp. 237–239.

48. F.P. Preparata and M.I. Shamos, *Computational Geometry*, Springer-Verlag, New York, NY, 1985.

49. M.J. Quinn, *Parallel Computing Theory and Practice*, McGraw-Hill, New York, NY, 1994.

50. S. Ranka and S. Sahni, *Hypercube Algorithms for Image Processing and Pattern Recognition*, Springer-Verlag, New York, NY, 1990.

51. K.H. Rosen, *Elementary Number Theory and its Applications*, Addison Wesley, Reading, MA, 1993.

52. A. Rosenfeld, "'Continuous' functions on digital pictures," *Pattern Recognition Letters* 4, 1986, pp. 177–184.

53. D. Sarkar and I. Stojmenovic, "An optimal parallel circle-cover algorithm," *Information Processing Letters* 32, 1989, pp. 3–6.

54. G.W. Stout, *High Performance Computing*, Addison Wesley, Reading, MA, 1995.

55. V. Strassen, "Gaussian elimination is not optimal," *Numerische Mathematik* 14 (3), 1969, pp. 354–356.

56. R.E. Tarjan, "Depth-first search and linear graph algorithms," *SIAM Journal on Computing* 1(2), June 1972, pp. 146–160.

57. R.E. Tarjan, *Data Structures and Network Algorithms,* Society for Industrial and Applied Mathematics, Philadelphia, PA, 1983.

58. F.L. van Scoy, "The parallel recognition of classes of graphs," *IEEE Transactions on Computers* 29, 1980, pp. 563–570.

59. B. Wagar, "Hyperquicksort: a fast sorting algorithm for hypercubes," in *Hypercube Multiprocessors* M.T. Heath, ed., Society for Industrial and Applied Mathematics, Philadelphia, PA, 1987, pp. 292–299.

60. S. Warshall, "A theorem on Boolean matrices," *Journal of the ACM* 9, 1962, pp. 11–12.

61. S. Yakowitz and Ferenc Szidarovszky, *An Introduction to Numerical Computations*, Macmillan, New York, NY, 1989.

Index

H

I

THE TERROR COURTS

The Terror Courts

Rough Justice at Guantanamo Bay

■

JESS BRAVIN

Yale UNIVERSITY PRESS

New Haven and London

Yale University Press books may be purchased in quantity for educational,
business, or promotional use. For information, please e-mail sales.press@
yale.edu (US office) or sales@yaleup.co.uk (UK office).

Designed by Sonia Shannon.
Set in Minion type by Keystone Typesetting, Inc.
Printed in the United States of America.

Library of Congress Cataloging-in-Publication Data
Bravin, Jess.
The terror courts : rough justice at Guantanamo Bay / Jess Bravin.
pages cm
Includes bibliographical references and index.
ISBN 978-0-300-18920-9 (clothbound)
1. War crimes trials—United States. 2. Guantanamo Bay Detention Camp.
3. Military courts—Cuba—Guantanamo Bay Naval Base. I. Title.
KF7661.B73 2013
345.73′023170269—dc23
2012034913

A catalogue record for this book is available from the British Library.

This paper meets the requirements of ANSI/NISO Z39.48–1992
(Permanence of Paper).

10 9 8 7 6 5 4 3 2 1